17-82

The Dynamics of Public Administration:
Guidelines to Current Transformations in Theory and Practice

GERALD E. CAIDEN
University of California at Berkeley

HOLT, RINEHART AND WINSTON, INC.

NEW YORK   CHICAGO   SAN FRANCISCO   ATLANTA
DALLAS   MONTREAL   TORONTO   LONDON   SYDNEY

Library of Congress Catalog Card Number: 74-163203
ISBN: 0-03-085232-3
Printed in the United States of America
1 2 3 4   090   9 8 7 6 5 4 3 2 1

Preface

Go to any high location and look around. You probably will see many things that offend the senses—abandoned trash, aging property and unsightly buildings, neglected land, smog, traffic jams, polluted streams. Scan the headlines of any newspaper. You will find many more things to trouble you—wars, strikes, crime, riots, price rises and unemployment, international conflicts, natural disasters, technical mishaps. All these are matters of public importance, for they affect society as a whole, not only the immediate participants. Counteraction requires community, not individual, resolution and effective changes in direction depend on public intervention. To get something done, the collective (or societal, community, or public) will must be cultivated through complex institutional frameworks. This is the domain of public affairs—the reshaping of relationships between man and man and between man and nature. Public administration is that part of the public domain concerned with the administrative aspects of the resolution of public issues.

What constitutes the public domain—public behavior, institutions and laws, as opposed to their private counterparts—varies in time and place, according to ideology, technology, political economy and administrative culture. Neither philosophers nor statisticians, or other technocrats—arguing from different conceptions, definitions, and ideals—have been able to agree. Further, ideas change fairly quickly. What was considered private fifty years ago may now be very much a public concern—for example, environmental pollution, industrial relations, international sport, and city growth. On the other hand, what is now considered a private preserve may be in the public domain in fifty years' time. While the industrial revolution may have enlarged the area of privacy, automation may diminish it.

Variations in the public domain among cultures, societies, communities, and even neighborhoods are paralleled by differing ideas of what should be included within the scope of public administration. Vagueness, indefiniteness, looseness, and imprecision are inevitable. Academics have tried to provide greater clarity and precision by defining boundaries, describing central concerns, and theorizing about perceived major consistencies. Practitioners tend to find this approach at best unrewarding, at worst dull and irrelevant. They see public administration as the implementation of communal decisions made in the political arena and the resolution of societal problems before the essentials of civilization are jeopardized. The questions they ask are concerned with practicalities. What does the public want in a specific instance, or what will be acceptable to it? How is public opinion shaping? How can opposing views be reconciled? How can principles, aims, and ideas be translated into reality? How well do existing arrangements, laws, programs and practices work, and how can they be improved? What should be given priority? How can resources and support for important public services be mustered? Practitioners are not too interested in matters of definition and theory. They want manuals of action, directions on what to do, and advice on how to improve on what they do. They seek a contemporary administrative companion to Machiavelli's *The Prince*. So far nobody has met their needs, and as far as this book is concerned, they will have to wait a little longer.

What, then, is the justification for producing yet another academic approach to public administration? Simply the gap between academic and practitioner is too wide and needs to be narrowed. The academics may have ignored much recorded experience and oral tradition passed on in the practice of public administration, but their work in the realm of definition, description, analysis, and theory has been significant in directing attention to misconceptions, superficialities, bland untested assertions, and inadequate results. The practitioners may have been performing satisfactorily by their own standards, but they might have done much better had they appreciated academic concerns and borrowed more from the growing volume of literature readily available to them. Just as the scholar has failed to study crucial functions, such as internal security and military-civil relations, the practitioner has failed to understand the purpose of administrative theory and comparative administration. Both sides need to exchange ideas and information and to combine forces for a concerted drive on the major challenges in the administration of public affairs.

Before a start can be made, a general survey of the field, current progress, unresolved issues and reliable research is needed. Several suitable texts already serve this purpose but the subject is expanding so fast that no single volume can suffice. I have found in teaching that newcomers to the subject need an introduction that guides them through the available literature, points out the major controversies, highlights, and shortcomings, reviews new and continuing research, and relates existing work to other knowledge. The present volume is the result. It is not intended to replace existing texts, but to introduce and supplement them. No attempt is made to cover the whole field in depth. Topics treated extensively in existing texts and specialized studies— such as managerial processes, intergovernmental relations, municipal administration, administrative law, and public personnel techniques—are mentioned only briefly, certainly not to the extent that their importance warrants, but no good reason exists to reproduce or duplicate in depth that which the interested reader will follow up for himself from original sources. The limited terms of reference preclude a comprehensive reshaping of existing knowledge within a new theory of public administration, although several elements that could compose a new framework for the discipline are represented. This book is designed to be read together with the established works and used as a foundation on which to build further knowledge by extensive reading and self-discovery. The intention is to encourage further exploration of a subject that daily gains in importance and that will soon become an essential part of every educated person's studies.

Because public administration is fragmented and often contradictory, the ordering of chapters does not follow any consistent logic, but to assist the newcomer in grasping the relationships between the various facets of public administration, the book is divided into five parts: Chapters 1 and 2 introduce the newcomer to the discipline as an independent area of study. Practitioners, impatient with academic wrangling and uninterested in identity problems, can skim these chapters and begin serious reading with Chapter 3. Chapter 1 covers the identity crisis—is there such a thing as public administration, and if so, what claims does its study have to autonomy? Public administration obviously exists in the real world. General prejudices and popular misconceptions about it distinguish it in the public mind, as do its peculiar features. Whether these are sufficient to set it apart for study is still being argued between those who believe its unity, scope, and theoretical potentialities suffice for academic autonomy and those who see it as an area for interdisciplinary approaches. A resolution to this problem is obstructed by the shifting base of the subject matter and the necessary accompanying changes in focus of the study. Chapter 2 assumes that if there is subject matter, then there is something to study. It examines the growth of public administration, the purposes behind its study, and the tortuous history of the study—with particular attention to American experience and with an overview of major trends in the current transformation of academic approaches by American scholars, who are by far the most innovative and productive.

Chapters 3, 4, and 5 show the political nature of public administration as a result of the transformation of the public policy arena and the unavoidable politicization of public arrangements. Although the politics-administration dichotomy that dominated thinking between the world wars has been thoroughly discredited, the possibility now exists that it will be reintroduced as a policy-administration dichotomy. Chapter 3 describes how public policy-making is fast becoming the new central core of the discipline of public administration, largely as a result of the need to improve existing public policies to meet contemporary societal challenges and of the failure of alternative societal institutions to public bureaucracies to provide a continual flow of workable public policies. Whereas the pre-Depression world could depend on political institutions to direct public administration, the post-Depression world largely depends on public administration to suggest alternatives from which political leaders can choose. The academic response has been to focus attention first on decision making, then on problem solving, and finally on policy analysis as an aid to the practitioner. Chapter 4 questions the concept of a depoliticized public bureaucracy and challenges the assumptions of neutrality by examining the political realities of life in the public service and the political implications of growing bureaucratic power. Chapter 5 examines the machinery of government as the living constitution, not a formal organizational apparatus to which strict scientific management principles can be applied without attention to the political context. Increased rationality is compatible with politicization and so too is administrative reform, providing that the political implications are appreciated by reform advocates.

Chapters 6, 7, 8, and 9 explore some of the unique aspects of public administration according to function, structure, process, and behavior. Chapter 6 reviews those societal functions in which public administration has a virtual if not absolute monopoly, namely, traditional governmental activities, nation building, management of the economy, social security, and control of the environment. Other societal institutions share in these functions only as minor partners. The functional expertise derived from these public activities is a mainstay of bureaucratic power. Chapter 7 looks at the blurring of the structural differentiation of public administration due to the government's wholesale entry into business and related activities, and the government's contracting out significant public services to private business and other private institutions. Chapter 8 concentrates on the processes of public financing, especially the peculiar nature of public revenue collection, debt management, and budgeting, which has no counterpart elsewhere. Chapter 9 investigates the special behavior patterns of public officials, again unique to public administration, and the requirements of public service.

Chapters 10 and 11 describe the progress being made in two relatively new areas, theory and comparison, which have yet to be fully assimilated by standard texts. Administrative theory has developed largely outside public administration, and much of it does not seem directly applicable. Nevertheless, as Chapter 10 indicates, theory has its place in the discipline and serves many practical purposes; there would be greater benefits if the status of public administration theory were elevated. The same is true of comparative studies in public administration. Chapter 11 highlights the theoretical significance of comparing and contrasting administrative systems and points out some of the practical benefits that have already flowed from development administration.

Chapter 12 is a personal overview of the state of the discipline as it enters the 1970s. I have used previously published sources in the *Journal of Comparative Administration* and *Public Administration* (Sydney) and comments, criticisms and exchanges of ideas among colleagues and students who have helped to shape the whole book. The essential binding theme is the constant change that has occurred, is currently taking place, and will continue to influence the scope of public administration in response to societal dynamics, and the need for the discipline of public administration to keep abreast of current events and shifts of emphasis in the practitioner's world. Public administration is what public administrators do, and what they do is determined by tradition and innovation. All too often the student gets bogged down in the knowledge of routines, laws, procedures, forms, and memoranda essential for an understanding of the traditional aspects of administering public affairs. He should keep reminding himself that there is another side — creative, ever changing, enterprising and dynamic — that is equally important. If he continues with his studies, one day he will be responsible for routinizing innovation and revitalizing routine.

Berkeley, California   **G. E. C.**
March 1971

Contents

Preface   iii

I   THE STUDY OF PUBLIC ADMINISTRATION   1

1. The Meaning of Public Administration   3
The Prejudice Against Public Administration   4
The Peculiarities of Public Administration   6
Four Approaches to Identification of Subject Matter   9
Attempts at Defining the Academic Discipline   12
The Shifting Base of Public Administration   19

2. The Study of Public Administration   23
The Growth of Public Administration   23
Why Study Public Administration?   26
The Evolution of the Discipline   30
A Discipline Transformed   42

II   POLITICS, POLICY, AND ADMINISTRATION   51

3. Public-Policy Making   53
The Transformed World of Public-Policy Making   55
The Response of Public Administration   61
From Decision Making to Problem Solving   68
From Policy Sciences to Policy Analysis   75

4. The Politicization Issue   82
The Depoliticized Bureaucracy   84
The Concept of Depoliticization   89
The Assumptions of Neutrality   94
Bureaucratic Power   102
The Measurement of Politicization   105

5. The Living Constitution   107
The Process of Rationalization   108
Political Control   113
Formal and Informal Structures   116
The Politics of Reorganization   118
Administrative Reform   123

III   FUNCTION, STRUCTURE, PROCESS, AND BEHAVIOR   129

6. Functional Expertise   131
Traditional Functions   133
Nation Building Functions   137
Economic-Management Functions   140
Social-Welfare Functions   144
Environmental-Control Functions   146
The Impact of Functional Expertise   152

7. Private Contractors and Public Entrepreneurs   154
The Decision To Contract   155
Private Contractors   159
Public Entrepreneurs   167

8. Public Finance   176
The Voracious Government   179
Meeting Governmental Costs   183
The Budget   188
Planning-Programming-Budgeting Systems (PPBS)   193

9. Public Service   199
Officialdom   201
Controls   203
Career Service   207
Public-Personnel Administration   210
Staff Relations   213
Employment Conditions   217

IV THEORY AND COMPARATIVE ADMINISTRATION   223

10. Administrative Theory   225
Why Theory?   229
Schools of Administrative Theory   231
Problems in Public Administrative Theory   240

11. Administrative Systems   244
International Systems   247
Comparative Political Systems   249
Comparative Administrative Systems   256
Developmental Systems   264

V ADMINISTRATION IN THE SEVENTIES   273

12. New Patterns in Public Administration   275
Public Administration in Ferment   278
Evolving Conceptions   282
A New Image for the Public Administrator   289
New Academies   292
Coping with Turbulence   294

Bibliographical Guide   298
General Bibliographies   298
Professional Journals   300
General Texts   304
Specialized Texts   311

Some Useful Addresses   335
Index   337

I

The Study
of Public
Administration

1
The Meaning of Public Administration

No one has yet produced a simple definition of public administration that is fully acceptable to both practitioners and scholars, certainly not one that is readily understandable to laymen without any preexisting knowledge of the subject matter. As in any other discipline, a simple answer to the basic inquiry "What exactly is public administration?" is impossible without detailed elaboration and numerous caveats. Knowledge is growing too rapidly and changing too fast to permit unaltered meanings and permanent boundaries. At one time the earth was considered the center of the universe, not a minor planet in a minor solar system in a minor galaxy. Likewise, the atom is no longer considered the smallest particle of matter. As our knowledge grows, our conceptions change. We do not require an exact meaning of the universe to comprehend its existence. Similarly, we do not require a precise meaning of public administration, an exact definition of its central core, and an acute identification of sharp boundaries vis-à-vis other subject matter to comprehend its existence and to single out its subject matter for independent scrutiny. This does not preclude the possibility that it may be part of or may imperceptibly spill over into another area.

At the present stage of man's evolution, public administration is indispensable. Contemporary civilization could not function without it. Urban society would be unbearable, law and

3

order meaningless, development impracticable, world trade impossible, and egalitarianism unattainable. Its growing pervasiveness in the conduct of human affairs is evident in the proliferation of public laws, the accumulation of huge arsenals for use by mass armies, the universal extension of the public sector of the economy, the wider accessibility of public amenities, the growth of public professions, and the increased depth and coverage of compulsory taxes. Opinions are divided as to the desirability of this trend. At one extreme, anarchists predict that it will end all individuality; the leviathan will order all human actions, and self-expression will be denied. To anarchists, every extension of public administration threatens to become totalitarianism. In opposition, social engineers envisage that the good society—the rational and responsive ordering of communal actions toward societal goals—will be achieved through public administration. They welcome its extension as a means of eliminating selfish private interests that exploit the common weal. Proponents of these opposite views wage their philosophical war in science fiction, romantic futuristic novels, political ideologies, party platforms, odd sects, and mass media. Both sides are successful in convincing everyone else that the truth lies somewhere between them. Just where is a matter of individual choice, related to past experience of public administration, personal estimation of cost-benefit ratio, general political disposition, and access to opinion makers. Personal interpretations are likely to be clouded by emotional issues and by the general prejudice against public administration.

THE PREJUDICE AGAINST PUBLIC ADMINISTRATION

The layman's understanding of the term "public administration" is influenced by the adverse images it usually evokes. In totalitarian regimes, it often is identified with the nefarious activities of the secret police, the abuse of discretionary power, and the regimentation of citizens by state functionaries. The mass media in democratic regimes frequently remind their audiences of the growing army of security-conscious, incompetent officials, who are supposed to spend much of their time manufacturing red tape to justify their occupancy of soft, unproductive jobs. Officiousness seems to be a spreading disease in newly independent states, where the public sector appears chaotic, replete with frenzied action without apparent results, and crass bungling of new programs. Corruption is still a way of life in low income countries, where public employment, dependent on one's having the right connections, is grossly overstaffed for the limited work load. Variations on these and similar themes are embodied in the folklore of many nations, and daily conversations are studded with criticisms of irritating conflicts with anonymous officialdom.

While citizens' grievances may be justified, a more intimate grasp of public affairs will probably show that the general impression of malfunctioning is greatly exaggerated and distorted. Public organizations rate among the best administered in the community, employing their share of the society's most talented people, and staffed by loyal, hard-working citizens, indistinguishable from their neighbors except for their place of employment. Ignorance of the context in which public administration works and of what really happens behind the scenes is largely responsible for the perpetuation of inherited myths, which were once a fairly accurate portrayal of public administration, when the conduct of public affairs was bad. Enlightenment about the true state of affairs is handicapped by official secrecy. Only Sweden has been bold enough to open its public records to its citizens, seemingly with few ill effects, but even there lampooning of public officials has been a traditional sport. The public seeks a whipping boy for failures in solving societal problems, and public officials are an obvious and easily accessible target on which to relieve inner stresses arising from the frustrations of daily living. Other traditional targets on which the public could vent its spleen have covered their more exposed features and have used the burgeoning public-relations industry to transform their public images. In contrast, few public authorities have embarked on elaborate public-relations campaigns. Nobody has been able to convince the taxpayer that the expenditure has been justified. Meanwhile, politicians continue to use public administration as their scapegoat while preventing insiders from speaking out. Unfortunately, public officials learn to live with criticism and adopt self-defensive mechanisms that fail to distinguish between just and unjust complaints.

The roots of prejudice go deeper than ignorance. Even if everyone became conversant with the problems of public administration and the difficulties of operating within a political environment, there would still be grounds for antagonism. The public remains on the outside, looking in. It judges performance purely by results, from the viewpoint of clientele needs and rising expectations that are derived in part from improvements on past successes and yearnings for unattainable perfection. New levels of achievement become new minimum expectations. No matter how well public administration performs, some people will never be satisfied. Moreover, it is likely that the majority has a lower tolerance level in respect to public authorities than other institutions; that is, most people will put up with more from private and voluntary organizations than their equivalents in the public sector. The prices of private services can rise without comment, whereas heated battles are fought over the smallest contemplated increases in the prices of public services. Patrons will queue longer and complain less in private banks than in public post offices. Businessmen may treat one another to expensive perquisites at the customers' expense, but high-ranking public officials of greater importance to the community will be subject to false economies. Such double standards obviously favor private enterprise, even when public enterprises outperform their private competitors in the same field of activity. This difference in attitudes is naturally fostered by entrepreneurs who fear nationalization. They are supported by others, who believe that even if the bureaucratic state could outperform private enterprise, a price has to be paid to preserve choice, which may be lost if the state assumes responsibility.

Behind the prejudice against public administration is a deep-seated resentment of the communal authority that it represents. Everyone would like to do his own thing within limits, but few succeed for any appreciable period. Life is otherwise conditioned, at least outwardly, by community expectations, behind which ultimately stands the coercive power of political institutions. As far as the individual is concerned, he is obliged to obey laws, pay taxes, conform to public decisions, obtain licenses, fill out forms, present himself for inspection at appointed times in designated places, and subject himself to countless inconveniences at the behest of the community. Should he fail to conform, sanctions will eventually be imposed on him — some inconsequential, others threatening his very existence. He may, of course, gladly conform to community expectations and never be confronted with community sanctions, though still aware of the sacrifices made and the irritations experienced in meeting his obligations to the community.

Whereas he may be conscious of the costs, he may be less aware of the benefits he receives — protection, security, cooperation, livelihood — which he never has cause to question. He may be unable to relate his contribution to the benefits, or if he does attempt to calculate the cost-benefit ratio, he may well find that his costs are disproportionate to the alleged benefits. As a taxpayer, for instance, he might prefer to keep his money for himself than to contribute to the education of others' children or to space research or a foreign regime that he opposes. Unless he has ideologically compelling reasons to support communal policy, right or wrong, he is inclined to lend passive support to community authority for causes in which he believes but is inclined to object actively when the authority is not used in his favor. Thus, few appear publicly to favor public administration and many are critical, even if on balance they have no real cause for complaint.

THE PECULIARITIES OF PUBLIC ADMINISTRATION

However vague the comprehension or perception of public administration, the citizen realizes that public administration is different from other societal institutions. First, he knows that it is unavoidable. He cannot escape communal authority: he has to come to terms with it. For the great mass of people there is no choice, other than willing acceptance or abject resignation. Other relationships can be made or broken at will. One does not have to pray, buy any particular brand of merchandise, attend spectator sports, or sleep at night — all these are voluntary and therefore avoidable activities. In contrast, the public will must be done. The tentacles of public administration reach all citizens and ensure this. Leaving the country will not help, as a passport is needed for entry into another country, nor is death a remedy. Just as one is not alive without a duly registered birth certificate, one is not dead without a death certificate (in the absence of which dead men are eligible to vote, draw rations, and pay taxes). Thus the official dictum prevails.

Second, the citizen knows that public administration can ultimately compel obedience; it has a legal monopoly of coercive power. The existence of other forms of coercive power indicates either ineffective performance by public administration or a deliberate decision by the political leadership to tolerate them. Otherwise, for any other body to enforce its will, it must employ the machinery of public administration—the law courts, police system, prisons, and, perhaps, militia. Governments try to avoid the use of repressive powers and, in their use of such powers, try to conform to community expectations. Their constant use and abuse would raise the specter of revolt, civil disobedience, and insubordination, which in turn would lead to more repression until all semblance of liberty would be lost. Only at times of extreme crisis do governments employ their ultimate powers to imprison people, draft young men, nationalize private enterprises, and direct workers to jobs. Other institutions cannot compel support: they have to attract it by convincing their clientele that they fulfill a need better than any potential rival.

Third, the citizen knows that the communal activities carried out by public administration have priority. Unless they are performed with some efficacy, other activities are jeopardized. Strikes of city policemen, firemen, and garbage collectors are accompanied by arson, theft, riots, disease, and filth. Similarly, breakdowns in public utility services bring normal life to a halt. The absence of emergency services leaves people at the mercy of earthquakes, hurricanes, floods, and fires, for pests and vermin, wildlife, and germs recognize no political or geographical boundaries. In crisis, people look to public administration and expect a quick and sure response. In turn, high-priority public services expect precedence over all other societal activities, being morally obliged to provide their services at all times and to have sufficient reserves to meet all anticipated demands. If prudent checks are not imposed, the demands of public administration could exceed capacity to pay. There never can be enough resources for communal activities. Weapons systems can always be improved; scientific, medical, and social research can always be expanded; emergency provisions can always be increased. The problem is where to draw the line to enable high-priority activities to be continued and improved without necessarily depriving other societal activities of needed resources.

Fourth, the citizen knows that in carrying out communal activities, public administration provides every citizen with a wide range of public services. Public administration contains the largest single multipurpose organizations. In most countries, public administration is already the largest single landowner, investor, employer, consumer, entrepreneur, and publisher. While public administration can take advantage of the economies of scale (specialization, professionalization, mechanization, routinization, standardization), it also experiences the disadvantages of scale and complexity (officiousness, red tape, regimentation, circumlocution, indifference). If unchecked, the disadvantages—in the absence of competition, measurable performance, political action, and self-corrective devices—could decline into bureaupathology, where purpose is subordinate to process, service to authority, reality to form, and adaptation to precedent. As other institutions reach the same size as public administration used to be (before it grew even bigger), they too begin to experience the same problems, but in solving them they are not so handicapped by diversity of purpose and expectation of consistency.

Fifth, the citizen knows that public administration is directly responsible to political leadership, for its top management is political. It is governed by political principles, promises, and expediencies, rather than academic theory, scientific principles, or business economics. The realm of public administration, the laws governing its operation, the distribution of functions among political institutions, the organization of public services, the size of public employment, and the principles governing financial and personnel administration are matters of heated political debate and compromise that are forever subject to change as political fortunes shift. Few other social institutions are so vulnerable to political pressure or so amenable to public opinion. A customer can complain about shoddy goods, but the private retailer or manufacturer is not obliged to heed his complaints; a member can criticize his voluntary association, but the governing committee is not compelled to accede to his wishes. But no politician can afford to ignore complaints and criticisms about the public domain, for he cannot tell how representative the complainant is or how his own political fortunes may be affected by his intervention or nonintervention.

> No action taken or contemplated by the government of a democracy is immune to public debate, scrutiny, or investigation. No other enterprise has such equal appeal or concern for everyone, is so equally dependent on everyone, or deals so vitally with those psychological intangibles which reflect popular economic needs and social aspirations. Other institutions, admittedly, are not free from politics, but government *is* politics . . . Each employee hired, each one demoted, transferred, or discharged, every efficiency rating, every assignment of responsibility, each change in administrative structure, each conversation, each letter, has to be thought about in terms of possible public agitation, investigation, or judgment.[1]

Sixth, the citizen knows that the political nature of public administration and the kind of communal activities involved make judgment of performance extraordinarily difficult. The ultimate objective is presumably the good society, incorporating many specific objectives such as peace, security, health, education, justice, prosperity, safety, liberty, and equality, few

[1] P. M. Appleby, *Big Democracy*. New York: Alfred A. Knopf, 1945, p. 7.

of which are susceptible to objective measurement. Will peace be better served by spending billions on a deterrent strike force or millions on disarmament conferences and mutual inspection teams? Will the public be better served by a communal park or subsidized fine arts? Is it worth saving babies to condemn them to lives of misery, starvation, and poverty? Can the efficacy of a social-welfare system be measured by the number of clients aided, the expenses of social services less overhead costs, or the speed of self-elimination? Can administrative performance be measured by the fewness of complaints, even when the public is scared to complain or when no facilities exist for the receipt of complaints?

Seventh, the citizen knows that he expects more of public administration than of other kinds of administration. He wants public officials to be paragons of virtue—honest, trustworthy, hard-working, loyal, competent, compassionate, and so on. Public morality should be above reproach, an example to younger generations. The citizen wants fair consideration, equal treatment, and consistency in his dealings with public authorities. He feels that the laws should be obeyed by all, officials and clientele alike, and that no one in public office should connive against the spirit and word of the law. Official discrimination should be confined. He wants the public domain to be conducted in the public interest, not for the advancement of special interests. The weak should be considered as well as the strong, minorities as well as majorities, unborn generations as well as present generations. He wants public officials to be optimistic and encouraging; they should show faith in a brighter future and act courageously in combatting defeatism and pessimism. He wants public officials to safeguard his money as if it were their own and to look after his interests as if he were present. They should have no secrets and should cooperate with public watchdogs set over them to ensure proper accountability.

The informed citizen knows that for all these reasons—unavoidability, ultimate coercive power, priority activities, size and multiplicity, political direction, unmeasurable purposes, and higher expectations—public administration is different, or if it is not, it *ought* to be, because of its public quality, concern for societal goals, compulsory powers, and relative openness.

FOUR APPROACHES TO IDENTIFICATION OF SUBJECT MATTER

How can the citizen recognize what is truly public administration? What exactly is the subject matter studied in public administration? Can precise boundaries be drawn around the subject?

One approach would be *the identification of communal activities subject to political direction.* In totalitarian regimes public administration is concerned with virtually all social activity. In low income countries, where much social activity is conducted within families, tribes, and self-sufficient communities, and where political direction is severely handicapped by language barriers and cultural diversity, public administration would be confined to a few activities conducted in the major towns and ports having contacts with the hinterland and foreigners. All societies do conduct certain activities communally—namely, the traditional functions of government, such as the conduct of external relations, defense, internal order, public works, social welfare, and taxation. These, then, are obviously in the province of public administration. In addition, there is a host of activities that all governments perform as monopoly services—postal communications, immigration controls, quarantine, currency, and weights and measures.

Beyond this point, there is no agreement. Some governments provide extensive public services and run large-scale public enterprises that elsewhere do not exist at all or remain in private hands, subject to varying degrees of public interference and political direction. For instance, most of the world's airlines, railroads, telecommunications, public utilities, and social services are government-owned, but in the United States of America they are largely privately owned, though subject to extensive public regulation. Further, some governments prefer to contract out many of their activities to private enterprise; that is, they finance the activities and provide guidelines, but leave details to the contractors. The superintending public authority nominally carries out the activity and assumes the responsibility for all programs conducted in its name. In the United States, space research and weapons production are carried out by contractors under the direction of superintending agencies, whereas the same activities in the Soviet Union and Australia are directly administered by public authorities. Thus, public administration cannot be identified by the nature of its activities alone.

A different approach at delineation would be *the identification of public institutions, grounded in public law, financed by public money, and staffed by career public servants.* These would be truly public authorities under political control. Government departments and ministries would be obvious candidates. So too would be regulatory agencies, statutory authorities, local governments, and public corporations financed by the public exchequer and staffed by career officials. Beyond this point, the boundary line is uncertain. In many countries, the government has joined with private enterprise and voluntary associations in mixed enterprises to provide community services. In others, where the government has contracted out large areas of public administration, the private contractors may have no other business. Withdrawal of the contract would render them redundant. They depend solely on public money, political connections, and technical expertise in the service they provide. Are these to be considered within public administration? In addition there are many bodies and organizations that the government subsidizes in order to keep them in existence, knowing that if they were to disappear, the government would be obliged to assume their activities directly. Should these be included for study in public administration? Further, the large body of public law and regulation effectively determines the fortunes of nongovernmental institutions as well as governmental ones. In low income countries, where bureaucratization has only just begun, communal activities directed by political leaders are not identifiable in governmental institutions (particularly where the term "communal" is identical with "racial" or "ethnic"). Public administration is not synonymous with political or governmental institutions.

A third approach would be a study of *administrative attitudes,* particularly those of decision makers and policy planners who take a public-minded, forward-looking view. Public administration would be distinguished by its outward-looking attitude — its concern for social repercussions, its awareness of political values, its reflection of community feelings, its expression of societal goals, its evidence of humaneness, its regard for truth, its confidence in the future, its abhorrence of social ills, its contribution to the quality of life, and its public accountability, responsiveness, and representativeness. Excluded would be inward-looking attitudes, concerned only with the private profit of the activity, institution, or process, irrespective of its external repercussions, which would be epitomized by the socialist's portrayal of capitalist robber barons.

Unfortunately, different attitudes coexist in varying shades of gray: it is rare to find either white or black. Just as some private entrepreneurs can be obsessed with the profit motive to the exclusion of anything else, others are public-spirited, concerned not only with their reputation among clientele but also with staff welfare and societal goals. Some public authorities are enlightened; others behave worse than the meanest private employer. Some units in the same organization are outward-looking, other units are inward-looking, and within an organizational unit, some administrators are outward-looking, and others are inward-looking. Publicly owned industries may operate no differently from their private counterparts. Private voluntary associations may be more responsive to community needs than public welfare agencies. Public administration has no monopoly of community concern.

A fourth approach would be to define public administration according to *the unique features of the processes employed in activating public policy.* This is the most common approach found in academic analysis of public administration. The unique processes include the nature of political controls and public accountability, the machinery of government and distribution of powers among the levels of government, the merit system and open competition, consolidated budgeting and public accounting, public enterprises, national planning, and local-government administration. The universal features include leadership, communications, delegation, planning, supervision, group norms, and teamwork. Presumably, should governmental institutions adopt the same processes as nongovernmental institutions or vice versa, the uniqueness of public administration would disappear.

All four approaches have something in common: they have a hard core that is unique to public administration. There are communal activities subject to political direction carried out by governmental institutions according to concepts of "publicness" through unique administrative processes. Beyond the hard core the distinctiveness of public administration gradually gives way to universals. At the perimeter, public administration merges into something else, perhaps better subject matter for administrative science, business economics, industrial psychology, or social welfare than a discipline of public administration. There is no sharp boundary line between public and nonpublic administration, and the subject matter can be approached from many different directions—administrative, political, economic, social, technical, philosophical, or psychological.

ATTEMPTS AT DEFINING THE ACADEMIC DISCIPLINE

Those who gain their livelihood in the study of public administration realize that the indeterminate nature of the subject matter of public administration leaves their students rather confused. They seek a sharper focus and a more precise definition of the central core of the discipline, without saddling themselves with outmoded conceptions or imposing on themselves a rigid definition. Several attempts to steer a path between imprecision and restriction follow.

> By public administration is meant, in common usage, the activities of the executive branches of national, state, and local governments; independent boards and commissions set up by Congress and state legislatures; government corporations; and certain other agencies of a specialized character. Specifically excluded are judicial and legislative agencies within the government and non-governmental administration.[2]

> A system of public administration is the composite of all the laws, regulations, practices, relationships, codes, and customs that prevail at any time in any jurisdiction for the fulfillment or execution of public policy.[3]

> At its fullest range, public administration embraces every area and activity governed by public policy . . . [including] the formal processes and operations through which the legislature exercises its power . . . the functions of the courts in the administration of justice and the work of military agencies . . . . By established usage, however, public administration has come to signify primarily the organization, personnel, practices, and procedures essential to effective performance of the civilian functions entrusted to the executive branch of government. In its general aspects, public administration centers its concern in those matters common to all or nearly all administrative agencies.[4]

> Public administration is decision making, planning the work to be done, formulating objectives and goals, working with the legislature and citizen organizations

[2] H. A. Simon, D. W. Smithburg, and V. A. Thompson, *Public Administration.* New York: Knopf, 1950, p. 7.

[3] L. D. White, *Introduction to the Study of Public Administration.* New York: Crowell Collier & Macmillan, 1955, p. 2.

[4] F. M. Marx (ed.), *Elements of Public Administration.* Englewood Cliffs, N.J.: Prentice-Hall, 1959, p. 6.

to gain public support and funds for government programs, establishing and revising organization, directing and supervising employees, providing leadership, communicating and receiving communications, determining work methods and procedures, appraising performance, exercising controls, and other functions performed by government executives and supervisors. It is the action part of government, the means by which the purposes and goals of government are realized.[5]

Public administration:
1. is cooperative group effort in a public setting.
2. covers all three branches—executive, legislative, and judicial—and their inter-relationships.
3. has an important role in the formulation of public policy and is thus part of the political process.
4. is more important than, and also different in significant ways from, private administration.
5. [as a field of study and practice, has been much influenced in recent years by the human-relations approach.]
6. is closely associated with numerous private groups and individuals in providing services to the community.[6]

Public administration may not have the conceptual or disciplinary cohesion we might like, but it is at least focused upon a definable area of study: the shaping and carrying out of public policy . . . . Public administration as a field is mainly concerned with the *means* for implementing political values. . . . Public administration may be defined as the coordination of individual and group efforts to carry out public policy. It is mainly occupied with the routine work of government.[7]

Public administration is the accomplishment of politically determined objectives. More than the technique or even the orderly execution of programs, however, public administration is also concerned with policy. . . . Public administration . . . must be sufficiently *practical* to solve problems and attain society's goals, but it must also be *exploratory and innovative* in its search for better methods based on broader understandings of what is involved in effective group activity.[8]

These post-1950 descriptions all emphasize the executive activities of public authorities, with special emphasis on public-policy making and execution. They generally concur (a) that public administration is part of cooperative human behavior, whose administrative aspects focus on the pursuit of rational goals in an organizational or bureaucratic authority structure, (b) that specifically governmental organizations can be differentiated in certain ways from other kinds of organization, and (c) that the study of pub-

[5] J. J. Corson and J. P. Harris, *Public Administration in Modern Society.* New York: McGraw-Hill, 1963, p. 12.

[6] F. A. Nigro, *Modern Public Administration.* New York: Harper & Row, 1965, p. 25. Section in brackets omitted from Second Edition, 1970, p. 20.

[7] J. M. Pfiffner and R. Presthus, *Public Administration.* New York: Ronald Press, 1967, pp. 5, 6, 7.

[8] M. E. Dimock and G. O. Dimock, *Public Administration.* New York: Holt, Rinehart and Winston, 1969, pp. 3, 11.

lic administration should concentrate on civilian organization in government, specifically executive organizations.

They differ over institutional boundaries, the major objectives of the study of public administration, the most promising approaches to reveal the true workings of governmental organizations, and the relationship between means and ends in public policy and between fact and value in decision making. The scope of the descriptions ranges from applied social science (if not all applied knowledge) to formal descriptions of individual administrative processes, from government (if not all political behavior) to routine activities of public bureaucrats, from the complete range of external relations of governmental organizations to exclusive concern with internal relationships in a closed system. They are obviously based on the formal structure of government in the United States of America—the distinction between church and state and between the civil and the military; the separation of powers; the primacy of the executive in conducting governmental operations; the federal nature of the American constitution; and the presuppositions of a democratic polity and the bureaucratic (or organizational) society. Some descriptions are meaningless outside American culture; others are far too narrow as definitions of a universal discipline. By limiting themselves in this way, they are unable to go beyond the American public-administration system or take full advantage of non-American contributions.

Is there any point in going further? Stein believes there is not. He believes administration is so complex and contains so many variables and intangibles that any highly systematic categorization is impossible. Administrative situations are so unique, so inherently disorderly, so unlike the highly conventionalized discipline of law that "public administration is a field in which everyman is his own codifier and categorizer, and the categories adopted must be looked on as relatively evanescent."[9]

Mosher is also inclined to doubt the worth of the effort:

> Public administration cannot demark any subcontinent as its exclusive province —unless it consists of such mundane matters as classifying budget expenditures, drawing organization charts, and mapping procedures. In fact, it would appear that any definition of this field would be either so encompassing as to call forth the wrath or ridicule of others, or so limiting as to stultify its own disciples. Perhaps it is best that it not be defined. It is more an area of interest than a discipline, more a focus than a separate science. . . . It is necessarily cross-disciplinary. The overlapping and vague boundaries should be viewed as a resource, even though they are irritating to some with orderly minds.[10]

He fears that public administration is growing so broad that it might be in danger of disappearing altogether as a recognizable focus of study.

[9] H. Stein, *Public Administration and Policy Development: A Case Book*. New York: Harcourt Brace Jovanovich, 1952, p. xxv.

[10] F. C. Mosher, "Research in Public Administration," *Public Administration Review*, 16 (Summer 1956), 177.

Parker goes much further and denies the very existence of a discipline:

> Anyone who has taught courses or conducted research under the rubric of "public administration" must have been troubled more or less frequently by two characteristics of his "field"—its nebulous scope and its lack of any distinctive technique. He must have felt himself a Jack of all trades as he pottered amateurishly about, now on the fringes of administrative law, now at the margins of accounting and budgeting, and then at the edges of industrial relations and occupational psychology. . . . Surely the man with a smattering of all these subjects could be master of none. . . . There is really no such subject as "public administration." No science or art can be identified by this title, least of all any single skill or coherent intellectual discipline. The term has no relation to the world of systematic thought.[11]

He argues that public administration should move on from its primitive stage, grounded in attempts to end maladministration in public affairs, of drawing attention "to a great new area of human action which called for the conscious attention of a number of social science disciplines, old and new," to the professional education of future administrators.

> The significance of the concept "public administration" is not academic or scientific, but vocational. It gives practising administrators a sense of community, and some common ground on which to exchange ideas and seek greater professional skills and maturity. It gives educators a focus around which to organize programmes for the professional preparation of practical administrators. It does not, in itself, offer any promising opportunity to widen or make more precise any single aspect of scientific knowledge.[12]

Truman also supports the idea of professional education of public administrators in applied social science relevant to public policy.

> The general features of such an education would involve a broad acquaintance with the theories, methods, and problems, including ways of stating problems, that characterize the several disciplines. . . . It must also . . . include some scientific work [for] a critical understanding of the difficulties, limitations and pitfalls of work in any social science. . . .[13]

The approach of these scholars fits well into Price's four estates in public-policy making, namely (a) the scientific, only concerned with discovering truth, not its application, use or moral effects, (b) the professional, which applied scientific knowledge to the practical affairs of men, (c) the administrative, which "must be prepared to understand and use a wide variety of professional expertise and scholarly disciplines [to aid] political superiors

---

[11] R. S. Parker, "The End of Public Administration," *Public Administration* (Sydney), 34 (June 1965), 99.

[12] Parker, "The End of Public Administration," p. 103.

[13] D. B. Truman, "The Social Sciences: Maturity, Relevance and the Problem of Training," in A. Ranney (ed.), *Political Science and Public Policy*. Chicago: Markham, 1968, p. 285.

attain their general purposes," and (d) the political, which used the skills of other estates but made decisions on basis of value judgment, hunch or compromise.[14]

In contrast, Landau not only believes there is a discipline of public administration around which organizing assumptions, concepts, and definitions can be systematically arranged, but he thinks it is important to "locate its center and clarify its principal points of reference."[15] He does not claim precision for any "field" of study, but unless such categorization occurs, the study of human behavior will be a mass of confusion, defeating any attempt "to group together, to classify certain activities, to make sense of them, and thereby, to impose a measure of order," and "to provide for a disciplined empirical study; to make possible a close and intensive focus, to render a knowledge of careful observation and record."[16]

> The "field," then, is a category of analysis; it is an area of focus upon a particular set of phenomena. It is an artificial construction, manmade and made quite deliberately. It constitutes an instrument or tool that, in modern dress, aims at providing empirically valid data. Through a process of "selective perception" we construct special fields, fence them off; we do so not to come to terms with the real world but in order to control our observation.
>
> Fields, therefore, must be treated as tentative and provisional; they are not "given" as the concrete categories of the real world are given. By their nature they are bound to undergo continuing reconsideration. Indeed, they provide the basis for their own alteration and modification, even for their replacement. And this is a measure of their success. If specialized analysis is initially productive, we are able to discover new variables, perceive new relationships, and construct new categories of analysis. Our focus shifts accordingly, our subject matter changes and leads again, we hope, to concepts that explain more than we were originally able to. This is the logic and perspective of specialization.[17]

Fields must overlap; their boundaries could not be defined precisely. Because public administration had not been conceived as a disciplined area of interest and as a field of scientific focus, it had neglected its definition and "the profession does not exhibit continuity in research, a rigorous methodology, or paradigms, theorums and theoretical systems."[18] A common unifying center must be established for systematic and disciplined inquiry. He rejects efforts to base the discipline on concrete institutions. That way it loses its flexibility and initiative and becomes "imprisoned in the institutional activity it presumes to study . . . the practical problems of the institutions become the problems of the discipline." Students, following familiar form, pile "fact upon

[14] D. K. Price, *The Scientific Estate.* Cambridge, Mass.: Harvard University Press, 1965, pp. 122–35.

[15] M. Landau, "The Concept of Decision-Making in the 'Field' of Public Administration," in S. Mailick and E. H. Van Ness (eds.), *Concepts and Issues in Administrative Behavior.* Englewood Cliffs, N.J.: Prentice-Hall, 1962, p. 2.

[16] Landau, "The Concept of Decision-Making," p. 3.

[17] Landau, "The Concept of Decision-Making," pp. 3–4.

[18] Landau, "The Concept of Decision-Making," p. 14.

fact and case upon case."[19] It fragments as conceptual categories take on a separate concrete existence. Thus the executive in the American polity becomes separated from the legislature and party, and itself splits into divisions. He also rejects efforts to identify the field with public policy, government, or executive. Instead, he supports attempts to construct the field in theoretical rather than practical terms, by centering public administration on decision making.

The decision-making approach to public administration had first been proposed by Simon[20] in the mid-1940s (see Chap. 3), but it had not received much support until Waldo revived it as the focus of the study of public administration in the mid-1950s.[21] Waldo, disillusioned with current definitions, set out to provide his own. He criticized those who glossed over the problem of definition altogether or proposed definitions that begged the question or compromised the issue "by failing to distinguish between the study of public administration and its subject matter." He saw public administration as one type of rational human cooperation "calculated to realize given desired goals with minimum loss to the realization of other desired goals."[22] Basically, it was concerned with the maximum realization of public goals. The administrative aspect concerned managerial behavior within organizations intended to achieve rational cooperation. The public aspect proved more difficult to pin down. For this he went beyond traditional American approaches to sociology for guidance. In structural-functional analysis, institutions and activities might be found that are associated with the identity of a group and with group life as a whole, having special coercive, symbolic, and ceremonial functions.

> This approach helps us to understand the special public quality of certain functions of government, for example, the apprehension and trial at law of persons accused of crimes, and the punishment or incarceration of the convicted; the manufacture and control of money; the conduct of foreign relations; or the recruitment, training, and control of armed forces. There is about such activities a monopoly aspect, and they are heavily vested with special coercions, symbolisms, and ceremonies. It is especially in such areas of activity that when a private citizen becomes a public official we expect him to play a new role, one which gives him special powers and prestige, but also requires of him observance of certain proprieties and ceremonies.[23]

These, then, would be the universals of the discipline. They would need to be seen in their cultural environment—"the entire complex of beliefs and ways of doing things of a society," emphasizing "the variety of human experi-

---

[19] Landau, "The Concept of Decision-Making," p. 6.

[20] H. A. Simon, *Administrative Behavior.* New York: Crowell Collier & Macmillan, 1947.

[21] See D. Waldo, *Ideas and Issues in Public Administration.* New York: McGraw-Hill, 1953; D. Waldo, "Administrative Theory in the United States: A Survey and Prospect," *Political Studies,* 2 (1954), pp. 70–86; D. Waldo, *The Study of Public Administration.* New York: Random House, 1955; D. Waldo, *Perspectives on Administration.* University, Ala.: University of Alabama Press, 1956.

[22] Waldo, *The Study of Public Administration,* p. 5.

[23] Waldo, *The Study of Public Administration,* p. 9.

ence in society rather than the recurrent patterns." Ways of doing things meant "patterns of activity with respect to food, clothing, shelter, courtship and marriage, child-rearing, entertainment, aesthetic expression and so forth,"[24] so that the student became aware of the differences in administrative systems (or subcultures), depending on the location, tasks, environment, and inhabitants of the system. The discipline would then break the bounds of American culture and be able to relate any administrative system to its environment and identify the interchange between them.

> Administration is a part of the cultural complex; and it not only is acted upon, it acts. Indeed, by definition a system of rational cooperative action, it inaugurates and controls much change. Administration may be thought of as the major invention and device by which civilised men in complex societies try to control their culture. . . .[25]

Finally, respect would have to be accorded to nonrational action—the irrational component in human psychology, unconscious adaptive social behavior, cultural conditioning, personal idiosyncrasies—that impeded rational order and prediction. Waldo's definition (or more realistically hints at an acceptable definition) has received much lip service, but it has not been developed further except by pioneers in comparative administrative systems (see Chap. 11). In 1967 Waldo was still complaining about the lack of consensus over boundaries and could still remark that "public administration is a subject matter in search of a discipline."[26] The crisis of identity has yet to be resolved.

From these attempts at definition, it can be seen that the discipline of public administration has outgrown its niche in political science (see Chap. 2), but maintains its distance from management science or any other discipline that studies the organizational society and administrative behavior in large-scale organizations. It has not developed a coherent body of systematic theory that justifies autonomy in its own right. Saddled with the intellectual baggage of the past, it has failed to maintain contact with the practical world of public administration and the transformation that has taken place in the subject matter as a result of organized genocide, technological prowess, internationalism, reaction against the organizational society and bureaucratism, revolution of rising expectations, proliferating public professions, and the relatively new phenomenon of turbulence that demands greater attention to the policies and outcomes of administration. The study lags behind the activity and needs to be updated to take into account contemporary happenings. Everything hinges on the "publicness" of public administration, which is a changing concept related to a philosophy of the public interest and normative administrative theory.

---

[24] Waldo, *The Study of Public Administration,* p. 10.

[25] Waldo, *The Study of Public Administration,* p. 11.

[26] D. Waldo, "Scope of the Theory of Public Administration," in J. C. Charlesworth, (ed.), *Theory and Practice of Public Administration: Scope, Objectives, and Methods,* Monograph 8, American Academy of Political and Social Science. Philadelphia: 1968, p. 2.

Among recent attempts to define publicness from questionable notions concerning sovereign power, public accountability, responsiveness and representativeness, absence of profit motive, and advocacy of public interest, Biller sought a new dimension based on an organization's relationship to its conditioning environment.[27] The organization's need for accurate and predictive information depended on the fluidity of its environment. The less fluid, the less the need; the more fluid, the more the need. But in conditions of extreme fluidity—in turbulent environments—no such information existed or could be obtained. Any organization that resided permanently in a turbulent environment or was frequently catapulted into it was a public organization, irrespective of its legal form, functions, activities, or other distinguishing characteristics. The adoption of this avant-garde definition would extend the scope of public administration to all participants in public affairs.

THE SHIFTING BASE OF PUBLIC ADMINISTRATION

The continuing controversy over the meaning of public administration reflects its changing subject matter. The field is being continually transformed. Traditional assumptions are frequently shattered by contemporary happenings. Now, more than at any other time in human history, public administration is in ferment. The subject matter is exploding in all directions. Communal activities subject to political direction are expanding fast in response to contemporary needs. New types of public organization are being created. New techniques and processes for improving the performance of public services are being discovered and adopted. The size of public budgets and staffs continually increases. Public laws multiply, as do the individual's contacts with public administration. Naturally, the academic study tries to keep pace; as it adapts itself to the changing nature of the subject matter, it must experience shifts in emphasis.

So much has happened in public administration since World War II that its study has been transformed. Some of the most important trends are summarized here; they and others are elaborated in succeeding chapters.

Shift from Work Processes to Societal Functions.

The work processes of public administration have been fairly well covered, and there is little more to say; all that is left is saying old things in a new way or the description of new processes, which may or may not be unique to public administration. In contrast, the societal functions provided by public administration are unique (see Chap. 6) and increase with the growing complexity of world civilization. They are conducted in many different ways, and

[27] R. P. Biller, "Some Implications of Adaptation Capacity for Organizational and Political Development," in F. Marini, (ed.), *Toward a New Public Administration.* San Francisco: Chandler, 1971, pp. 103–105.

comparative analysis may provide exciting clues to the nature of man and society.

Shift from Staff to Line Activies.

While the study of public administration has confined itself largely to the common administrative processes of governmental operation, other disciplines—such as education, economics, criminology, public health, law, social welfare, and military science—have filled the vacuum in the study of the societal functions provided by public authorities and have made valuable contributions to their respective fields. Some boundary activities have not been so fortunate, and the administration of important areas such as defense, foreign affairs, environmental control, and consumer protection have been neglected. Public administration, sometimes under the rubric of "public affairs" or "public policy," has begun to move into those areas inadequately covered by other disciplines.

Shift from Government Bureaucracy to Other Forms of Communal Activity.

Preoccupation with public bureaucracy—that is, large-scale governmental organizations financed entirely by public monies and staffed predominantly by career officials, linked by common political leadership and identical public laws—has obscured the rapid proliferation of other kinds of organization through which communal services are provided, such as community corporations, mixed enterprises, civic corps, and voluntary associations. It has also neglected the search for alternatives to bureaucratization. Public-administration scholars in the past, following Weber,[28] have tended to idolize bureaucracy and to exaggerate its importance even in the organizational society.

Shift from Professional Administrators at the Apex of Public Bureaucracy to the Whole Administration.

Most students of public administration, like administrative scientists, have viewed the provision of communal activities exclusively from the viewpoint of the full-time administrators, with advice on how to improve the latter's standing with politicians, pressure groups, community, and subordinates. They have been less sympathetic toward the clientele of public services, subordinates, or public-service associations. The behavioralists have turned their attention to public officials at middle and low levels, particularly those who directly confront the clientele.[29] The industrial-relations specialists

---

[28] See H. H. Gerth and C. W. Mills, *From Max Weber: Essays in Sociology.* New York: Oxford University Press, 1946.

[29] P. M. Blau and W. R. Scott, *Formal Organizations.* San Francisco: Chandler, 1962. B. Crozier, *The Bureaucratic Phenomenon.* London, Tavistock, 1964.

have discovered the public servant as employee and the government as employer. The internal politics of public organizations are now being exposed.

Shift from Scientism to Normative Public-Policy Making.

The American study of public administration began with normative policy analysis and reformist aspirations (see Chap. 2). Then it became scientific, with emphasis on identification of universal principles of management. It rediscovered politics, only to return via behavioralism to describing the "what" rather than the "why" or the "ought." Now, while advances are taking place in scientism, there are longings to return to social relevance, societal awareness, practical guides to better public administration, normative administrative theory, and controversial public issues.

Shift from Internal Relationships of the Public Administration System to External Relationships.

The practice of abstracting the public administration system from its peculiar environment and treating it as if it existed in a vacuum is disappearing fast. Not only is there more attention to the conditioning influence of the environment, but also the impact of public administration in changing its environment. This is a new ecological approach.

Shift from the National to the Transnational.

For too long American scholars ignored the rest of the world, but the United States' role as leading world power, technical assistance missions, and the ease of foreign travel have broken the isolation. As yet, however, the traffic is predominantly one way. Americans are discovering new vistas and dimensions in public administration, but non-Americans do not have similar facilities at their disposal. Nevertheless, cross-fertilization is taking place, and the discipline of public administration is becoming more international. As a result, its status in underdeveloped countries is rising, thereby encouraging study of their administrative needs in the new subdiscipline of development administration (see Chap. 11).

Shift from Intradisciplinary to Interdisciplinary Approaches.

Not long ago, scholars came to public administration from history, political science, and law. Today, they come from a wide range of diverse disciplines —mathematics, anthropology, linguistics, biochemistry. The public domain is open territory; public administration, far from preempting it, has encouraged other disciplines to explore its many ramifications in the life of the community. Each discipline introduces its traditions. In the meantime, the public administrator learns new insights and techniques from the proliferating variety.

These shifts in emphasis indicate that a change in the aims of the discipline of public administration is taking place. Both academics and practitioners want to improve its contribution to the alleviation of human problems. They want to demonstrate its intellectual worth. They want to develop interactional as well as content skills.[30] They want to reopen the debate over the good society. They want to rid the discipline of numerous false dichotomies that once dominated it as the basic issues—whether public administration was an art or a science, whether politics could be separated from administration, whether line and staff could be identified, whether specialists or generalists should head bureaucratic organizations, whether informal or formal relationships were more important, whether fact and value should be divorced —as they have rid it of the simplistic proverbs or principles that once constituted its normative administrative theory. They want to open up new frontiers and explore the new roles of government in contemporary society. They want to enhance its disciplinary status and its academic reputation. They want to attract creative minds capable of breaking present barriers to progress. In short, they want to transform the adverse image of both the study and practice of public administration. They hope that more people will appreciate that its study is a coherent discipline demanding first-class talent and that the subject matter is evidence not of man's imprisonment, but of his growing freedom over his environment.

[30] R. P. Biller, "Some Implications of Adaptation Capacity," p. 118.

2

The Study
of Public
Administration

The controversy over the definition, scope, objectives, and core of public administration has obvious bearing on its study. If the accent is placed on the word "public," the study might be subsumed within the traditional mother disciplines of history, law, and political science. If the accent is placed on the word "administration," it would be more comfortable associated with the newer disciplines of management science, behavioral science, and computer science. At the present time, it is wavering between these other disciplines, unable to claim full autonomy, because of its shifting basis and unresolved methodological problems, yet growing too large in itself to be accommodated easily within any other discipline. In the past its scholars limited their concerns, but now they are reaching out, moving into areas where others have already staked a claim, and are abandoning self-imposed limitations. The new impetus is strengthened by the expansion of the subject matter into uncharted territory, requiring new dimensions in the study and threatening to swallow related subdisciplines.

THE GROWTH OF PUBLIC ADMINISTRATION

Public administration, however defined and with whatever emphasis, increases in importance as civilized society develops in complexity and as societal institutions become increasingly specialized and differentiated. Its scope has expanded considerably with the rise of the modern administrative state. Today, there is hardly any aspect of contemporary living that does not involve public administration or increased public control over private concerns. Society is becoming more dependent on the political system, which in turn is becoming more dependent on the administrative system, or, put differently, the individual's freedom of action is being limited by political institutions, whose freedom of action in turn in being limited by public bureaucracies. For instance, the control of nuclear weapons and the reduction of armaments will require a system of detection, inspection, and safe disposal. In the absence of voluntary agreements to disarm, based on lessening fear of preemptive strikes, some kind of international apparatus with sufficient power and adequate sanctions will be necessary. Large-scale industries that fail to live up to public expectations will be subject to greater public regulation or will be threatened with nationalization. Egalitarianism will require a wholesale redistribution of income and wealth through public authorities and the provision of uniform national services. It seems likely that the present trend of heaping more and more demands on public administration—from medical research to consumer protection, from storing food surpluses to alleviating poverty, from space exploration to offshore drilling—will continue, and people will want public administration to anticipate their demands in advance.

The continuing expansion of public administration is readily explainable. First, people want more out of life; they want to share in the latest advances in knowledge. Their world extends beyond the radius of a day's walk to embrace the whole planet and perhaps soon the solar system as well; their relationships with their fellow men and the natural environment multiply. Of the many devices employed to maintain order in the system, public administration is crucial in reconciling competing demands and conflicting interests.

Second, other societal institutions which once assumed more of the burden, are declining in influence, and public administration has had to fill the gap. The extended family is being atomized in the mass society. Feudal relationships between master and servant are being swept away by mechanization, proletarianization, specialization, and consolidation. Aristocracies, kingdoms, tribal systems, and other paternal regimes are being replaced by bureaucratic states. Religion is a declining force, and organized clergies are fast shedding nontheological functions. Few private businesses, professions, and voluntary associations have been able to fill the vacuum.

Third, all mass movements since the eighteenth century have enormously increased the number, variety, and complexity of public-administration functions. The agrarian, industrial, and commercial revolutions brought government into business. Nationalism, imperialism, and internationalism extended the scope of government, while larger populations, urbanization, diversified communications, and greater mobility intensified governmental activities. The development of democratic, totalitarian, and socialist ideologies, accompanied by mass liberal, labor and anticolonial followings, transformed the concept of government.

Fourth, technology made big government possible. Ability to exert public control over communal activities has probably lagged increasingly behind the need. The closing of the gap will necessitate both technological advances and further expansion of public administration.

Fifth, the public in whose name public administration is conducted demands higher-quality performance and better public services. Every year more people must be served with a greater variety of activities to a higher standard. The expansion would be even greater were it not limited by competing societal institutions, scarce resources, public controls, more efficient processes, and confining professional ethics.

An examination of the crucial roles assumed by public administration in contemporary society as the instrument of the polity—local, regional, national, and international—and as a key power constituent in its own right further reveals the relationship between modernization and an expanding public administration:

a. Preservation of the polity—employment of representative symbols, inculcation of loyalty to the polity, celebration of political successes and honor of political heroes, promotion of unifying elements, bestowing of legitimacy, and resistance to involuntary external absorption

b. Maintenance of stability and order—preservation of tradition, conservative attitude to innovation, continuity of services, underwriting of societal activities, defense of the status quo, prosecution of nonconforming extremists, superiority over competitive coercive force, imposition of legitimate sanctions, peaceful reconciliation of disputes, and mediation

c. Institutionalization of change—arbiter of competing interests, implementation of reforms, provision of planning mechanisms, development programs and creative research, orderly transformation and exchange of mobile resources, and enforcement or provision of minimum standards

d. Management of large-scale communal services—public protection, social services, public enterprises, public utilities, conservation, land registration, marketing, and leisure facilities

e. Ensuring growth—protection from natural elements, wildlife and rival polities, provision of research information and statistics, promotion of optimistic ideology, public investment, and exploration and discovery

f. Protection of the defenseless—welfare programs, institutional charity, egalitarian influences, standardization, redistribution effects, nondiscriminating laws and practices, free services, and paternal attitudes

g. Formation of public opinion—provision of intelligence, control over mass media, preservation of cultural heritage, propaganda, representation of interest groups, public relations, functional feasibility, bureaucratic attitudes, and support to cultural events

h. Influential political force—strategic position, functional expertise, intelligence and research, clientele support, administrative discretion, priority resources, coercive power, leadership and inspiration, and crisis management

No settled society could exist without the competent performance of these roles according to community expectations, taking into account available mobile resources and the nature of the environment. Each role assumes a certain level of technical and communication skills. Some are shared with other societal institutions, while others are exclusive and monopolistic. Some demand little of the community; others require considerable effort from all. Some have barely changed in form throughout history; others are repeatedly transformed. Some are closely related and mutually reinforcing; others are distinctive, competitive, and even contradictory. Each has a different impact on society, but when they all expand, as they have over the past century, the stresses and strains have wide ramifications.

Nothing is preordained in the growth of public administration, nor is there inevitability about its continuing expansion, although collectivist ideologies and social turbulence are major determining factors for the immediate future. As alternatives to public bureaucratization are still relatively weak, the autonomous power base of public administration grows and poses a serious challenge to other political mechanisms (see Chap. 4). This is particularly true where public administration is highly centralized under the direction of an immobile self-selective elite corps, geographically concentrated in one place (for example, a capital city) and isolated professionally and socially from other power centers. In certain circumstances, the administrative elite could usurp effective political power. The basic requirements for such an event would include critically weak political institutions, lack of political consensus, mass political apathy or neutralization, bureaucratic unity, inept politicians, and full exploitation of bureaucratic power. These would enable the administrative elite to insist on strict obedience, to extend its hold over clientele, to infiltrate rival power centers, to capture supposedly independent watchdogs, to destroy civil liberty, and to displace its own service orientation.

WHY STUDY PUBLIC ADMINISTRATION?

The possibility, weak though it is, that public administration could turn into a tyrannous leviathan is reason enough to justify its study. Ceaseless vigilance is necessary to prevent political usurpation, abuse of discretionary power, and maladministration. The existence of a well-informed body of public opinion not only constitutes a safeguard against bureau-pathology in public administration, but also acts as a corrective to distorted images and false charges. Ignorance of public administration leaves the citizen dependent on officialdom—on its impartiality, honesty, efficiency, and correctness—and on knowledgeable middlemen who may favor officialdom against the best interests of the clientele. Even if the intermediaries are trustworthy, economical, and unavoidable (because the citizen does not have the time and competence, or the issues are so complicated that professional specialization is required), there are many occasions when the citizen must come into direct contact with public administration and should know how to act. More people are now finding employment in the public sector, and presumably they are obliged to learn more about their work environment as a matter of course. Possibly they might improve their professional capacity and acquire new skills useful not only within their own administration, but of assistance to other administrations too. Even if they fail to learn practical skills, they can improve their intellectual skills in grappling with a highly relevant and stimulating body of knowledge, which demands an open mind and an interdisciplinary perspective.

These are compelling enough reasons to justify the teaching of public administration, whether or not it is accorded disciplinary status by the academic profession. But what can the student expect from his studies? When medical students attend medical school, they know that after the successful completion of their courses they will qualify as doctors. Similarly, students of law, music, linguistics, and chemistry know they will study the great masters in the subject and the requisite skills that will make them, after a period of practical work, proficient in their chosen specialization. But potential students of public administration do not know what to expect from their courses or for what their studies will fit them afterwards. Some hope to be good public administrators; others are content with only an explanation of what goes on behind the scenes in public bureaucracies. Much will depend on the institution running the course (whether it is a university, training school, research institute, or government department); the background and knowledge of the instructors; and the experience, academic ability, and professional requirements of the students.

Although a smattering of knowledge may have been acquired at school, in youth movements, or in military training, serious study for most only begins at a higher education level or after a promising start in an official career. The fairly mature student finds two basic approaches: one academic, the other vocational. Although these are not wholly distinct, their aims are quite different. Academic teaching stresses the importance of passing on the accumulated knowledge of the discipline and different ways of thinking about it and uses management techniques mainly as research tools or illustrations of theoretical points. Vocational training, however, teaches specific managerial techniques and aims at producing better practitioners or at fitting people into vocational slots. The vocational trainee and the undergraduate are not expected to contribute anything original, but to concentrate on learning the basic vocabulary, the most important ideas, the different approaches, the principal texts, and some knowledge about their own administrative culture and official environment. The potential executive and the postgraduate cover much the same ground, but with greater sophistication, and they are expected to demonstrate a greater awareness of interrelationships; a higher sense for detecting relevant detail; a broader knowledge of ideas, values, approaches, theories, and limitations;

and a capacity for original research and creativity. Mature judgment counts for more than breadth of knowledge, and the emphasis switches from learning from others to the ability to work independently with minimum guidance and to impart independent learning to others.

At the introductory level, the stress is on a broad understanding of public administration. The aim is to develop the mind of the student by getting him to think analytically about an important contemporary phenomenon that daily affects his life and about which he may be unconsciously prejudiced by socializing influences. The teaching is designed to widen intellectual horizons, to question personal attitudes toward public affairs, to develop an interest in contemporary administrative problems, and to provide a minimum basic framework of information upon which the student can develop his thinking capacity. More specifically, it seeks the following:

a. To stress the ability to speak and write effectively—that is, clearly, precisely, and concisely
b. To develop intellectual, research, and practical tools
c. To acquaint the student with the literature of the subject and with ways to find new writing when his formal courses are completed
d. To promote an awareness of the importance of public administration, its operations, traditions, practices, and embodied values and trends
e. To link the discipline to other disciplines, show the connections between them, and compare and contrast their different approaches
f. To emphasize realism, the pragmatic-empirical foundation of the subject matter, and the dynamic nature of administration
g. To educate for intelligent citizenship, to promote increased participation in public affairs, to create a better understanding of the national culture and dominant social values, and to develop future public leaders
h. To prepare students for public employment by encouragement and inspiration, guidance in the values of the administrative culture, acculturation, simulation, and acquaintance with public administration (through projects or guest instructors)

Further, but more questionably, it seeks these goals:

a. To project values, promote reforms, and stimulate unorthodoxy
b. To channel students to understaffed public authorities
c. To present blueprints for administrative action

All these goals seem demanding, but they are encompassed in the whole range of teaching methods now available—lectures, seminars, tutorials, class discussions, case studies, essays, seminar papers, and book reviews, projects, syndicates, field trips, demonstrations, group and individual assignments, T groups, management-simulation games, internships, textbooks, and administrative novels.

On completion of his courses, the new student should be expected to know something of the following: the national administrative culture, the history of bureaucracy, the political nature of public administration, the main schools of administrative theory, comparative administration, public-personnel administration, public finance, administrative law, organizational theory, policy making, administrative history and biography, and public enterprise. He should be familiar with the main textbooks, other major books, and the leading journals. He should know how public administration has been conducted in his own country and in selected other countries, but not in any great detail. If he is set a problem in the subject, he should know where to look for information relevant to attempting some solution. Any practical ability, however, other than specific skills and management tools, would have been picked up incidentally or outside the courses.

The more advanced student learns actively rather than passively. The numbers are reduced, and a greater intimacy between instructors and students is encouraged. The basic aims are modified: coverage gives way to depth, courses are more specialized, and techniques and skills are given more prominence. The student is expected to find his own way in the literature and to apply what is relevant to individual projects, which are more problem-oriented. The students have more outside contacts, and usually the number of ancillary subjects is reduced. The courses are designed to widen horizons, to cultivate creativity, to encourage a scientific approach, to search for rational guidelines, and to promote vitality and diversity in developing the discipline. The student is expected to grapple with complicated sets of concepts, to have a thorough understanding of academic controversies, to comprehend the essence of administration, to recognize the stages of the administrative process, to be aware of current trends, to have a detailed knowledge of a specific area, and to make an original contribution. By this time, the student should have developed a philosophy of administration and methods for coping with administrative problems, as well as academic attributes such as testing the accuracy of asserted facts, the consistency of stated assumptions, the validity of drawn inferences, and the worth of value judgments.

Since teaching and research are inseparable, as part of the learning process the student is also expected to do independent work that can be loosely described as research, although in fact it is preparatory to research. The subject matter is changing so fast that instructors have difficulty in keeping abreast of current developments; moreover, the output of books, articles, and papers is so great that an instructor could be fully occupied only with new material that should be incorporated into teaching. But beyond this, his function is to advance new knowledge. The main concerns of his research can be classified as follows:

a. Teaching methods—investigations into the most effective methods and techniques, the composition of student body, staff-student relationships, organization of courses, and innovations

b. Documentation—collection of information and organization of records in a depository, research bank, or clearing house, including the search for teaching material and lost evidence in administrative history

c. Behavior—analysis of administration in action and the recording of nondocumentary evidence

d. Publication—compilation of bibliographies, journals, textbooks, readings, and lengthy exploratory studies

e. Cross-fertilization—exchange of information through conferences, debates, and discussions

f. Methodology—examination of vocabulary, techniques, criteria, sources, and logic from which results flow

g. Empiricism—concentration on the practical, problem solving, forecasting, and reform advocacy

h. Theory—concentration on the universals, model-building, hypothesizing

i. Interdisciplinary approaches—investigation of links, casual relationships, effects, and consequences.

Research interests may lead across the world and into large investments, or a pad and pencil in a quiet place may be sufficient.

Teaching and research bring instructors and practitioners together to their mutual benefit. Often their roles are interchanged or concurrent. The instructor learns of current developments and hears the latest administrative gossip, which may indicate shifts in policy and attitudes. He may also follow the progress of former students and discover through feedback where courses are failing. Without exchange of information with practitioners, teaching might be divorced from contemporary reality and the courses become increasingly outmoded and irrelevant. The instructors know they have yet to agree on the best methods for teaching administration or solving research problems. They are also aware that the discipline has to hold the attention of its students and the prospective employers and to build up a reputation for effectiveness. Only through self-criticism can the blocks to further progress be removed.

THE EVOLUTION OF THE DISCIPLINE

Systematic study of the various manifestations of public administration began only in the eighteenth century, and official university recognition did not arrive until World War I, when professorial chairs in the subject were established and instructional textbooks were published. Yet, public administration is as old as civilized society: almost every prominent figure in human history has expressed his thoughts on the nature of politics, government, and public administration at some time in his life, and all great books devote some space to the conduct of public affairs and reflect on the nature of public administration. Scattered thoughts, however, do not constitute a discipline, though it is important to note that, even without systematic teaching and study of public administration, the sages built great cities, constructed massive public works, fashioned huge armies, managed vast territories, and codified numerous laws. Snatches of their administrative know-how can be gleaned from recorded history, which reveals that public administration was rarely singled out for special treatment. Instead, it was considered part of political economy, military organization, or religious practice. Only when governments could be differentiated from other societal institutions and their activities developed to the point where professional administrators were indispensable for their effective performance, could modern public administration emerge. The term "public administration" began to creep into European languages during the seventeenth century to distinguish between the absolute monarch's administration of public affairs and his management of his private household. The contemporary discipline arose out of the bureaucratization of the nation-state when the church was separated from the state and government was superimposed on all other societal institutions within a definite territory.

The first systematic studies in modern public administration were designed to prepare potential public officials in Prussia for government service. They were largely descriptive accounts of the formal machinery of government, the work of public servants, and the code of conduct expected of public officials, compiled and taught by professors of the cameral sciences, which then covered all knowledge deemed necessary for the governance of an absolutist state. The Prussian example was copied elsewhere in Europe, but the discipline was confined to aspiring candidates to public service among the intelligentsia. The cameralist approach continued to influence European studies in public administration into the twentieth century, until it was super-seded by administrative law and legal studies.

Ideologically, cameralism lost support to liberalism and socialism, and arbitrary government gave way to bureaucratic administration of public laws. Aspirants to public office needed administrative law, a subject taught in Sweden and Austria not long after administrative studies had commenced in Prussia. The administrative law in cameralist courses increased at the same time as the law facilities broadened the content of administrative law courses to cover nonjuridical matter pertaining to the administration of public affairs. Eventually the law faculties assumed major responsibility for public administration, with emphasis predominatly descriptive, although comparative analysis was taught in legal theory and administrative jurisprudence. Civil-service training schools, within universities and the public bureaucracy, copied the same mixture of juridical and nonjuridical aspects of administrative law. Not until after World War II was public administration accorded independent status. In the meantime, the European administrative-law tradition had been exported to African and Asian colonies, Latin America, Turkey, and Japan, where it still remains strong, as it does in the European communist regimes.

In English-speaking countries, the social sciences and public law were slower to develop, with the exception of political economy. Potential public officials went straight into their chosen profession without undertaking special preparatory courses beforehand. Their academic studies had no direct bearing on the work they might perform in the public bureaucracy, except in highly specialized areas such as public health and engineering. There were no civil-service training schools, although there were high schools noted for preparing potential public servants in general skills and character formation. Few law faculties offered administrative law or constitutional law as anything more than a specialty with the non-juridical aspects virtually excluded. Administrative study was largely vocational training on the job or in specialized internal courses for customs officers, telegraphists, and the like. Circumstances were less favorable to the emergence of a discipline of public administration. The scope of governmental administration was traditionally narrower than in Europe, governmental administration was less centralized, bureaucratized and legally oriented, and administration was considered more of a pragmatic art than something that could be taught and learnt.

When the need for public-administration studies became more apparent with the enlargement of government services in the latter half of the nineteenth century, the British and American approaches differed considerably. In Britain, official circles resisted formal training programs in administration until after World War II. The older universities too resisted any move to develop administrative studies, whether on European or American lines. It was left to newer institutes of higher education, oriented to the social sciences, such as the liberal University of Manchester and the Fabian-based London School of Economics and Political Science, to pioneer public-administration studies, and to professionally-minded public servants to encourage the exchange of ideas through the Royal Institute of Public Administration. British Commonwealth countries shared much the same experience, lagging behind academic developments despite a flair for pragmatic innovation in the practice of public administration. The British approach remains largely descriptive and analytical, freely interpreting public administration to include anything of relevance to the administration of public affairs that might help policy makers, practitioners, and administrative reformers.

The American approach departed from the legal bias of Europe and the unstructured British interpretation. Because the United States has been so influential in the formation of the discipline of public administration, the evolution of the American approach to the discipline is explored here in detail.

Origins in the Movement for Administrative Reform

In the second half of the nineteenth century, the United States was beginning to experience the growing pains of economic development and enhanced international standing. A large public investment was required to support private initiative and to ameliorate dislocations accompanying rapid change. Public services lagged behind needs, and their quality was poor. Public finances were disorganized, permitting considerable seepage both in collection and disbursement. Quality staff were insufficiently supported at top political levels or by subordinates. Public morality left much to be desired, and frequent scandals and disasters hardly improved the public image of officialdom. Something had to be done to reform the administrative system of government more in keeping with contemporary needs, to improve the standard of public services, and to root out inefficiency and corruption.

Administrative reformers could not derive much benefit from reform movements outside the United States, where the political environment was so different. They had to build a climate of opinion favorable to reform and focus public opinion on this key issue. They had to study the facts of American public administration, examine how it worked, evaluate its good and bad points, and propose workable and politically acceptable solutions. They had to seek allies, impress political leaders with their case, and exert sufficient political pressure to upset prevailing arrangements. They had to give status and respectability to reform and provide ideological underpinning for pragmatic suggestions. Theirs was a political movement intent on achieving reform through influence rather than the direct exercise of power. They were in the political arena for specific limited purposes, unwilling to get involved in anything bigger or anything that would identify them with partisan political machines, on which they blamed much public inefficiency.

Between 1870 and 1917, the Mugwumps and then the Progressives provided the reform impetus outside the established party machines by going straight to the public via the press, educational societies, and professional associations until they grew strong enough to challenge the parties from within. The reform movement nurtured the embryo discipline of public administration, first outlined conceptually by Woodrow Wilson, a young academic in the Progressive movement and leading member of the National Civil Service Reform League, in an article entitled "The Study of Administration," published in the June 1887 issue of the *Political Science Quarterly*. The reform movement sought funds, staff, students, publicity, and social recognition for the study of public administration. It promoted comparative studies, particularly with Britain and Europe, from which it derived its idealized model of a politically neutral, professional, morally irreproachable, and efficient public bureaucracy. To counter partisan manipulation of the public domain, it emphasized rational analysis and a scientific approach. Yet it was as much concerned with results as with processes, with end products as with methods, with all branches of government as with the executive, with the whole range of public issues as with housekeeping functions, with moral imperatives as with scientific principles.

Although Wilson pointed the way, it was Goodnow, a professor of administrative law at Columbia University, who earned the title of "father of American public administration" for his deep involvement in public affairs, his drive to gain disciplinary recognition for public administration, his original contributions to American administrative law and practice, and his pioneering efforts in establishing special research institutes for public administration. Goodnow, another Progressive academic had acquired, like other Amherst graduates in moral philosophy, knowledge of the cameral sciences, administrative law, and nonpartisan bureaucracies in Germany, and had begun to teach public administration in history, public-law, and political-economy courses about the time that Wilson wrote his essay. His *Politics and Administration* (New York: Macmillan, 1900), intended as a theoretical introduction to comparative administrative law, was actually a polemic on the need for an extensive overhaul of the American system of government. In it he drew a functional distinction between politics and administration, the former having to do with the policies or expressions of the state will, the latter with the execution of these policies. He believed that political control was too strong in the United States; it subverted the popular will to partisan interests and undermined efficient administration. Direct democracy should be strengthened and nonpartisan administrative functions, which he carefully designated, should be depoliticized. Like Wilson before him, he recommended the strengthening of the executive over internal administration and the reduction of legislative control and interference. He equated party politics with corruption and inefficiency and denigrated professional politicians. He hoped to improve the quality of public business by replacing the spoils system with nonpartisan bureaucracies. He was sure a division between political control and administrative execution existed and could be used to delineate depoliticized officialdom from partisan politicians. This distinction was to haunt the study of public administration in the United States until after World War II.

The civil-service reform movement had been groping in this direction, and Goodnow's book had immediate effect in guiding President Roosevelt's administrative reforms. But the removal of immoral spoilsmen, corrupt politicians, aggressive entrepreneurs, and lazy party functionaries from public office did not ensure that public administration would be conducted with greater efficiency or economy. The structures and processes were still antiquated, and moral men with inadequate knowledge and skills were no more qualified to run large-scale public services than immoral men, as the many public inquiries conducted on partisan lines at the time attempted to show.

Development through Scientific Analysis

What was needed were impartial investigations into the facts of public administration. Several voluntary groups formed by citizens interested in good government existed to educate public opinion on municipal administration and to assist objective research stripped of popular muckraking and fault-finding and unprejudiced by preconceived ideals. They had only a marginal impact until the New York Bureau of Municipal Research was founded in 1906 to promote efficient and economical municipal government and the scientific study of municipal administration. Early success against Tammany Hall gained the Bureau official recognition, and it was employed by public authorities to carry out research and to undertake administrative reforms.

The Bureau's director, F. A. Cleveland, was appointed chairman of President Taft's Commission on Economy and Efficiency, and the Bureau became the model for similar research bureaus in major cities. It began to produce handbooks and manuals of administrative practice, and in 1911 it established a Training School for Public Service to train professionals in the study and administration of public business. The Bureau published *Municipal Research* "to promote the application of scientific principles to government," and some of its trustees formed the Efficiency Society (of New York). The Bureau was solidly behind Taylorism, the application of scientific method to administrative processes associated with F. W. Taylor, the management-science pioneer who came into prominence in the decade before World War I.

Taylor believed that his scientific principles of management were universally applicable. He was keen to apply them to public administration and supported attempts by his disciples to employ scientific management techniques in defense establishments. One of the first tests of applicability occurred when the Taft Commission on Economy and Efficiency (directed by Cleveland, Goodnow, W. F. Willoughby, and others) undertook the first comprehensive investigation of federal administration. Its recommendations closely followed scientific management principles, but little was done about them. Meanwhile, similar public inquiries and numerous private research groups mushroomed. The search for facts was accompanied by the growth of specialized libraries in public administration, bill-drafting services, and the proliferation of public-administration studies at the universities. In 1913, the American Political Science Association acknowledged the university's role in training students for public service and the need for more practical emphasis in teaching political science and economics. These efforts led to the formation of a clearing house under the auspices of the National Federation of Governmental Research Agencies in 1916.

A marked feature of the research movement was the attempt to avoid undersirable publicity, unconstructive muckraking, partisan politics, personal considerations, and political campaigns. It worked through self-enlightenment, citizen education, and influence. Another feature was the narrowing of concepts and objectives to scientific management principles and virtually exclusive preoccupation with management processes and structures. The message was clear: effective public business could be attained by following the principles and practices of effective private business. If irresponsible political bosses and invisible government were removed, government could be reconstructed as if it were a private business. Government should contain a strong executive with full administrative powers, a watchdog legislature, an independent auditor, unifunctional administrative units, a standard all-inclusive budget, and a merit civil service. Mastery of the scientific laws on which these proposals were based was to constitute the discipline of public administration between the world wars. The political environment of public administration was not overlooked, merely glossed over.

The scarcity of teaching materials was not overcome until the mid-1920s. Early attempts to provide textbooks were cut short by World War I, but after

1917 the deficiency was soon remedied by the New York Bureau and a new research institute established in Washington, D.C., in 1916, the Institute for Government Research (The Brookings Institution). In New York, the Bureau was in the hands of Cleveland, then C. A. Beard, and after 1921 L. Gulick, who became the first director of the National Institute of Public Administration when the Bureau and its training school merged. The emphasis of the NIPA continued on municipal affairs, although it made frequent forays into other levels of government. It concentrated on general principles and methods and issued several texts on personnel administration, public budgeting, police administration, and health administration, as well as the first bibliography in public administration.[1] Its spirit was that of scientism—to discover the laws that govern men and society through the same techniques that discover the laws that govern atoms. More progress could be achieved "through an application of the scientific spirit, through impartial research, through the testing of ideas, and the discovery of principles of administration than through any program of political reform which mankind has yet adopted."[2] This approach led to the collection of essays on administrative science, *Papers on the Science of Administration,* edited by L. Gulick and L. Urwick, published by the Institue in 1937 for the use of the President's Committee on Administrative Management, after the Institute had affiliated with Columbia University to survive the Depression.

In contrast, the Institute for Government Research, under W. F. Willoughby, concerned itself with federal administration and embarked on an ambitious publications program. Under Willoughby's directorship, over one hundred books were issued, of which he wrote fourteen, including *The Principles of Public Adminstration* (Baltimore: John Hopkins Press, 1927). Like Gulick, he was interested in ideal guiding norms, the range of available alternatives, the measurement of the practice against the ideal, and ways of bringing the actual and the ideal together. He was not concerned with the political implications of analysis, and he persistently and dogmatically proposed changes in the American system of government based on the scientific principles. He departed from orthodoxy by enthroning the legislature rather than the executive. Otherwise, he spent much of his time formulating and elaborating the scientific principles according to which public administration should be reconstructed. The doctrine of the research institutes was clear; it has been summarized by Sayre as follows:

    1.   The politics-administration dichotomy was assumed both as a self-evident

---

[1] P. Studensky, *Public Pension Systems.* New York: Appleton, 1920; A. E. Buck, *Public Budgeting.* New York: Appleton, 1921; B. Smith, *State Police.* New York: Crowell Collier & Macmillan, 1925; C. Heer, *The Post-War Expansion of State Expenditures.* New York: N.I.P.A., 1926; S. Greer, *A Bibliography of Public Administration.* New York: N.I.P.A., 1926; and C. E. McCombs, *City Health Administration.* New York: Crowell Collier & Macmillan, 1927.

[2] L. Gulick, *The National Institute of Public Administration.* New York: N.I.P.A., 1928, pp. 101–103.

truth and as a desirable goal; administration was perceived as a self-contained world of its own; with its own separate values, rules, and methods.

2. Organization theory was stated in "scientific management" terms; that is, it was seen largely as a problem in organization technology—the necessities of hierarchy; the uses of staff agencies, a limited span of control, subdivision of work by such "scientific" principles as purpose, process, place, or clientele.

3. The executive budget was emphasized as an instrument of rationality, of coordination, planning, and control.

4. Personnel management was stressed as an additional element of rationality (jobs were to be described "scientifically," employees were to be selected, paid, advanced by "scientific" methods).

5. A "neutral" or "impartial" career service was required to insure competence, expertise, rationality.

6. A body of administrative law was needed to prescribe standards of due process in administrative conduct.[3]

This doctrine constituted public administration orthodoxy between the world wars. Its influence persists.

The research institutes in New York and Washington, D.C., were not the only bodies sponsoring academic research and publication. The public professions and reform advocates were doing their share too. In Chicago, C. E. Merriam, Professor of Political Science, took a different attitude from his academic colleagues, who refused to participate actively in politics. He encouraged his staff to engage in public controversy and reform advocacy. It was from his department that L. D. White produced the first undergraduate textbook, *Introduction to the Study of Public Administration* (New York: Crowell-Collier-Macmillan, 1926), which evidenced less enthusiasm for basic principles and scientific management and endeavored to take into account the political environment of public administration. White went much further in *The City Manager* (Chicago: University of Chicago Press, 1927), which questioned the separation of politics from administration and the applicability of universal principles (see Chap. 3). The Chicago department was impressed with John Dewey's doubts that facts alone could lead to principles and doctrines, for doctrines could prejudice the interpretation of facts. What was needed was not dogmatic doctrines, but flexible scientific thinking as an experimental tool of inquiry. Ideas derived from special circumstances ought not "be frozen into absolute standards and masquerade as eternal truths."[4]

Further doubts about the validity of the principles approach were raised by the onset of the Depression, when the divergence between theory and practice, ideal and reality, could not be denied. Many textbook maxims were inapplicable, contradictory, unrealizable, and invalid. The dogma of the one best way was highly suspect, and the principles approach seemed inap-

---

[3] W. S. Sayre, "Premises of Public Administration: Past and Emerging," *Public Administration Review*, 18 (1958), 102–103.

[4] J. Dewey, *The Public and Its Problems.* New York: Holt, Rinehart and Winston, 1927, p. 203.

propriate for the most pressing issues of the day in American public admin-istration. With severe cuts in research grants, many research bureaus dis-appeared, and those that struggled on switched to empirical problem solving.

Disillusionment with the scientific-principles approach was evident soon after the New Deal came into being, when Harry Hopkins responded to a budget-bureau inspector who sought an organizational chart of his relief program with the comment, "I don't want anybody around here to waste any time drawing boxes." In a few quick strokes, Roosevelt undid the manage-ment orthodoxy of the past decade. Every move was disowned by the public-administration establishment, notably The Brookings Institution (formerly Institute for Government Research) and the National Civil Service Reform League. Their criticism evoked public fears that the bad old days of political bossism, spoils system, and wholesale corruption would be revived. To quiet opposition, Roosevelt accepted a proposal from the Social Science Research Council that it carry out an independent inquiry into public-service personnel. The 1933 Commission of Inquiry on Public Service Personnel was not the first SSRC inquiry conducted for a President. Merriam had been instrumental in setting up the Spelman Fund to finance SSRC and to per-suade President Hoover to conduct research on social trends. Now he and Brownlow (head of the newly formed Public Administration Clearing House, established by several government professional associations in Chicago), with Gulick as director of research, conducted a similar project and by 1936 had published twelve monographs on public-personnel administration, in-cluding L. D. White (ed.), *Civil Service Abroad* (New York: McGraw-Hill, 1935); C. J. Friedrich *et al., Problems of the American Public Service* (New York: McGraw-Hill, 1935); and L. Wilmerding, *Government by Merit* (New York: McGraw-Hill, 1935). These, like the final report, *Better Government Personnel* (New York: McGraw-Hill, 1936), were traditionally overlaid with preconceived theory and without compromise on principle.

Reconciliation with Politics

The first to realize the impact of the New Deal on the study and practice of public administration was Gulick.[5] To him, the government had become the "super-holding company" of American economic life. It would be required to assume greater responsibilities and functions, create planning mechanisms, redistribute powers, specialize, professionalize, and reorganize. Politics and administration could not be separated; administration could not be taken out of politics, and politics could not be taken out of administration (see Chap. 3, 4, and 5). Further doubt about the politics-administration dichotomy was expressed by the Chicago department, which charged that public admin-istration had been conceived too narrowly and that the formal separation between politics and administration had gone too far and made public ad-

---

[5] L. Gulick, "Politics, Administration and the New Deal," *Annals of the American Academy of Political and Social Science,* Vol. 169.

ministration detached and unreal.[6] Public administration involved more than a mere study of techniques and general principles; it was the "state in action," as broad as government itself. The good administrator participated in public-policy making, and he was an organizational politician. Herring's study of the relationships between pressure groups and federal officials[7] was ample testimony. The political nature of public administration was more important than the scientific analysis of administrative structures.

The clash between scientific analysis and politics in public administration was highlighted by the President's attempts between 1936 and 1941 to reorganize the federal machinery of government, whose ramshackle structure was an obvious target for reform (see Chap. 5). Previous inquiries had been fruitless. Roosevelt decided against another Social Science Research Council research project and appointed a Committee on Administrative Management (consisting of Brownlow, Merriam, and Gulick) to review the federal administrative apparatus and advise on the principles of a reorganization. Briefly, all that the committee did was to apply traditional management orthodoxy through the principles approach and make a few concessions to the constitutional setting, dominant political values, and democratic processes.[8] Roosevelt could hardly reject a report that followed his known wishes and exaggerated central bureaucratic leadership at the expense of congressional supervision. In contrast, a Brookings Institution report for Congress put Congress at the head of executive power and viewed the President as a general manager responsible to Congress through strong independent audit. Despite a great deal of common agreement in the two reports, their respective supporters attacked each other and challenged the other's intellectual honesty, political impartiality, and administrative principles. The reorganization issue was caught up in the political fight between the President and Congress, and the scientific principles of the President's committee were eroded by political considerations. Politics, not administrative science, had triumphed.

The episode of the President's committee divided public administration scholars. Those who were struck by the similarities with business administration and were deeply committed to scientific management theory believed that, although public administration worked in a political context, the similarities were more important than the differences. Those who were convinced that the differences were more important and were critical of the principles approach believed the political environment to be the deter-

[6] J. M. Gaus et al., Frontiers of Public Administration. Chicago: University of Chicago Press, 1936.

[7] P. Herring, Public Administration and the Public Interest. New York: Russell and Russell, 1936.

[8] The detailed operations of the Brownlow committee have been well documented by B. D. Karl, Executive Reorganization and Reform in the New Deal. Cambridge, Mass.: Harvard University Press, 1963; and R. Polenberg, Reorganizing Roosevelt's Government. Cambridge, Mass.: Harvard University Press, 1966.

mining factor. The former preferred general model building and theorizing; the latter returned to empiricism and political concerns. Possibly more than any other event, World War II demonstrated that general administrative principles, derived from business or scientific analysis, had limited applicability in public administration whose size, functions, growth rate, and composition depended on the societal requirements of the political system and reflected political ideology, constitutional arrangements, and communal expectations.

The reconciliation with politics during the 1940s did not occur without a struggle. During that time the study of public administration was in disarray. It could not adjust itself properly to the transformation that was taking place in the practice, and no administrative philosopher with the status of Keynes in economics emerged to reshape the discipline in line with current events. Instead, several different developments took place, which, in one way or another, marked a change of direction.

Initially, there was a backlash reaction to big government and the growth of a leviathan—represented by right-wing, laissez-faire and liberal philosophizers such as F. A. Hayek in *The Road to Serfdom* (Chicago: University of Chicago Press, 1944) and L. Von Mises in *Bureaucracy* (New Haven: Yale University Press, 1944)—but public opinion firmly supported more government.

The principles of public administration were attacked. They were not scientific but normative, embodying questionable values. They were not universal, but culture-bound. They were not grounded in evidence but based on misplaced corporate analogies and autocratic assumptions. For every principle, there was an equally plausible and acceptable contradictory principle. According to Simon, they were only criteria for describing and diagnosing administrative situations, and they suffered from superficiality, oversimplification, and lack of realism.[9] Until the principles became truly scientific, public administration could not be recognized as a science, if indeed it were ever possible to exclude normative considerations from administrative problems; to separate ends from means in government; to develop a science of man; and to base principles on limited culture-bound experience without recourse to comparative study.[10]

The assumption of rational efficiency was superseded by concepts of social efficiency, quality of government, political ends, and public wants. The study of public administration should not be concerned "chiefly with the most successful exploitation of manpower, money and materials in the service of any master, for any purpose, subject only to the direction of politics" but

[9] H. A. Simon, *Administrative Behavior.* New York: Crowell Collier & Macmillan, 1947, pp. 20–38.

[10] R. A. Dahl, "The Science of Public Administration: Three Problems," *Public Administration Review* 7 (1947), pp. 1–11.

with "the process of social change and the means for making such changes best serve the ends of a more truly democratic society."[11] The problem of democratizing the organization of authority was tackled philosophically by O. Tead in *Democratic Administration* (New York: Association Press, 1945); ideologically by C. A. Beard in *Public Policy and General Welfare* (New York: Holt, Rinehart, and Winston, 1941); and pragmatically by A. Leiserson in *Administrative Regulation* (Chicago: University of Chicago Press, 1942). Their aim was to blend big government with democratic mores, to humanize large-scale organizations, to improve the morale of hard-pressed staffs, to train people to resist the temptation to bureau-pathology, and to evolve a new management ideology emphasizing democratic values.

The politics-administration dichotomy, like the "proverbs" of administration, was irreparably damaged. It was described as "misleading," "a fetish," "a stereotype," and the term "politics" was replaced by "policy," which denoted something more positive and less partisan and deceitful (see Chap. 3). At the beginning of the war, the Reed Committee had given up the attempt at drawing a rigid line between political and career executives in extending the merit system in the Federal Civil Service. The new theorists argued that the public bureaucracy had always had an important policy-making role and that policy formulation was inextricably interwoven with managerial functions. Case studies were produced to show that no distinction could be made in practice.[12] The old dichotomy was buried in postwar textbooks, such as F. M Marx (ed.), *Elements of Public Administration* (Englewood Cliffs, N.J.: Prentice-Hall, 1946), which admitted the political nature of public administration, the political role of administrators, and the existence of bureaucratic power.

The philosophical bases of the discipline were irreparably damaged. Waldo's assessment of American public administration theory at the end of World War II, contained in *The Administrative State* (New York: Ronald, 1948), found existing theory wanting in many ways—its view of the good life, its presumption that action flowed from facts or pressures, its enthronement of an administrative ruling class, its acceptance of the separation of powers, and its penchant for dichotomies rather than continua. He questioned the validity of the principles approach, the heavy stress on formal organization, the scientific adequacy of factual research without reference to values, and the meaning of "efficiency and economy" in the pyramid of values. His book refuted the theoretical worth of much that then constituted the core of the discipline, without providing a new core or constructive proposals about

[11] E. S. Wengert, "The Study of Public Administration," *American Political Science Review* 36 (1942), p. 316.

[12] P. H. Appleby, *Big Democracy.* New York: Alfred A. Knopf, 1945; J. D. Kingsley, *Representative Bureaucracy.* Yellow Springs, Ohio: Antioch Press, 1944; D. E. Lilienthal, *TVA Democracy on the March.* New York: Harper & Row, 1944; and A. Leighton, *The Governing of Men.* Princeton: Princeton University Press, 1946.

where the discipline ought to head. Written with "a certain animus toward, even contempt for, the literature of Public Administration,"[13] it constituted an indictment of public-administration theory, whose shock waves had the unfortunate and unintended effect of turning scholars away from theory for at least a decade.

The contemporary study of public administration began to take shape during this confusing period when so much that had been written on it was superseded by events accompanying the New Deal and World War II, and when much that had been thought about it was debunked by politicians, practitioners, and younger scholars who had participated in those events as administrators and advisers. At this point, the discipline was ripe for innovation.

The remainder of this book is concerned with the nature of postwar developments and the transformations that have since taken place in both theory and practice. Before turning to these exciting happenings, it is necessary to remember that much of the past was not abandoned overnight or at all and that the overreaction of postwar disillusionment with the principles approach and the politics-administration dichotomy has since been corrected a little by the rediscovery and reworking of valuable material bequeathed by the pioneers. The reformist drive behind the study of public administration still persists, although it is somewhat disguised under new academic approaches. People want to improve public administration and hope that they will derive practical benefit from its study as well as intellectual stimulation. The scientific bent is much more sophisticated than the early principles approach, with more scientific hardware available and a greater variety of relevant scientific techniques (see Chap. 3). Administrative theory has expanded in its search for universal principles, but it remains separate from public administration, and little cross-fertilization has taken place (see Chap. 10). Finally, the study of public administration has continued uneasily as a branch of political science, less concerned with the inner workings of public bureaucracies and focused more on public policy.

A DISCIPLINE TRANSFORMED

Before the study of public administration in the United States changed direction in the 1940s, it was at least traveling an identifiable route. Since then it has been pursuing different paths at the same time. If anything, it is more confused now than it was then, for too much has happened too quickly. No single person or group has been able to assimilate everything that has happened, let alone code, classify, and arrange in a coherent unifying framework. Innovations followed too closely on one another, and the discipline lost its

[13] D. Waldo, "The Administrative State Revisited," *Public Administration Review* 25 (March 1965), p. 6.

bearings; nobody yet has appeared capable of restoring any semblance of order. Other disciplines have experienced similar upheavals, disconcerting events when they occur, but healthy in the long run. The shake-up, however, has not been erratic, but has centered on several definite trends, which together have transformed the study of public administration throughout the world.

Internationalism

Before World War II, European, British, and American studies kept strictly apart, with little exchange of ideas or transnational review. They still go their own ways, but the barriers have been breached. The proliferation of international organizations has brought a new dimension, that of international administration. The technical-assistance program of the United Nations in public administration has financed several international seminars and issued administrative handbooks for use by underdeveloped countries. It has taken experts to needy countries and brought students to developed countries. Some United Nations agencies have provided extensive training and research facilities and assisted international efforts in establishing institutes of public administration throughout the world. The International Institute of Administrative Sciences, a nongovernmental organization located in Brussels, has performed invaluable service in bringing together east and west, developed and undeveloped, rich and poor. Isolation is now strictly self-imposed.

Wider Horizons

A universal feature in the postwar years has been the rapid acceleration of the size and scope of public administration. In communist regimes, it covers practically every conceivable aspect of community life. Elsewhere, governments have increased the range of their services to include large-scale monopolistic industries, uniform social services, economic development, conservation of resources, population planning and control, science and technology, international aid, and environmental control; in the meantime their traditional functions of internal and external security, law and order, public works, and social regulation have been transformed by technology, population growth, urbanism, and automation. Public administration is booming: there are not enough experts available to meet the escalating demand. In these circumstances, the discipline has had to raise its sights beyond housekeeping functions and to encompass the functional transformation taking place and the enhanced role of public administration in meeting societal needs. Even within the scope of traditional boundaries, attention must now be focused on the prominence of the military; the extension of quasi-autonomous public authorities, mixed enterprises and government contracting; public financing of science and technology; technological revolutions in every governmental activity; shifting lines of authority between different levels of government: the great growth of public financing and public employment and the impact on the private sector, the government as investor, consumer, and employer; and the repercussions on individual liberty, particularly the need for citizen redress against unwarranted intrusion into private affairs and maladministration. The discipline grows more complex and compelling daily.

Search for Autonomy

The enlargement of public administration made it unsuitable for subservient status within the traditional disciplines, which grew increasingly reluctant to shelter it under their rubric. Political science, for instance, moved in a different direction. The American Political Science Association went so far as to drop it altogether from its 1967 Annual Meeting, having excluded it from the four major areas of study in a 1962 committee report, "Political Science as a Discipline." In the search for a continuing place in the sun, some instructors do not care where the discipline is taught or under what title, claiming that it is part of the organizational aspects of modern life dealing with institutions involved in public affairs. To others, "public administration is administration that is public"[14] or "a public process . . . in which there are varying degrees of publicness,"[15] or "macroadministration," not identifiable with government or bureaucracy, but with any large-scale organization or complex of organizations with public-policy objectives. This view is close to the functional approach in comparative administration, spearheaded by F. W. Riggs,[16] and the search for the boundaries of administrative systems in diverse cultures. The publicness constitutes the basis for autonomy from administrative science (dominated too much by business administration) and organizational theory (dominated too much by sociologists).

A different view, although with much the same object in mind, is a return to the idea of public administration as a profession and multidisciplinary schools of public administration as training grounds for potential public servants in all governmental functions—that is, to bring under one roof that which is now separated into many different postgraduate schools in the United States. Although not specifically advocated, it would have an occupational or vocational emphasis. It would not cater to all potential public servants, only to those whose jobs would have a high administrative content. It would teach low-key administrative generalists a new style of positive thinking and show that contemporary public administration demands

---

[14] H. Emmerich, "The Scope of the Practice of Public Administration," in J. C. Charlesworth, ed., *Theory and Practice of Public Administration: Scope, Objectives and Methods,* Monograph 8, American Academy of Political and Social Sciences. Philadelphia: 1968, p. 95.

[15] L. Caldwell, in J. C. Charlesworth, ed., Ibid. p. 236.

[16] See F. W. Riggs, *The Ecology of Public Administration.* New York: Asia Publishing House, 1961; *Administration in Developing Countries.* Boston: Houghton Mifflin, 1964; and *Thailand.* Honolulu: East-West Center Press, 1966.

creative administrators who are able to move in and out of government, being aware of public psychology and political strategies; capable of being reformers, social changers, crisis managers, and political initiators; skilled in negotiation and advocacy, public relations, consultation, policy analysis and evaluation; versed in complex decision making; ready to lead, with deep concerns about ethical values, responsible power, personal liberty, public interest, and the moral issues of their time. In short, it would provide a suitable discipline for a new guardian class behind political leaders.

Return to Reality

Having cast off the proverbs of public administration, the discipline looked anew at the subject matter and saw it for what it was, not what it purported to be, or what it should have been. The new realism appeared in the Case Reports of the Committee on Public Administration of the Social Science Research Council, which were case studies of selected administrative problems of the New Deal and World War II. These were followed by the Committee on Public Administration and the Inter-University Case Program associated with H. Stein and E. Bock, from which have resulted objective accounts of administrative situations suitable for analysis and role playing in the classroom. The case-study approach has been described in the introductions to H. Stein, *Public Administration and Policy Development: A Case Book* (New York: Harcourt, 1952) and F. C. Mosher, *Governmental Reorganizations* (Indianapolis: Bobbs-Merrill, 1967). The assumption is that administrative actions must be viewed in context as part of the totality of human behavior, and administrative situations as part of the wider social system. This is similar to behavioralism, but employs literary talents rather than scientific methods.

Behavioralism itself came to public administration through H. A. Simon, first in his *Administrative Behavior* (New York: Macmillan, 1947), and then in a significantly different textbook: H. A. Simon, D. W. Smithburg, and V. A. Thompson, *Public Administration* (New York: Knopf, 1950). Although written in public administration, the analysis in these two books of human behavior within governmental organizations could be applied equally to human behavior in any bureaucratic organization, governmental or non-governmental. Indeed, since the early 1950s, behavioralism has come to public administration largely from sociologists and psychologists working in related fields, and few behavioralist studies in public administration have been exported in exchange, except in bureaucratic theory.[17] Rather

---

[17] Among the most significant are P. M. Blau, *The Dynamics of Bureaucracy.* Chicago: University of Chicago Press, 1955; P. M. Blau and W. R. Scott, *Formal Organizations.* San Francisco: Chandler, 1962; R. T. Golembiewski, *The Small Group.* Chicago: University of Chicago Press, 1962; W. J. Gore, *Administrative Decision Making.* New York: John Wiley & Sons, 1964.

than accept things at their face value or reproduce official self-images, the new realism goes behind the scenes and attempts to describe what really goes on and to test the findings scientifically.

From Process to Results

Postwar public administration still devotes much attention to the general administrative processes outlined in Gulick's 1937 POSDCORB formula, representing planning, organizing, staffing, directing, coordinating, reporting, and budgeting. The emphasis has since switched to a process first analysed in detail in Simon's *Administrative Behavior,* namely, decision making. Simon's book is an attempt to refocus the discipline of public administration on rationality, as opposed to the folklore of scientific principles, and on a logical positivist bent to behavioralism, centered on the concept of rational decision making that minimized nonrationality content. Right, that is, rational decisions, he argued, were more important than efficient and economic means of carrying them out. The heart of all administration, public and nonpublic, was decision making, and the vocabulary of administrative theory should be drawn from the logic and psychology of human choice. Simon's later work on decision making, like most other research in this area, was conducted on the borders of public administration, although many of the techniques that have been developed to ensure greater rationality in decision making—operations research, game theory, cybernetics, system analysis, program budgeting—originated within public administration and were incorporated into military decision making.

Simon's concern with the end product of administration—decision making —coincided with the redefinition of public administration as a study of public-policy making and application (to which Simon was opposed, as it would lead to public administration swallowing political science and possibly other social sciences too). The two were united in P. Appleby's *Policy and Administration* (University of Alabama Press, 1949), which confirmed much of Simon's decision-making analysis in public-policy making and mapped out the role that the public officials (administrators) played in the political system as policy makers. Public officials were influential decision makers in the public-policy arena and gained strength as governmental decision making became more demanding. Were they any more objective or rational than their political masters? Nobody really knew, as there were no scientific measures by which policies or decisions could be judged. Planners, fiscal economists, military strategists, systems engineers, and others set out to find ways of thinking the unthinkable in nuclear warfare, devising appropriate policies for defense, and measuring functional performance in public administration. Their concern was no longer process, but the end results of public administration, the cost-benefit ratio of public programs, and the objectives of public policy. From Program Performance Budgeting Systems (PPBS) and policy analysis, the next step was policy planning and long-range forecasting of future states to assist in the formulation of present policies and objectives and the evaluation of current actions.

More Sophisticated Theory

As previously noted, Waldo and Simon virtually destroyed public-administration theory at the beginning of the postwar period. The return to realism was an attempt to start all over again by examining the facts and by working up to more realistic theory. The results, from a theoretical viewpoint, have been disappointing. The number of truly original thinkers in public-administration theory is very small. Most are imitative; they borrow their ideas from other disciplines and apply them to public administration. Because the ideas have already been tried elsewhere, the general level of public-administration theory has improved on prewar efforts.

In chronological order, the first reconstruction in theory occurred with the sociologists' rediscovery of Weber and his ideal bureaucracy, which was derived from a study of public-administration history. Weber's model has since become the starting point of theoretical explorations in public administration. Bureaucratic theory has explored the formal and informal characteristics of large-scale formal organizations, the relationship between the formal and informal networks, different typologies of bureaucracy, bureaucratic behavior and bureau-pathology, bureaucratic power and bureaucratic weaknesses, bureaucratic confrontations, irrationality in bureaucracy, bureaucratic personality types, and the wider process of rationality in government—all of which are relevant to understanding public administration. The external relations of bureaucracies have been explored in S. N. Eisenstadt, *The Political Systems of Empires* (New York: Free Press, 1963), which is again largely based on public-administration history. The idolization of bureaucratic authority is being questioned, and with the recent onset of the antiorganization movement, alternatives to bureaucracy are being explored.

Closely allied to bureaucratic theory has been organizational theory, a field that has experienced a remarkable growth in the postwar era. Again, its findings concerning organizational dynamics, small-group behavior, communications, leadership patterns, decision making, open systems, human relations and morale are highly relevant to public administration. New insights are being provided from the highly rational field of the management sciences and cybernetics to explorations of the irrational and abnormal in clinical psychiatry, but there is a time lag before they are applied to public administration by theorists and a much greater time lag before they percolate to the practitioners.

Cultural Breakthrough

Although much of public-administration theory is imitative and culture-bound, the study of comparative public and development administration, a field virtually unknown before the war, except for cursory country-by-country descriptions, has broken through cultural barriers and is stimulating much original thinking. The impetus came from great-power competition, international humanitarianism, and appeals for help from backward countries and newly independent states. The transference of administrative know-how proved more difficult than was anticipated. Public administration had to be seen in context, but western bureaucratic concepts were inadequate. New perspectives were badly needed, and F. W. Riggs pioneered a new administrative vocabulary to describe different societal typologies, administrative cultures, and administrative systems. The theoretical side of comparative public administration has paralleled developments in comparative politics and modernization, while the practical side has followed developments in economic analysis, social anthropology, and planning theory. In both cases, it has been necessary to construct theoretical models and to indulge in much speculation. The result has been a questioning of the traditional framework of public administration and western egocentricity. The developed nations are beginning to learn from the so-called undeveloped nations, particularly in coping with a wide range of comparatively new problems that have long been assimilated in poorer countries. Transnational administrative reform is no longer only from rich nations to poor.

Excising Discredited Material

Despite frenzied activity now taking place in public administration, no new synthesis has occurred, an adequate science of administration is as elusive as it has ever been, and a fundamental and comprehensive theory is still missing. Public administration has yet to prove it is a theoretical or practical science. Instead, partial theories abound, and a body of data and theory is becoming distinguishable from other organized knowledge, which may be integrated and synthesized into a true discipline. More importantly, dead ends, false dichotomies, and inadequate theories are being discarded. For instance, the politics-administration dichotomy has been thoroughly discredited, and so have the principles of public administration. In recent years, the line-and-staff dichotomy has been challenged.[18] Currently under fire are the generalist-specialist controversy[19] and the efficacy of bureaucratic organization in conditions of rapid change and turbulence.[20] A new generation of scholars is once again challenging the present orthodoxy and its relevance to the social order.[21] From the stimulation of this debate and controversy, public administration emerges in better shape.

At the present time, the most disturbing features are the inapplicability

---

[18] G. G. Fisch, "Line-Staff is Obsolete," *Harvard Business Review,* 39, No. 5 (1961), 67–79.
[19] Y. Dror, *Public Policy Making Reexamined.* San Francisco: Chandler, 1968.
[20] W. G. Bennis, *Changing Organizations.* New York: McGraw-Hill, 1966.
[21] F. Marini, ed., *Toward a New Public Administration.* San Francisco: Chandler, 1970.

of much of the study to nondemocratic regimes and the failure to bridge the gap between theorists and practitioners, who seem to be traveling parallel courses without ever getting any closer. The former challenges the status of the study as a universal discipline; the latter challenges its right to exist at all. If it is really true that practitioners can get along well without any help from the theorists, and the theorists can exist without reference to practice, something is radically wrong. Reciprocity is not lacking, but until it increases, the study may continue to wander aimlessly in all directions. Perhaps the quickest way of recapturing direction is to concentrate on the probable rather than the possible and to look at the obvious rather than search for the obscure. Likewise, the practitioners may be reattracted by a return to practical operating problems, not to "snidely deprecate what is being done . . . and freely criticize and gratuitously advise those who do"[22] but to help them constructively and operationalize theoretical concerns.

[22] D. Waldo, "Scope of the Theory of Public Administration," in J. C. Charlesworth, ed., *Theory and Practice of Public Administration: Scope, Objectives and Methods,* Monograph 8, American Academy of Political and Social Sciences. Philadelphia, 1968, p. 19.

II
Politics, Policy, and Administration

3

Public-Policy Making

Public-policy making—the determination of the general direction of publicly resolved societal issues—is the most important area of public administration and still the most neglected aspect in the discipline, although in recent years valiant attempts have been made to remedy this defect. Public-policy making determines the whole shape of the discipline, the division of resources and responsibilities between public and private sectors, the distribution of communal goods, the scope of government, and the extent of public controls. It covers the most crucial and fundamental decisions of the contemporary world, which determine the future of civilization, man, and the planet—for instance, whether man will annihilate himself and perhaps all life in thermonuclear holocaust; whether man will so pollute and poison the atmosphere that the delicate ecological balance is adversely disrupted for animal life; whether man, in his reckless exploitation of natural resources to maintain and improve living standards for greater and greater numbers of people, will exterminate and destroy all that he cannot use for himself; and, perhaps, whether the mistakes will be repeated on other planets. Until World War II such issues were left to philosophy and science fiction. Now they are the practical concern of international bodies and the great powers. Actions have been taken in the past without adequate thought to community repercussions, then or in the future; once accepted, these have become the norm, despite subsequent realization of their hastiness or shortsightedness. Actions now being taken may have similar effects for future generations, but the difference is that we are more aware of the possibility, more conscious of impending doom, and more reluctant to be history's villains.

Nineteenth-century optimism in the inevitability of progress and twentieth-century technical know-how have transformed the world. They have brought into man's grasp all that he has longed for, yet he is no more secure, and the greater majority of people still live as their ancestors used to do, in the same wretched, diseased, illiterate, half-starved, downtrodden condition. Man sends sterilized instruments to the moon, but cannot keep his streets clean. He builds fearful destructive weapons, but cannot ensure humane treatment of prisoners of war and refugees, survivors of battle. He produces poisonous chemicals and gases in vast quantities, but cannot supply enough vaccines for the needy to prevent communicable illness.

The contrasts are obvious; they are the end products of public-policy making. It is not suprising that "policy" and "development" have been redis-covered in the past two decades in public administration. They dominate the practitioner's world. The one tells him what his general direction is and where he is heading. The other tells him where he ought to be heading and how he might be able to speed his progress. The attention that is now being given to both concepts in public administration, less by traditionalists than by the avant-garde, less by the mainstream than by intruders from other disciplines, demonstrates an accelerating shift in direction in both theory and practice from process to direction and from technique to purpose, which is a reversal of the trend between the world wars.

Process and technique in public administration—the traditional core—still remain the center of interest in the bulk of public-administration liter-ature, and they are not likely to be replaced by direction and purpose or anything else for at least another generation. They are invaluable in the con-temporary world. They tell people how to administer public policies within a going system and how to establish new public programs from the beginning. They translate vague ideas and principles into tangible reality. They are indis-pensible tools in civilized society. But in these changing times, they are no longer considered sufficient in themselves. Practitioners need to know not only where they are, but where they are heading; they are not content to accept what they are doing without knowing why. They want to improve on past performance. While some public-administration theorists have flirted with behavioralism, a value-free administrative science and a logical-posi-tivist approach to the facts of public administration, the reformist motivation has remained strong in public administration theory, and in recent years emphasis has swung back to values, morality, ethics, ideas, ideology, beliefs, and feelings.

In any fair view of the facts of administrative life the establishment of policy con-sensus and the search for politically acceptable values is a highest priority endeavor. To abandon this process as something essentially arbitrary and capricious beyond, above, or below reason, is as fatal to significant inquiry in politics as in ethics. Only an empty manipulation of logical concepts can result from this evisceration of the subject. A meaningful study of administration cannot shy away from values. . . . The view of administration as sheerly instrumental, or even largely instrumental, must be rejected as empirically untenable and ethically unwarranted.[1]

The current search in the western world is for a more sophisticated philosophical rationalization of a socially aware, change-oriented, democratic public administration, to replace the simplistic theories that were produced in the 1930s and 1940s in reply to the threat of totalitarianism, and to combat the value-free, logical-positivist behavioral scientists in public administration.

The reemergence of public-policy concerns in public administration is due partly to the fear of putting administrative technicians in politically sensitive positions, and partly to increasing social demands for better public-policy making. People have always turned instinctively to leaders, political or otherwise, who they believed knew what to do and could issue practical instructions promptly, even if the decisions later appeared disastrous. Today, even greater importance is attached to decisions and decision makers, simply because so much more is at stake. In the past, crucial decisions took considerable time and organization to implement, and recall was possible before the process was far advanced. Today mass media and bureaucratization promote instant action beyond recall. Examples of far-reaching decisions in the twentieth century that have reshaped contemporary history include the unleashing of both world wars, the use of atomic weapons, the United States intervention in Vietnam, and the isolation of Communist China as positive-action decisions, and the standstill at the Yalu River in the Korean War, the blockade of Cuba in place of invasion or air bombardment of Cuban missile sites, and foreign nonintervention in civil wars and wars between bordering states as negative-action decisions. This kind of epoch-making decision is of quite a different order than that encountered in egocentric administrative theory. These decisions concern all humanity, not just the participants or the bureaucratic elites involved in the final stages. They shape the future, just as past decisions shaped the present. Most, if not all, take place within the public arena and rely predominantly on public authorities for effect.

THE TRANSFORMED WORLD OF PUBLIC-POLICY MAKING

Public-policy making is never easy: it requires a high sense of responsibility and a willingness to take the initiative as well as to assume risks. There are many other difficulties as well—complete information is unobtainable; the evidence is rarely conclusive; different interests urge different courses of action; outcomes are unknown; feedback is sporadic; the processes are not properly understood, not even by major participants. Moreover, few have

[1] N. E. Long, *The Polity.* Chicago: Rand McNally, 1962, p. 79.

penetrated the processes in depth; most have to be content with the story as related by mass media. Consequently, they never know what the sub-editor cut out of the reporter's version, how much the reporter left out of his copy, what the official interviewer failed to relate to the reporter, how much the official spokesmen's superiors did not tell him, what they, in turn, did not know about informal influences, how much their political masters concealed, and what went on in the minds of the rulers in whose name action was taken. Great men issue decisions, but rarely relate how or why they arrived at them. Others can only conjecture from what little they can glean from intimates, gossip, memoirs, depth interviews, and officially recorded evidence (which is not always trustworthy). Moreover, witnesses contradict one another. Thus, in spite of sparse information, public-policy making seems to have become more complicated in time.

Widened Public Arena   The society of man has gradually grown from the small group to the tribe, to the nation, to the international order. Individual actions have had repercussions in a widening social context, while that social context has had increasing influence over individual actions. Ten thousand years ago, emergent caveman was probably unaware of different races and colors in warmer regions of the world. Five thousand years ago, hunters did not know the existence of farmers. Five hundred years ago, the Old World did not know of the existence of the New World. One hundred years ago, the white man was still discovering new worlds unaware of his existence. Fifty years ago, the bloodiest war ever fought did not touch the major part of the planet. Today, however, the public arena exempts none. Chance contact with the stray traveler may wipe out societies unable to resist new germs as effectively as an off-course nuclear warhead can destroy any part of the globe. Finds of rare minerals and precious resources invite immediate foreign invasion, whether in Arctic icelands, the high mountains of the Andes, or the barren Sahara deserts. No man is an island unless he renounces society altogether, and more importantly, society is prepared to renounce him. Even a person's intimate thoughts in his subconscious can be revealed if society so deems.

Complicated Public Arena   Complexity is less a function of vastly increased populations than increased external influences upon private concerns. As societies link, relate, exchange, cooperate, and integrate, the scope of communal interest widens. The volume of public business mounts beyond the capability of any one person or group of people to master; specialization and delegation are imperative. Even so, the ceaseless flow of matter requiring a decision by someone in public authority and the urgency with which each item is expected to be dealt by those awaiting the decision preclude thorough investigation, deep-seated analysis, and foresighted thinking in all but a fraction of decisions. Decision making must be institutionalized and routinized — hence there is government and public bureaucracy. As the public arena continues to grow more complicated, routinization fails to cope with the volume of business or produce satisfactory decisions. New areas of public business cannot be routinized at all, and other arrangements have to be made. Public-policy makers have to cope with both routinized and nonroutinized decisions and develop a facility for moving quickly from one to the other. Their task is to maintain the output of decisions.

Complex Problems　The nature of the problems requiring decision changes with the size and diversity of the public arena. Small, homogeneous societies are fortunate, compared with the contemporary international order, which is faced with problems never before experienced and for which new solutions, new directions, new guidelines are needed. Some examples follow:

a. *Population explosion.* Modern science is conquering death so that more people are surviving for longer periods of time. It is also conquering life so that fewer unwanted babies need be born and fewer wanted babies need be born without a proper chance of survival. How will the newcomers support themselves?

b. *Total war.* Modern weapons are capable of destroying the planet in minutes and, if manufactured in certain ways, they can make the planet uninhabitable. Sufficient stock piles already exist to obliterate man, and freak accidents could well spark world genocide. How are such weapons to be controlled? How can wars be fought without their deployment? How can they be ended without a fight to the finish?

c. *Galloping technology.* Innovation has been institutionalized. Scientific ideas are quickly translated into products, and they have an immediate impact on living styles, possibly more important than the influence of social institutions. Can the products be adequately tested for safety before general release? Can institutionalized innovation be controlled? How can people be educated to overcome technological enslavement?

d. *Rising expectations.* The latest and newest inventions are known instantaneously through mass media. Rich and poor alike want to share in technological progress: the rich can no longer do without what they have been accustomed to, and the poor crave to catch up with the rich. Failure to satisfy rising expectations is an inherent destabilizing force that could upset the social order. How can that force be channelled into creative rather than destructive activity? How can minorities be accorded equality? How can majorities be prevented from exterminating deviant minorities? How can the gap between rich and poor be narrowed?

e. *Turbulence.* The pace of change is so fast that nothing is stable. No assumptions can be made about the future. Existing trends cannot be projected, as everything is in flux. Familiar landmarks disappear with disconcerting rapidity. How can people cope? How can institutions adapt? How can societies build on turbulence?

These problems constitute the challenge of our times.

Variety of Public-Policy Makers　The very existence of a problem denotes either that no solution has been found or that nobody can agree on the best solution, in which case, lacking compromise and consensus, a search will be made for a different solution altogether. Where nobody within institutionalized public-policy making knows what to do or how to translate ideal, ambition, or principle into action, irregular policy-making sources are employed. In traditional societies, the local chiefs may consult with the medicine man, soothsayer, or self-proclaimed prophet. Modern counterparts are astrologers, fortune-tellers, academies of science, second chambers, and religious fanatics. Modern societies also have more sophisticated public-policy making supports outside the governmental framework. Public-spirited citizens offer their services, and public authorities contract policy formulation activities to non-public groups. The acuteness of contemporary problems has been accompanied by the proliferation of temporary research groups engaged in public-policy formulation and planning and semi-permanent public-policy making bodies, outside both the institutionalized public-policy framework and the routinized decision making. They are better placed to experiment and innovate, but they do not have responsibility or authority for adoption and implementation.

Shared Public-Policy Making   In simple societies, a few people or even one person can make all necessary decisions and know most things that happen, but in more complex societies, decision making is shared, delegated, and institutionalized in routine channels. Public-policy making is a concern of different institutional elites and their various entourages. The institutional elites may or may not be interlocking through common ancestry, tribal affiliation, or political party, but no matter what they share, their different interests, functions, and clientele will divide them and cause them to compete like rival nobles in medieval days. Within each sphere of competence, differential recruitment, personal idiosyncrasies, professional rivalry, social mobility, and diversity of opinions further complicate public-policy making, particularly where contending groups seek outside allies, power brokers, middlemen, opinion makers, and mass support. Power is diffused, not concentrated.

Multi-dimensional Problems   Routinization caters well to the problem that falls within defined channels, but it cannot handle problems that cover multiple channels. For instance, bureaucracies, the optimum form of institutionalized routine decision making, cope well with problems that fall within their competence, but not with problems marginal to them or outside their competence. In post-industrial societies, more problems are multidimensional and unsuitable for bureaucratization. Often, the first essential is to clarify the problem and to ensure that interested groups recognize the existence of a problem before attempting a solution.

Governmental Leadership Entailed   Whereas simple problems can be handled routinely or cooperatively between different power centers, solutions to multidimensional problems require the backing of legitimacy and ultimate coercive force. Private interests are not expected to assume responsibility for communal problems, for they are self-centered and inward-looking; their main considerations are survival and betterment, and their concern for communal repercussions and their response to other communal needs are secondary. They are unable to command the resources or wield sufficient powers to cope with multidimensional problems, and they, themselves, are largely dependent on government support. Similarly, voluntary associations are marginal, although still valuable mobilizing forces. Political parties are super-voluntary associations where they are vote-getting machines, but they may develop into states within states where they extend their activities to commerce, industry, agriculture, social services, and cultural facilities. To complete their goals, they still have to command the governmental apparatus, as do military elites, religious orders, and any other group that wants to tackle multidimensional problems.

Increasing Dependence on Bureaucratic Infrastructures   When the scope of government was limited in pre-industrial societies, political rulers were their own public-policy makers, aided by bureaucratic infrastructures. The expansion of government overloaded the political rulers and forced them to rely increasingly on enlarged bureaucratic infrastructures ready to engage in public-policy planning in their spheres of competence. In post-industrial society, political rulers have largely contracted out of policy planning and implementation. They rely on bureaucratic infrastructures to undertake such activities, while they concentrate on policy selection. Even in this area, the background and experience of political leaders may not qualify them to choose between alternative policies suggested by bureaucratic infrastructures in highly specialized technical and professional fields such as weapons systems, environmental controls, social service administration, and computer hardware.

> There is a distinct risk that the quality of politicians will not keep abreast of either the more difficult problems or the new policy knowledge, so that either public policy will lag more and more behind what it should or could be or politicians will influence policy making less. Comparing the roles of politicians in policy making a few decades ago with their roles today does show that in modern countries most of them (but not the central political leaders) have less influence, especially on critical problems of military and scientific policy. Some of this decline in their influence may be desirable, or unavoidable, but some of it is caused by their being less and less qualified for their jobs.[2]

The vacuum is being filled by the bureaucratic infrastructures, and public servants are exhorted in contemporary textbooks in public administration to recognize their leadership and decision-making functions.

> By "public administrator" we mean "policy-making" civil servants, including chief executives, department heads, and staff officials in personnel, finance, purchasing and public relations. Given the similarity of roles between those at the top polit-

[2] Y. Dror, *Public Policy Making Reexamined.* San Francisco: Chandler, 1968, p. 247.

ical levels and their immediate career subordinates, our analysis covers both politically appointed and permanent administrators. While top administrators are clearly more occupied with the legislature, party matters, and overall policy, those at the upper levels of middle management require a similar generalizing capacity in order to recommend new policy which often arises from their work with specialists at the operating level.

In a behavioral context, the generalist administrator is mainly involved in making decisions, that is, in determining the operating policies of the organization and the best ways of achieving its major programs . . . his major considerations tend to be political and strategic, as contrasted with the mainly technical orientation of his specialist subordinates. . . . The political element in organizational decisions grows more significant as one moves up the hierarchical ladder.[3]

Public-policy Planning and Implementation Centered on the Public Bureaucracy Whereas most public-policy decisions are taken in the political arena, most policy planning and implementation takes place in the bureaucratic arena. That portion of decision making not undertaken in the political arena is shared between the public bureaucracy and private institutions. That portion of planning and implementation not undertaken in the bureaucratic arena is shared between public political institutions and private institutions. In multidimensional problems and technical decision making, planning, decision, and implementation are so closely associated that it may not be possible to differentiate among them. Hence, the public bureaucracy, because of its strategic position, functional expertise, and associated policy planning and implementing mechanisms may make public-policy decisions in defense and related matters, economic and political development, and social-welfare programs involving large sums of public money. In these and other fields, the public bureaucracy has a monopoly of policy talent or the information on which policy formulation depends. Because it performs so well in these areas, it is often called upon to supply the thinking in other public-policy fields, for which it may not be so qualified. This is especially true in new fields of public-policy where the only policy talent available may be outside the public bureaucracy in universities (research scientists, academic lawyers, behavioral scientists); research institutes (policy analysts, scientific advisers, professionals); and voluntary societies (technical expertise, policy advisers). Even so, the public bureaucracy is likely to be made responsible for implementation unless strong outside pressures are exerted to prevent further bureaucratic aggrandizement.

The higher executives and professionals of the federal service stand, with the President and the Congress, at the center of the nation's policy process. Much of the process of decision-making is in their hands. The assemblage of information, the discovery of alternatives, the analytical appraisal of these choices, the synthesis of risks and opportunities into innovative yet realistic recommendations, the

---

[3] J. M. Pfiffner and R. Presthus, *Public Administration,* fifth ed. New York: Ronald Press, 1967, pp. 103, 108.

process of bargaining and accommodation which transforms proposals into accepted policies, the executing of resulting plans and programs—in each of these stages effective participation by the higher executives and professions is indispensable to the President and the Congress, being essential to the creation and execution of viable public policies.[4]

The overall trend in policy making from the public political arena to the not-so-public bureaucratic infrastructure and its associates raises several important issues currently under debate. Where wilwthe trend stop? Is it inevitable? Will political institutions lose their effective means of control over the bureaucratic infrastructure? Will the political arena shift from open forums such as mass media, party conferences, and legislatures to closed forums, such as committee meetings, bureaucratic conferences, and confidential memoranda? Can the politician be rescued from the technocrat? How can professional public servants be sensitized to the political aspects of public-policy making? How far should the public servant substitute for his political master? How can the technocrat be controlled from without, and how can he control himself? How can the community participate in the public-policy making processes? How can public-policy making be improved? How can public policies be evaluated?

THE RESPONSE OF PUBLIC ADMINISTRATION

The transformed world of public-policy making has overturned public administration since the Great Depression. Before then, government was relatively confined in scope and area, and the public bureaucracy had many rivals in the public arena. It was turly subordinate to political institutions; its world was much narrower, with fewer outside contacts, less understanding of causal relationships, fewer societal repercussions, and less concern with mass media and public opinion. Now big government is here. Potential rivals to the public bureaucracy are either dependent on it or so intertwined in public processes that their autonomy is greatly reduced. It is problematical whether political institutions are able to subordinate the public bureaucracy as they once could. The contrast is quite sharp, particularly when we recall that the transformation occurred in one generation.

The response to this transformation varies from country to country. Only the experience of the Soviet Union, western Europe, and the United States need be considered, as most other countries derived their expectations and attitudes from them. In the Soviet Union, immediately after the revolution, the public bureaucracy provided continuity in the public-policy arena until new political cadres mastered their unfamiliar environment. Officials who could or would not conform to the new orthodoxy were demoted or dis-

[4] W. S. Sayre, "The Public Service," in President's Commission on National Goals, *Goals for Americans.* Englewood Cliffs, N.J.: Prentice-Hall, 1960, pp. 292–293.

missed. Academics were employed to justify decisions. In western Europe the administrative-law tradition prevented a ready acceptance of active policy-making roles in deference to strict political subordination. Such reluctance to enter the public-policy arena was not evidenced by bureaucratic elites drawn from upper-class backgrounds, particularly in unstable and weak political regimes where policy vacuums were frequent. In Great Britain, public administration was given a wider interpretation, to include policy issues as well as administrative methods. The ends of government were legitimate concerns of public officials brought up in a liberal tradition and performing a generalist role. Although institutionally a clear line was drawn between political and official careers, socially politicians and top administrators were close. The academics were active in public affairs and in policy making. The transformation was in the British tradition and did not cause the heart searching that occurred in western Europe. In the United States the transition was also accomplished smoothly, both in politicized bureaucracies and at the apex of merit civil services, where the line between politics and administration had never been clear. In contrast to Britain, the American academics were slow to adjust, but when they did, they overreacted.

Between the world wars the academic study of public administration preached a strict dichotomy between politics and administration in the public sector. Academics deliberately chose to confine the area of the discipline and drew narrow boundaries. They wanted to establish their autonomy from political science, law, and other related disciplines by concentrating on the internal relationships of the public-administration system, which were not being covered by any other discipline. More importantly, they wanted to improve public administration in the United States without entering the political arena themselves, working with local party bosses in party machines, joining the public service, or involving the administrative-reform movement in partisan political controversy. Their model was a depoliticized, professional, morally irreproachable, and efficient public bureaucracy, and their method was scientific inquiry accompanied by adequate publicity and constant repetition of the same simple themes, with few notable exceptions. They abhorred politics and would not involve themselves in public policy, except over administrative reform. Yet, they did not ignore the external relationships of the administrative system altogether; introductions and prefaces to major writings invariably apologized for limiting the scope of their coverage. Nevertheless, in contrast to non-American scholars, they rarely investigated policy matters, major functional areas (for example, education, health, police); noncivil executive administration; and public-private overlays. Instead, their preoccupations were civil-service legislation, governmental reorganizations, budgeting systems, and innovative management techniques. In this way, they protected their embryonic discipline while meeting a felt public need. They did not exaggerate the originality or the worth of the discipline, and the search for universal scientific laws governing administrative systems seemed promising. If they failed, they could redraw the parameters and adopt a different approach.

By stripping the discipline of political (and much academic) controversy, removing the lifeblood of politics, and confining themselves in their own intellectual straight jacket, the American pioneers made their discipline appear somewhat dull and pedestrian for their students. Public administration was perceived as an instrument connecting the rulers and the ruled. Decisions flowed downward from the rulers, to be executed by career officials within the formal governmental structure, while information flowed upward from the ruled, to be assimilated by career politicians. By concentrating largely on administrative generalists and bureaucratic elites, the academics exaggerated the importance of bureaucratization in the political system and oversimplified the administrative system by neglecting its social dynamics. Supposedly objective, they injected their own values into the discipline —belief in rationality, one best way, and goals of efficiency and economy.

This introverted definition of public administration did not go unchallenged at any time, but serious objections were only raised with the New Deal. White had been troubled by trying to fit his knowledge about the workings of public administration into a rigid theoretical framework that ignored human behavior. Significantly, he ended his *Introduction to the Study of Public Administration* (1926) with a reference to morale, the key to which was to be found in trusted political and administrative leadership and the "recognition and gratification of the universal human aspirations of the multitude of men and women who toil, often in obscure positions, for the common weal."[5] In *The City Manager,* he found that the city-manager system failed to keep politics and administration apart, partly because improvement policy could not be separated from politics. He stated the classic dilemma of city managers as follows:

> If [city managers] follow the strict theory of the manager plan and conceive themselves primarily as professional-technical administrators, they achieve the prerequisites of permanence in their position and lay the foundation of city administration of an order of excellence hitherto unequaled. But they do this at the cost of being forced to observe the needs of the city ignored, or misrepresented, or so ineptly set before the voters that they are defeated at the polls. If they set themselves the task of supplying the deficiencies of the council and directly or indirectly attempt to direct public opinion in favor of the needs of the city, they may easily achieve the temporary leadership of their community, but only at the serious risk of becoming involved in politics and of forfeiting the privilege of giving uninterrupted technical service of a high order of excellence.[6]

[5] L. D. White, *Introduction to the Study of Public Administration.* New York: Crowell Collier & Macmillan, 1926, p. 478.

[6] L. D. White, *The City Manager.* Chicago: University of Chicago Press, 1927, p. 230.

Yet, he optimistically believed that it ought to be possible to separate politics and administration: "Sound administration can develop and continue only if this separation can be achieved."[7]

The New Deal ended such notions. As Gulick pointed out at the beginning of the Roosevelt era, his programs would involve "a new and revolutionary extension of the practice and the theory of administration . . . concerned not with checks and balances or with the division of policy and administration, but with the division between policy veto on one side and policy planning and execution on the other."[8] In reaching this conclusion, Gulick demolished the politics-administration dichotomy. It had not been possible to take administration out of politics. Autonomous agencies had introduced self-perpetuating elites and had so fragmented public-policy making that balanced programs, economies of scale, and internal cooperation were difficult to achieve. Legal prohibitions had not eliminated abuses. Likewise, it had not been possible to take politics out of administration without killing democratic government. Although a theoretical distinction could be made, no practical division existed, as both political and administrative acts were seamless webs of discretion and action, "a continual process of decision-action-discretion-action," in Gulick's words. The distinction grew not from the nature of the things done, but out of the division of labor; it revolved around social psychology.

> The reason for insisting that the elected legislative and executive officials shall not interfere with the details of administration, and that the rank and file of the permanent administration shall be permanent and skilled and shall not meddle with politics, is simply that this division of work makes use of specialization and appears to give better results than a system where such a differentiation does not exist.[9]

With these brief strokes, the existing assumption at that time behind academic writing about public administration collapsed.

A new direction for American public administration was suggested in a slim volume, *The Frontiers of Public Administration* (Chicago: University of Chicago Press, 1936), containing essays by L. D. White, J. M. Gaus, and M. E. Dimock, who were to ensure its acceptance in the next decade. Their points were that the United States should quit copying foreign models. Americans should not feel guilty if their public administration system was peculiar. Public administration was not the managerial aspects of enforcing the law and discharging governmental responsibilities but the "state in action," as broad as government itself, its scope being determined only by whatever was needed to fulfill the ends and objectives of the state. The politics-administration dichotomy had made public administration "detached

---

[7] White, *The City Manager,* p. 301.

[8] L. Gulick, "Politics, Administration and the New Deal," *Annals of the American Academy of Political and Social Science,* 169 (1933), pp. 65–66.

[9] Gulick, "Politics, Administration and the New Deal," p. 63.

and unreal," "giving too little weight to the propulsions, policies and attitudes which run throughout government."

Research and teaching in public administration involve more than a mere study of techniques and general principles, which may be thought to be applicable to all levels and conditions of administration. Public administration is to be isolated from the whole process of government only for the sake of convenience in research, teaching, and training. Admitting that the formulation of hypotheses and principles is necessary and desirable, the worker in the field of public administration should be constantly on his guard against generalizations which bear no close relation to the solution of the particular problem and situation which he is exploring. Public administration, like government, is a human activity and, like the activity of humans, is complex and often unpredictable. So much depends upon the personal factor. Public administration is not an end in itself, but is merely a tool of government and the servant of the community — as such it may be expected to grow and to change as society itself changes.

Generalizations relative to public administration are hazardous. Although there are common elements in every type of administrative situation, such as organization, finance and personnel, it should always be recognized that the requirements of a given situation and the differences in subject matter should be given a great deal of weight in prescribing solutions in the field of public administration. Then, too, the functions of government are growing rapidly both in scope and in extent. Allowances frequently have to be made for distinctive conditions obtaining in the performance of a new governmental function or arising from the increased size and areal variations of old functions. Finally, as those who have made administrative surveys soon discover, there are important differences in place, time, local tradition, and objective which need to be given their full weight by a realistic researcher in public administration. Instead of expecting standardization, simplicity and complete parallelisms, a student of public administration should expect to find a great variety of problems and likewise varying formulas. Public administration should be elastic. Its principles are convenient guides to future action, but they should be conditioned in their application by time and place factors, by sound judgment, by intuition, by willingness to experiment, and by regard for the distinctive conditions and differing objectives of the particular case.[10]

The objective of public administration was not blind obedience to the master's dictates as the helpless pawn of the governmental elite or mechanical business efficiency, "tantamount to economy, penny-pinching and profit-making." It was "the good life," humane, warm, progressive, and protective of individual rights. The good administrator was a political participant in public-policy making. Herring had provided proof of official involvement in public-policy making and partisan politics in his investigation of the relationships between pressure groups and federal officials, following a study of the relationships between pressure groups and congressmen.

[10] J. M. Gaus et al., Frontiers of Public Administration. Chicago: University of Chicago Press, 1936, pp. 4–5. Copyright 1936 by the University of Chicago. All rights reserved.

Herring found that officials had to weigh the pressure groups against the general interest and nonrepresented interests. From his case studies, he concluded the following:

> The official cannot escape the political climate of his bureau but he can learn to weather the storm of politics and to cultivate his garden when under the sunny rays of public approbation.[11]

> Officials cannot be removed from the storms of politics by erecting an independent commission over them in umbrella fashion.[12]

> Where a special interest is identified with a certain bureau, officials often unite with allied forces on the outside in obstructing change. For them administration in the public interest means the promotion of the interests of a certain group.[13]

> Special interests cannot turn aside the general political trend dominating the administration as a whole. Where they are in harmony with this trend, they can accelerate movements for their own benefit and override other group interests less fortunately placed.[14]

> Behind the army and behind the navy there are political machines of no mean strength. When either department is meddled with, these machines swing into action.[15]

> The administrative structure of the federal government cannot be rationalized in accordance with any a priori scheme. It is bound to the inequalities of our economic order and to the inconsistencies of popular government.[16]

> The federal machinery of administration has been beaten out on the anvil of Congress by the hammer and tongs of selfish forces, which shape matters, now one way and now another, in the heat of conflict and controversy. That the finished product is not well-articulated structure, but rather a distorted and lopsided maze, is the inevitable consequence.[17]

There could be little doubt that public officials had an active political role in public administration from regulation to conflict resolution, from planning to public-opinion formation.

Herring's testimony was further strengthened during World War II and afterwards. Academics became part of the public bureaucracy and discovered for themselves the inseparability of politics and administration and the public-policy making role of the public official. Postwar public administration was a new world. Democratic representative government was more important

---

[11] Pendleton Herring, *Public Administration and the Public Interest* (1936), New York: Russell & Russell, 1967, p. 68.

[12] Herring, *Public Administration,* p. 107.

[13] Herring, *Public Administration,* p. 257.

[14] Herring, *Public Administration,* p. 316.

[15] Herring, *Public Administration,* p. 338.

[16] Herring, *Public Administration,* p. 343.

[17] Herring, *Public Administration,* pp. 343–344.

than economical public management. The United States, the world leader, was confronted with the spread of communism and the rise of anticolonial movements. The federal government had assumed responsibility for the active shaping of the future of American society. Private and public sectors were partners, not competitors. Public administration was more than a tool for implementing political ideas: it was an integral part of those ideas and was tied to the citizens' search for a sense of security, of belonging, and their reliance on governmental action for the realization of basic human desires in an impersonal, disorganized world.[18] More effective public administration implied constitutional and political reforms and prior shifts in political values. Efficiency of means was replaced by notions of social efficiency, quality of government, political ends, public wants, and democratic values.

Already "policy" was replacing "politics" in the literature of public administration. Policy denoted something positive: it emphasized political initiatives and programs and indicated that the people involved really cared about what they were doing. Politics, however, was still suspect and associated with power seeking and deceit. The textbooks continued to reflect the old dichotomy, but after 1939 it was assaulted from every direction and academically finally laid to rest by Appleby, who maintained that public-policy making was shared by all branches of government throughout the public bureaucracy. Where a decision was finally made depended on political evaluation. As government in action, public administration was subject to political processes to attain consensus or an approximation of the public interest. No boundary line could be drawn between political officers and public servants. Public officials handled all matters up to the point where the political parties and elected representatives wanted their way. Public administration was itself a basic political process by which the people achieved and controlled governance.[19] Since Appleby, nobody has denied the political nature of public administration.

Confronted with the obvious concern of public administration with public-policy making, the textbooks revised their definitions to reflect the public-policy orientation.

> Public administration consists of all those operations having for their purpose the fulfillment or enforcement of public policy.[20]

> Public administration may be defined as the coordination of individual and group efforts to carry out public policy.[21]

---

[18] E. S. Wengert, "The Study of Public Administration," *American Political Science Review,* 36 (1942), p. 314.

[19] P. H. Appleby, *Policy and Administration.* University, Ala.: University of Alabama Press, 1949, p. 170.

[20] L. D. White, *Introduction to the Study of Public Administration.* New York: Crowell Collier & Macmillan, 1955, p. 1.

[21] J. M. Pfiffner and R. Presthus, *Public Administration,* p. 7.

As a study, public administration examines every aspect of government's efforts to discharge the laws and to give effect to public policy.[22]

As a result, public administration was equated with government or political science. "In the effort to define the field, the field evaporates."[23] In fact, academics in the discipline of public administration have not gone this far, but have kept mostly within older boundary lines. Having rediscovered public-policy making, they bequeathed it to behavioral scientists concerned with decision making and policy sciences.

FROM DECISION MAKING TO PROBLEM SOLVING

One of the first critics to challenge the redefinition of public administration as the study of public policy was Herbert Simon, who warned that it would range as wide as governmental problems and would eventually swallow political science and possibly other social sciences as well. Eventually it would become applied social science.[24] He preferred to see scholars concentrate less on public policy and more on the behavior of those who made decisions in the public arena and the processes by which they defined public policy. Administrative theory "should be concerned with the processes of decision as well as with the processes of action."[25] A general theory of administration should "include principles of organization that will insure correct decision-making just as it must include principles that will insure effective action." Decision making was the heart of administration; it pervaded the entire administrative process as much as the art of getting things done.

Simon's emphasis on decision making was not new. Economists had long been concerned with the problem of choice from available alternatives. In administrative theory, Chester Barnard, who wrote the foreword to Simon's *Administrative Behavior,* in which the theory of rational decision making was first outlined, had in *The Functions of the Executive* (Cambridge: Harvard University Press, 1938) suggested that organizations were systems of decision making because organizational action was based on careful calculation, and a crucial function of the executive (that is, administrator) was decision making.

Simon, much influenced by Barnard, carried these ideas further in his attempt to redirect public administration away from the nonoperational principles approach to behavioralism, that is, the ability to describe "exactly how an administrative organization looks and exactly how it works." For

[22] M. E. Dimock, G. O. Dimock, and L. W. Koenig, *Public Administration.* New York: Holt, Rinehart and Winston, 1958, p. 12.

[23] M. Landau, "The Concept of Decision-Making in the Field of Public Administration," in S. Mailick and E. H. Van Ness, eds., *Concepts and Issues in Administrative Behavior.* Englewood Cliffs, N.J.: Prentice-Hall, 1962, p. 9.

[24] H. A. Simon, "A Comment on The Science of Public Administration," *Public Administration Review,* 8 (1948) pp. 200–203.

[25] H. A. Simon, *Administrative Behavior.* New York: Crowell Collier & Macmillan, 1947, p. 1.

him, a scientifically relevant description of an organization would designate for each person in an organization the decisions he made and just what influences affected his decisions. Existing descriptions, confined to form, were superficial, oversimplified, and unrealistic because they did not deal with the allocation of decision making functions. A proper vocabulary for describing the administrative organization as a decision system and empirical studies of the limits of rationality in decision making were needed so that operational criteria for administrative evaluation could be developed.

Simon's *Administrative Behavior* was an attempt to provide a proper vocabulary. Decisions, he noted, were made at every level within an organization. They contained varying degrees of factual (administrative, pertaining to means) and value (policy, pertaining to objectives) judgments. Differentiation was difficult because most value judgments were made in terms of intermediate values, which involved factual questions. Further, sanctions were needed to ensure that experts deciding factual questions followed democratically formulated value judgments. He proposed that, ideally, the factual and ethical elements should be separated as far as possible and allocated between representatives and administrators according to their relative importance and the degree to which the ethical issues were controversial. Insofar as decisions led to the selection of final (organizational) goals, they were "value judgments," and where they implemented such goals, they were "factual judgments." Where representatives made factual judgments (semiscientific, quasi-judicial, quasi-business), they should be supplied with information and advice. Where administrators made value judgments (social policy, politics), they should be responsive to community values and answerable for their decisions. In practice, representatives often requested administrators to make decisions with a high policy content for them; administrators, in deciding questions with a high political content, followed their own values. In short, fact and value could not be separated institutionally, and individuals could not separate completely factual and value components in a decision. Goodnow had come to similar conclusions more than forty years earlier.

Simon's point of departure was his emphasis on correct decisions, as well as right ways of doing things; the one could not be divorced from the other. Efficient decision making was not the attainment of absolute perfection or the ruthless pursuit of mechanical efficiency in means, but that choice of alternatives that produced the largest results for the given application of resources. It was a relationship between the ends desired and the means used to achieve the desired ends. The ideal was unattainable perfect rationality, by which all objectives would be defined and arranged according to priority, all possible alternative strategies would be listed together with their consequences, and comparative evaluation taken of the strategies and their consequences, so that the maximum results would be forthcoming from the resources employed in terms of opportunity costs. In practice, however, complete information was unobtainable, man was not an exclusively rational being, and both the objectives and the consequences in public policy were not susceptible to quantitative measurement or even approximate evaluations. In addition to objective rationality, there was also subjective, conscious, deliberate, organizational, and personal rationality. Empirical studies would reveal how people actually made decisions and what most influenced them, but Simon believed that his preliminary conjectures had revealed the possibility of measuring and evaluating efficient decision making and the need to define, quantify, and measure administrative choice.

Simon failed to convince his public-administration colleagues. His work was considered too avant-garde, too much in the realm of administrative science, too narrowly defined, and somewhat peripheral to the central core of public administration. It was more favorably regarded in business administration and management science. Simon continued his work virtually single-handed, without active encouragement from the public-administration establishment.

In collaboration with D. W. Smithburg and V. A. Thompson, Simon produced the first behavioralist textbook in public administration, designed to show how American public administration worked "through a realistic, behavioral description of the processes of administration."[26] It concentrated more on the informal side of public administration, introducing and applying concepts in sociology and psychology to public administration. Although it was not specifically designed around a decision-making approach, it repeated much of the argument of *Administrative Behavior* and went much further in challenging the notion that the ideal in public administration was rationality in pursuit of mechanical efficiency. But as more empirical evidence about how decisions were actually made began to accumulate, Simon dropped the notion of optimal rational choice altogether and opted for bounded rationality and a satisficing model of decision making—that is, people accept what is good enough or satisfying to them and do not search for all possible alternatives. Their expectations limit their search, and they adopt the most satisfying perceived alternative. In a new introduction for the second edition of *Administrative Behavior* in 1957, he put forward the satisficing model as a better description of reality than the maximizing model. In *Models of Man* (New York: Wiley, 1957), he predicted mathematical models of program feasibility within bounded rationality, once time limits, value systems, and factually available alternatives were known. He was already engaged in the application of computers to decision making and general simulation models of individual decision making that might be susceptible to computer programming.

Computer work had suggested the possibility of distinguishing between routine decisions that might be programmable and problem-solving decisions that were more complex. In an overview of organization theory, March and

[26] H. A. Simon, D. W. Smithburg, V. A. Thompson, *Public Administration.* New York: Knopf. 1950, p. vi.

Simon distinguished between routinized and problem-solving responses to environmental stimuli in a decision-making continuum.[27] Routine responses developed from repeated experiences, whereas problem-solving responses occurred when the environmental stimulus was novel and involved a search for alternatives and consequences of action, which could be dispensed with once a performance program had been adopted. The problem-solving processes were aggregations of large numbers of simple thought-action elements concerned with the search for relevant information and the screening of that information for possible solutions in hierarchically structured procedural and substantive programs. Problem solvers began with variables within their control and gradually extended their programs until a satisfactory, not optimal, solution was found. On the whole, problem solving in groups was less error-prone, speedier, more competent, and conformist, although it involved group dynamics. A distinction should be made between abilities to devise solutions and abilities to evaluate their correctness.

These seminal ideas were further developed by Simon in a series of lectures given in 1960 and published in *The New Science of Management Decision* (New York: Harper and Row, 1960). The decision-making process was again broken into intelligence (searching the environment for conditions calling for decision); design (inventing, developing, and analyzing possible courses of action); and choice (selecting a course of action), execution being indistinguishable from making more detailed policy. The skills of each were learnable and trainable, providing that a distinction was made between personal and organizational decision making. Decisions occurred along a continuum between *programmed decisions* that were repetitive and routine, and for which a definite routine had been worked out so that they were not treated anew every time, and *nonprogrammed decisions* that were novel, unstructured, and consequential, for which there was "no cut and dried method for handling the problem because it hasn't arisen before, or because its precise nature and structure are elusive or complex, or because it is so important that it deserves a custom-tailored treatment."[28]

In nonprogrammed situations, solutions relied on general capacity for intelligent, adaptive, problem-oriented action, which enabled problem solvers to fill in gaps in special problem-solving skills and to reason about any kind of situation in terms of ends and means. Different techniques were used for handling the programmed and the nonprogrammed aspects of decision making. Programmed decisions were traditionally handled by habit, operating routine (bureaucratized habit), and organizational structure, while nonprogrammed decisions were traditionally handled by personal skills (judgment, intuition, creativity), improvisation, and sensitized administrators freed from routine. Since the publication of *Administrative Behavior,* several

[27] J. G. March and H. A. Simon, *Organizations.* New York: John Wiley & Sons, 1958, pp 139–142, 178–182.
[28] H. A. Simon, *The New Science of Management Decision.* New York: Harper & Row, 1960 p. 6.

new techniques have been developed to handle both programmed and non-programmed decisions, most originating in public policy to solve specific problems, particularly in war strategy. As Simon's enumeration covers progress up to the end of the 1950s only, it has been updated and rearranged to include more recent developments in decision making, as applied to problem solving in public administration.

Computers

Routinized, programmed decisions and habitual operating routine are most susceptible to mechanization and automatic processing. From high-speed mechanical calculations, the computer has graduated to data processing, information retrieval, and programmed decision making in routine operations. Whereas public authorities at one time employed large numbers of white-collar workers to process routine operations in census coding, income-tax collection, stock control, and similar repetitive paperwork requiring the application of standard decisions, they now use computers and employ white-collar workers to process the computers and technicians to service them. Wherever data can be represented by mathematical or other symbols, computers can be introduced.

Simulation is a prime example. The laboratory optimum can be simulated and the outcomes used as guidelines for the real world. Alternatively, the real world can be programmed and aggregated into a comprehensive, consistent model of the entire system, whose theory elements can be manipulated. A computer program that describes the municipal budgetary decision process is contained in J. P. Crecine, *Governmental Problem-Solving: A Computer Simulation of Municipal Budgeting,* (Chicago: Rand McNally, 1969). Computer technology has developed so fast that computers can be programmed to correct their mistakes and learn from past errors so that in their field of competence they develop simple thinking processes capable of making decisions. Thus, computers can be programmed to compose music, play chess, and design machines.

Management-science tools

Just as physical scientists construct mock-ups and small-scale models, management scientists construct mathematical models and theoretical simulations as symbolic representations of the problems to be studied. Model construction entails identification of significant variables and the relationships between them; specification of the objectives and the criteria by which the objectives may be measured; and listing of restrictions and restraints, including uncertainties, all expressed in explicit and quantitative terms. Some models, which are designed to represent symbolically the real world, include (a) linear programming, used to determine the optimum use of resources to meet stated objectives within specified restrictions (for example, minimize transportation costs); (b) simulation models, used to narrow alternatives and identify consequences of particular policies (for example, business decisions);

(c) game theory, used to designate strategies in a competitive situation, designed to minimize loss (for example, military strategy); (d) Monte Carlo method, used to approximate unpredictable real-world situations (for example, fire occurrence); (e) queuing theory, used to find the optimum balance between costs of facilities to meet demand and costs associated with delays in a waiting-line problem (for example, toll bridges); and (f) dynamic programming, used to solve problems with many stages (for example, road systems). They reduce rule-by-thumb and other costly trial-and-error methods. They are essentially normative, not descriptive, models. They have been elaborated in analyses of decision making in situations of conflict, rivalry, and bargaining in military strategy and foreign policy; a good example is T. C. Schelling, *The Strategy of Conflict* (Cambridge: Harvard University Press, 1960). Collectively they have contributed much toward a pure theory of rational choice in conditions of certainty and uncertainty, stability and instability, simplicity and complexity.

Systems approach

In contrast to the mathematical models of management science, the systems approach allows for information exchange between parts of the system. The idea of system can be used to denote the relationships between component parts within defined boundaries—as in the case of an organization or a problem—or an organized means of controlling an operation incorporating indicators that show divergence from an accepted norm or standard and self-regulating mechanisms with ability to adjust to change and to correct errors (like thermostatic heaters) or an overview of a hierarchy of component parts (such as a pyramid), where the whole is different from a sum of the parts. The systems model is abstract (in that symbols stand for reality), holistic (in that structure is unimportant), dynamic, and pragmatic.[29]

Systems approach is basic to operations research, system analysis, critical-path scheduling, PERT (Program Evaluation Review Technique), cybernetics, flow charts, cycle regulation, performance measurement (input-output), and stochastic processes (choice behavior). It also provides the backing for operational models of self-regulating systems, adaptive control processes, and information systems. In these ways, the systems approach has improved the quality of problem solving and decision making, provided standards for evaluation and measurement, and contributed to more accurate prediction and description of administrative behavior.

Heuristic methods

Many problems are not susceptible to quantification or systems analysis, yet solution is no longer a matter of pure inspiration, guesswork, or chance. Studies have been made of problem solving and decision making by individ-

---

[29] J. Haberstroh, "Organization Design and Systems Analysis," in J. G. March, ed., *Handbook of Organizations.* Chicago: Rand McNally, 1965, p. 1172.

uals alone and in groups to discern whether shortcuts could be made and whether some factors were more important than others. Simon himself has pioneered laboratory experiments of thought processes for translation into computer programs that simulate human thought. Several programs have been developed jointly by the Carnegie Institute of Technology and the Rand Corporation, and independently by computer manufacturers and designers. These programs enable machines to make nonprogrammed decisions, as well as programmed decisions, but so far their performance and cost have not justified their replacement of human problem solvers. Like other heuristic methods, they may not produce a solution at all, or the solution they produce may not be good enough, but they do have a built-in ability to choose from alternatives, which the management-science tools lack. They are an artificial intelligence that may eventually tell much about successful problem solving for unstructured problems, that is, nonprogrammed decision making.

Applied decision-making theory

Decision-making theory has had an important practical impact on public administration. In planning, the optimal model of the rational man had long been suspect. Soviet national planning between the world wars had revealed the impractical nature of optimal planning, further confirmed by Allied war planning. The satisficing model proved a more feasible basis for national planning, and indeed all planning undertaken by public authorities, by reducing the search for alternatives and the detailed specification of planning objectives. In public finance, decision-making theory, in conjunction with management-science tools, the systems approach, and welfare economic theory led to Planning-Programming-Budgeting Systems (see Chap. 8), cost-benefit analysis of public projects and urban development planning, public-sector investment programming, developmental balance sheets and the goals-achievement matrix, and other public-policy planning aids. Field studies within public organizations have begun to break down the formalistic image of the public service by revealing much about small-group decision making, particularly the importance of leadership roles, influence and power structures, communications, group norms, and cohesiveness and atmosphere, but they have yet to make any significant impact on public-personnel practices in general or on the structuring of public authorities.

Decision-making models

By 1960, Simon had identified three major models of decision making, namely, (a) nonprogrammed decision making based on instinct, judgment, intuition, and other extra-rational factors, (b) pure-rationality optimal decision making, and (c) satisficing decision making. In the 1960s, Simon added the maze model of decision making: problem solvers follow different sets of paths, some of which lead to a payoff solution, others merely to additional sets of paths. It was similar to the tree concept in game theory and to Klein's sequential-decision model at the Rand Corporation of concurrent multiple-path analysis until one path proved superior.

Lindblom suggested a "muddling-through" model of incremental policy changes or successive limited comparisons. Problem solvers limit their search to incremental departures from existing policies because support is unlikely for more radical departures whose full consequences are unknown and unforeseeable. Lindblom claimed that his model was a closer approximation of practices in American public administration than other models.

Dissatisfaction with the conservatism of Lindblom's model led Dror to construct an optimum public-policy making model, which was largely a fusion of nonprogrammed decision making and economic rationality that limited the search for alternatives until the law of diminishing returns set in.

Etzioni suggested a mixed-scanning approach, which combined high order, fundamental policy-making processes, and incremental strategies, which prepared for and implemented fundamental decisions. The first would scan the decision area in general and the second would focus on specific points requiring deeper investigation. Such mixed scanning could take place at different levels, with varying degrees of detail and coverage.[30]

These decision making models probably influence the actual behavior of problem solvers, who study them as a guide to how decisions are or should be made and how public-policy problems are or should be approached.

FROM POLICY SCIENCES TO POLICY ANALYSIS

Policy making[31] is probably the most important aspect of decision making. An inefficient organization working in the right direction is better for society than an efficient organization going in the wrong direction; the latter's efficiency only compounds the policy-making error. Possibly Simon's work,

---

[30] A. Etzioni, "Mixed-Scanning: A 'Third' Approach to Decision-Making," *Public Administration Review,* 27 (Dec. 1967), pp. 385–392.

[31] A clear definition of public policy has been provided by A. Ranney, "The Study of Policy Content," in A. Ranney, ed., *Political Science and Public Policy.* Chicago: Markham, 1968, p. 7.

A particular object or set of objects—some designated part of the environment (an aspect of the society or physical world), which is intended to be affected.

A desired course of events—a particular sequence of behavior desired in the particular object or set of objects.

A selected line of action—a particular set of actions chosen to bring about the desired course of events: in other words, not merely whatever the society happens to be doing toward the set of objects at the moment, but a deliberate selection of one line of action from among several possible lines.

A declaration of intent—whether broadcast publicly to all who will listen or communicated secretly to a special few, some statement by the policy makers as to what they intend to do, how, and why.

An implementation of intent—the actions actually undertaken vis-à-vis the particular set of objects in pursuance of the choices and declaration.

more than anything else, did much to highlight the importance of correct decisions in preference to correct arrangements, with which administrative science was (and still largely is) preoccupied. The bulk of decision-making theory, however, is concerned with organizational policy, which may suit unifunctional organizations, but is insufficient for multifunctional organizations and public-policy making that involves many different organizations. The optimization of organizational policy in the public sector may impede overall public policy by detracting from more important public goals and by ignoring public policies that are not represented in organizational competition. For instance, military conscription, a desirable public policy to boost depleted military forces and perhaps to discipline unruly youth, may work counter to technological needs by depriving society of the very people who are most qualified to benefit from technological education. Although public-policy making bears much resemblance to decision making and problem solving, it is of a different order.

John Dewey first conceived the idea that public policy could be studied systematically. In *Logic,* he drew attention to the experimental nature of policy measures, which represented plans of action selected from alternatives and had observable consequences that could serve as validation tests. When they were treated as isolated independent measures, improvision was encouraged and their consequences were inadequately observed.

> The result is merely that [a policy] works or it does not work as a gross whole, and some other policy is improvised. Lack of careful, selective, continual observation of conditions promotes indefiniteness in formation of policies and this indefiniteness reacts in turn to obstruct definiteness of the observations relevant to its test and revision. [32]

Dewey's idea was taken up by Harold Lasswell, an experimental political scientist who found that political-analysis techniques were insufficient for a proper understanding of public policy. His search took him further and further away from political science into behavioralism and the physical sciences, until he broached the idea of policy sciences. But instead of promoting a separate discipline of policy studies with its own distinct subject matter, he proposed a field of study that would draw on relevant knowledge from other disciplines, which he termed policy sciences when they contributed understanding for the control of events. [33] The policy sciences could clarify practical problems, and practical experience in dealing with policy problems could test policy-science concepts.

> The policy sciences study the process of deciding or choosing and evaluate the relevance of available knowledge for the solution of particular problems. When policy scientists are concerned with government, law, and political mobilization,

---

[32] Quoted by V. Ostrom, "Public Policy Studies: An Approach to Governmental Research," paper to the Conference on Research Functions of University Bureaus and Institutes for Government Related Research. Berkeley: University of California, August 1959.

[33] H. D. Laswell and D. Lerner, eds., *The Policy Sciences.* Palo Alto: Stanford University Press, 1951.

they focus on particular decisions. Policy scientists also study the choosing process of non-governmental organizations and individuals and consider the significance of current stock of knowledge for specific issues. Since an official decision or a private choice is a problem-solving activity, five intellectual tasks are performed at varying levels of insight and understanding; clarification of goals; description of trends; analysis of conditions; projection of future developments; and invention, evaluation, and selection of alternatives.[34]

The policy scientist was concerned, for instance, with value goals (his own and others'), the role of the policy scientist (or adviser) in history, the factors that favored the evolution of the policy sciences (urbanism, bureaucratization, trained intelligence, empiricism, scientism, perceived conflict, and others), decision analysis, open intelligence networks, and communications. He was an intellectual committed to public affairs and to personal concern and involvement with contemporary events. His duty was to interest specialists in the public repercussions of their work.

Lasswell's plea for a responsible and responsive intelligentsia was slow in producing results. The main body of noncommitted specialists preferred to keep out of public policy. The complex problems of public policy in the 1950s were left to public authorities and whomever they chose to consult. The number of policy-oriented specialists in public employment increased, in addition to which special public-policy analysis organizations, both public and private, were established, and more use was made by the public service of universities, private organizations, and contracts in public-policy making. In the 1960s these trends were accelerated, and more specialists of their own volition entered the public-policy making arena concerned about urban problems, environmental controls, scientific funding, aerospace enterprises, weapons systems, poverty programs, and civil rights. With attention focused on student protests, increasing faculty involvement in public policy was overshadowed. In the wake of the new alliance between politicians, public servants, and socially aware intelligentsia, several new journals were established to cater to their common interests and to bridge the gap between specialists and policy scientists. Within the public service, as policy became the key word, researchers gained access to high levels. The pioneer studies of decision making and public-policy making that had been undertaken in difficult circumstances were strengthened by in-depth research, detailed memoirs by participants in public-policy processes, and personal experience in public office or in advisory capacity.

In public administration, studies of public policy had been infrequent during the heyday of the politics-administration dichotomy. With the demise of the dichotomy in the 1930s and 1940s, policy studies became more popular. Significantly, the first case-study text was entitled *Public Administration and Policy Development,*[35] which was soon followed by detailed histories

---

[34] H. D. Lasswell, "Policy Sciences" in D. L. Sills, ed., *Encyclopedia of Social Sciences,* vol. 12. New York: Crowell Collier & Macmillan, 1968, pp. 181–182.

[35] H. Stein, ed., *Public Administration and Policy Development.* New York: Harcourt Brace Jovanovich, 1952.

of public-policy making during World War II and specialized monographs on specific organizations or policy programs. These early studies were largely descriptive or critical analyses of policies, organizations, or processes. It was often difficult to build from them or adapt their knowledge to other circumstances. Gradually researchers began to generalize and theorize about the process of public-policy making itself, using models developed in normative economic theory, decision-making theory, political behavior, weapons systems, and international systems. Policy formulation about policy making was termed "metapolicymaking" by Dror in his survey, *Public Policy Making Reexamined* (San Francisco: Chandler, 1968).

As in decision making, much of the original work in public-policy making has been contributed outside the public-administration establishment in the behavioralist tradition. It has stopped short of recommending policies or evaluating them on moral grounds. Well-placed theorists have not been able to share their knowledge because of their strategic position in public life. Few techniques have been evolved to aid public-policy makers. Policy science, however, has had an impact and is likely to have more influence in the real world as more knowledge is gained and as interest in scientific approaches to societal problems spreads and applied social scientists enter public-policy making. The study of policy making is likely to contribute most in the following areas.

Policy framework

Although public-policy making reaches back to the dawn of human society, very little is known about it apart from snatches of information, some detailed studies, a few suggestions for general frameworks, and general gleanings at different levels. New knowledge enables checklists to be constructed of all the factors that potential policy makers should consider—goals, values, sources, actors, environmental influences, strategies, and so on. The checklists provide a basis for empirical testing, theoretical constructs, and validation. What is now a mysterious art may eventually have a scientific foundation, and what now constitutes personal charisma may be studied and learned as acquired skills. Future policy makers will be able to locate themselves within existing knowledge and spot relevant landmarks and paths that should make their job much easier than current muddling through unknown territory. In this way, they will be less dependent on history and patterns that they did not mold and more capable of guiding their own processes in terms of downward controlling factors (knowledge, decision making, and power) and upward consensus-forming process in active societies.[36]

Policy strategies

Enough is already known to show that early normative work in public-policy making was narrowly conceived, overgeneralized, and unsophisticated. The

[36] A. Etzioni, *The Active Society: A Theory of Societal and Political Processes.* New York: Free Press, 1967.

strategies failed to take into account the complexity of public-policy making in a dynamic (and now turbulent) situation; they assumed too much about the efficacy of bureaucratic instruments and political processes. More recent studies of public-policy making refer to several complexities that have to be examined first. What exactly is the problem for which a practical policy is sought? How do the problem and its possible solutions dovetail with other problems and their possible solutions? Whose interests are affected? Which combination of interests will be satisfied by this or that policy? Which would constitute the public interest? How much would have to be compromised to keep future options open or to pay off past and expected future favors? Consideration of such questions may defer obvious strategies. The best policy may be no policy at all—that is, a decision to do nothing—as no feasible solution may exist, strategic political leverage points may oppose any action, the policy environment may be too unpromising, or the society—its values, institutions, social composition, ideology, resources—may be changing too fast for consistent policy making. The policy selected will probably reflect historical continuity in the problem area, the societal power structure, charismatic qualities of policy participants, and the institutional instruments available for policy implementation.[37]

Clarification of public interest

In public-policy making, problems are never solved; they merely change shape. The problem of employment becomes a problem of affluence, leisure, and inflationary pressure. The problem of war becomes a problem of peace. One area of public-policy making may become relatively tranquil by pushing more serious problems onto other areas. What is right or good is relative to concepts of the public interest, which is the abstraction of the idea of the good society at any particular point of time. A public policy is considered in the public interest if it matches individual perceptions of what constitutes the good society. The clarification of the abstract public interest aids legal definiteness, limits ambiguous discretionary power, sets middle-range goals, and confines conflict. It also reveals the underlying value premises of policy makers, their conceptions of the role of public servants (that is, whether as instruments, guardians, conflict resolvers, interest articulators and mediators, or social engineers and political manipulators), and their interpretations of administrative ethics.[38] Certainly it challenged the idea that the public bureaucracy could or should be value neutral.

Different levels of policy making

Apart from the mapping of general frameworks, most studies distinguish between three different levels of policy making: (a) individuals alone and in small groups, (b) organizational policy making, and (c) metapolicy making

---

[37] M. Kroll, "Hypotheses and Designs for the Study of Public Policies in the United States," *Midwest Journal of Political Science,* VI, No. 4, pp. 363–383.

[38] G. Schubert, *The Public Interest.* New York: Free Press, 1960.

and multiorganizational problem solving—corresponding to individual politicking, bureaucratic politics, and macropolitical processes. The first category is very much the province of psychologists, sociologists, and behavioralists. The second category attracts not only serious studies of the formulation of organizational policies and implemented by bureaucratic politicians, but also humorous critiques. Both categories lend themselves to high-quality fiction, which may reveal more about public-policy making at these levels than academic studies studded with unfamiliar words and straight gobbledygook masquerading as theory. The third category is the political scientists' concern both at national and international levels. All three categories overlap and share some features. The most ambitious attempt at linkage is Dror's optimal policy-making model, which identifies seven metapolicy-making phases, seven policy-making phases, three post-policy-making phases, and an interconnecting communications and feedback phase.[39]

Institutionalization of public-policy making

Several studies have referred to the inadequacy of existing structures in coping with contemporary problems and of institutional obstacles to better policy making. Their suggestions, some of which have been acted upon, include the creation of policy-making units, the redesign of organizations around major problems, the establishment of independent policy-research institutes and institutes for the future, which would explore long-range policy implications by generating realistic pictures of future states and by demonstrating how their realization depended on currently available policies, the measurement and evaluation of existing policies, policy planning, PPBS, and relaxation of censorship and official secrets laws that prevent nonparticipants from knowing, let alone judging, public policies made in their name.

Policy content and evaluation

The study of public-policy-making processes has invariably been based on actual policies, but whereas early studies held the policy content as the dependent variable, later studies have considered it as the independent variable. The first approach investigated the power plays, participants, and policy actors to explain policy variables. The second approach examined the policy content in determining the actors, their relationships and the strategies, and the outcomes as influencing the social system and objectives. Growing involvement in the public arena by academic policy analysts as activists and advisers has blurred the line between normative and objective studies, but clarified the possibility of political cost-benefit measures as a professional skill.

New profession of policy analysts

Outstanding public figures have demonstrated that it is possible to transfer between problem areas, to apply similar policy-making techniques in both

---

[39] Y. Dror, *Public Policy Making Reexamined,* pp. 163–196.

public and private spheres, and to bridge the gap between theory and practice. Barnard and Vickers went from practice to theory, while Hitch and
Kissinger have gone from theory to practice. Independently, several universities and policy-research institutes conceived the idea that policy analysis
should be institutionalized and professionalized to fill the obvious gap between theory and practice and to create a reservoir of trained policy analysts who are able to devise and evaluate policy, policy-making processes
and techniques, and policy needs in the community. Policy analysts would
be neither a new breed of generalist administrators, specialists who had
become generalists through social awareness or sensitivity training, nor
program budgeters. Instead, they would be specialists in policy-making
knowledge, employed basically on emerging problems and improving public
policies and on public-policy-making capacity in general.

Although policy studies challenge the disciplinary qualifications of public
administration as a distinct subject rather than a general field of interest in
which people trained in relevant disciplines can specialize, they attract a
new wave of socially aware students anxious to improve the world around
them by changing public policies and the institutions and influences that
shape them. Concerned scholars find that in many new areas there is a policy
vacuum waiting to be filled by creative minds and trained intelligence, and
a widening gap between what could be done and what is being done by practitioners steeped in outmoded bureaucratic management values. They find
some encouragement in that part of the American public administration
establishment that never abandoned its reformist philosophy and its belief
in the attainment of the good society through democratic public administration. The problem is to reach the professional politician and the professional
bureaucrat, whose routes into public policy do not bring them in touch with
the new knowledge, and which, to the detriment of all, they may never properly understand.

By rejecting the attempts to transform public administration into public-
policy making, the mainstream has pushed the problem-solvers and policy
analysts toward a new discipline of policy sciences. The two disciplines may
be reunited by the new style political economists centered on the journal
Public Choice and the work of G. Tullock, J. M. Buchanan, A. Downs and
V. Ostrom,[40] concerned with public investment, communal goods and
services, opportunity costs in public finance, and welfare economics. They
apply political and economic analysis to the processes of collective action
(and inaction), the politics of public agencies, the public expression of individual preferences, the articulation of unorganized demands, public enterprise operations, and the organization of public service delivery systems
serving different collectivities. By concentrating on such practical problems
as metropolitan services and public utility distribution, they bring operating
specialists together with new public-policy making knowledge.

[40] See V. Ostrom and E. Ostrom,"Public Choice: A Different Approach to the Study of Public
Administration," *Public Administration Review,* 31 (1971). pp. 203–216, and L. L. Wade and R. L.
Curry, *A Logic of Public Policy.* Belmont, Calif.: Wadsworth, 1970.

4

The Politicization Issue

Because of their strategic position between political leaders and citizens, public officials have always been influential in public-policy making. Even those without direct outside contacts knew they could influence decisions and public actions by altering recommendations and distorting advice. Political leaders could not tell to what extent they were exercising political power without extensive feedback, ranging from personal spy systems to airing public grievances. Citizens approached public officials to intercede on their behalf before the political leaders and to seek an exercise of discretion in their favor. Public officials have never been seen as mere catalysts, ciphers, or instruments, whatever image they may have held of themselves. They are political actors and they are expected to be political actors. Political leaders use them for personal and party interests. Qualification for public office depends on compatibility with political leaders. In short, the public bureaucracy is politicized.

Only in western democracies and some of their former colonies is a different conception advanced. In them, the ideal is that politicians should take a self-denying ordinance, put aside their personal and party ambitions, and ensure that their decisions are executed in a rational, universal, egalitarian, and impersonal manner through a neutral or depoliticized bureaucracy. Public officials should serve their political masters without fear or favor and willingly contract out of active political life. Their personal political opinions should not be projected into their jobs, and they should take pains not to have their political views known publicly. They should be neutral instruments in the conduct of public affairs, speaking publicly if at all, in the voice of their political masters.

Depoliticization is the theme of the great bulk of literature on public administration, particularly in public-personnel administration, where it is often equated with the merit system. If the public bureaucracy is not depoliticized, then it ought to be.

> The genuine official . . . will not engage in politics. Rather, he should engage in impartial 'administration'. . . . The honor of the civil servant is vested in his ability to execute conscientiously the order of the superior authorities, exactly as if the order agreed with his own conviction. This holds even if the order appears wrong to him and if, despite the civil servant's remonstrances, the authority insists on the order. Without this moral discipline and self-denial, in the highest sense, the whole apparatus would fall to pieces.[1]

> As the arm of political choice, public administration is expected to make that choice fully effective in the discharge of the government's continuing functions. It forfeits public confidence by being indifferent as well as being inept. But unreserved acceptance of political direction must not lead the career man to turn into a zealous partisan of the government of the day. He cannot commit himself personally to particular policies without compromising the basic purpose of the administrative system as an instrumentality of equal use for any government coming to power lawfully.[2]

> There are spheres of activity legitimately open to the ordinary citizen in which the Civil Servant can play no part, or only a limited part. He is not to indulge in political or party controversy, lest by so doing he should appear no longer the disinterested adviser of Ministers or able impartially to execute their policy. He is bound to maintain a proper reticence in discussing public affairs and more particularly those with which his own Department is concerned. And lastly, his position clearly imposes upon him restrictions in matters of commerce and business from which the ordinary citizen is free.[3]

> The Hatch Act is designed to prevent those subject to it from assuming general political leadership or from becoming prominently identified with any political movement, party or faction or with the success or failure of any candidate for election to public office. . . . Any political activity that is prohibited in the case of an employee acting independently is also prohibited in the case of an employee acting in open or secret cooperation with others. . . . Political activity, in fact, regardless of the methods or means used by the employee, constitutes the violation.[4]

---

[1] M. Weber, "Politics as a Vocation," in H. H. Gerth and C. W. Mills, *From Max Weber: Essays in Sociology.* New York: Oxford University Press, 1958, p. 95.

[2] F. M. Marx, *The Administrative State.* Chicago: University of Chicago Press, 1957, p. 130.

[3] Report of the Board of Enquiry, Cmd. 3037, HMSO. London, 1928, paragraph 57.

[4] United States Civil Service Commission, *Political Activity,* Pamphlet 20. Washington, D.C., 1961, p. 10.

The message is clear—the public bureaucracy should be staffed by neutral professionals.

Western scholars have promoted their depoliticized model throughout the world, and so well have they denigrated the politicized bureaucracy that few can be found to defend it. Yet, despite their heavy propaganda over the past fifty years, they have not been very successful. Even in western democracies, practice is at variance with the lip service paid to the ideal. Only parts of their public bureaucracies have been depoliticized. Currently, there is a reaction against the depoliticized model or instrumentality thesis. The issue is by no means resolved.

THE DEPOLITICIZED BUREAUCRACY

Before a depoliticized bureaucracy is possible, a society has to be able to maintain a modern bureaucracy and to distinguish between political and administrative office holders. First, political functions must be differentiated and institutionalized into a readily identifiable governmental system with (a) agreed methods for determining political leaders (rulers), (b) a legal system through which the rulers' authority is expressed, (c) a military-police force at the ruler's call, capable of enforcing authority, and (d) a tributary tax system enabling the rulers to reward and punish without recourse to violence, build symbols of authority, and provide minimum communal services for the preservation of society and the safety of life and property. Second, the scale of governmental operations must require bureaucratization, and a sufficient number of persons must be willing to devote themselves fully to public service and accept a subordinate relationship to the rulers. Third, public officials must be adequately skilled to conduct governmental operations. These requirements were met in bureaucratic empires, theocracies, city states, and kingdoms before the modern bureaucratic state came into existence. They were largely absent outside Europe and the British Empire until the nineteenth century, and there are some contemporary societies that cannot meet them yet.

Once a corps of officials exists, successive rulers can inherit loyal servants skilled in public affairs on whom they are initially reliant until new appointees reach the same level of competence. Providing that they give the rulers no reason to doubt their loyalty and that they do not use discretionary power to embarrass the rulers publicly, they can increase their power. They can establish a monopoly over their expertise, confine the secrets of their trade to themselves, and insist that they alone select and teach initiates. Thus they begin to regulate themselves, develop insiders' symbols, decide on standards of official conduct, and discipline one another. They can decide among themselves the limits of partisan activity to prevent the security of all from being jeopardized by the recklessness of a few. They realize that, if purged, they have no ready alternative employment, little possibility of reemployment, scant resources on which to live until a new job is offered, and few means of combatting social disgrace. Neutrality is prudent, whereas partisanship offends either rulers or the ruled. If it is unavoidable, it should preferably be exercised in displays of loyalty, unless current rulers will be soon replaced or otherwise unable to employ sanctions.

The prudent policy for career officials in the bureaucratic state has been buttressed by a public-service ideology that was first expounded during the French Revolution:

a. Public administration is a machine for the implementation of the general will, as conceived by the representatives of the people. Government is a public trust to be used in the general interest and not for the benefit of particular sectional interests.
b. The public official is the servant of the public; he is there for their benefit, not they for his.
c. The public official should be the embodiment of all public virtues—he should be hard-working, honest, impartial, wise, sincere, just, and trustworthy. Official conduct should be beyond reproach.
d. The public official should obey his superiors and subordinate his personal interests, unless objection is based on conscientious grounds, whereupon he should leave public office before publicly declaring his opposition to govern-mental policy.
e. The public official should perform his duties efficiently and economically.
f. Appointment to public office should be on the basis of merit of the person and not on the privilege of his class.
g. Public officials should be subjected to the law in the same way as other citizens.

These ideas suited the political climate of western Europe during the nineteenth century for several reasons. Absolute monarchy was collapsing or conceding to revolutionary movements. The need for strong centralized executive government was apparent, and weak legislatures were an ineffective counterweight. Real power was passing to various combinations of upper- and middle-class blocs that expected and exacted obedience and respect from below. Rational administration was being extended as state activities expanded. Reformed and revitalized public bureaucracies retained the respect of the public. The public service continued as a high-prestige career, attractive to upper- and middle-class power blocs, as well as to aspiring social classes for whom new opportunities were available with increased physical and occupational mobility, higher literacy, wider civil liberties, and greater accessibility to public office. The concept of nonpartisan bu-reaucracy was further aided by a strong administrative-law system, profes-sionalization of technical services, middle-class dominance of the public professions, and close affinity between political and official elites, which smoothed the way toward equality before the law, equal consideration to all citizens, uniform national services, exclusion of public officials from the public political arena, bureaucratic self-government under political direction, and a reduction of official corruption and misuse of discretionary power.

The British took a slightly different path to reach the same ends. In Britain, the public bureaucracy had been depoliticized to prevent the monarch and the aristocracy from manipulating the electoral system and official patronage to thwart Parliament and underrepresented power blocs. Middle-class accession to power brought much-needed reforms and an institutionalized merit system. Democratization made no appreciable impact on official neutrality, and no party sought to gain political advantage from the exploitation of official patronage. Neutrality was again buttressed by an elaborate code of professional ethics that enshrined nonpartisan behavior and political subordination.

Nineteenth-century politicians in western Europe and Britain decided to forego the political advantages of a partisan bureaucracy, simply because partisanship became more a liability than an asset. Democratization made it impossible to guarantee public office to the upper and middle classes alone or to satisfy all those who sought public employment either as a high-prestige occupation or as a secure job. More office seekers were disappointed than satisfied. Political support had to be gained in other ways—by clarification of political ideology, codification of political programs, organization of national vote-getting machines, control of mass media, and manipulation of electoral systems, all of which promised greater returns in terms of political investment. To ward off revolution, the established power blocs made concessions and embarked on sweeping reforms entailing increased governmental intervention in economic affairs and social-action programs. Government work became complicated, specialized, and professional, and its proper performance required highly qualified, public-spirited citizens prepared to stay in public employment. The inefficiencies of the public bureaucracy could cost a country its independence, stability, progress, and well-being. Politicians were forced by disaster or the threat of disaster to ensure competent public services by restructuring the machinery of government and instituting merit systems independent of political organizations. Thus, politicians were shielded from the liabilities of patronage and were guaranteed effective execution of their decisions in socially acceptable ways. After all, given a rigid social structure and privileged educational opportunities, the merit system preserved the bureaucratic elites for established power blocs. Only revolutionary and radical lower-class political representatives would be handicapped, if at all, by the social composition of the bureaucratic elites.

Within the public bureaucracy, officials were prepared to forego all public political activity in return for the benefits of public office—namely, social status, security, good working conditions, and fair employment practices. They knew when they joined that they were committing themselves for life. Most officials were temperamentally unsuited for political life or uninterested in politics. The work alone was enough to attract and satisfy them, and they were prepared to accept unreservedly the conditions of employment, including limitations on their civil rights and codes of official conduct. At the apex, they shared in public-policy making and managed the machinery of government under the guidance of responsible politicians. They became increasingly responsible for the detailed direction of large-scale enterprises providing a wide range of goods and services once their political masters felt sure that public officials could be relied on to apply their political values, anticipate their concerns, and parry public criticism. On the whole, mutual trust prevailed. In the final event, the officials could always rely on the politicians to assume full responsibility for all actions taken on behalf of the government and to defend them in public against criticism.

The compact between politicians and officials was supported by a citizenry prepared to make sacrifices for strong, effective, and responsible government, given external threats, internal divisions, and weak, splintered legislatures. Genuine concern existed for the safety of the nation and the preservation of the regime. There was also general awareness of the repercussions of violence, war, civil strife, economic depressions, disease, and hunger in a confined area. Discretionary government was not new, although certain safeguards had been incorporated. In reaction to the corruption of absolutist regimes, representative governments were expected to rid themselves of waste and immorality in public business and to reduce nepotism, corruption, and patronage. Sordid politics were separated from moral, efficient public administration through such devices as professional ethics, merit systems, and neutral bureaucracies.

American visitors to western Europe were impressed by the public bureaucracies they found, which were orderly, efficient, honest. At home, in contrast, the politicized bureaucracies were disorderly, inefficient, and corrupt. Public morality fell below European standards. The blame was put on the spoils system, although it was only one of a number of contributory factors. In turn, the spoils system was blamed by the gentry on Jacksonian democracy, while ignoring the wider political environment, particularly the strict separation of powers and an elective chief executive that made effective government difficult without the manipulation of public monies and offices.

Long before Jacksonian democracy, political and official positions had been fused at the apex of government and public office had been considered something more than a patriotic, secure livelihood for social aspirants. Jackson widened access to bureaucratic and political power used for partisan and personal ends. He democratized public service, until then a preserve of the gentry and, like Jefferson before him, made the bureaucratic elite more representative of political ends. Rotation of public offices enabled more people to participate in government and prevented bureaucratic usurpation of political power. After all, the duties of public office were so simple, he claimed, that any intelligent person was qualified. An alternative to rotation was the transference of appointing and retiring powers to Congress. Another was to replace patronage with an examination system on Chinese lines. Both, however, were impractical in American politics. After the 1830s, every swing of the political pendulum was accompanied by a noticeable turnover of partisans. Thus a spoils system was institutionalized outside the region that became the Confederacy where pre-Jacksonian government by the gentry survived. Politicization showed its worth in the Civil War by obtaining the support of dissidents and frontiersmen to the established regime. It suited entrepreneurial politics. It enabled a strong two-party system to survive. It mobilized a politically apathetic citizenry preoccupied with other pursuits.

Actually, the bureaucracies of the United States and western Europe were not very different before the Civil War. Merit systems were not yet firmly established anywhere on a national basis. Jacksonian democracy notwithstanding, public office demanded education and skills confined to a relatively small section of the population, and job requirements narrowed selection still further. Even relatively low-level positions were considered middle-class occupations, and their incumbents shared a common outlook with the politicians whom they served. Political protégés could be accommodated in new positions, as bureaucracies grew, without entailing the dismissal of nonpartisans. Embryonic merit systems and in-service training courses were used in specialized areas. The major difference was in tenure. European officials were appointed for life, and their low turnover contrasted with American officialdom's limited tenure positions, frequent reorganizations, and greater occupational mobility. No valid comparisons in staff quality, however, have been made. While European commentators dealt harshly with their nineteenth-century administrations, Americans were less concerned or may have had less reason to be alarmed.[5]

After the Civil War, the divergences widened as Europe reformed and the United States continued with the spoils system. Public morality declined, according to respectable folk who were being squeezed out by political manipulators and unscrupulous party bosses. Morality—not efficiency and economy or better public services—was the rallying cry of the administrative reformers, whose simplistic solution to the problem was a European nonpartisan bureaucracy. The Pendleton Act of 1883 became the symbol of an effective stand against public corruption, the spoils system, and party bosses. Since then, the reform movement in the United States has firmly supported depoliticization, although it has not achieved the measure of success attained in Europe or even of some of the newly independent states that have followed European practice.

Depoliticized western bureaucracies have persisted in essence despite social and political revolutions, foreign occupations, violent swings of the political pendulum, economic disasters, and radical transformations of the

[5] See L. D. White's studies in federal administrative history—*The Federalists* (1948), *The Jeffersonians* (1951), *The Jacksonians* (1954), and *The Republican Era* (1958), all published by Crowell-Collier-Macmillan and later released as paperbacks by the Free Press in 1965—and P. Van Riper, *History of the United States Civil Service*. New York: Harper & Row, 1958.

public domain. So far the experience of newly independent states has been too short to assess whether their depoliticized bureaucracies are likely to continue unaffected by their turbulent environments. In the older states, depoliticization seems to have fared best (a) in prosperous countries with relatively little actual and disguised unemployment, rising living standards, and high literacy levels, where people are not very dependent on public employment and where political leverage from spoils is low; (b) in democratic regimes with ideological emphasis on civil rights, rule of law, equality, and compromise, where people have rights against the state, are assured of equal access to public office, and may choose from several competing parties; (c) in organizational societies where people are used to dealing with impersonal authority and to working within bureaucratic frameworks: (d) in socially mobile societies where class barriers are uncertain and the family is atomized so that people rely more on themselves than family connections for advancement, based on achievement rather than ascription: and (e) in highly sophisticated societies, where people can distinguish between political and official career routes separated by well differentiated political and governmental systems and strong political institutions. Depoliticization has emphasized professionalism, which in turn has stressed rationality, efficiency, and service. It has demanded competence in public employment and has guaranteed permanency, reliability, and continuity in public affairs. Political leaders have been assured of a reliable corps of experts and professionals behind them. The public has been treated to uniform, impartial, and competent treatment. The public officials have been offered a rewarding career, secure in tenure and sheltered from political and public criticism.

THE CONCEPT OF DEPOLITICIZATION

The concept of depoliticization is simple. Politicians should rule; public officials should do their bidding. Political offices should be filled competitively in the political arena; bureaucratic offices should be filled competitively in the bureaucratic arena. The political official should be selected on the basis of his political competence; the bureaucratic (or public) official should be selected on the basis of his bureaucratic competence. The separation of political and official career routes should be institutionalized by legal or constitutional prohibition on concurrent office holding and interchange. The politician should be judged by the electorate or his political peers; the official should be judged by his political overseers or his bureaucratic peers. Political office should be of limited tenure and subject to frequent elections; bureaucratic office should be of unlimited tenure, subject to good behavior. The public bureaucracy should be a career service, staffed by experts and open to all qualified citizens. Officials should not be political partisans, political appointees, or party spoilsmen; on appointment they should not take any further part in active politics. In return for restriction on their civil rights, they should be shielded from outside criticism. In different words, public officials obey their political masters and carry out their will. They are anonymous ciphers or instruments. They are professionals doing their duty, career officials who are not dependent on political leaders for their positions or security. As experts, they look after the administrative details and refer political matters, political values, and policy changes upward for decision.

The concept has much to commend it. Ideologically, few could support the subordination of politics to officialdom. The guardian bureaucracy or bureaucratic polity is essentially an aristocratic concept advocated by those who would presumably qualify as the guardians and who believe themselves better able to rule than the elected representatives of the people. Bureaucratic rule, no matter how representative, altruistic, and self-effacing, would be autocratic and arbitrary, permitting no change of regime except by armed revolt. Under the concept of depoliticization, the politicians really rule and make the decisions. The state apparatus relieves them of the routine and permits them to concentrate on the important matters of government. When things go well, they can take the credit, but when things go wrong, they can always blame the anonymous, silent career officials for acting contrary to instructions. Public officials have a sense of security unknown to politicians, for they do not have to defend themselves publicly. They can eschew partisan politics and offset partisan distortions in government. By blindly following orders, they can salve their consciences.

The concept simplifies governmental studies by delineating a clear boundary between political science and public administration. By separating politics from administration, it aids administrative science. It is readily understood and provides comfort to a public worried about the possibility of bureaucratic usurpation of political power.

> Policy decision is the responsibility of Ministers and the Cabinet. The Civil Servant's essential role is to implement to the best of his ability decisions handed down to him by his Minister or the Cabinet, and provided the relative roles of Minister and Civil Servant are well understood, there need be no conflict between them. . . . The Civil Servant must, therefore, be in a position to serve all governments of whatever complexion with equal loyalty and obtain the confidence of Ministers irrespective of their political affiliations.[6]

> As an instrument of government, public administration occupies a central place because of its capacity for achieving results by its own operations. It is eminently suited to function as an agent of policy, to give policy immediate meaning by affecting economic and social behavior.[7]

---

[6] A.L. Adu, *The Civil Service in New African States.* New York: Praeger, 1965, p. 26.

[7] F. M. Marx, "The Social Function of Public Administration," in F. M. Marx, ed., *The Elements of Public Administration.* Englewood Cliffs, N.J.: Prentice-Hall, 1959, p. 99.

If the concept is carried to its logical conclusion, the depoliticized bureaucracy, full of officials just following orders (that is, agents, instruments, tools), could destroy liberty and vanquish civilization should government fall into the hands of tyrannous psychopaths. The obedient bureaucrat's role was many a Nazi's justification for perpetrating genocide.

But no public bureaucracy exists in a vacuum; none can be abstracted from its societal context. The public instrumentality is a tangible mix of organizations, laws, physical plant, and people, conducting observable and identifiable activities, drawing resources from society, and transforming them into public services. It is under pressure from many different sources. The *political leaders* want to use it to advantage—to consolidate their position and to enhance their reputations. They want a subservient body, whether composed of partisan supporters or neutral professionals, not a potential rival government. The *major social classes* also want to exploit it for advantage or at least to obtain favorable treatment from it, through infiltration and social contacts. The *public officials* have their own ideas about their role. They want a higher social status and higher rewards for their services. *Special interests* want to preserve their autonomy while obtaining the maximum support from the public bureaucracy. *Unorganized interests* want the public bureaucracy to represent them in public-policy making. *Citizens* want a competent service bureaucracy open to all. These pressures converge on the bureaucracy, and whose instrument it is at any time or place cannot be answered simply by reference to constitutional theory or concepts of depoliticization. Rarely will it be the exclusive instrument of the political leaders. More likely, each function will indicate different compromises between opposing forces. Within the complex, there may be little agreement about anything, and outcomes may be due less to orderly structuring by interlocking elites than to shifting compromises and unholy alliances between conflicting units pursuing contradictory goals.

According to the concept of depoliticization, the question of divided loyalties hardly arises. The official's first and only duty is to his political master, right or wrong. If he cannot abide by his master's decisions, he should resign.

This master-servant relationship suited well the early days of the bureaucratic state, when public officials were instruments of an absolute monarch or their aristocratic patrons. Today, the answer is not so easy. Conflicts of loyalty are frequent, and nobody can categorically state which should be preferred among the following:

a. *Humanity.* The public bureaucracy or community power should be used to benefit all mankind, not only one country or region. The goal is to improve the quality of life generally on the planet and to foreswear national rivalries. (International officials are expected to put humanity above national considerations.)

   b. *Nation.* Loyalty to nation, discredited by Nazi Germany, which gave it racial overtones, still appeals to the altruistic who wish to serve their fellow men. More recently it has been used by leaders of newly independent states to maintain the people's confidence in new polities where there are few cohesive factors.

   c. *State or polity.* Although more concrete than the idea of nation, the state or polity also has its metaphysical features. First loyalty is to the state, not the international order or self.

   d. *Regime or constitution.* This loyalty is questioned in revolution or foreign occupation.

   e. *Government or political leaders.* The masters determine what should be done; the servants only follow, although they may advise, warn, persuade, and encourage.

   f. *Party.* Public officials may depend on a political party for their positions. The party bureaucracy may be integrated with the state bureaucracy in dominant one-party states, or ideologically, the party may capture a member's total loyalty.

   g. *Social class, tribe, religion.* The official is expected to protect and advance his ascriptive group.

   h. *Profession or program.* The needs of the public service provided become paramount, and in any clash of loyalties, the program or profession has priority.

   i. *Trade union.* The official as a public employee may be entitled to protect his personal interest like any other employee.

   j. *Clientele, public, public interest, community or public responsibility.* Loyalty to notions of a general will, the common interests of all citizens, publicness, or underdogs and underprivileged is often part of official ideology.

   k. *The good society.* The official is loyal to his personal conception of the ideal.

Which one of these possibilities predominates is a question of individual conscience. Whenever conflict arises between political dictum and personal choice, resolution is not simply resignation by dissenting officials. Individual resignations barely make any impression. Mass resignations would jeopardize the polity, reduce the efficacy of public services, and threaten the security and well-being of society. Voluntary resignation unrealistically assumes ready alternative employment, some private means to cover transitional unemployment and removals, and absence of social repercussions on leaving governmental service. More likely, the dissident will take to passive resistance; he will take no action, but disguise his inactivity in many ways. If vehemently opposed, he may resort to active sabotage and risk the consequences. Depoliticization, by denying political activity to officials and expecting absolute loyalty from them, is more applicable to robots than human beings in our troubled times. As a solution to the problem of politicization, it is increasingly unrealistic and unrealizable.

The conditions under which the depoliticization concept can be strictly applied are diminishing. The public bureaucracy is too valuable a prize in contemporary society to be left solely to the professionals. It can make or break other political institutions. It holds the keys to national development. The fortunes of political leaders are tied too closely to bureaucratic performance. Pressures for politicization are increasing. Administrative systems are subject to greater external influence. The impetus in society, its dynamics and enterprise, is no longer found chiefly outside the governmental system. Political leaders and their public instruments act as something more than referees; they attempt to channel social forces in given directions. Major rewards (for example, spoils, pork barrel, contracts) and sanctions (for example, differential use of discretion, legal prosecution) of the political system are contained in the public bureaucracy: it is more worthwhile to exploit bureaucratic partisanship. Within the political system, the politicians are not so overwhelmingly superior to public officials, whose exercise of discretionary powers is increasing. Perhaps fifty years ago, most policy initiatives came from the political elite. Today, the public bureaucracy has replaced the political elite as the source of policy initiatives.

In theory, ministers decide policy, and civil servants carry out their decisions. This is strictly true from a constitutional standpoint; but in reality it is a conventional half-truth. Ministers seldom have the time, or knowledge, and sometimes not the skill, to formulate policy unaided. They must rely on their senior officials for advice, and still more for knowledge of the basic facts and figures on which policy must be based. They have a right to expect that civil servants will do their utmost to make proposals which will reflect, or at least be compatible with, the political philosophy and the programme of the party in power.[8]

Whether or not the trend is desirable or reversible, the fact remains that few would want to return to the passive bureaucracy of the past—its conservative approach, adherence to the strict letter of the law, reluctance to depart from precedent, weight given to respectability (that is, good connections), reliability (that is, reputation for avoiding innovation), and seniority (that is, length of routine service), and group conformity. Such traits might have suited the temper of past times, but they had to be changed to meet modern needs. Administrative reform is now concerned mainly with injecting initiative, enterprise, and managerial ability, without too much dislocation. Old structures are being revamped and streamlined. New structures are being superimposed. Closed career structures are being opened. No official is expected to be neutral about his job; instead, he must believe in what he is doing. He must adjust to changing social values and goals. If he wishes to maintain his self-respect, mix with his fellow citizens, uphold the prestige of his chosen profession, and perform effectively, he cannot be anybody's passive instrument.

[8] W. A. Robson, "Bureaucracy and Democracy," in W. A. Robson, ed., *The Civil Service in Britain and France.* London: Hogarth, 1956, p. 8.

THE ASSUMPTIONS OF NEUTRALITY

The concept of depoliticization has been rejected in many states as being undesirable and impracticable. Public officials are expected to be partisan on the side of the ruling parties: the public bureaucracy is a legitimate extension of party organization. In contrast, excessive party partisanship by officials in multiparty democracies strengthens the appeal of neutrality. A depoliticized bureaucracy saves political parties the trouble and expense of rebuilding the public bureaucracy with every change of political composition in the government. The public has confidence in a public bureaucracy loyal to every government and obedient to political orders without discrimination. The government is saved the expense of strict supervisory mechanisms to ensure obedience. The public officials are secure and can devote themselves to their duties. They freely accept limitations on their political activity as a necessary employment condition. The assumptions on which all of this is based should be examined closely in the light of modern conditions.

The Assumption that an Open Public Bureaucracy Will Better Reflect Society

A politicized bureaucracy restricts entry to the public bureaucracy by confining selection to those favorably disposed to the ruling parties. An open public bureaucracy abandons political restrictions, broadens the range of selection, and makes the public bureaucracy more representative of the society it is supposed to serve. But even with the best intentions, no public bureaucracy can ever mirror society, and its unrepresentative nature has a distorting effect on the exercise of discretion. The public bureaucracy is a middle-class profession and is largely staffed by the middle class, more so at its upper levels than lower levels. The middle-class bias arises from (a) the unrepresentative cross section of applicants, reflecting differential occupational images, job opportunities, employment conditions, and personal motivations, and (b) the distortion effects of bureaucratic requirements such as nationality, sex, education, health, loyalty, age, location, and job qualifications. The poor are unable to qualify. They lack education or good health, particularly in countries where most of the population is illiterate and diseased. The middle class is qualified and has aspirations that public office can fulfill, namely, upward social mobility, status, and security.

The requirements of a merit system, reflecting a middle-class disposition, build into the public bureaucracy a set of values that give it a stabilizing effect, but unconsciously prejudice officials against certain sections of the public that do not accept those values. Hence, revolutionaries condemn public officials for upholding establishment values to which they are opposed. This also accounts for a strong antigovernment, antiauthority, antipublic service attitude among the lower classes and dispossessed minority groups, who feel that they do not receive equal treatment from officialdom. They have few allies within the public bureaucracy, and they do not know how to master bureaucratic mores to ensure equal consideration. Even if the merit system were designed to ensure that the public bureaucracy was an exact image of society, discounting lower performance standards and the exclusion of the very young and elderly, it would be truly miraculous if every administrative unit were so composed. The exact balance of political forces within a neutral bureaucracy would not matter anyway, if it were only an instrument or catalyst between rulers and ruled. Considerations of social composition are important precisely because it is much more (see Chap. 9).

The Assumption that the Public Bureaucracy Will Accept Neutrality

The distortion effects of an unrepresentative bureaucracy would not be serious if public officials accepted neutrality in word and deed and acted as if they were political eunuchs. Rarely have they been denied all political rights or refused to exercise those they had. The act of voting denotes a definite political prejudice, particularly in countries where electoral systems are new and balloting is public. Public officials are political animals with partisan prejudices. They may not be passionately involved, and they may not consciously permit their personal opinions to affect their work, but they are not neutral. Certainly any top official who does not think politically, appreciate the political problems in public administration, or understand the political implications of official business is not suitably qualified. The political content of bureaucratic work rises rapidly beyond routine performance and is high even in relatively low-status positions, in politically sensitive areas such as foreign affairs, public relations, censorship, and immigration. Noncontroversial is not nonpolitical. Further, when public officials see themselves as employees entitled to the same rights as employees everywhere, they chafe at political restrictions. They, too, want to unionize, conduct pressure group activities, and associate politically with the wider labor movement. The public employer can be just as bad as (even worse than) private employers who can participate in political life.

The Assumption that the Public Bureaucracy Will Be Accepted as Acting Neutrally

Even if the public officials try to act impartially and contract out of active politics, the public or pressure groups with which they come into contact do not believe them. Public confidence in a public bureaucracy is hard to cultivate because of ingrained antiauthoritarian mores and lingering adverse images of partisanship, corruption, and inefficiency. It is easily destroyed too by isolated incidents and by the deliberate distortions of antibureaucratic and antigovernment groups. Mass media are more concerned with the sensational than with routine competence. One slip, and the whole public sector is condemned. In such circumstances, with the public wanting to believe in partisanship and others willing to supply the evidence, the public bureaucracy can do no right. If it faithfully supports the politicians in power, the opposition sees collusion. If it supports the opposition, the government suspects treason. In all governments, partisan advantage is a factor in decision making, however much it can be disguised, and public officials are involved as advisers and executors. Outsiders cannot believe that officials serve their different masters equally. It may be better to reveal internal divisions within the public bureaucracy and identify the sources of political advice; they are known to interested and concerned parties anyway.

The Assumption that It Is Desirable for the Public Bureaucracy to Be Neutral

Politicization would seem to be detrimental where (a) political decisions were ignored or deliberately sabotaged by public officials, (b) frequent shifts of the political pendulum were accompanied by wholesale changes of staff to disrupt the smooth running of government, and (c) knowledge of political alignments within the public bureaucracy profoundly affected public attitudes toward the political system, government, and public services. If a polity were so weak that it could not detect resistance and sabotage within the public bureaucracy or discipline offenders, depoliticization would hardly strengthen political institutions. On the contrary, it is likely to jeopardize existing governmental operations and open the polity to extraneous influences ready to fill political vacuums. Frequent changes of government do not have to be accompanied by wholesale displacement of staff, certainly not in the bulk of routine government operations, where policy is settled and the opinions of public officials have no influence on technical operations. In politically sensitive areas, all that is required is the permanent exclusion of extremists dedicated to the overthrow of the regime by force and the temporary reshuffling of staff. If the public does not care about the political views of doctors, salesmen, plumbers, and keyboard operators, which they need never know, why should it care about the political views of mailmen, lighthouse keepers, customs inspectors, and tax checkers, all public officials, whose personal opinions they may never know? Neutrality or the appearance of neutrality may be desired in relatively few positions. Much depends on public attitudes and political education. Australia, for instance, has demonstrated that political freedom can be permitted to all public officials without damaging the reputation of official impartiality.

On the other hand, it would seem desirable to place politically sensitive officials in many of the newer functions of government not undertaken in a law-and-order state. There are numerous policy programs in modern government that require a political commitment by all involved to ensure their success. The staff must be enthusiastic and parade their optimism. Much the same applies to development projects. The public officials should believe in development through public initiative. Within public bureaucracies, strong personalities are needed to withstand pressure groups that threaten political blackmail or seek favors in public policy. Ideological politics are becoming more important in countries that never before had a modern political system, political parties, or mass political movements.

The Assumption that the Advantages of a Neutral Public Bureaucracy Outweigh the Disadvantages

Granted that a neutral bureaucracy may have the advantages of permanency, continuity, reliability, and professionalism (advantages that are not the monopoly of depoliticization), they may not be sufficient to outweigh other considerations of more importance to the political system and the society. A depoliticized bureaucracy may be too conservative for a dynamic society. Its reluctance to depart from routine and its preference for incremental change may obstruct public-policy making in a turbulent environment. Crisis demands unusual action and requires wide flexibility. A society in which the public bureaucracy is a dominant political institution may need to use it for political unity and societal stability. There may be no other unifying force at all or no other political institution able to command public loyalty. If any group is underrepresented or not represented at all, it may revolt and form its own polity or remain a persistent nuisance within the existing polity. To stabilize the polity, it may be necessary to build up a representative party system, using the spoils of public office, and only after a party system has been established on an independent basis move toward a depoliticized public bureaucracy with built-in safeguards against inbreeding and isolation.

The Assumption that the Public Bureaucracy Can Be Politically Neutral

The possibility of bureaucratic neutrality needs to be tackled on two levels: (a) that the public bureaucracy can be party-politically neutral, and (b) that it can be politically neutral.

Party political neutrality   The success of the merit systems in western democracies proves that the public bureaucracy can be nonpartisan, providing certain concessions are made. It is impossible to recruit only nonpartisans. To prohibit from public employment anyone who has a political record is patently absurd in a politically active society. It would involve an intensive investigation of every applicant. The nearest attempt at political screening in nontotalitarian regimes is the investigation of persons with suspect backgrounds in subversive and extremist organizations to prevent their employment on security grounds. Even this limitation raises the prospect of blackmail or blacklisting without adequate opportunity of rebuttal and overlooks the person who holds subversive views without formally associating with extremists. Much more common is the commitment, on entering the public bureaucracy, to drop all past associations and abstain from active politics. All employers oblige their employees to forego some aspect of their individual rights, and most make active political participation difficult if not impossible for many employees. Relatively few people have the time, income, or facilities for politics. Blanket prohibitions on public employees, such as the Hatch Act in the United States of America, are probably more severe than anything imposed on other citizens. They are overreactions to the spoils system, justified on the grounds that otherwise the public bureaucracy would be corrupt, unstable, discriminatory, unprofessional, and unable to give the same loyal service to all governments. Other countries have been less strict, by placing prohibitions only on top officials and lesser-ranking officials in politically sensitive areas. A few have permitted full political activity, providing official duties were not compromised, confidential public documents were not revealed, and comments on the immediate work area of the officials were restricted.

The effect of political restrictions is to exclude an increasing proportion of the adult work force from the political arena, to reduce public officials to the status of second-class citizens, to limit the effectiveness of public-employee unionism, to censor the public expression of officials, to maintain the government's monopoly over official information, and to deny mass media and political parties access to many intelligent, well informed citizens and so deprive the public of information that might help it to decide on important public issues. The democratic spirit is denied needlessly, as there are alternatives for preventing the dysfunctions of a spoils system and for maintaining public confidence in the public bureaucracy, without blanket prohibitions. In practice, political pressures prove too strong. Restrictions are observed in the breach, and sanctions are used only as an ultimate weapon against abuse. A calculated risk is taken that public officials can be trusted in the main to be discreet about partisan politics in off-duty hours and that political parties will not embarrass public officials.

Formal prohibitions ignore political socialization processes that prejudice an official's political outlook, whether or not he publicly adheres to a political party. These socialization processes commence in the family and cover friends and spouse, schooling and other formal education, military service, youth movements, clubs and associations, hobbies, and contacts. Mass media play a part in shaping attitudes to current events, and the official is influenced by discussions with colleagues and contacts on the job. Psychologically, too, he may be predisposed politically, and he may be affected by the social environment of public bureaucracy. Some officials are pushed into public service by their ascriptive groups as a duty. Others are attracted to it from idealistic motives. They may view it as a stepping stone to something else. If they stay, they can be expected to favor politicians and parties that are disposed toward them—that is, political activists who support government intervention, public enterprise, public employment, social programs, official aggrandizement, and public-employee unionism. At elections, parties compete for the growing public-employee vote by offering to improve employment conditions.

Even if he wants no part in partisan politics, the public official may be drawn into the political arena. He is carrying out the government's decisions, and these are partisan-political, irrespective how widely supported they may be and how much accord there may be with the opposition. The government parties hope to extract as much political gain as possible, while opposition is not adverse to making political capital out of official mistakes. At any time, the official can be singled out for special political attention either for something he has done that he should not have, or something he omitted to do that he should have. Toward the apex, the political pressures increase. The political masters may delegate much of their work to subordinate officials. They may be incompetent or unable to do much work, so that officials have to fill the political vacuum. In other words, the official may become his own political master or work as if he were the politician. Only those in the very center of government know to what extent bureaucracy and partisan politics are fused, and how captive or dependent are the political masters. Occasionally leakages occur, but on the whole such things remain secret.

Political neutrality The politics-administration dichotomy denies any political role to public officials. It assumes that there is an identifiable distinction between politics (or policy or value) and administration (or execution or fact) and that people will consciously act according to the distinction. These are convenient assumptions that most people would like to accept. It simplifies the study of government and provides a comforting ideology, and it fits well into a value-free science of administration. Politicians like to believe that they rule and that officials are meek ciphers, and the officials want the public to believe that the politicians really rule. It has been instrumental in devising organizational forms in public administration such as the city-manager in local government, the public corporation in public enterprise, and the ministerial department in central government. It dominated the study of public administration in the United States before World War II, and it is still found in textbooks, political speeches, and official mores. Even if it does not exist, people want to believe it does.

Unfortunately, nobody has yet defined either "politics" or "administration" satisfactorily, and no definition has been generally accepted.

> But it is to be emphasized that in its early stages, systematic investigation must employ lexical terms—those with conventional meanings. These frequently, if not always, result in paradox: their denotations are much clearer than their designations. By custom and convention, that which they point to is recognizable, the things they denote are relatively clear, but the *grounds* upon which identification is made remain quite implicit. Investigation, therefore, appears to be loose and ambiguous, shifting and imprecise, and loaded with bias.[9]

In public administration, politics is seen as the realm of the politician, concerned with values, policies, decisions, ends, judgments, and respon-

[9] J. M. Landau, "Political and Administrative Development: General Commentary," in R. Braibant, ed., *Political and Administrative Development.* Durham, N.C.: Duke University Press, 1969, p. 326.

sibility, while administration is the world of the official, who is concerned with facts, execution, means, accountability, methods, laws, and structures. The two overlap, and in many instances they are fused; politicians perform administrative duties, and officials assume political responsibilities. Political and administrative content vary with position and personal predilection. One politician will handle everything himself, while another may be happy to delegate everything to subordinates. One official will refer anything out of routine to his superiors, while another will assume responsibility for making a decision and only report to his superiors after taking action. Changes in direction and emphasis in public affairs take place at every level within the public bureaucracy and enter the political arena from any point. The importance of a decision is not dependent on the status of the initiator or whether it concerns ends or means (if these can be separated), but its political repercussions and the extent of departure from previously accepted norms. The politics-administration distinction is not a dichotomy but a continuum; between the extremes, there are various gradations of fusion.

This fusion has long been acknowledged in democratic theory. Political leaders have not accepted any distinction between politics and administration in public affairs, but have accepted responsibility for all matters. Attempts to disclaim responsibility have not been successful, as opponents have accused them of shifting the blame on silenced officials unable to answer for themselves. If they did not know what officials were doing, then they *should* have known, and they remain responsible for remedial action. The strictest interpretation is the principle of ministerial responsibility, which holds the minister responsible for everything within his formal jurisdiction. Ministers take the attitude that, if they are responsible for everything and if their critics fail to recognize any distinction between politics and administration, important and unimportant decisions, known or unknown actions, then they ought to keep an eye on everything and ignore any distinction themselves. In practice, however, the position is more fluid. Some ministers refuse responsibility for a subordinate's action taken without their knowledge. Nevertheless, their reputations depend to some extent on their familiarity and control of the area of their jurisdiction. By the time politicians have reached ministerial level, they are fairly sophisticated in the ways of officialdom and bureaucratic defense mechanisms. They know what they want and what the public will not tolerate. They believe that they are the rulers, that they understand the public and the public understands them, that they are the people's representatives, the protectors of cherished values, and the guardians of the weak and underprivileged. Therefore, it is their duty to interfere in all aspects of the public bureaucracy to see that their will is being done and that the officials know their place. Nothing is too small if political capital can be made from it. No theoretical distinctions between politics and administration should prevent them from doing what they believe is right, and no bureaucratic defenses are safe from political charisma.

Both politicians and officials are bound by notions of public propriety. They share similar ideas about public trust, public responsibility, public property, public interest, and political feasibility. They are mutually obliged to warn one another of potential abuse. The politician watches for bureaucratic excesses. The official draws attention to political excesses. Both share responsibility for ensuring that government operations are properly maintained and capable of bearing all but the most unexpected demands. This responsibility goes beyond the mechanics of government into public-policy making. The politician rectifies errors as they occur and rebuilds when the bureaucracy fails. The official indicates policy vacuums and hastens to fill them when politicians fail to react. In public administration, the deficiencies of one are corrected by the other, neither being reluctant to step into the other's province when necessary. Indeed, as the work load on politicians has increased, officials have been encouraged to assume more of the burden and undertake activities that were once the cherished preserve of the politicians. The official has to think politically and may be called upon to substitute for his political master, even to fight his political battles for him. In turn, the politicians are brought directly into bureaucratic infighting, as in a growing area of government, officials make and carry out their own political decisions, and the politicians settle for a supervisory role over an innovating bureaucracy.

> A modern administrator . . . must ever be on the alert to see whether the particular function of Government entrusted to his care meets the current needs of the public. This means that a public administrator must show initiative and enterprise. Every public administrator must keep his ears open to hear the voices of the people as they express their changing needs. Of course he will recognize that the people will demand of their legislative representatives more services and lower costs. The enterprising administrator must be able to come up with the ideas that will help meet these conflicting demands at least in part. A public administrator in effect must be a salesman selling his new ideas and new methods to the people and then to their representatives. In this way he can adjust himself to the changing circumstances. [10]

Imagination, planning, articulation of ideas, and stimulation are part of the official's job. He no longer confines himself to things that somebody else has decided should be done:

> To be successful every government official needs to be aware of outside considerations, available to the concerned committees of the Congress, willing to work in a goldfish bowl, earnest in cultivating his public relations—because his personal public relations are the relations between the people and their government. He

[10] F. P. Zeidler, "The Administrator and Public Policy," *Public Administration Review,* 14 (Summer 1954), pp. 180–182.

must be adept—increasingly so as he rises in rank and responsibility—in helping to build the coalition of outside forces which will provide a "political base" for the program in his charge. He must therefore not be afraid to advocate new policies if he thinks the old ones are worn out, nor can he flinch from becoming identified with the administration of which he is a part and defending his program in public.[11]

The *expected* politicization of the public official the higher he goes in the public bureaucracy indicates the formal acceptance of bureaucratic power.

BUREAUCRATIC POWER

Max Weber, from whom theoretical conceptions of bureaucracy are derived, identified three types of authority—traditional (custom), charismatic, and legal-rational. For him, bureaucracy is a legal-rational staff, functioning within a pluralistic power structure; it is a means or an instrument. Weber did not seriously envisage that the bureaucracy might assume authority in its own right and perhaps constitute a ruling class with a monopoly of power. Such a prospect, however, was raised by J. Burnham in *The Managerial Revolution* (New York: John Day, 1941). He feared that managers would become a self-perpetuating ruling class through their control of the instruments of production in both public and private enterprise once ownership and control were separated. He drew attention to the growth of autonomous bureaucratic power able to influence the daily lives of people. Managers and officials not only followed orders; they also made them. If politics is concerned with who gets what, when, and how, then they are political actors very much involved with the market place and price mechanism of societal demands, and concerned with preserving a community grown too complicated for either tradition or arbitrary rule alone to preserve, without undue use of coercion.[12] Whether or not officials view themselves as political actors, they play a very important part in maintaining the stability of the polity, which is needed for the play of politics and the avoidance of continual coercion.

The public bureaucracy is a political instrument strategically placed in the political arena. It is the embodiment of the polity and the living constitution (see Chap. 5). It is governed by politics, and everything about it is political. Its powers rely on political concurrence. Its management competence enlarges the area of effective political action. Moreover, in all these things, it is not a passive tool. It has its own definite ideas, principles, policies, and objectives derived from experience, functional activities, and social composition. As a body, it will counteract its critics and oppose hostile

[11] H. Cleveland, "Executives in the Political Jungle," *Annals of the American Academy of Political and Social Science,* 307 (Sept. 1956), p. 44.

[12] See B. Crick, *In Defense of Politics.* London: Weidenfeld and Nicholson, 1962.

proposals through official replies, informal approaches to supporters and opponents, manipulation of bureaucratic sanctions, and public demonstrations organized by public-employee associations and concerned allies. To favored proposals, on the other hand, little opposition is offered. On the contrary, assistance will be given and past favors remembered. These partial attitudes will be conveyed by word and deed through contacts, so that pressure is exerted on the rulers to stand by the status quo or to push for reforms.[13] As an action group, the public bureaucracy may obstruct governmental policies with which it is in disagreement, as happened in Saskatchewan, when the Cooperative Commonwealth Federation took office in 1944,[14] or it may keep prodding the government into more adventurous action, as usually happens during political immobility.

The bases of bureaucratic power, besides the weaknesses of other political institutions and low-caliber political leaders, include the following:

a. *Resources.* Whatever resources a public bureaucracy consumes, the costs should be measured in foregone alternatives. No society ever has enough resources to accomplish a fraction of its objectives. The priority given to the public bureaucracy in resource allocation enables it to lord over dependent institutions and to provide stiff competition to rivals. In all modern societies, it commands an appreciable portion of the community's talent and wealth.

b. *Expertise.* Many of the functions carried out by the public bureaucracy are monopolistic. The public bureaucracy employs most (if not all) functional experts, who cannot be replaced easily from outside. It contains unique occupations and professions indispensable to quality performance, as well as many experienced administrators peculiar to public employment (see Chap.6).

c. *Legitimate monopoly of instruments of coercive power.* Political leaders depend on the loyalty of the military and the police, for which a price must be paid, usually in the form of special treatment or concessions, to prevent their usurpation of political office.

d. *Status.* Despite adverse images of the public bureaucracy, the standing of top officials is high in the social structure. Top officials are part of the aristocracy, the power elite, the ruling class, or their equivalents. The social position confers authority—particularly if it is supported by an ideology of public service, responsibility, rationality, credibility, loyalty to the regime, and devotion to the public interest.

e. *Discretionary powers.* In routine areas, marginal activities, and technical functions, the political leaders maintain only weak supervisory control and delegate freedom of action to the public bureaucracy. Thus, public officials run public enterprises without much political interference. Sometimes, when politicians are reluctant to decide on public issues, they prefer that public officials decide for them, and then they resume responsibility after public reaction is known.

[13] See F. M. Marx, "The Higher Civil Service as an Action Group in Western Political Development," in J. La Palombara, ed., *Bureaucracy and Political Development.* Princeton: Princeton University Press, 1963, pp. 62–95.

[14] S. M. Lipset, *Agrarian Socialism.* New York: Doubleday, 1968, pp. 307–331.

f. *Confidential information.* The public bureaucracy is a storehouse of state secrets, access to which may be denied both to outsiders and political leaders. Nobody else may have alternative sources of information, in which case their effectiveness in public-policy making depends on access to the public bureaucracy's storehouse.

g. *Strategic position.* As the link between the rulers and the ruled, the public bureaucracy is responsible for the manner in which political orders are carried out and for the conformity of end results with expectations. It may thus be in a position to negate political intentions and distort feedback. The rulers may be misled or deceived by the suppression of complaints, appeals, difficulties, and problems. The political leaders are dependent on the honesty and openness of the public bureaucracy. Otherwise, they may have to rely on strict control, spy systems, and politicization.

h. *Reputation.* The treatment meted out by the public bureaucracy influences the citizen's perception of the polity, government, and political leaders. It is a major factor in public-opinion formation.

From these bases, the public bureaucracy derives further power over environmental transformation, cultural maintenance and transmission, systematic goal gratification, scientific experimentation, applied technology, and societal arrangements. Much of its political power is latent and apparent only in crises. There can be little doubt, however, that it must grow with the complexity of civilization and the widening dimensions of public administration.

The public bureaucracy is expected to be a political force. Several illustrations indicate that it is more than a neutral instrument. (a) Public officials compose political speeches and sometimes have to substitute for their political masters at short notice. (b) They advise political leaders and are consulted by electoral strategists. (c) They participate in governmental decision making and may exclude outsiders in technical areas. (d) They draft laws and issue bylaws. (e) They manipulate budgets in closed sessions. (f) They explain government policies and reconcile clientele groups to them. (g) They participate in national planning processes that determine political objectives. (h) They leak information to mass media, to judge political reactions to contemplated policies. These examples can be multiplied, but the common theme is the expectation that the public bureaucracy should be used politically, even in highly differentiated societies. In undifferentiated societies, the political power of the public bureaucracy is more obvious.

The power of public bureaucracy is only one of many political forces, strong and weak, that can be offset in the political arena. Possibly more than most, bureaucractic power is fragmented; rarely is the official elite united on all issues. More likely, it is fractured by intensive in-fighting between competing organizations, policies, programs, and values. The rank and file add horizontal to vertical divisions. The splintering of bureaucratic power makes outside control much easier. Each part can be harnassed by political parties, pressure groups, trade unions, even foreign agents. Because bureaucratic power is not independent, the public officials play by the accepted rules of the political system; once they depart from the rules, they invite instant retaliation and undermine their own power base. They work within acknowledged political constraints, which tend to have a stabilizing effect on the polity, except where public officials overthrow the existing regime and create a bureaucratic polity.

THE MEASUREMENT OF POLITICIZATION

No single measure accommodates the different facets of politicization. The complete absence of politicization only occurs under a slave or serf system with abnormal personalities, or under a system that isolates officials from all external contacts and outside influence. Assuming that the individual is free to join and leave the public bureaucracy, and that his life style differs from his neighbors only in respect to the peculiar nature of his employment, departures from strict neutrality can be viewed from three directions. The first is the degree of political abstinence by officials:

a. Denial of all public political activity
b. Permission to vote
c. Participation in public meetings
d. Membership of political organization
e. Active political membership
f. Full political activity, including concurrent holding of official and political offices

Except in the last instance, officials are penalized on the grounds that, if their political views were public knowledge, political opponents would distrust them, or political supporters might seek them out and extract favors.

The second is the amount of personal influence exercised by officials in their work:

a. Political apathy
b. Injection of personal views
c. Political commitment to political leaders, programs, or policies
d. Political discrimination between supporters and opponents in conscious manipulation of bureaucratic power
e. Political connivance to exceed bureaucratic powers for partisan ends
f. Political usurpation

Except in the first instance, officials abuse the trust reposed in them that they will act impartially. Their political masters may profess ignorance of discrimination unless the actions complained of adversely affect their own public standing.

The third is the extent to which political leaders interfere with a merit system and professional ethics:

a. Bureaucratic self-regulation
b. Differential treatment of misconduct; only actions adversely affecting political leaders punished
c. Political conformity in top officials; promotion dependent on political compatibility with political masters
d. Political appointments; entry based on political qualifications and merit system bypassed
e. Spoils system; tenure dependent on political fortunes of patrons
f. Political entrenchment of partisans, with purges of suspected opponents or neutrals

Increasing political interference with a self-regulating merit system eventually breaks down any distinction between official and political careers. All three are quite separate. Denial of political rights to officials does not prevent their being used for partisan ends by political leaders. Strict adherence to professional ethics does not prevent an official from aspiring to political office.

In applying these measures to a specific public bureaucracy or segment, certain difficulties must be faced. First, the different parts of the bureaucracy may display no regular pattern of politicization; there may be no meaningful average or mean. Second, relations between politicians and officials may be confidential, and serious political consequences may flow from breaches of confidence. The outsider may be given only a superficial or misleading guide. Third, the relationships are dynamic. They change continually, sometimes quite drastically, and revelation may itself be the catalyst for immediate change. Fourth, it is not easy in practice to distinguish between actualities and intent, legality or imagery. Fifth, none of the measurements can be precise. Sixth, the boundary line of the public bureaucracy is imprecise, and the transition zones are likely to show considerable variation. The fact that one state's public bureaucracy is more politicized than another does not make it any better or worse, or reflect in any way on performance. Each state must choose the path that best suits its peculiar environment.

5

The Living Constitution

All modern bureaucratic states have some kind of constitution, whether written or unwritten, strong or weak, federal or unitary, which embodies the formal arrangements of the polity and its political ideology. Constitutional doctrines and laws are formal manifestations of the polity. The reality is the living constitution—that is, the state in action. "The State is as its officials are."[1] Hence, the machinery of government—the ever changing form, arrangement, and operation of governmental organs, public authorities, and politically directed private institutions—is not the plaything of administrative experts but the starting point of political analysis. It conditions and is conditioned by the rules of the political game as played within the state. It transforms decisions into actions and policies into practices. It distills inarticulate political demands and filters articulate political demands. The efficacy of its operations and the competence with which it carries out its special functions affects (if not determines) the stability, well-being, and progress of the polity. The citizens' impression and image of how well political leaders perform are largely derived from contact with and information about the machinery of government. Today so many people are caught within its processes as servants or clients that thinking about it occupies much of their time.

The political nature of the machinery

[1] J. Dewey, *The Public and Its Problems.* New York: Holt, Rinehart and Winston, 1927, p. 69.

of government is best illustrated in new states, where the living constitution is the main instrument through which nationhood is being shaped and societies modernized. In itself, the machinery of government represents rebirth and rejuvenation of pre-colonial polities or the creation of something completely new, above and beyond traditional institutions, and the symbols it uses are designed to reinforce nation building and to promote the integration of diverse peoples into an enduring compact. It is a unifying factor, enabling political extremes to coexist, while emphasizing agreement and consensus, which is further strengthened by bureaucratic norms and administered political values. Government organs are spearheads of development, promoting progress, strengthening security and stability, improving living standards, and encouraging enterprise and private initiative, while preserving cooperativism and collectivism, and extending the range of their services. The machinery of government overshadows all other social organizations, which depend on it for recognition, support, legal status, financial aid, information, manpower, protection, and guidance, either directly or through interlocking intermediary groups (including political parties, trade unions, voluntary societies, joint enterprises), and multiple office holding. Thus the consequences of its malfunctioning are much higher than in older states, for if any part disintegrates, the country could be overrun from the outside or beset with chaos. Alternatives or substitutes are inferior, and its reserve capacity is already taxed by just coping with everyday problems, let alone recurrent crises.

Outwardly, the machinery of government is a political instrument conducting extensive administrative activities. Inwardly, it is a complex organization made up of large bureaucracies that are loosely coordinated and controlled by political mechanisms. These two perspectives, however, are never wholly reconcilable. One is a reflection of political values, the other a mirror of administrative practices. One measures performance according to political objectives, the other according to administrative efficiency. One has greater regard for political leaders and public clientele, the other for official convenience. Often one of them has to be sacrificed to the other. Paradoxically, increased rationality in organizing the machinery of government has not apparently interfered with increased political sensitivity.

THE PROCESS OF RATIONALIZATION

The application of rationality to the machinery of government is best seen in the history of the modern bureaucratic state from its earliest days to the present, and beyond to forthcoming applications of modern technology now being planned. Obviously it is impossible to describe in any great detail the different paths taken by every state. Instead, a general composite model based on western experience is used here to demonstrate the different stages of development.

Stage 1: Pre-Rationality

The genesis of modern public administration is to be found in the organization of the king's household in a country where he had many rival contenders and where the church assumed responsibility for social services. Household officials could be divided into two groups: one responsible for personal services to the king and the other, distinguishable by education, special skills, and superior functions, responsible for the administration of the king's lands, his finances, justice, and the raising of armies. Amenable to the king's will and dependent upon his pleasure, the latter group exercised delegated powers. They were drawn from the educated classes—the bourgeois and the clerics—and enjoyed, in practice, permanent tenure and a certain amount of discretion. They gained their positions through patronage and purchase, in return for which they kept the fees and perquisites of office. Over the course of time they often developed proprietary claims to their positions. Their sole business was to make the king the richest and most powerful man in the country, although they could also make use of their powers for their own ends. The aim of the king was to be master of his household, have full control over his officials, and enlarge his power.

As the king grew more successful against his rivals, government by the king in person merged into government under the king, exercised in his name. He employed more officials, who regarded the authority delegated to them as their inheritable freehold. They filled vacancies by cooptation, and in this way produced self-perpetuating family dynasties of nobles in such profit-making enterprises as farming taxes, billeting of troops, contracting supplies and communications, and placing relatives and friends in sinecures. Gradually, state administration and finances became separated from the management of the king's household, and the complex duties of state were consolidated into compartments headed by ad hoc bodies of officials who emphasized collective leadership. In this way a greater measure of uniformity was produced at the center. Field administration still remained largely autonomous. State administration at this stage was confused, cumbersome, and slow.

The scope of government depended on the king's will and inclination, and the extent to which he could persuade his rivals among the clergy, nobles, and burghers to accept his authority. Decision making was centered on the king's court, but depended on local enforcement. Public services were small, confined to law and order, regulatory activities, and selected public works. Even warfare was limited to small armies, which equipped themselves and fed off the land. Administrative methods were rather crude, with a premium on ritual. Technological aids were simple. Governmental functions were integrated with other societal institutions and barely consolidated internally into specialized areas.

Stage 2: Movement Toward Rationality

The eighteenth century heralded the age of reason, with the scientific challenge to religion and the application of scientific thought to human society.

This created a favorable climate of opinion for the reorganization of the machinery of government to meet the challenge of rural displacement, industrialism, technological advances, large-scale warfare, and middle-class professionalism. The divine right of kings was one of the first victims. Kings in some countries were deposed altogether by republicans, or their absolute powers were strictly regulated and controlled by the aristocrats and/or middle class. The king's household either disappeared altogether or was more closely defined. Persistent threats to the polity from within and without forced the central authorities to extend their influence over local administration. Previously contracted services were now directly assumed by the central authorities. The state began to establish its own education system in competition with the church and to seek competent staff outside traditional sources. Antiquated methods and procedures were exposed and more efficient methods and techniques substituted.

Governments needed bigger armies; better weapons; surer supplies; more money; different forms of taxation; new organizations for the administration of social services; better policing and more inspectors; greater coordination, uniformity, and standardization; and higher efficiency. Moreover, the people demanded better communications and postal facilities; relief from poverty, oppression, distress, and insecurity; and equality before the law, with the abolition of legal disabilities and ancient privileges. The French Revolution advanced the causes of liberty, equality, and fraternity against the suppression, inequality and social cleavage that had been embodied and epitomized in the administration of absolute monarchy. New social classes and changes in social structure brought demands for participation in government and the employment of more businesslike methods in public administration.

In response, the increasing range of public services was consolidated into related specialties such as war, finance, foreign affairs, navy, colonies, trade, interior, and justice. Proprietary positions were reduced or abolished as sinecures and perquisites were eliminated. Professional public servants introduced budgeting techniques, proper accounting, and auditing practices. Field administration was taken out of the hands of the aristocracy and placed under career officials who were appointed by the central administration or transferred to local self-governments. Working methods were overhauled, statistics were introduced, and record keeping was expanded. New kinds of organization were established, with elaborate rules and regulations. New public buildings were constructed to house the expanding governmental activities and the increase in scale of operations, particularly in the military field, where conscripted armies up to one million strong were equipped, trained, and accommodated by the state. Power and authority passed to leading politicians and top-ranking officials drawn from the elite social classes. Collective leadership was continued only in matters of the highest importance as leaders became specialized. Boards and councils were superseded by departments headed by ministers, and duties and responsibilities were clearly defined among authorities; within the departments, clear chains of command and accountability were established. New administrative structures formed separate ministries or were attached to existing ministries. Field services were made more dependent on the central administration through their consolidation into a ministry responsible for internal affairs or through the creation of new regional units of the central administration.

The increase of governmental administration was accompanied by an equally impressive growth of legislation. The king and his officials no longer were above the law, free to act in whatever way they pleased. They were now subject to the law like any other individual and more so, since the law laid down detailed instructions as to what could or could not be done by officials in the performance of their duties. A great body of public law grew up, and special bodies were created to adjudicate between aggrieved citizen and the public official as the representative of the impersonal power of the state. New laws governed the consolidated fund into which all revenues were deposited and out of which all expenditures were paid, but only on the agreement of the people's representatives and the finance minister. Officials who handled public money were ordered to pay sureties, take oaths, and give other guarantees, so that effective action could be taken against corrupt practices. High standards of conduct and efficiency were ensured by elaborate rules and instructions and by the enforcement of severe penalties for offenses and misconduct. In return, public officials—because of their specialized skill and knowledge, standing, authority, and importance—were guaranteed permanent tenure and granted pensions on retirement. Government service was made into a full-time career by the prohibition of outside employment and restrictions on outside interests.

Stage 3: Rationality

The trends of the pre-rationality stage intensified and revitalized the whole administrative structure of government. Kings and aristocracies gave way to representative chambers and to political leaders who were responsible and responsive to the electorate. The functions and activities of government expanded in all directions. Existing organizations were enlarged and localized into field and regional offices. Alongside them new organizations came into existence and were assimilated into the system through multiple coordinating mechanisms. The distinction between political and administrative office was clearly marked, and the two careers separated. The official had to qualify through an elaborate examination system designed to eliminate political influence and to produce the most competent applicant. Advancement similarly depended on performance alone, not influence with patrons. The merit system was ruled over by an elite corps of generalists, conscious of their position at the apex of the public bureaucracy and in close proximity to the political leaders. Subordinate to them were vertical career channels of specialists, professionals, and technicians governed by elaborate staff codes administered by personnel experts.

Despite some experimentation with organizational forms, bureaucracy predominated. Each part was responsible for specific functions within the bounds of legal-rational authority. Formally, everything was structured, seemingly well ordered, sensibly arranged, and working with clockwork precision. Everyone knew his place within the hierarchy and followed scientific management methods, enlisting the aid of productivity and efficiency experts. In decision making, statistics became more elaborate, and the budget was developed into a sophisticated control mechanism and policy coordinator. New functions were allotted their rightful place, according to rational criteria, and the whole was supervised by special control agencies directly subordinate to the political leaders. Among these, planning assumed an increasing importance in policy making, together with computer technology (in data storage and retrieval), mathematical models, behavioral studies, and public-opinion polls.

Stage 4: Post-Rationality

In response to the persistence of turbulence and antiorganizational movements, bureaucratization was modified. Several local functions were allocated to community control in various forms of direct participative democracy. Large bureaucracies were split up and reorganized into competing autonomies, with greater freedom of action as detailed rules were generalized. Large units decentralized their operations. The use of temporary, problem-oriented organizations was accelerated. The generalist elite corps was diversified, with the incorporation of professionals, scientists, and policy analysts, all familiar with cybernetics, computerized decision making, long-range forecasting, and new techniques to measure political feasibility of alternative strategies. No separation was possible between human and technological resources. Political leaders and top administrators had to be periodically retrained to master the complexities of a quickly changing world, and tests for knowledge or content skills were replaced by searches for adaptive skills through applied social psychology. Planning, budgeting, and policy making were fused. Automative techniques replaced unskilled and semiskilled labor, which was freed for continual career retraining programs. To maintain public confidence, mass media provided more information about the operation of government, and a wide range of self-correcting mechanisms was incorporated within the machinery of government. Measurements of governmental performance enabled the citizen to judge the efficacy of governmental operations, and institutionalized reform bodies provided remedies for defects. The citizen's rights were protected by competent public watchdogs able to compensate for administrative errors that could not be righted.

From a historical perspective, rationality is appealing for it produced results. Although it may not have produced optimum results, it certainly brought results more quickly and directly than anything else. Rational arrangements eliminated much time-consuming meandering and preserved scarce resources that might otherwise have been dissipated. Moreover reason appealed to the intellectual, who attached to it an imperious righteousness. Politically, it curbed emotion and limited violent fluctuations. Rationality was compromising, accommodating, stable, amoral. The rational administrator did not meet obstacles head on, but sought to avoid confrontation by finding ways around them. He was constructive, creative, innovative, farsighted, and flexible. In short, rationality was many things that politics was not or that political activity was reputed to lack. Reasonable people supposedly seek to maximize consensus, harmony, unity of interests, collaboration of diverse groups for the common good and to denigrate conflict, factionalism, power struggles, and ideology. Rational experts in public affairs promise immediate substantial gains—less partisanship, elimination of wasteful spoils, a higher level of professional competence, coherent policies, integrated structure, better decisions. Yet political leaders and the general public have rarely been convinced that the anticipated results would be forthcoming or that they would be worth the loss in political control and partisan policies. They fear the consequences of further shifts in power from the political arena to scientism and self-appointed guardians of the public interest not directly responsible to the people. They are willing to adopt rational arrangements, but not to be governed by them.

POLITICAL CONTROL

Only in bureaucratic polities do officials control themselves and arrange the machinery of government as they like. Elsewhere they are firmly subordinate to political leaders, and they are expected to abide by the arrangements laid down for them. They may influence the political leaders into accepting their recommendations and proposals, but the final say belongs to the politicians, who consider rationality along with other equally important factors. Political strategies are likely to predominate, although increasing bureaucratic power may force concessions. The very size of the machinery of government and its integration with other societal institutions reduce the possibility that it will depart significantly from communal expectations and political values.

The machinery of government is a political creature. Its size and scope are determined by the range and frequency of governmental decisions. Formally, it is the mechanism by which governmental decisions are implemented. Informally, it is indispensable in the formulation, determination, and evaluation of governmental decisions. The number and arrangement of its component organs are politically controversial. The whole business cannot be determined simply by scientific management principles; this is an area where efficiency, objectivity, rationality, and other such values embodied in management science are subordinate to political ideology, personal ambition, and intensive power play between contending forces. Similarly, the distribution of functions between levels of government cannot be determined by their functional requisites. Overriding factors are the strength of local feeling, the distribution of communal power, attitudes toward centralization or separation of powers, and the charisma and ambition of political representatives at different governmental levels. The allocation of resources between functions is not a matter of sliderule calculations of needs and benefits, but a reflection of political values, communal priorities, and power play between bargainers. Scientific management techniques are advisory aids, not policy determinants.

Even if rationality triumphed at program level, the need for political determination would not diminish. There are no absolute boundaries between governmental functions; they overlap and merge into one another. Someone has to settle conflicts of jurisdiction and coordinate and integrate separate aspects of the same problem area. Usually, the political leaders can rely on the officials concerned to settle their differences amicably and to resolve issues through partisan mutual adjustment; but not all conflicts are settled in this way. Adjudication is required from an authority that all officials will accept. Political leaders are also needed to allocate responsibilities for new functions, problem areas, and political vacuums. Their decisions are made in the light of events at the time, not in anticipation of what future historians might say or what the optimum might be if they had access to all the facts. They hope they will be right most of the time, but they also realize that, if they should make mistakes, they will have to live with them, but not as long as the permanent officials who are also involved. More important to them is ensuring that the whole apparatus performs according to their expectations and instructions. Their role is to guard against arbitrariness, to correct contradictions, abuses, and distortions, and to show who is really boss.

Obviously the small group of political leaders at the apex of the structure can handle only a minute portion of their heavy supervisory functions; they are busy people with many distractions. Consequently, they are forced to delegate the bulk of their administrative authority. They may formally contract large areas of government to private bodies to execute on their behalf for a fee or other compensation. They may persuade other societal organizations to undertake government functions. They may delegate authority to agents who act in their stead. They may so arrange the organizational forms of government that most of the work is performed by subordinate bodies and trusted servants. They may decide to divest themselves of immediate responsibility by abrogating power to direct democracy. Whatever they choose to do, they are free to intervene at any time and resume direct responsibility. Their self-denial ordinance exists only so long as it is politically profitable: it is revoked the moment it becomes a political liability. Merit civil services, independent statutory authorities, autonomous local governments, and self-governing public enterprises are not exempt. Their special status reflects political consensus on the limits of partisanship at program level.

The more societal resources commanded by the machinery of government, the greater the political prize in power, services, contracts, positions, and ideological leadership,[2] and the greater the returns for partisan political investment. For instance, control over information emanating within the governmental apparatus can be used to hide mistakes, corruption, spoils and bad decisions, to shield the public from bad news or impending crisis, to project favorable images, to deny knowledge to political opponents, and to persuade the public into a desired course of action. The political leaders in power command the combined talents of officialdom and associates to fill political vacuums, solve political problems, and generally create a favorable impression of their rule. Few opponents can match the political advantage that office bestows; they cannot draw on the societal resources of the machinery of government and must rely on exposing mistakes and cultivating whatever countervailing political forces that have not been preempted by office holders. The fortunes of the political leaders and the governmental apparatus that they head are tied together by their mutual dependence, joint cooperation, toleration of vices, and combined efforts to ensure effective results and security of position. After all, the public's view of public administration, political leadership, and the polity is largely derived from clientele treatment at the hands of officialdom and the extent of general knowledge about and participation in the machinery of government. Are officials responsive, inspirational, creative, friendly, and effective, or are they rude, corrupt, dull-witted, slow, aggressive, and aggrandizing? Are they so secretive, distant, isolated, and forbidding that information has to be gathered secondhand by those who are in the know and its dissemination unwittingly distorted by prejudiced outsiders? Are they willing to represent unpopular views and minority interests, and to expose political chicanery, public deceit, and corruption in high places? How protective are they of political leaders, and how protective are political leaders of officials?

The governmental apparatus is only as good as its political leaders want it to be. They can block action at every turn. They can ignore all proferred advice. They can insist on their will being done. If confronted with passive resistance or active sabotage, they have the means to crush any revolt, providing they are prepared to pay the political price. They risk further escalation of the crisis into full-scale revolution if they misjudge the extent of revulsion against their rule. In other words, the machinery of government reflects the political style of the leaders. Ideological commitments take precedence, and political charisma outshines official pragmatism. People within the system work so closely together that they learn to read one another's minds, to anticipate their reactions and to plan accordingly, to trust one another when absent, and to retire secure in the knowledge that public affairs are in capable hands. Individual dynamism and inspiration are infectious, but so too are sloth and indifference. The contrast in styles between sets of leaders will be reflected

---

[2] W. S. Sayre and H. Kaufman, *Governing New York*. New York: Russell Sage Foundation, 1960, p. 1.

administratively in tendencies toward liberalism or autocracy, openness or secrecy, informality or formality, individual or group decision making, showmanship or reticence, action or avoidance of action, economy or extravagence. Subordinates can do much to bolster their superiors, but they can never quite replace them.

FORMAL AND INFORMAL STRUCTURES

Even in highly bureaucratized societies, the machinery of government is not easily defined. At the top, bottom, and sides it shades off into nongovernmental institutions. The situation is further complicated by the crisscross network of informal relations. Changes in social patterns are likely to be reflected in alterations in the machinery of government, and alterations in the machinery of government have wide social repercussions. The whole arrangement is an ever shifting network of alliances and compromises. It is a combination of ideology and pragmatism, rationality and emotion, old and new, legal and extralegal. There is a formal facade, easily described, and an informal backing, much of which is known only to participants. Constitutions, laws, ethical codes, organizational structures, accounts, filing systems, and committee reports are accessible to all and are the most publicized. Interpretations, informal agreements, loopholes, confidential memoranda, chance meetings, temporary groups, and unstructured sessions, however, which may have more bearing on what actually happens, are inaccessible and are the least publicized. Short of having all public confidences exposed, an imbalance is unavoidable. Hence, nobody can describe the living constitution fully or accurately; and all accounts are personal interpretations subject to correction as further information comes to hand.

The central core, however, is identifiable and fairly stable. It is composed of public laws, ranging in importance from a formal constitution to local-authority bylaws; public institutions enbracing huge departments of state and subordinate post offices located in retail stores; public officials (both elected and appointed), from chief executives to coach drivers; public property, comprising airports and weapons-testing ranges, as well as pen-nibs and paper clips; and public accounts, incorporating finance laws and single-item receipts from public sales. The boundaries are defined differently from one state to another, and the definitions change with every budget, census, stock taking, and annual report. Nevertheless, a broad measure of agreement exists that, whatever they cover, they all belong to the machinery of government. But they are not exclusive to government, for public officials are members of many nongovernmental bodies and may subordinate loyalty to their employer to other social institutions. Public property may be used for nongovernmental purposes, as when public halls are hired for private functions.

Beyond the core, identification of the limits of the living constitution is virtually impossible. At the apex, the machinery of government becomes the government itself, the constitutional arrangements, the political system, the structure of coercive force, and supranational institutions. Merit systems draw a distinction in career pattern, but they do not prevent interchanges of personnel. In one-party states, the party and public bureaucracy may be formally integrated. Elective officials bridge the political and bureaucratic worlds. At the sides, the public domain merges with the private domain through pressure-group representations, consultative committees, contracted activities, delegated responsibilities, mixed enterprises, universities, trade unions, collectives, and professional societies. The area untouched by the machinery of government is shrinking fast as more outside interests seek formal inclusion into the governmental apparatus. At the bottom, bureaucratic structures give way to direct citizen participation, composite bodies, and volunteer groups. In less bureaucratic societies, where functions are fused and institutions not so well differentiated, the boundaries are barely discernible.

Further difficulty in identification is caused by the informal structure, which cuts across the formal arrangements. Informal patterns are aided by small territorial area, ease and frequency of personal contacts, good communications, and a homogeneous society, all of which enable people to cut through bureaucratic ritual by employing personal contacts derived from their upbringing, schooling, military service, private associations, residences, or previous employment. In intensely politicized societies, where a sizable proportion of the population is politically active and belongs to political movements, political parties provide the contacts, introductions, and middlemen. In less politicized societies, religion, race, tribe, caste, lodge, and overseas military experience may perform the same service. In some polities, the informal structure may concentrate effective political participation on relatively few key positions, as may be the case in military regimes, or it may open up the confined councils of government to wider community participation, as may happen in closely-knit neighborhoods. Contacts take place outside business hours at house parties, informal gatherings, trade conventions and conferences, religious celebrations, national events, and chance events. Telecommunications have yet to replace personal meetings, recorded correspondence, and third-party presence. Within business hours, informal structures are strengthened by overcrowded accommodation, concentrated physical location, informal working methods, ad hoc committees, and frequent travel.

For those who can use it, the informal structure is advantageous. It shortens communication routes, gives access to influential decision makers, obtains quicker decisions, and spreads confidential knowledge. For them, it smooths the way through the governmental maze and discriminates in their favor. In underdeveloped countries, where the margin between life and death is small, it may be the crucial factor in survival. In this case, those on the outer edge may be prepared to make huge sacrifices to gain access to the influential, who, in turn, may exploit their modicum of power to the full. Elsewhere, it is likely to perpetuate distinctions and work in favor of established interests.

The fact that it is confidential or hidden from outsiders denied access to it invites gross distortions of formal intent and paves the way for corruption. On the other hand, it is more flexible than the formal structure, certainly more accommodating to change, and to this extent more realistic and perhaps more responsive to shifting trends. Politicans and rationalists vie with one another in both structures.

THE POLITICS OF REORGANIZATION

The conflict between rationality and politics is best illustrated in the frustrating history of the federal reorganization movement in the United States. The American constitution is unclear about whether the President or Congress has final responsibility for administrative arrangements. One side argues that Congress is the final arbiter; the President is required to follow congressional initiatives, and while he may propose, Congress disposes. If the President were permitted full control, the presidency would become a dictatorship, and public opinion as represented by Congress would be ignored. The other side insists that Congress is not a suitable body to decide on administrative arrangements, partly because it lacks the proper perspective, and partly because it has a vested interest in spoils. The President is in a better position to decide, as the bureaucracy is more representative of the community than Congress, and he should be given a free hand. Caught between the two, the federal machinery of government has grown haphazardly, like a multicolored patchwork, as first one side took the initiative and then the other, neither being disposed to undo the other's handiwork or to disrupt a working system by radical overhaul. From time to time, pressures for rationalization, simplification, and economy have been accompanied by demands for a thorough review of the executive branch of government by administrative experts. Before the Great Depression, little had come of them. Presidents had not been too keen to push administrative reform, and Congress had let the issue die in committee.

Roosevelt's New Deal program did not silence demands for action. On the contrary, his use of patronage, his multiplication of agencies, his elaborate personal checks-and-balances system in competitive policy making, and his bypassing of existing structures horrified the administrative experts brought up on scientific management principles. Every move was disowned by the public administration establishment as inviting waste, corruption, high costs, lawlessness, and partisanship. Roosevelt pacified his critics with the Social Science Research Council's inquiry into public-personnel administration, but not for long. Herring, in his study *Public Administration and the Public Interest* (New York: Russell and Russell, 1936), was particularly critical of the federal machinery of government, with its "tangle of alphabetical monstrosities," lack of coordination between the general-purpose executive departments and subordinate bureaus, and excessive particularism and internecine warfare. The federal government had to be seen as a whole and developed as an institution for executing policy in the public interest and for promoting the general welfare. To this end it should be reorganized, properly staffed, and better directed by detailed policies. New bodies were needed for administrative overview, policy coordination, financial integration, and national planning. Prophetically, he made a warning:

> Schemes for reorganization cannot be superimposed without consideration of the political and economic factors that are affected thereby. Experts have burned the midnight oil in devising Utopian plans; in vain have they rubbed their student lamps looking for an almost magical reordering of the bureaus and departments. Major changes must come slowly and even indirectly. The possibility of reorganizing the federal administration depends upon an understanding of the social forces and group pressures that stand in the way.
>
> As a practical matter, what the theorist might regard as ideally best in administrative organization must be reconciled with what is politically possible. Democracy means that our federal structure shall be the product of what politically effective individuals and groups are able to get. If the government is to act as an impartial arbiter among all groups and if the administration is to serve all classes and interests, how can this be accomplished in the face of our political structure?[3]

The Social Science Research Council proposed to Roosevelt that, on the completion of the public-personnel administration study, it should review the federal machinery of government. Roosevelt preferred a committee of his own, containing people sympathetic to the New Deal and thereby excluding the critical Brookings Institution. In March 1936, the President's Committee on Administrative Management, composed of Brownlow, Merriam, and Gulick, commenced operations and worked independently of the President. Its task was to advise him on the principles of a reorganization, not the details. It worked in secrecy and kept apart from the congressional committees that had been appointed to work with it. The Senate committee thereupon approached the Brookings Institution for research assistance. Because the Brownlow committee submitted its draft report to the President and redrafted sections to his liking, the final report was earmarked as a presidential policy statement when it was presented to Congress on 12 January 1937.

The Brownlow committee's report opened with a reaffirmation of the virtues of American democracy and a warning about the need to maintain the efficiency of governmental administration, whose foundations were grounded in those principles "drawn from the experience of mankind in carrying on large-scale enterprises," namely, "a responsible and effective chief executive as the center of energy, direction and administrative management; the systematic organization of all activities in the hands of a qual-

---

[3] P. Herring, *Public Administration and the Public Interest.* New York: Russell and Russell, 1936, p. 347.

ified personnel under [his] direction; and to aid him in this, appropriate managerial and staff agencies." The existing arrangements did not fulfill such requirements and needed modernizing by (1) expanding White House staff; (2) strengthening managerial agencies, particularly those concerned with the budget, efficiency research, personnel, and planning; (3) extending the merit system to all nonpolicy-determining posts and making federal service an attractive career; (4) reorganizing all agencies into a few large departments; and (5) revising the fiscal system in the light of the best governmental and private practice. The objective was to make democratic government modern, efficient, and effective in carrying out the national will, and to this end economy, simplification, symmetry, better methods, and higher official salaries were needed. The remainder of the report elaborated on the five major action areas just noted.

1. White House Staff. The President should have more executive assistants (up to six) to act as his overall watchdogs and funds to enlarge his staff. Moreover, the President should have direct control over personnel, finance, organization, and planning. The central agencies—Civil Service Administration, the Bureau of the Budget, and the National Resources Board—should be part of the Executive Office to provide the necessary administrative leadership.

2. Personnel management. The merit system should be extended to all positions other than policy determining, which should be filled by presidential partisans. Personnel matters should be administered by a single executive, not a board, and aided by a nonpartisan citizen board. The Civil Service Administrator should be appointed from the top three in nonpartisan competition. Top salaries should be raised.

3. Fiscal management. The Bureau of the Budget should have effective control over all aspects of finance, including efficiency audit and scrutiny of proposed legislation. The Secretary of the Treasury should prescribe accounting administration and fiscal management, with the Attorney General as arbitrator between the Treasury and departments. The Auditor General should conduct his work simultaneously with disbursement, and disputes between him and the Treasury over exemptions should be referred to Congress.

4. Planning. The National Resources Board (of which Merriam was a member) should become an advisory central planning agency and a clearing house in national resource planning, based on scientific study, not "uninformed judgment and political expediency."

5. Administrative reorganization. All agencies should be consolidated into twelve departments (ten existing ones plus two new ones), and the President should accept responsibility for continuing reform. Within the departments, some agencies should be allowed more independence than others. The judicial functions of existing autonomous agencies should be exercised by impartial, independent bodies, except where the volume of business was very large, in which case the administration would decide and the judicial body would act as an appellate body. Public corporations, also integrated in the departmental structure, should assign the task of corporate administration to a general manager.

6. Accountability of executive to the Congress. Congress should employ an independent audit, not impose detailed requirements.

The report emphasized better service to society rather than economy, with no attempt to recommend which functions could be discontinued. The ultimate test of reorganization should be "human happiness and values."

Congress was not convinced. The adoption of management orthodoxy in public administration exaggerated central bureaucratic leadership at the expense of congressional supervision. Roosevelt could hardly reject a report that he had instigated, followed his known wishes to bring the autonomous agencies under cabinet supervision, strengthened his hand over the federal executive, deprived Congress of spoils, reduced the influence of the Comptroller-General—a noted critic of the New Deal, and granted the President the initiative in future reorganizations. From the congressional viewpoint, however, the report did not promise substantial savings or propose the abandonment of emergency agencies. In this it was contradicted by the Report of the Brookings Institution presented to the congressional Committee on Governmental Organization on 23 March 1937. The Brookings report put Congress at the head of executive power and viewed the President as the general manager responsible to Congress through strong independent audit and control. The report had examined the details of governmental operations and revealed the extent of duplication. It recommended a slower, piecemeal, lower-level reorganization and supported a strong Comptroller-General. It barely dealt with higher-level executive problems, which had been the main concern of the Brownlow committee.

Roosevelt, fully aware of the political implications of the Brownlow committee's proposals, decided to stick to the report's theme that reorganization was good management. He denied that his powers would be increased or that he had any definite plans for detailed transfers of functions and agencies. He stressed that the merit system would be extended and that, where necessary, the independence of regulatory commissions would be maintained. He realized that not all the Brownlow committee's proposals were practicable or politically feasible. Already Senator Byrd, chairman of the Senate Committee on Government Organization (and a trustee of both Gulick's Institute of Public Administration and Brownlow's Public Administration Clearing House), had broken with the President over fiscal policy and government economies. The abrupt manner in which the Brownlow committee report was released also had not helped. In view of the opposition's strength, members of the Brownlow committee were prepared to compromise, but their reluctance to go into details brought much criticism at the Joint Committee hearings. This was but a prelude to congressional stalling throughout 1937 and increasing public resistance throughout 1938, as the reorganization issue got caught up in the general debate over Roosevelt's leadership. At a strategy meeting on 8 December 1938, attended by Merriam and Gulick, modified proposals were split into separate measures, and most of the controversial features were dropped. Roosevelt recalled the Brownlow Committee to draft new plans after the passage of the relatively weak Reorganization Act 1939. Its new plans, minor in nature compared with the original report, were accepted by Congress.

The continual expansion of the federal machinery of government since the early 1940s has divided the sides even further. Periodically the Brownlow committee's recommendations are revived, and Presidents try to implement them without congressional approval through their wide executive powers, but suspicions of presidential initiatives provoke heated debates in Congress. Succeeding presidential reorganization inquiries have been less bold in their approach and have retreated from scientific management principles, which exaggerated bureaucratic initiatives. Meanwhile, Presidents have strengthened their hold over administrative arrangements and have been supported in this by the administrative scholars, policy initiators, pressure groups, pro-statists, and liberals and opposed by constitutionalists, conservatives, anti-statists, and spoilsmen. Reorganization was acknowledged by the Brownlow committee to be a complex political issue, not a debate between administrative scientists. Attempts at reorganization since then have confirmed the many variables:

a. Motives (change of policy, centralization of control, change in status of administrative agency, accommodation to personal preferences of valued officials, recognition of potentialities of technological innovation, conflict resolution)
b. Purposes (economy, efficiency, law enforcement, coordination, consolidation, elimination of duplication)
c. Processes (formal presidential committes large and small, informal advisory committees, consultants, mixed public commissions)
d. Attitudes (Senate, President, agencies, pressure groups, mass media)
e. Issues (policy coordination, decentralization, field administration, autonomous agencies, grants-in-aid, contracts)[4]

While much has been accomplished, a good deal has been left undone. Failure has been variously ascribed to political opposition, bureaucratic resistance, impracticable recommendations, exaggerated expectations, unjust criticism of working arrangements, and the inevitable nature of modern government, which are a far cry from the rationalist's assumptions that all problems have solutions, that all objectives are reconcilable, and that man is master of his destiny.

Case studies of reorganization at organizational level, contained in F. C. Mosher's *Governmental Reorganizations* (Indianapolis: Bobbs-Merrill, 1967), reveal how success and failure have been related to internal tensions arising from different views about organizational purposes, centripetal and

[4] H. C. Mansfield, "Federal Executive Reorganization: Thirty Years of Experience," *Public Administration Review,* Vol. 19., No. 4, 1969, pp. 332–345.

centrifugal drives for control over programs and operations, conflicts of opinion over expansion or maintenance of programs, conflicting aspirations of different specialized groups, interpersonal competition, and clashes between old and new. Reorganizations were produced by many cumulative decisions seeking changes in image, policy, and program. Where they depended on formal study, the nature, composition, methods, and auspices of the study groups significantly conditioned their proposals as well as the likelihood of their success. Otherwise, few generalizations could be made, as the circumstances of each case varied so much and opposite conclusions could be drawn from different cases. Mosher warns about the hazards "involved in transferring research findings and theoretical propositions developed in one context to situations and behaviors in another one."[5] The attempt "may result in faulty emphasis, and in conclusions of doubtful relevance or even of total inapplicability."[6] The public bureaucracies examined seemed to differ more than they agreed; each had to be treated on its merits. Rational analysis provides a checklist of all the factors that should be considered and may point to optimum strategies, but it cannot substitute for the political skills needed to pilot administrative reforms, particularly in the public sector.

ADMINISTRATIVE REFORM

Reorganization is an aspect of administrative reform, which, in turn, is part of societal reform, the continual debate in society about the whole culture. It is unlikely that there has been a society where everybody was perfectly content and no one was pressing for changes of some kind. Men are by nature reformers, "endeavoring to change others in order to maintain or create desired situations for themselves, or to change themselves in order to accommodate to unyielding circumstances or to realize a new dream."[7] The living constitution of every society is being reformed continually in response to the changing environment, new ideas and innovations, powerful drives to progress by eradicating observable social ills, and natural inclinations to compare one's own society with somebody else's society. Successful reforms in the living constitution set in motion a whole series of chain events that lead to reforms in other institutions, and these reforms in turn may generate the demand for further reforms in the governmental apparatus. To succeed, reforms need to be preceded or accompanied by cultural changes that permit their accommodation and assimilation. When the culture changes slowly, reform may be impeded. In turbulent societies, where the culture is changing very quickly, reform may be indispensable and institutionalized.

[5] F. C. Mosher, *Government Reorganizations.* Indianapolis: Bobbs-Merrill, 1967, p. 535.

[6] Mosher, *Government Reorganizations,* p. 536.

[7] W. H. Goodenough, *Cooperation in Change.* New York: Russell Sage Foundation, 1963, p. 15.

Differentiated modern societies have separate organizations responsible for overlapping political and administrative reforms. One way to distinguish between them is to confine the use of the term "administrative reform" for those reforms in the living constitution for the implementation of other kinds of reform. They would include attempts to (a) change purposes and goals, (b) alter the mix of resources, (c) transform attitudes and methods, (d) improve relationships and standards, (e) speed decisions, (f) alter patterns of authority and communication, and (g) achieve a higher level of efficiency. Some are unavoidably political, with administrative ramifications. Others are mainly administrative, with political repercussions. After all, reform entails political activity, ideological rationalizations, power plays, campaign strategies, and concessions. Invariably, response reflects political disposition toward change in general and personal evaluation of contemporary events. This is particularly true of public administration, where almost everything is political or could be made into a partisan issue.

No administration is perfect, least of all public administration, which is a political compromise between contending forces and as such not wholly rational, logical, ideal, stable, or satisfactory. There is always room for improvement and a permanent place for administrative reform. When a public body fails to meet the demands put on it, things do not get done at all or are done in a manner below previous or potential standards of performance. Although it may be able to meet current demands, it collapses under extraordinary demands or unexpected events. It cannot adjust to abnormal situations and fails to anticipate future demands, being too occupied with the immediate. It does not adopt the most effective methods and is out of touch with the latest developments in its field. These are all indications that a public body could do better if it tried. But tolerance of maladministration is high. People are so used to what they habitually receive that they can conceive of nothing else or they do not know how to improve matters. They may realize just how difficult it is under the circumstances to alter things without sufficient resources to overcome the resistance of vested interests in the status quo, or they may have good reason to doubt the motivations, skills, and objectives of the reformers. Short of institutionalized reform (for example, Bureau of the Budget, Civil Service Commission, Management Services Unit, Ombudsman), individual initiatives may be blocked or offset.

Institutionalized administrative reform has many advantages over noninstitutionalized reform. It is continual, not sporadic. It is part of the system, and not viewed as an outside attack on the system. It has access to inside information denied to the outsider. It can stress constructive criticism and extol the virtues of change without appearing to threaten anyone's status or security. It can build on past experience. The loyalty of the people involved is proved and their qualifications tested. A network of support for it already exists. It is less likely to be disruptive, pursuing incrementalism and concerned with its continuing relations. On the other hand, concern for existing relationships may blunt its effectiveness, and it may fail in situations where nothing but sweeping reforms will suffice. What really counts is not the quantity and quality of the reform proposals or the intensity of the reform struggle, but the end results, in terms of permanent transformation for the better. Permanent watchdogs are more likely to succeed than temporary commissions and other once-and-for-all efforts.

Reform is a difficult process. It requires recognition of need, formulation of feasible correctives, and inspired advocates willing to overcome the many obstacles—geographical, historical, technological, cultural, economic, social, political, and administrative. Each society has its own peculiar set of problems. Underdeveloped societies may be isolated from reform currents, culturally divided, technologically backward, poor in resources, lacking in administrative skills, dependent on political charisma, and organizationally ill-equipped. In contrast, developed countries may be changing so fast that nobody can tell what is going to happen next, and until the pace of change slows, reformers may be unable to formulate practical proposals, or by the time they get around to implementation, events may have overtaken them. Reforms are bound up with such general social traits as disposition toward risk taking, the existence of unprogressive power elites with a self-image of omnipotence, cultural homogeneity, and the quality of the administrative system. When account is taken of all the environmental, organizational, and personality obstacles, it is not surprising that many reforms, reform movements, and reformers fail, and that those who do succeed receive the attention given to them. Even in the most favorable circumstances, reform is tricky. Yet, even though signs may point to failure, reformers may surprise themselves and bring off a major historical triumph. Modern societies value trail blazers to whom all are indebted; if they had adjusted to the world as they found it, they could never have changed it.

Who are administrative reformers? With some, it is a matter of character: they are born rebels, perfectionists, nonconformists, geniuses, eccentrics; they are not conservative, cautionary, dependent, or masochistic. They are naturally disposed to reform by some inner compulsion. With others, it is environmental pressures coupled with a predisposition to sympathize with the underdog, a social conscience that revolts against exploitation, poverty, ignorance, suffering, misery, and pain, and a moral doctrine favoring action and outspokenness. They may be dreamers and martyrs; responsible, compassionate, charismatic individuals willing to fight for others; or strategists placed in a situation in which logic demands reform. In essence, their reforms are normative and rooted in values. They believe that administration is important and that an improvement in administration will pay handsomely in the attainment of other objectives. Improved administration is wanted less for itself than for the results that are supposed to flow from it in adding to the quality of life.

A current administrative reform movement in the United States that seeks societal ends rather than administrative efficiency concerns decentralization. Although ideologically the decentralization movement is partly a reaction against technocracy and impersonal bureaucratic instruments, it follows such respectable American traditions as federalism, states' rights, local home rule, and grass-roots democracy. The movement claims that technocrats and rationalists have carried centralization to the point where decisions are made so far from the people for whom they are intended that they appear dehumanized, rigid, and insensitive. The people at the end of the line feel alienated from the anonymous "them," their own social institutions, and would like to resume more direct responsibility for ordering their own lives and environment. The movement consists of conservatives who resent concentrated power that is not in their hands or who oppose big government in principle, southerners who want to be free of northern interference via Washington, radicals and minority groups who want to control some part of the living constitution by themselves, and liberals who still prize individualism or who are disappointed at the failure of centralization to solve societal problems. They combine to demand (a) political decentralization from the federal government to other levels of government, (b) administrative decentralization in the federal agencies dealing with urban problems, and (c) greater individual and community participation in public-policy making.

Politically, the movement believes that the federal government has preempted decision making and lessened the power of the state and local governments. It wants to strengthen these two tiers against the federal government by various revenue-sharing and tax-credit schemes that would return fiscal dividends to state and local governments to be used for urban problems, and by a shift from special-purpose grants to bloc grants that could be used freely by state and local governments as they saw fit, not as directed by Washington. The issue is whether federal or local schemes are more likely to improve urban life. The movement believes that the fragmented and uncoordinated approach of overlapping federal agencies detracts from amelioration of urban ills. Administratively, decentralization within the agencies would reduce delays in getting programs started, eliminate much confusion in grants-in-aid, rationalize functional boundaries, and encourage regional and local coordination in federal government activities.

Administrative improvement of this kind, however, will not guarantee greater local participation in decision making. Too many resources are spent *on* the bureaucracy, not *by* the bureaucracy, and too many decisions are made *for* recipients, not *by* them. Societally, according to the decentralization movement, there is too much administration and too much dependency on administration, in contrast to too little individual and community responsibility and self-control. Proposed remedies take two major forms: greater community participation in bureaucratic decision making and eliminating bureaucracies altogether. Community participation in bureaucratic decision making already takes many different forms. In the United States, it may currently be seen at work in grand juries, selective-service boards, the Peace Corps, parent-teacher associations, police-review boards, community action programs, model-cities programs, and little town halls (in New York). Probably it will continue to expand. As to bypassing bureaucracies, one proposal at federal level is to abandon bureaucracies with a vested interest in poverty through income maintenance systems (for example, negative income taxes and family allowances), adult retraining, and full employment. At neighborhood level, community control is advocated as an alternative to bureaucracy through such forms as communes, cooperatives, neighborhood councils, and community corporations. Here the aims are the furthest removed from *administrative* reform and directed more at political mobilization of apathetic citizens, psychological uplift of dispossessed groups, "power to the people," more effective recipient demands on public authorities, and greater responsiveness of public services to constituents' needs, priorities, and feelings at the local level; and defusing ghetto tensions, increased minority representation, greater equality, and increased legitimacy for the polity, from the national viewpoint. Advocates of community control are really demanding a fourth level to the living constitution.

Growing demands for drastic changes of the living Constitution have been accompanied by widespread recognition that reform is long overdue. In response, different interests have proposed numerous plans for structural overhaul, reminiscent of the suggestions made by the Brownlow Committee and its successors, ably traced by Harold Seidman in *Politics, Position and Power*. In contrast to past experience, it is likely that some fundamental reforms will succeed, but only after bitter struggles between rationalists and politicians, managerial scientists and pressure groups, bureaucrats and democrats. Formal administrative changes alone will not make much difference without constitutional amendments, attitudinal changes, political realignments and imaginative programming, in view of the complex historical relationships involved.

We will compound the problems if we demand simple answers. The growing interdependence of the Federal Government, state and local governments, and many private institutions; increasing reliance on administration by grant and contract; and the greater utilization of multi-jurisdictional programs have added new dimensions to public administration. Whatever strategy is devised must be as sophisticated as the problem which it seeks to solve and retain sufficient flexibility to permit rapid adjustment to changing circumstances.[8]

[8] H. Seidman, *Politics, Position and Power,* New York: Oxford University Press, 1970, p. 286.

III

Function, Structure, Process, and Behavior

6
Functional Expertise

The enhanced political role of the public bureaucracy and its integration with other societal institutions through the living constitution and notions of "publicness" is largely the result of functional expertise. Ideological imperatives would not have been so strong if public administration had not demonstrated its capacity for assuming additional roles. Initial failures would have forced the ideologues to search for alternatives to the bureaucratic state and to oppose any further heaping of functions on the machinery of government. Had the bureaucratic state been less successful, some of the declining societal institutions might have been revived or their regression slowed down. Instead, the bureaucratic state has shown a remarkable ability to absorb more and more burdens, so that most solutions to societal problems involve extending the bureaucratic state even further. No real alternative has yet emerged capable of coping with the complex issues of modern society in nonbureaucratic ways outside the public domain. Lenin's vision of the eventual withering away of the state is further from realization than when it was formulated in the early part of the twentieth century, and ideological rationalizations of small-scale communal enterprise have not prevented their advocates from adopting large-scale bureaucratic devices at the first opportunity in Israel, China, and India. The bureaucratic state has the power, coverage, resources, organization, and professional competence to give it functional superiority.

The laissez-faire image of government, with which the contemporary state is compared, never corresponded to reality. At a time when governments may have been abandoning tariffs and poor law relief and contracting out of economic entrepreneurship, they were also becoming involved in bigger wars, military research and intelligence, public utilities for growing cities, cultural amenities, and institutionalized welfare. Public investment grew, and governmental regulation of private enterprise expanded. Practical politicians and empirical administrators were ahead of the philosophers. The very people who demanded an end to government prohibitions and public charity were the first to demand ample police protection, safe streets, proper sanitation, pure water, and adequate gas and electric supplies. Even today, major critics of the burgeoning public bureaucracy demand more and better public services that would enhance the public bureaucracy even further. Economy campaigns are doomed before they begin, unless politicians can persuade the public or different sections of the public to go without something to which they have become accustomed. The trend seems set in the following directions:

a. There are increased public expectations that the public bureaucracy will meet growing demands for more and better public services.
b. The public bureaucracy assumes a greater importance in the life of the community.
c. Public officials respond to their changing environments and seek to satisfy public demands, while improving their administrative and technical proficiency.
d. Public occupations and governmental professions proliferate.
e. Contacts between citizens and public officials multiply.
f. The need to exercise greater control and supervision over public administration is apparent as the opportunities to exercise discretionary power increase.
g. The ability of outsiders to regulate the living constitution diminishes.
h. The balance of government alters as administrative law vies with the legal system, legislatures become little more than sounding boards of public opinion, the need for quick and decisive action accelerates, and more work devolves on public officials.
i. As loopholes in public law are blocked, greater sophistication is employed to outwit public authorities, which sets in motion a vicious circle of check and countercheck.
j. Government becomes increasingly complicated and confused, permitting wider possibilities for dysfunction and requiring formal training for a thorough understanding of its operations.
k. New roles are institutionalized, and new functions eventually gain political acceptance as indispensable to modern life.

The trend could be slowed down by antiorganization movements, reaction to bureau-pathology, reform and revitalization of other societal institutions, and self-imposed bureaucratic limitations. It could be halted by the sudden emergence of a worldwide anti-statist movement, a temporary evening out of public demands together with a halt in human knowledge, or a thermonuclear holocaust. Unless a dramatic breakthrough in social organization occurs, it is unlikely to be reversed.

As big government continues, the public bureaucracy can be expected to strengthen further its dynamic role and its deep involvement in the political system as the administrative arm of executive government and a political power in its own right. It will play a basic part in establishing, determining, and implementing political goals and major policy directives. It will adapt to new societal goals, new spheres of activity, and new social needs arising from diversification of the social structure and extension of political participation. It will remain a major instrument of social change and political socialization, entailing new learning roles between citizen and official. It will become, where it has not already done so, the principal channel of economic and social mobility and advancement through its central place in economic development, its ability to satisfy rising expectations, its influence on the education system, and its status among white-collar workers. In conjunction with firm political leadership and a high measure of political consensus, it will facilitate stability and continuity in the political system, induce and develop new types of economic entrepreneurship, and generate both professional competence and political initiative. These bold claims can be substantiated by a brief review of the functional expertise of public administration.

TRADITIONAL FUNCTIONS

In terms of money spent and people employed, the fastest growing area in public administration is in those activities that governments have always carried out, not in the newer functions that they have assumed in the past century. With the possible exception of the protection of the defenseless, increased governmental operations have not resulted from the collapse or inability of other societal institutions, but the radical transformation of the functions themselves.

External Relations

A century ago, external relations was a relatively simple affair, conducted directly between visiting statesmen or delegated to resident ambassadors who conducted personal diplomacy in an aristocratic setting. States conducting external relations on their own behalf were confined to Europe, America, and parts of Asia. The only standing international organization was the embryonic International Postal Union. Today, external relations is an academic discipline in its own right, concerned not only with the complicated relations among an ever growing number of sovereign states, but also with the multiplication of international bodies dealing with subjects ranging from international law to civil aviation tariffs, from peace-keeping operations to atomic-energy research. The diplomatic corps is rarely responsible for personal diplomacy. Instead, it is more concerned with the issue of visas and passports, the protection of tourists and businessmen, the gathering of information, and the bolstering of foreign trade. Outside the diplomatic corps, other governmental agencies have representatives abroad attached to the embassies or working independently, on trade, intelligence, migration, and tourist activities, but more likely on technical assistance, mutual defense pacts, espionage, cultural exchanges, quarantine, and scientific research. Every state provides staff for permanent international organizations, ranging from the United Nations complex to regional headquarters of defense-treaty organizations.

Internal Law and Order

In rural settlements before the industrial revolution, the maintenance of law and order was the responsibility of the local aristocracy, whose word was law. As mobility was low, most people knew one another and knew among themselves who was suspected of committing crimes and generally disturbing the local peace. Thus the community itself enforced the peace, sometimes justly, through elaborate legal procedures, other times unjustly, through vigilantes and star chambers. Towns also relied on self-protection and community control, except in the case of large-scale revolt and organized crime, when the militia would be employed. Since then, civilian police forces have grown out of the town watchman and the rural sheriff. The police experimented with crime detection and prevention techniques until, along with similar concern in the prison system, the field of criminology came into being. The law-court system was elaborated and differentiated, and the state branched into administrative tribunals separate from the judicial system. To enforce the law, inspectorates were established, and from these small beginnings, a large statistical, research, and census organization was developed. The state also began licensing and performing marriage ceremonies and issuing divorces, registering all land dealings and property rights, regulating all weights, measures, and commercial standards, and conferring legal monopolies on creative work, where it had not done so before. As populations grow, all these activities expand. The militia is still held in reserve, in case the community takes the law into its own hands.

Defense

Only two centuries ago, wars were fought between small mercenary armies assisted by local volunteers and led by aristocrats. The mercenaries largely equipped themselves, except for heavy armor, and lived off the land as best they could, taking loot as their reward for victory and killing off the injured and diseased. Since then, mass conscripted armies have replaced mercenaries. Weapons, with the aid of modern science and technology, are now capable of destroying the whole planet and of ensuring the absence of life from large parts of the land mass for generations afterward. Military and civil industries are integrated. Less distinction is made between military combatants and innocent civilians. Warfare is conducted around the clock on land, sea, and air, in a variety of new ways, including gases, chemicals, and germs. On the other hand, the injured are saved and rehabilitated, and restitution made to defeated enemies. These transformations in warfare necessitate a permanent war organization responsible for all aspects of defense policy and strategy (planning, intelligence, espionage, propaganda, research, mobilization, logistics, and so on), professional military training (national service, military camps, training grounds), supplies and maintenance (weapons research, armaments and repair industry, supply depots), civil defense, and rehabilitation. The aim of the defense complex in peace is to improve its proficiency and weaponry by constant drills and practices to test the speed of mobilization; the degree of mechanization; the speed, precision, and destructive capacity of armor; the suitability of equipment, uniforms and supplies; the level of health, literacy, and morale of the armed forces; the efficacy of psychological warfare; and the depth of reserves.

The modern military complex has an important impact on society. It is big business, even in countries that cannot afford the military hardware fostered on them by aggressive sellers. It absorbs a sizable proportion of the gross national product the world over for problematical returns, while provoking arms races that may result in exactly that which the countries concerned purchase arms to avoid. It is big technology, embracing automation, computers, electronics, atomic energy, ballistic missiles, space research, communications satellites, metallurgy, and engineering design. It is big investment, advantageous to developed countries in stimulating research, development, and peaceful spin-offs, and perhaps to underdeveloped countries by injecting economic accelerator effects and building a technological infrastructure. It is big politics, with repercussions on political ideology, foreign relations, nation building, economic policy, occupational status, resource ownership, allocation and distribution, and civil liberties. Not all polities are capable of handling the modern military complex. This is particularly true of newly independent states with weak political institutions, poorly developed political ideologies, lack of political consensus, and depressed economies. They may become praetorian states, in which the militia is the ruling group and serves as the recruiting ground of political leaders.[1]

Public Works

The spectacular public feats of the past—the seven wonders of the world, large-scale irrigation, flood control and drainage schemes, ports and harbors, religious shrines—have been matched in every generation within the limi-

---

[1] A. Perlmutter, *Military and Politics in Israel.* New York: Frederick A. Praeger, 1969, p. 123.

tations of the culture. The past century has witnessed large-scale subway systems under major cities, vast river-valley development schemes, networks of superhighways and railroads, public broadcasting services, communication satellites, suspension bridges, airports, undersea exploration, and reforestation. But these spectacular public projects should not eclipse the steady advance along a wide sector of traditional public concerns, such as transportation and communications, public buildings, civic amenities, public utilities, market places, cemeteries, and similar activities that fill the agenda of local authorities without raising much political enthusiasm.

Taxation

A national taxation system requires an elaborate infrastructure of records, inspection, cooperation, collection, and accounting. Many countries still lack such an infrastructure and rely on methods since abandoned or reduced in rationalized administrative systems. The simplest form of national taxation is customs and excise—charges on tangibles as they enter or leave the country —which requires inspectors at all ports and a preventative service around the coast and borders to apprehend smugglers. Even simpler is the delegation of taxation to private entrepreneurs. The government contracts with a private entrepreneur to provide either a service for a fixed sum (and he profits from cost economies), or a sum of money levied on persons, property, or goods (and he profits from the excess he raises). Alternatively, the government grants legal monopolies for a consideration or it resorts to loans and devaluation.

Rationalized administrative systems with centralized taxation have confined it to public authorities, integrated it with national economic policies, and coordinated it with social and welfare schemes. Customs and excise continue to be major money raisers, but their administration is complicated by the wider range of commodities covered and integration with tariff and protection policies. Customs and excise have been joined by taxes on personal income, sales, property, and profits (see Chap. 8), collected directly from the taxpayer or through intermediary bodies such as employers, wholesalers, and retailers. The government is in the loan business through central banking services, domestic banking, post-office savings banks, and loan authorities, and it has further supplemented taxation with proceeds from the sale of public lands and the surpluses of public enterprises. In these ways, it can estimate with some accuracy taxable capacity and reduce tax seepage, thus maximizing revenues and mobilizing resources for community purposes.

Protection of the Defenseless

Even laissez-faire philosophy allowed for humane treatment to those unable, through no fault of their own, to look after themselves. Before the bureaucratic state assumed the responsibility, the burden fell upon the family, religious institutions, and charity. The bureaucratic state institutionalized welfare by providing, through taxation, special institutions for orphans, physically handicapped and mentally deranged persons, and war widows, where they were kept alive at public expense without being expected to provide any societal return. Attitudes to the defenseless have since been transformed by the welfare state, but it is important to note that the original humanitarian motives, however executed, have been extended to aborigine minorities, who until recent decades were decimated as a nonhuman species, and to social minorities, who were exploited or denied full participation in community life as serfs, servants, or second-class citizens.

In each of these traditional functions, public administration possesses an expertise unmatched elsewhere in society. Some are by nature governmental monopolies. Others are shared with other societal institutions, in which case public administration does not have exclusive expertise. In most, there is no ready substitute for officialdom, as alternatives have disappeared or been dismantled altogether and improvisation would take too long or fail through sheer lack of experience, know-how, competence, and public support. In these traditional functions, the government commands respect. It has built up a reputation of competence and fair dealing. No one is quite prepared to see anyone else handle these activities simply because on past performance, they failed in their trust.

NATION BUILDING FUNCTIONS

Nationalism was able to use the traditional functions of government to promote nation building. For instance, the ideology of the militia was transformed from pecuniary gain and military prowess to patriotism and chauvinism when civilian conscripts replaced hired mercenaries. Public works boosted the national image, but the success of nationalism was largely due to other factors. Today many new states are trying to employ public administration for nation-building purposes without the aid of other compelling factors. They may have to create a nation virtually out of nothing if they are to survive as sovereign entities. Their peoples may have little in common, except that through historical accident they find themselves inhabiting the same land area designated as a new state. Their independence movements, where such existed, may not have been nationalist or may have since split into many factions at cross purposes with one another over the next step. Their economic enterprises may be in the hands of foreigners. Their leaders may be ideologically committed to international movements that disclaim nationalism. Their public bureaucracies, reflecting cultural divergences, may be divided houses. There may not be time to wait until the people reconcile their differences and unite under common symbols. In short, they may have to concentrate on nation-building functions long institutionalized in older states.

National Symbols

Patriotism needs something more than a distinctive flag, a national anthem, a unique coat of arms, and public insignia, but such symbols are an indispensable beginning. The government, through public administration, and perhaps with the aid of other societal institutions, impresses these national symbols on the citizenry until the people identify themselves with them. Flags are flown on public buildings; national symbols head all official documents; public officials wear uniforms embossed with national symbols; national symbols are paraded on all public occasions; official languages only are used in the conduct of public business; public buildings, streets, squares, and thoroughfares are named after national heroes; public holidays and ceremonies commemorate national events. Nationalism is particularly impressed on children through the education system and on conscripted youth through the military system. Public officials are constantly reminded of their national importance, and they may be required to demonstrate publicly their loyalty to the nation by taking oaths of allegiance. Citizenship is conferred as an honor at naturalization ceremonies, and treason is condemned as one of the worst offenses a citizen can commit. Finally, there are national prestige projects of variable utility, ranging from national airlines and national hotels to the sponsoring of international conferences and sports events.

National Unity

Public administration is one of the major representations of national unity in any state. A public-service career attracts capable people who are willing to devote themselves to the commonweal in the service of their fellow men. They are expected to uphold national policies and national values above sectional and partisan interests. Their self-image highlights their role in unification, consolidation, continuity, and national integration. In national emergencies, they are the first on the scene. In fact, so reliable are they that the public expects them to provide the initiative at all times, and private citizens continue their usual activities safe in the knowledge that not only is something being done, but it is being done to the best of one's ability. Public officials foster national unity by the way they handle the public and by their adherence to nondiscriminatory bureaucratic procedures. By their personal example, they may remind others of national self-awareness, merely in their attitudes of pride in national accomplishments and faith in the national future. As representatives of the state, they signify the unity of the nation, adherence to one government, and support of common objectives. To promote national unity, recruitment may be based on representative quotas to ensure that each region, religion, creed, class, or political movement is adequately represented in government and has a firm stake in the system. If any important minority were excluded or discriminated against, it might be tempted to break away and form a state of its own.

National Socialization

National self-consciousness is awakened early by the education system and by the way academic subjects are taught, particularly history and geography. After school, young adults are further impressed with national consciousness through state-supported youth movements and clubs, and more obviously in full citizen rights, governmental elections, jury service, military service, and various forms of voluntary civic activity. To build a wider measure of national support, the state may favor the dominant religion or protect all religions. Where the state opts for the majority religion, religious doctrine may become part of the state ideology, and religious practices may be incorporated into law. State officials may be inducted in religious ceremonies, and prayers may precede all governmental business. Religious holidays may be appointed state holidays (for example, Sunday closing, Christmas, Buddha's birthday). The state may support religious institutions directly by building places of worship, paying the clergy, subsidizing religious schools, supplying religious articles as a free service, and specially favoring religious bodies in taxation and property laws. The state may also have special concern for co-religionists in other countries. Similarly, in the cultural sphere, the state may actively prefer the dominant culture or protect minority cultures. It may insist on one standard language or one form of dress. It may encourage indigenous arts and promote national orchestras, theaters, folk-dance groups, arts festivals, literary competitions, and leisure activities, as well as subsidizing national celebrities, national designs, and national exhibitions. Most states will preserve the cultural past in monuments, museums, archives, libraries, and art galleries.

National Development

The objective of national development is improving the quality of life for all citizens through self-sustained growth, equitable distribution of societal products, wide political participation, and individual self-fulfillment. Few countries can attain this objective without artificial stimulation by public authorities. The government has to ensure that the essential prerequisites for national development are obtained—security, stability, social cohesion, mobile resources, and so forth. It must stimulate private enterprise to expand and innovate or fill the gap with public enterprise. It must diversify the economy through commercial cash crops, industrialization, commerce, and service industries, and may need to employ national planning techniques, public investment measures, and public initiative in education, research, training, and publicity. It must promote greater productivity, higher standards, and prompter action, and it may have to begin with its own administration. Enhanced economic participation by the public bureaucracy may, however, detract from other goals, such as the strengthening of viable social and political institutions. Public officials, as social change agents, may teach their clientele new cultural styles and, as pacesetters, spearhead modernization by example. For instance, they participate in communal affairs and elections and encourage others to do likewise. They limit the size of their families and extol the virtues of the small family. In these ways, public administration acts as the innovator.

Nation-building functions, though not new, present difficulties. The fact that they have to be performed at all indicates the existence of severe obstacles to nationalism that have to be overcome. They aim at an end product that is intangible and, if attained, may be outmoded by internationalism. They may require different administrative styles and structures from the traditional functions. Public administration may not be the most competent institution to handle them, but in many new states, it has no option. Societal vacuums must be filled, and public administration is best positioned to do so. By the time other societal institutions are sufficiently mature to assume much of the responsibility, its functional expertise in nation building may be uncontestable.

ECONOMIC-MANAGEMENT FUNCTIONS

Governments have always reserved certain economic powers to themselves, such as control of the currency supply, the regulation of trade and commerce, and the sale of public lands and monopoly franchises. With the expansion of traditional functions and the assumption of nation-building functions, public authorities have grown more involved in economic matters, if only to assure a ready supply of weapons and limitations on economic exploitation of the defenseless. Their economic role has increased in response to the revolution of rising expectations. People expect the government to do more. They have always looked to it for action in solving community problems; that is what governments are for, and that is what no other societal institutions can do better. Community problems have grown with the agrarian revolution (which displaced people from the land), the industrial revolution (which transformed landless people into an urban proletariat), and urbanization (which brought problems of overcrowding, slums, disease, hard-core poverty, sanitation, transportation, civil disorder, and so on). War technology has assumed a momentum of its own, enlarging its coverage to include ports and harbors, airports, supply factories, research establishments, and stockpiles of essential matériel. Democratization of the political process means that the demands of the middle and lower classes have to be considered, besides those of elites. The rise of collectivist ideologies has further enhanced the economic-management functions of public administration.

Public Enterprise

The government has become a major economic entrepreneur, providing a wide range of economic products and services directly to the consuming public (See Chap. 7).

Economic Regulation

Nowhere has the institution of private property been wholly enshrined. Governments have always intervened to regulate private transactions, property exchanges, master-servant relationships, market prices, and working conditions. The extent of economic regulation has been transformed over the past century in response to trade cycles, monetary fluctuations, infant-industry protection, migration, labor organization, pressure group activity, and a host of other factors, best illustrated from a sectoral breakdown of economic regulation.

Primary industries   A century ago, most people were engaged (as they still are in low income countries) in self-sufficient primary occupations on privately owned land, and their living standards were governed by uncertain yields, subject to violent fluctuations. Since then, industrialization has provided alternative employment, has improved productive methods, and has opened new markets. In response, governments have intervened in the following ways:

  a. *Land redistribution.* The seizure of private property and the breakup of estates; land nationalization; high property and inheritance taxes; encouragement of co-operatives; support to small farmers; relocation of industry to rural areas to raise local employment levels.
  b. *Protection.* Prohibition on food imports; sliding scale tariffs; government storage of surplus; government purchase of surplus for distribution; guaranteed markets and prices; public marketing authorities; bulk purchase agreements; agricultural planning.
  c. *Subsidization.* Disease prevention; food inspection; research; cheap freight rates; subsidies and price supports; free and cheap loans; losses on government services in rural areas (posts, power supply, water).

In combination, governments have greatly reduced the risk factor in primary industry, in some cases to the point where private enterprise has been eliminated.

Extractive industries   Some governments have reserved to themselves the exploitation of valuable mineral deposits. Elsewhere, they provide survey and mapping services, subsidize exploration, regulate production through quota systems and royalty payments, inspect mining and forestry practices and plants, set prices, and renovate exploited areas (by reforestation and land reclamation).

Public utilities   Because of their importance to the community and their monopolistic features, public utilities are either publicly owned or strictly regulated in most countries. They are not permitted to exploit consumers or reap extraordinary profits. They are obliged to serve all adequately, without discrimination, at continuously reasonable rates.

Secondary industries   In addition to protection, subsidization, labor regulation, and safety precautions, governments have enacted a large body of law governing private corporations and their practices, the quality of merchandise, the nature of advertising, marketing conditions, overseas trade dealings, and permission to operate. Similar arrangements may be in force for secondary industries as apply to primary and extractive industries.

Small service industries   Small service industries are probably subject to less regulation than other economic sectors, but large service industries such as banking, insurance, advertising, commerce, broadcasting, entertainment, and distribution are probably subject to more legal regulatory bodies, inspection, licensing, compulsory government transactions, and incentive schemes.

Labor regulation   Apart from work-place controls, the government protects professional organizations and employee unions (which may be monopsonies), provides employment bureaus, vocational training and apprenticeship schemes, and supervises employer-employee relations.

In many respects, the functional expertise developed in all these areas is unique to public administration. It is not easily replaced and once institutionalized, it is usually taken for granted unless performance is really defective. The regulated institutions adapt themselves and experience difficulty in readjusting if the regulations are removed.

Economic Planning

Since the Great Depression, there has been a move away from the negative connotations of economic regulation to the positive approach of economic planning based on detailed intelligence and sophisticated planning techniques. Economic planning has taken three main forms, as follows:

Macrocollectivist planning   In reaction to the laissez-faire market philosophy, legal rationalists, technocrats, and collectivist ideologues believed that macroplanning could eliminate the wastes of free competition. Macrocollectivist planning involved the detailed planning and control of every aspect of the economy, including demand (viewed as the capacity to buy, a matter of income distribution, consumer research, and restrictive choice), investment potential, labor supply, foreign-exchange balance, and economic targets. It required control over all economic activity, a large intelligence network, a permanent planning organization, and effective rewards and sanctions for the enforcement of targets. Its introduction in the Soviet Union gave it a totalitarian slant, from which it has not recovered outside the communist bloc, despite relaxation of the formal framework and a retreat from centralization.

Post-Keynesian adjustment planning   Keynes did not reject the market mechanism, but sought to use it to overcome trade cycles and mass unemployment. The solution was not detailed macroplanning, but the maintenance of effective demand through fiscal, monetary, and banking policies, backed by readily available public-works programs that could be adjusted to meet fluctuations in employment and monetary values. Keynesians accepted the principle that the government was responsible for ensuring full employment through control of money supply, variable budgeting (which meant abandoning the concept of a balanced budget), flexible rates of interest, public-works programs, unemployment relief payments, and international agreements on money and trade. Governments control movements; they do not determine them. Control mechanisms involve government participation in banking, money, and credit supply, investment and savings, trade patterns, consumption trends, taxation policy, and social-welfare adjustments. Post-Keynesian economic planning has extended to prices and incomes policy, technological growth rates, international tariff agreements, labor supply, and containment of international corporations. Economic intelligence replaces centralized planning organizations.

Development planning   Impoverished new states lack the human resources for detailed macrocollective planning and a strong innovative private sector for post-Keynesian adjustment planning. Instead, they try to steer a course somewhere between them. Central planning agencies collect economic intelligence data, from which they define national economic goals and devise plans for government investment that they hope will be effected through public finance, public projects and programs, and technical aid on the one hand, and public controls and restrictions, political sanctions, and pressure on foreign nationals, on the other. Sometimes the plans are little more than codes of current projects in hand. Other times they are highly sophisticated economic models that cannot be translated to economically feasible programs or politically acceptable projects. Their propaganda value may be just as important as their economic impact, for they really intend to go beyond economics into political ideology, communal norms, social attitudes, moral standards, and behavior patterns.

Taken together, economic-management functions become more impressive as economic life grows more complex and as partisan mutual adjustment—on which the market mechanism depends—becomes increasingly inadequate to cope with contemporary economic problems. The management of the national economy requires a different outlook from the management of a subsystem organization, although the economic techniques may be the same. The differences are best highlighted whenever economic managers shift from micro to macro level, as, for instance, when private entrepreneurs offer themselves for wartime planning. Some adjust easily and make a success of their jobs. Others are miserable failures who have to be saved to avoid disaster. The art of getting things done through other people requires different talents according to what has to be done, the circumstances, and the people.

SOCIAL-WELFARE FUNCTIONS

Except for the protection of the defenseless, governments left social welfare to other societal institutions, if indeed anyone bothered at all with the illiterate, diseased, poverty-stricken, unemployed, and deserted. Social misfortune was considered as divine retribution for sins committed in the past or divine tests of character that would reap just rewards in the hereafter. Unemployment—the major cause of poverty—was looked upon as a person's own fault for being work-shy; there was always work around for lively hands. If the government was to intervene to protect the just from the rebellious unjust, public charity was not to be made enjoyable but degrading, stripping a social outcast of any self-respect in return for being kept alive.

These ideas still limit extensions of the concept of the welfare state, which developed in response to the breakdown of social-welfare services provided by other societal institutions and the obvious need for alleviation in the contemporary society. People could no longer fall back on the land. They could not rely on employers to meet their needs when unemployed. The church would not administer to nonbelievers. Private charity, after taxation and materialism had taken their share of private wealth, could not meet the growing welfare problem resulting from large-scale warfare, heavy seasonal and cyclical unemployment, international trade fluctuations, technological displacement, and natural disasters. While the upper classes could escape the social repercussions by isolating themselves in special areas or journeying abroad in times of crisis, the middle classes had to face increased crime (particularly theft, prostitution, and drunkenness), intruding slums, raging epidemics, low labor productivity, and corrupt charity systems. Their response was an immediate demand for more public services, such as (a) better local police, street lighting, paving of roads, public utilities; (b) establishment of separate institutions for the sick, mentally ill, orphans and widows, old and infirm, war-wounded; (c) provision of inspection to maintain proper standards for construction, town planning, markets, public thoroughfares, factories, mines, and public institutions; and (d) concern for preventative as well as remedial measures (insurance and savings, education, vaccination, pure water and so on).

To justify increased governmental concern with social welfare, philosophical justification was found from several different sources. The religious took their stand on the basis of moral improvement, puritanism, humanitarianism, and paternalism. The laissez-faire economic liberals believed that the government was justified in giving everybody a fair chance to compete as individuals. Democratic theorists stressed equal rights, equal consideration, belief in the individual, and the responsible use of power by the majority. From political democracy, they went into social democracy and economic democracy with notions of equality, public ownership, cooperative enterprise, and collectivism. Socialists began with the premise that man was master of his own destiny and each man's life was entitled to equal consideration. The community was higher than the individual, and the state was the instrument of social action. The guiding principle should be "from each according to his capacity, to each according to his need." With the merging of these various ideas, the concept of the welfare state recognized social welfare as the responsibility of the state, not the private concern of the individual. Social diseases were the fault of society, not the individual. The state should seek to eliminate all social diseases by remedial action. It should eliminate the threat of social diseases by preventative action. It should improve the welfare of all as national income rose and more knowledge became available. It should guarantee a minimum standard of welfare for everybody, and that standard should rise higher than the general increase in welfare.

In practical terms, the welfare state carries out social-welfare functions according to a "womb to tomb" policy. Before a baby is born, its chances of survival are improved by the provision of prenatal clinics, domestic help, and special foods for the mother, who receives a subsidy to cover the costs of pregnancy and confinement. When the child is born, if he is deformed or otherwise abnormal, the state cares for him in special institutions. If he is normal, the mother is assisted in the initial stages of child care, and should anything happen to the child's parents before he is mature, the state will care for him. As a young person, the state provides his parents with a special allowance to cover the extra expenses, and if they mistreat or neglect him, he is withdrawn from their care. If he commits a crime, he is not treated as a criminal but given special attention to assist him toward normal development. His health and education are provided by the state, free of charge. As a working adult, he is guaranteed employment as far as possible and retrained regularly to fill vacancies. He is provided with medical treatment, hospitalization, and convalescence, but should he become disabled, the state will care for him, as it does when he is unemployed. Social diseases—drugs, alcoholism, cigarettes, venereal disease—are attacked as social problems. Nonworkers without other means of support are assisted by the state. When people die, they are buried by the state, or their funerals are subsidized.

National Health Services

Medical health services are government-run; medical practitioners are public officials, and their facilities are predominantly public property. Included are preventative as well as remedial services, pure research as well as applied practice, and even ancillary industries serving the needs of the national health services.

National Welfare Services

Whereas health services deal with physical and mental well-being, the national welfare services are concerned with those who cannot support themselves or need help in other ways. The services may be delivered to the needy citizen, or the needy citizen may be taken out of his normal environment and placed in special institutions or relocated in more congenial surroundings.

National Insurance, Pension, and Superannuation Schemes

To assist the citizen through temporary misfortune or to subsidize the cost of national health and welfare services, the able-bodied employee is compelled to contribute from his current earnings, a proportion to be used by him personally when in need or by others when placed in a general fund.

National Education System

The state provides at least a schooling system for all children between the ages of five and fifteen, extending the system downward to kindergartens from the age of two, and upward to high schools, technical colleges, trade schools, universities, research institutes, and comprehensive adult-education courses. The basic school system is universal, free, secular, and nondiscriminatory (that is, unsegregated) to the children, but outside the school system the parents and/or students may have to contribute directly for the services provided. Those capable of benefiting from the courses offered, but unable to afford the direct charges, may be excused the charges, subsidized by scholarships, or lent money repayable at a later date. The education system may extend into mass media, publishing, and other ancillary industries.

Public Housing

Where private housing is inadequate or too costly for deserving citizens, the state provides adequate housing at subsidized rents and acts as a good landlord. The housing may include recreational facilities, cultural amenities, and local services.

Special Group Services

The state caters to those seeking employment, young adults, criminal offenders, social misfits, deserted families, migrants, war victims and ex-servicemen, lonely people, and victims of natural calamities.

Social-welfare functions are among the fastest growing categories of public administration. They employ large numbers of professional workers in large-scale complex organizations. In many areas they still compete with the private sector, and their functional expertise is not unique.

ENVIRONMENTAL-CONTROL FUNCTIONS

Compared with a century ago, most people in developed countries live longer, eat better, stand taller, and possess more goods. They enjoy a standard of living far above that experienced before. The poor live better than the rich of yesteryear. For them, enormous progress has been made and is being made at an accelerating pace. Affluence is now within the reach of millions, and millions more expect to attain it within their lifetime, certainly within their children's lifetime. This achievement is due to man's increasing mastery over his environment. Scientists and engineers are unraveling the secrets of nature and subjecting the total environment to human influence. We can remake "our lives at a breathtaking and even accelerating rate."[2] We can do anything we want—farm the seas, eradicate slums, prolong life, explore the heavens, and live without want, drudgery, and disease if we are prepared to meet the economic and political costs, if we are prepared to share our secrets with our fellow men, and if we are prepared to tackle the social diseases of galloping technology, such as terrifying destructive power, overpopulation, urban overcrowding, pollution of the air, sea, and land, and societal instability, to name but a few contemporary problems. Already a gross imbalance between scientific and societal progress exists, epitomized by thermonuclear weapons and starvation side by side, or by spacecraft and widespread slums. Technologically induced social changes occur so rapidly that people and societies cannot adapt, and the whole fabric of society is challenged by ceaseless turbulence.

Public authorities have always been deeply involved in environmental control. They have encouraged control over nature and promoted science and technology by supporting the intelligentsia, incorporating them within the governmental structure, and cooperating with researchers. They have had to cope with the problems of research successes. Some have destroyed the findings and the scientists or prohibited the application of theoretical breakthroughs, as in the Middle Ages. Others have resorted to regulation rather than outright prohibition, and still others, embracing scientism, have opted for constructive alleviation through directed research. Periodically statesmen have had to question whether increased environmental control has really contributed to progress or improved the quality of life. Is there "some law of nature which states that the danger to human life remains constant, so that as one source diminishes another must take its place"?[3] Are people happier, safer, and surer now that they have more goods, better health, greater mobility both physically and socially, and more opportunity to join large-scale organizations? The answer may be straightforward to the affluent, but the vast majority of mankind is still no better off than it was a thousand years ago, and in some respects worse off. The rich may be getting richer, but the poor do not change in most parts of the world. The whole effort may only tie more and more people to complexity and "enlarge their dependence on science, technology, and the men who understand how to use them."[4] This point is seen in a closer examination of environmental-control functions.

[2] J. D. Frank, "Galloping Technology, A New Social Disease," *Journal of Social Issues,* XXII, No. 4 (1966), p. 1.

[3] Frank, "Galloping Technology," p. 3.

[4] C. F. Stover, *The Government of Science.* Santa Barbara: Center for the Study of Democratic Institutions, 1962, p. 8.

Research and Development

Public administration has always been in the vanguard of science and technology. Rulers have wanted to master the latest discoveries and advances in knowledge to secure their position. Failure to appreciate the value of new information has led to many a downfall. More practically, rulers have promoted military science, particularly research into explosives and weaponry. They have tried to prolong their own lives with medical aid administered by court physicians. They have financed voyages of exploration and discovery. They have sought better farming and manufacturing techniques and improved building, construction, and engineering skills. Science has brought prestige. Only the ignorant and foolish have neglected to cultivate the intelligentsia and derive added power through the application of new knowledge. But the scientists' response has been mixed. The academic scientist has sought intellectual freedom to devote himself to discovery, without concern for societal repercussions of his work, governmental restrictions, or application, but he has shown willingness to be consulted on technical aspects. The practical scientist, on the other hand, no less interested in discovery, has sought ways of securing resources for scientific endeavor, enhancing the prestige of science, and using new knowledge for the advancement of humanity. The one has tended to stay outside public administration, except in a technical capacity; the other has been intimately involved in public-policy making.

Today research and development is very big government business, particularly in developed countries, where substantial sums are spent on military science, medical research, atomic energy, and space exploration. While much may be contracted out to private enterprise and universities, a considerable part is performed directly in scientific organizations run by governments. Currently governments are conducting research and development in every conceivable area of scientific knowledge, from telecommunications to animal breeding, from oceanography to weather forecasting, from computer technology to neurophysiology. Among the heaviest annual investments in the United States of America are the Department of Defense ($8.5 billion); National Aeronautics and Space Administration ($3.75 billion); Atomic Energy Commission ($1.5 billion); Department of Health, Education and Welfare ($1.25 billion); and the National Science Foundation ($0.5 billion). At the end of the 1960s, the United States Government was spending over $17 billion on research and development, compared with just over $7 billion by private investors. Of the million or so professional scientists and engineers, about one third was engaged on research and development in private industry and another 150,000 in federal government research and development. Before the Korean War, the United States government spent less than $1.5 billion on research and development. Thus, at least a fivefold increase in real terms had occurred in less than twenty years. It is doubtful whether such large expenditures will be reduced, unless large missile programs and space ventures are abandoned and the money not re-allocated to other research.

The rapid growth of governmental research and development raises many new problems. Much of it is secret. The scientists employed cannot pass on their discoveries, and nobody outside knows what they are working on and to what use their discoveries are being put. To maintain the supply of vast resources, the scientists have to publicize their more spectacular achievements and to sell their research as if it were some brand of merchandise. The organization of scientific research calls for different arrangements than those usually found in government and different ways for handling creative people. The demands of scientism may conflict with political expectations. Evaluative techniques may fail when applied to preliminary research designs and reports in progress. The allocation of scarce resources between worthy scientific projects may be irrational or subject to a scientific spoils system more nefarious than a political spoils system. As in all speculative ventures, the results may bear no relation to the resources invested. More difficult still is the calculation of societal return and the estimation of social impact. Birth-control pills change sexual mores. Automatic machines free men from work. Replaceable body parts prolong life. All these social repercussions may be incalculable and of grave political concern. Science is too important now to be left to the scientists alone.

Conservation

The conquest of nature has involved overkill. Man has destroyed irreplacable natural beauty, exterminated whole species of animals, created deserts where vegetation once flourished, and polluted his environment with his own waste products. "He simply ripped and tore and gouged and slashed what he needed from a seemingly endless supply. In the process, he killed, ruthlessly."[5] When he had exhausted nature, he moved on to some other place to repeat the process. In his trail he left ravaged forests with half-sawn trunks, eroded soils, disused mines and land slips, ugly scenic scars, piles of discarded litter, and

> gross misuse of national waters—the discoloration of rivers due to chemicals contained in industrial waste effluents; the shorelines made hideous by stinking organic sewage material; the algal blooms which have produced a malodorous, falsely solid surface on what may have once been sparkling streams or crystal ponds; the sometimes mysterious kills of fish left to float bellies up, dead and rotting under a summer sky.[6]

[5] United States Department of the Interior, *The Third Wave.* Washington, D.C., 1966, p. 7.

[6] R. Starr and J. Carlson, "Pollution and Poverty: the Strategy of Cross-Commitment," *The Public Interest,* No. 10 (Winter 1968), p. 105.

The first reaction was to protect species of flora and fauna in danger of extinction by prohibiting hunting and designating certain areas as wildlife preserves. Disappearing wildlife was also preserved in botanical and zoological gardens.

The next step was to set about restoring what had been destroyed. Conservation was based on the notion that, since there was only a limited amount of natural resources, wasteful, needless, and exorbitant exploitation would exhaust nature and condemn future generations. Natural resources had to be harbored through more efficient methods of usifacture and replacement of nonexhaustible resources. Conservation had three aspects—the better utilization of exhaustible natural resources, the reclamation of waste, and the renewal of nonexhaustible resources through reforestation and soil renewal. It soon branched out to include the preservation of historical sites and monuments, nature studies, recreational facilities, water conservation, and forestry fire protection. It became a general nature protection movement—to preserve rare resources, to protect natural environments, to improve the quality of life for urban dwellings denied esthetic pleasure, peace and quiet, fresh air, and living room.

Urban Design

The crowding of people into cities, which is a relatively new phenomenon in mankind's history, raised new problems, covering a wide range of amenities, open space, housing, shopping centers, transportation, public utilities and services, employment, law and order, migration, race relations, political activity and community participation, land use, access routes, recreation, entertainment, and tourism. Cities could not be allowed to happen. They had to be controlled and designed. New cities were to be planned and old cities redesigned. As town planning could not be considered apart from the suburbs and surroundings, regional planning joined urban planning and later still incorporated satellite town schemes, whereby big cities were deliberately reduced in population by the creation of new self-sufficient planned towns retaining direct rail and road links. Physical planning was finally extended to rural land use and wildlife regions.

Environmental Controls

Conservation and land use planning do not halt man's destruction of his own environment. Environmental controls are advocated by those who believe that man lives in a closed system—a spherical surface of fixed diameter with but a few miles of depth, its only exogenous input being the sun's energy.

> The atmosphere is not only the air which humans, animals, and plants breathe; it is the envelope which protects living things from harmful radiation from the sun and outer space. It is also the medium of climate, the winds and the rain. These are inseparable from the hydrosphere, including the oceans, which cover seven-tenths of the earth's surface with their currents and evaporation; and from the biosphere,

with the vegetation and its transpiration and photosynthesis; and from the lithosphere, with its minerals, extracted for man's increasing needs.[7]

Despite the vastness of water, air, land and life, man's environment is finite. For every gain, there is a corresponding loss.

> We start with the fact that the total weight of materials taken into the economy from nature must ultimately equal the total weight of the wastes discharged, plus any materials recycled. This means that a reduction in any one kind of waste, such as particulate matter into the atmosphere, must be accompanied by an increase in some other kind of waste, such as dry solids or solids discharged into waterways, or else by a continual recycling of this material.[8]

Man lives in a dynamic system that relies on a self-regulating equilibrium. His accelerating technology has upset the balance. Metals and plastics are indissoluble. Man-made poisons accumulate. Carbon in the atmosphere (burnt fossil-fuels) admits radiant heat and keeps convection heat close to the surface, thereby raising temperatures sufficiently to melt the ice caps, raise sea temperatures, and change rainfall patterns.

The long-range implications of man's destructive nature helps to focus attention on more immediate concerns, such as smog, smoke, oil and water pollution, sewerage and garbage dumps, uncapped oil wells, scarred landscape, radiation hazards, poisoned foodstuffs, untested drugs, noise, transportation and disposal of poison gas, networks of overhead wires and pylons, land slips, dangerous roads and transportation, shoddy goods, unsightly buildings and billboards, junk heaps, regimented housing, overcrowding, traffic jams, high-rise apartments, and faulty industrial zoning. These problems are being tackled by prohibition, regulation, education, research, engineering projects, and public-works programs. Unfortunately, public authorities are some of the worst offenders, particularly in radiation hazards, poison gases, thermal pollution (from nuclear reactors), and untreated sewerage disposal. The emphasis is moving toward a more positive approach to the quality of life and to a modernized version of the good society, which includes mass rapid-transit systems, outdoor recreational facilities, cultural centers, clean air, water and food, reliable and safe products, drug and chemical controls, and even a challenge to such communal traits as competition, profit taking, materialism, and egocentricity.

Personal Well-Being

Environmental hazards are nondiscriminating: they affect all human beings. Social hazards are discriminatory, as the burden falls unfairly on certain groups in the community—the rural poor, urban slumdwellers, unorganized labor, homosexuals, the elderly, and conscripted youth. Civil rights have

---

[7] Lord Ritchie-Calder, "Polluting the Environment," *The Center Magazine,* II (May 1969), 10.
[8] U.S. Congress, "Toward a Social Report: Our Physical Environment," *Congressional Record,* March 4, 1969, p. S2324.

assumed a new direction, away from political participation to personal well-being, which takes into account economic and social discrimination, cultural needs, and protection of individual privacy. The restoration of human dignity is becoming institutionalized as a public-administration function through such devices as fair employment practices, ombudsmen, citizens' advice bureaus, legal aid, consumer protection, Alcoholics and Drugs Anonymous (where publicly supported), and rehabilitation of criminals. Once again, public administration is a main offender, particularly in census questionnaires, wiretapping and bugging, and new tools for the manipulation and control of action and thought.

Environmental-control functions, like social-welfare functions, are relatively new to public administration, but nonetheless essential in the modern bureaucratic state. Their province is the realm of publicness, the general concern of all unrepresented by partisan political movements, vested interests, sectional pressure groups, and bureaucratic self-protection. In many cases, the dangers are unobtrusive; they are insidious but gradually accumulating until they reach the point of intolerance. A dramatic event —such as the explosion of a "dirty" weapon or bridge collapse or political assassination—will focus immediate attention on the problem and galvanize action. Although the drama subsides, the slow relentless buildup continues until it reaches the intolerance level again. Then DDT is banned or slum clearance begins.

THE IMPACT OF FUNCTIONAL EXPERTISE

The functional expertise now being developed within public administration is truly impressive. No other societal institution can compete in scope, depth, and variety. In many communities, no other combination of societal institutions can match the governmental apparatus in quality and quantity of public services. None of the functional expertise is dispensable under present conditions. Somebody has to be knowledgeable in all these areas and it so happens that public administration is deemed the most suitable place for the experts. Further, it is usurping fields that were once the preserve of other societal institutions and assuming sole responsibility in many new fields. Not only is its functional expertise growing, but the monopoly element is increasing. No other societal institution is capable of challenging its experts or of reassuming functions once nationalized. Once government has intervened, it is difficult, if not impossible, to exclude it without an overwhelming case against political interference or a dramatic change in circumstance.

Public administration is fast becoming the predominant employer or contractor of professionals, scientists, and technicians, that is, the new technological intelligentsia. Most new professions are public professions: their practitioners are public officials, as nobody else employs them at all or in numbers insignificant for any appreciable effect on employment conditions. The government lays down the ground rules for employee observance. The practitioners have no ready alternative employer or employment. They are truly public servants, for they can never be anything else without changing their expertise. On the other hand, their public employer is as much dependent on them as they on him. He has no alternative source of expertise and must, to some extent, accept the peculiarities of the new technological intelligentsia. They may want more freedom of action, freer discipline, fewer organizational restraints, separate and distinctive working conditions, and more self-determination than has been customary in public bureaucracies. There may be greater conflicts between functional expertise and political limitations. There certainly will be conflicts between experts in different fields and between experts who take a narrow or broad view in the same field. Harmony and peace are not to be expected in public administration when experts compete with one another and disagree in their own specialized fields.

The political problems of control escalate. Who decides when experts disagree? Who confronts experts when they are united? Are political leaders sufficiently capable of understanding the technical issues to make a reasonable decision? How does the career expert gain access to the political arena when he is in fundamental disagreement not only with the political leader, but also with career supervisors who do have access to the political arena? How do career experts reeducate the public to appreciate the need for political action in their specialized fields? What safeguards can be built into the living constitution to prevent the usurpation of political power by functional experts? Will public administration eventually swamp its competitors and reduce the functions of other societal institutions to insignificance? Will every other societal institution eventually become a pawn of functional experts in the governmental apparatus? These are the political issues behind debates on weapons systems, medical ethics, engineering programs, research proposals, scientific reports, and police methods. They cannot be left to functional experts to resolve.

7

Private Contractors and Public Entrepreneurs

When governments assume responsibility for a new activity, they may decide to contract its operation to other societal institutions, to conduct its operation within the apparatus of the bureaucratic state, or to combine public and private performance. Weak governments have veered to contracting out functions. Strong governments have centralized performance in impressive bureaucratic frameworks. Historically, governments have had little option to contracting out until they have built up sufficient functional expertise to wrest full control and operation from other societal institutions. A period of bureaucratic aggrandizement has followed until bureaucratic mismanagement, bureau-pathology, and fear of authoritarianism have reversed the process. Decentralization and private abuse of the public weal have brought their problems in turn. On the whole, the modern bureaucratic state has tended to aggrandize; only in the most developed countries is there a move away from centralization. Elsewhere, bureaucratic aggrandizement is still in progress, as professional armies and conscripted reserves replace mercenaries, taxing powers are removed from private contractors and assumed directly by public officials, essential industries and monopolies are nationalized, and environmental controls are taken out of private hands. Even in developed countries, the move away from bureaucratic aggrandizement has not been particularly marked, and successes are few, for rarely does a government shed an activity once it has acquired it.

154

Reaction has been strongest after wars, during periods of economic prosperity, and when anti-statist movements have been politically and economically powerful.

THE DECISION TO CONTRACT

The decision to contract public services to private bodies rather than assume direct governmental supply is much more complicated than a simple choice between economic and political reflections of individual preferences, as recorded in the price system and market place on the one hand, and elections and politics on the other. The pricing mechanism does not apply to noneconomic institutions and is distorted by income distribution, immediate choice, monopoly, imperfect competition, fragmentation, and egocentrism. The electoral system does not apply to nonrepresentative institutions and is distorted by apathy (or nonparticipation), infrequency, limited choice, power distribution, and ignorance. The distortions of the one need the correcting influences of the other. Economic criteria require political manipulation, just as political valuations require cost accounting. Moreover, no two countries are likely to react identically on all issues. Their different responses, reflecting differences in circumstances, resources, cultures, and societal objectives, provide contrasting styles of government. Among the most important factors that have to be considered are those that follow.

Control

Functional expertise accompanies resources, authority, responsibility and power. If too many activities are contracted, the government will not be able to attain or match the knowledge and experience necessary to perform assigned functions, and it will always be dependent on contractors. It may lose control over the contracted activities altogether, without abdicating responsibility for the proper expenditure of public funds. This could be a serious threat to the polity in the fields of weaponry, policing powers, and taxation.

Adequate Control Mechanisms

To perform new activities, governments must be capable either of conducting the operations themselves—which means that they must command the necessary resources and expertise—or of adequately supervising the contracted operations—which means that they must possess the necessary legal, budgetary, administrative, and intelligence controls. Contracts give them access to resources and expertise that would otherwise have to be compulsorily annexed, but they also imply weakness, particularly when governments are uncertain of their exact requirements.

A government that cannot provide adequate administrators for the comparatively minor operating subdivisions of its program is bound to have difficulty in tying those pieces together into a general program that makes sense. It is proper enough to insist that each private institution ought to be given latitude in a research or development contract and not be bound by unnecessary specifications or requirements. But in a broad sense the program must be based on a coherent system of governmental requirements and public policy, or there is no justification in supporting it with public funds. The basic question is whether the government has an adequate system of top management and enough foresight and experience in preparing in advance plans to unify the vast scientific program into a coherent whole.[1]

Economy

Taxpayers presumably want cheap public services. If contractors now provide identical or better services than estimates indicate public authorities could achieve if they invested in comparable facilities, the extra costs of direct governmental operation would seem wasteful and unwise, unless market valuation failed to allow adequately for social costs or beneficial spill-over effects, such as investment multiplier or technological breakthrough. Cost considerations may have to be modified further by political overlays, such as preference for a national contractor ("Buy American" or "Buy British"), protection of small business against concentrated economic power, utilization of unused capacity, geographical distribution of contracts, preference to depressed areas, conservation, and redistribution of income.

Quality

Governments want assurance that public services will conform to expected standards and that public work will be adequately performed. Two separate considerations are involved. Can the work be done at all? If so, can it be done to expectations? In research and development activities, there is no guarantee that the work can be done at all, that is, whether a breakthrough will be made or the prototypes will actually work, or certainty which of different approaches to a problem is likely most to succeed. If something is being done for the first time, a price has to be paid for experimentation. Decision is a matter of trust in a team of problem solvers, tried or untested, old or new, conservative or innovative. Should a breakthrough be made, the solution may not be economically feasible, politically practical, or technologically proficient. Consideration might also be given not only to getting a job done, but strengthening the prestige, image, and standing of the institution doing it, building a reserve of functional expertise for use in emergencies, and improving on existing effectiveness and efficiency.

[1] D. Price, *Government and Science.* New York: New York University Press, 1954, p. 92.

Perception of Time Span

Often when governments enter new fields, they do not know whether they will stay, and they are therefore reluctant to commit themselves to permanent arrangements. Temporary activities have a habit, however, of hardening into long-term commitments.

Size of Activity

The task may be beyond the capacity of any nongovernmental organizations to perform without assuming governmental powers, for they may not have the compulsory power, property rights, capital, scope, sanctions or status.

Political Ideology

The community may be prejudiced for or against private property, economic competition, profiteering, public ownership, collectivism, or planning.

Secrecy

In certain activities, such as espionage and nuclear fission, an overwhelming need for secrecy prevails. These activitites must therefore be performed by institutions of the highest integrity, out of public notice.

Nature of Objectives

The goals may be either intangible, unmeasurable, indivisible, and abstract, or concrete, divisible, and measurable. The goods and services may already be provided by other societal institutions, and governmental demands may be a minority share ("on-the-shelf"), or they may be designed solely or predominantly to government specifications ("off-the-shelf"). The off-the-shelf products may have no alternative uses, as in the case of weapons systems, or they may be applied and adapted to nongovernmental uses, as in the case of electronics, ship building, airplane design, and chemicals.

Time Lag

Governments may want instantaneous results or lowest possible lead-in time compatible with good performance. Thus, many governments have their own presses geared to produce printed bills and other public documents for legislators, judges, espionage services, and militia.

Propaganda

Irrespective of political ideology, the community may be persuaded that this or that institution is superior in performance, trustworthy, speedy, or capable of doing whatever it is called upon to do, although no justification may exist in fact. Similarly, labor organizations may believe that they have more (or less) bargaining power with public authorities than with private employers, without analyzing past results.

Conflicts of Interest

Governments may wish to lessen the risk of interest conflict and divided loyalties and reduce interlocking elites and multiple officeholding that might increase the risk.

In mixed enterprise western democracies since World War II, several experiments have been made to get the best of all worlds. Governments have created nonprofit private organizations for greater flexibility in providing new activities to eliminate the defects of bureaucratic centralism. They have contracted out routine administration of public bodies. They have assumed the management of nongovernmental organizations for greater control over contracted activities. They have established mixed and joint enterprises and financed independent "think tanks" to review public policies and strategies. They have provided matching funds to encourage other societal institutions to conduct community services that would not otherwise be available or that the government itself would not perform so well. Tax exemptions and reimbursements have been designed for the same purpose. As a result of these and other attempts to merge public and private sectors, the distinction between public and private law, like that between proprietary and governmental functions, is anachronistic. In contractual relations, the government has more difficulty in putting itself in a favored legal position vis-à-vis private parties on grounds of sovereignty alone, while constitutional concepts, such as the due process of law, are being extended to large business corporations. The increase in public contracts has made business a partner of government, with a corresponding reduction of countervailing power. A further prediction is the following:

> A concept of cooperation will increasingly supplant the concept of competition which for so long dominated social and political thinking. Within the business community this development is already clearly evident; witness, for example, the demands for fair-trade laws, the outlawing of "unfair" competition, the administered-price system, and the growing recognition that a community of interest exists among the components of those huge private collectivities, the corporations.[2]

On the other hand, cooperation could disguise dictation through governmental control over the purse strings and threat of public ownership. In the United States, where the distinction between public and private sector has become very blurred, public authorities concerned with defense, scientific research, and atomic energy already determine the economic fate of some of

---

[2] A. S. Miller, "Administration by Contract: a New Concern for the Administrative Lawyer," *New York University Law Review*, 36, May 1961, pp. 957–990.

the largest business corporations and some of the most important political regions, and they impede academic freedom and individual rights in their controls over contracted activities performed by universities, voluntary associations, and private corporations. Murry Weidenbaum has outlined the implications of fusion in *The Modern Public Sector* (New York: Basic Books, 1969).

PRIVATE CONTRACTORS

Before the bureaucratic state, most governmental functions were performed by other societal institutions or contracted to private entrepreneurs. The rulers would arrange with private bankers, noblemen, city merchants, and foreign traders to have a service provided at a certain price, not necessarily in cash terms, but perhaps in return for concessions, monopolies, and land grants and titles. Once the terms were settled, the rulers had little control over the quality of the services provided or the excess profits made by the contractors, except in withholding the promised rewards. In raising armies and providing goods, the contractors would hope to get away with the minimum. In collecting taxes, they would extort more than was necessary and pocket the difference, being able to invoke the majesty of the polity to punish those who complained. Where the bureaucratic state is still weak, as in some newly independent countries in Africa and Asia, the situation has barely changed for centuries. Even in highly sophisticated countries, it is still difficult to reduce political spoils in contracting, to prevent excess profits, to ensure quality performance, and to eliminate kickbacks. Other deficiencies have been eliminated by bureaucratization and public administration, or they have been institutionalized through legal tax seepages and subcontracting.

General Characteristics and Problems

The extent of contracting cannot be accurately gauged. On-the-shelf purchases are not usually considered contracted activities. These are goods and services normally supplied by commercial outlets, irrespective of the customer, and do not involve special arrangements whereby the government provides capital, lends staff and public property, and maintains quality process controls. They are purchased by individual agencies or a centralized supply and stores agency (for economies on bulk purchase), without special processing or contracts. Another area largely excluded is secret contracting and other subterfuges employed by governments to hide certain activities that they wish to keep secret. The number of legal contracts, however defined, does not indicate the scope and extent of contracting or provisions for renewal. Progress payments and open-ended contracts hinder the calculation of total costs, and taxation laws affect the return to government sources of contract payments. Even more difficult to measure is the extent of contracting and subcontracting between governments and among different governmental units, and the division between public and private sectors of contracts to mixed enterprises.

Accepting at face value the claims of communist regimes to minimize private contracting, and of newly independent states to prefer bureaucratic aggrandizement, it seems that private contracting is a diminishing influence outside the western world. Arms contracts, which is a large component of governmental expenditures everywhere, is more a government business, although private-arms manufactures still sell their products in the international market, both legally and illegally, Large-scale developmental projects, such as the Aswan Dam, Snowy Mountains Hydro-Electricity scheme, British Channel tunnel, and Concorde, are likely to be carried out by governments and parts contracted out, whereas once, like the Suez Canal, they may have been private ventures or have been wholly contracted out.

In the western world, private contractors still play an important part, and in some areas, such as research and development, policy analysis, and management of public facilities, their role is increasing. They undertake public-works programs, capital projects, building and construction, repairs, cleaning and maintenance, printing and publishing, rural postal facilities, garbage collection and sewerage disposal, custodian services, data processing, fuel supply, and medical facilities. The most important of the new areas of private contracting are weapons systems, research and development, automative equipment, and stockpiling. In some cases, private entrepreneurs will not sell outright to governments, but will insist on lending their wares by contract. In other cases, private entrepreneurs depend entirely on government contracts and have no other market.

Some estimation of the worth of private contracts can be gained from possibly the world's largest contracting public authority, the federal government of the United States of America, which spends over $50 billion a year on procurement, of which over 85 percent is spent by the Department of Defense. Between 1951 and 1967, the Department of Defense spent $431 billion on military procurement and property-management activities from private entrepreneurs, about 50 percent of the entire budget, and 9 percent of the gross national product. In research and development, the annual expenditure is about $17 billion, showing an even faster proportionate rise than military procurement, although, of course, the two are interrelated, as the bulk of the money has gone toward weapons systems such as intercontinental ballistic missiles, antimissile missiles, supersonic aircraft, atomic weapons and carriers, and radar systems, obtained from large companies such as General Dynamics, Lockheed, Boeing, General Electric, North American Aviation, and General Motors, and concentrated in five industries—aircraft and parts, communications equipment, electronic components, ordnance, and shipbuilding. Over 90 percent of ordnance work and of aircraft and missile construction, 60 percent of shipbuilding, and 40 percent of communications equipment before 1967 were attributable to military procurement, and the counties most heavily dependent on defense contracts included Box Elder

(Utah), Fairfield (Connecticut), Tioga (New York), Ellmore (Idaho), Stephens (Texas), and Newport News (Virginia).[3] Over four-fifths of the business of Republic Aviation, McDonnell, Grumman, and Lockheed depended on government contracts. Put differently, for every public official, there may be three others employed by private contractors on government work.

The expansion of military contracting has largely been due to the adoption of the concept of the complete weapon system, which includes all related equipment, materials, services, and personnel required for the major element of the system, support systems and subsystems, considered as a single unit and given to a prime contractor or team. The concept of the complete system differs substantially from the traditional concept of several companies competing for the patronage of several buyers in an open, free market. Instead, there is only one buyer and one prime contractor for an unmarketable product, which requires considerable effort in unpredictable research and development within the bounds of fluctuating defense policies, which can be changed without warning. The prime contractor may attempt to handle the entire task himself through horizontal and vertical integration with associated industries, competitors, and suppliers, or he may subcontract different parts of the task to other companies, which are tied together temporarily by complex agreements, trade pacts, and information exchange. Whereas previously the government might contract separately for an airframe and supporting equipment, which would be assembled at one point, the tendency now is to centralize the control of the airframe and its supporting equipment to the one weapon-system contractor who is responsible for its whole operational performance, not just the airframe, engine, or weaponry. Thus, the prime contractor decides how he will organize the project, rather than the government, which may, however, insist on competitive subcontracting. The potential contractor must investigate beforehand the possibilities of industrial integration, teamwork, subcontracting and subsystem competition, and he must also decide whether he will participate cooperatively in research and development, while competing for processing and manufacturing rights. The complete weapon system may eliminate all competition by creating a weapons cartel, in which case "the pretext of competitive procurement" might have to be abandoned to simplify contract arrangements, and weapons procurement and the whole weapons industry nationalized or treated as semipublicly owned monopolies.[4] The danger is that the complete weapon system may create vested interests in mass weaponry that prevent alternative strategies in foreign affairs and defense, and insist on the manufacture and foreign sale of weapons that are outdated or have no useful purpose other than to maintain the manufacturers in business, to prevent adverse economic and political repercussions, nationally and locally.

[3] E. Benoit and K. E. Boulding, eds., *Disarmament and the Economy.* New York: Harper & Row, 1963, p. 48.
[4] J. S. Livingston, "Decision Making in Weapons Development," *Harvard Business Review,* Vol. 36 (Jan.–Feb. 1958), pp. 127–136.

The United States federal government does not contemplate any change of policy; it will continue to contract enormous sums of public money to large, temporary combinations of private entrepreneurs. First, it strongly believes in the efficacy of private enterprise and has no intention of building a mammoth public arsenal of its own. Despite past failures, some of which were more the fault of the contracting authorities than the contractors, the record of technological success has been satisfactory. Targets have been achieved. A man has been put on the moon before 1970. Nuclear armed submarines have been built, as well as large numbers of supersonic aircraft and missiles. Military personnel have been transported comfortably and quickly around the globe. Moreover, no alternative system anywhere else has outperformed United States industry. Results count, and in solving public problems, one resorts to the most appropriate bodies and people, wherever they are found. "A partnership among public and private agencies is the best way in our society to enlist the Nation's resources and achieve the most rapid progress."[5]

Second, an alternative system of public enterprise is not politically acceptable. The taxpayers seem to prefer to pay the same scientist more in private industry or in a government-controlled contract organization than in public service. The flexibility of the contract system suits the political system and the need to satisfy political demands. An arsenal system would reduce political leverage over economic power. It would also reduce the level of business activity and create organizational monsters that would dwarf existing establishments.

Third, the government reduces its risks. Greater responsibility rests on private enterprise, while eliminating governmental concern with routine details. Public authorities retain control of key points without undertaking the management of the whole system. Centralization is reduced by built-in partisan mutual adjustment and self-controls. The problem of controlling the uncontrollable is bypassed, as is that of managing the unmanageable. The contracting authority does not have to know all details or maintain complete control over all aspects, yet it retains large discriminatory powers over potential contractors and leaves its options open.

Fourth, the government can call on all the community's resources when necessary; it has a wider range of selection and choice; it can modify, vary, and change at will. It is not committed to any set pattern or prearranged framework. Its own standing is less damaged by failure. It can always blame the contractors rather than inadequate policy preparation, control networks, and product evaluation systems.

Fifth, the contract system does not diminish the government's ability to impose political directions. Indeed, the contracting authorities can incorporate political demands in their contract requirements, such as preference

---

[5] Bureau of the Budget, "Report to the President on Government Contracting for Research and Development," Senate Document 94 (May 1962), p. vii.

to small business, fair employment practices, labor regulation, hidden subsidies, ethical standards, use of local materials, and good safety practices. In intergovernmental relations, contracts can be used to delegate detailed operations to a lower level, while retaining policy responsibility.

Finally, costs may be a secondary consideration. The government might be able to do things cheaper itself, but speed may be the essence rather than cost; this is especially true in wartime and crisis. There is no time to stop and consider alternatives when something has to be done quickly before the situation worsens. The government may not even know what it wants, but is prepared to accept anything feasible, and here the contract system is most susceptible to abuse by contractors. Thus the issue is not the abolition of the system, but the need to improve safeguards.

In theory, the contract system is its own safeguard. If the contract is not fulfilled, the government does not pay and loses nothing. This is possible when the government can refuse to pay until the contract is completed, knows exactly what it wants, and writes into the contract exact specifications. Very often, however, the government has to provide advance capital that it will not be able to reclaim, lend its facilities at nominal or no charge to private entrepreneurs, and write contracts in very vague terms, as nobody knows beforehand what the outcome will be. Moreover, the contract is supposed to be awarded to the lowest tender likely to complete the contract to satisfaction. There may be no competition at all, and no private entrepreneur may be willing to undertake the work without guarantees and concessions. Thus the tenderers may deliberately conspire to defraud the government or to quote inflated prices. The public authorities may have no way of estimating what a reasonable offer should be, what profit markup has been made, who has been prevented from tendering, or how much is intended to be subcontracted or incorporated into nongovernmental contracts. It is unlikely that public authorities will ever block all subterfuges; they will always be one step behind the inventiveness of the unscrupulous.

Recent Improvements in the Contract System

Since the 1950s, public authorities have improved their contract management in a number of ways:

Review of need   Before a contract is let, a careful search is made of existing stocks for disposal. In the past, superficial checks have led to needless contracts that have merely increased stocks of unused materials. Public authorities buy only what they really need, using the latest scientific management techniques to determine requirements.

Calculation of cost   On-the-shelf items are readily calculable, although it is known that public authorities have let contracts for identical products above market prices. Further intelligence and investigation may enable a public authority to make a fair estimate of the probable costs and profit margins. It may be able to negotiate lower contract prices or threaten to supply its own needs internally. Thus contractors may be obliged to disclose all necessary information about their tender.

Economies of scale   Procurement is centralized to prevent internal competition and to obtain the best deal for collective requirements. The procurement agency lets a single contract and then distributes the product among several agencies.

Increased competition   The letting agency seeks to extend competition by extensive advertising, propaganda campaigns, splitting contracts among several suppliers beginning with the lowest tenders and working upward until requirements are met, and if necessary, going outside the country altogether. It may insist on competition in subcontracts and enforce antitrust legislation.

Onus on the contractor   The agreed contract price is final and nonnegotiable, in the event of unforeseen snags, the contractor bears the risk. In addition, a ceiling is set on expenditures in research and development where the results are uncertain.

Limited profits   Public authorities agree to meet all reasonable costs, but they fix the fee beforehand. The costs may not be minimized, but the profits are not linked to them, as in markups and percentage profit margins. Profit margins are also limited by law.

Incentive contracts   Where it is possible to estimate costs, product performance, reliability, quality and delivery dates, contractors are awarded incentives for superior performance according to a sliding-scale bonus and penalized if they fall below targets. They may also be granted permission to adapt the results for commercial use. Cost reimbursements can be planned with much the same intent. However, the elaborate accounting involved and the complexity of estimates may nullify any savings to the government, and there may be legal complications in paying more than the agreed contract prices or changing the terms of a contract before its completion.

Contract management controls   The letting agency manages the contract to cut out middlemen expenses and the pyramiding of profits by subcontractors and prime contractors. When needless costs or excess profits are discovered, contracts are renegotiable or new contracts incorporate higher targets. Both the letting agency and the contractor may work closely together in planning and execution, but either or both may lack the requisite techniques.

Breaches of contract   The government may protect itself against the mistakes of its own contracting officers and exclude itself from business law, as interpreted by the courts. It may provide an administrative disputes procedure to bypass the courts without necessarily circumscribing contractors' rights to recover and to challenge unilateral change orders.

Patents and copyrights   Public authorities may reserve all rights to new discoveries made under their contracts.

Cost-reduction programs   The public authorities attempt to standardize their equipment, promote common user services, restrict contract or use of public property, reduce unnecessarily large stocks and multiple storage locations, coordinate requirements of closely related products, improve contract specifications and contract administration, and directly procure items for contractors and subcontractors from existing stocks. They also share contract information and intelligence, limit spare-part clauses, test the real life of short shelf-life items (for example, goods subject to spoilage, deterioration, and obsolescence, dated by the contractor to ensure full use), recoup on sales of surplus products, protect subcontractors against prime contractors, review sole-source claims, delay start of work before contract is signed, evaluate the quality of research and development work, eliminate conflicts of interest, and improve the quality of procurement staff. They can further reduce costs by strictly monitoring kickbacks and other fees or commissions received by politicians, procurement officers, and prime contractors in the award of contracts.

Obviously contractors dislike these improvements, for several reasons. Their profits are limited, Their opportunities for diverting public money and property to private business are diminished. Their freedom in selecting subcontractors is reduced, and kickbacks may be eliminated. They are forced to adopt different accounting practices and to accommodate themselves to government intelligence demands. They must permit detailed examinations of their operations and access to trade secrets. Their rights of redress may be impeded. If they do too well financially, they may be penalized in follow-up contracts, but if they do not perform well enough, they may be publicly exposed, and their commercial business may suffer as a result, or they may lose their public business. They may be forced to adopt unfamiliar public-administration practices on behalf of the government, which add unduly to overhead expenses. They resent the additional risks imposed on them. Their development programs may be held back until the government formally establishes a use or before they have had the opportunity of demonstrating the worth of prototypes. They may be confronted with a stop-and-go type of development, which is highly inefficient and expensive, because the government changes its policies, cuts budgets, or loses patience. In short, some contractors are not at all pleased with stricter governmental controls over contracts and resist attempts to encroach further on their preserves.

How the battle of wits stands between the contractors and procurement agencies can again be gauged from the military procurement area of the United States federal government, as revealed by the evidence of the Economy in Government Procurement and Property Management hearings before the Subcommittee on Economy in Government of the Joint Economic Committee, under the chairmanship of Senator Proxmire during the 1960s. The Department of Defense had implemented most of the contract controls previously mentioned and had secured large economies during a period in which annual procurement expenditures were nearly doubled and individual transactions topped 15 million. Nevertheless, the Proxmire committee was highly critical of the Department of Defense's "loose and flagrantly negligent management practices." Until 1969, less than 13 percent of all contracts had been advertised, and although the Department claimed that 40 percent had been competitive, it was evident that even in much of that area there had been no meaningful competition, which was further confirmed by legal retreats from competition under 10 USC Section 2304. At least 60 percent of all military procurements had been negotiated with a single contractor. As the Department had largely ignored the Truth in Negotiations Act, which required the production of information before the award of significant contracts, and had not maintained detailed price inventories, it had been unable to challenge the costs claimed by the contractors. Not only had the government been overcharged consistently, it had not known what stock it had had on hand to prevent the letting of unnecessary contracts.

Despite the increase of fixed price contracts and incentive contracts, major expenditures had been incurred on cost-reimbursement contracts going to oligopolies (immune from antitrust laws), which had dominated contracts. The top one hundred contractors had accounted for about three-quarters of government expenditures and the top twenty-five, most of whom had retained their standings over twenty years, had received over one-third of the expenditures. At the end of the 1960s the top one hundred had $150 billion worth of contracts in hand. In contrast, small business had accounted for only 18 percent of government expenditures (although it was not known how many small businesses had benefited from subcontracting to primary contractors) and had been the first affected by cutbacks. The prime contractors had made excess profits compared with nonmilitary business, attributable in part to their cheap use of $15 billion worth of public property (a "back-door subsidy"), high progress payments (which had enabled them to use public money not their own), reimbursed leased property (again not their own investment), and unduly protective practices of the Department in shielding American producers from foreign competitors. The ability of the Renegotiation Board to tackle excess profits had been handicapped by political and industrial opposition, legal restrictions, and general administrative hamstringing.

In response to these findings, the Department of Defense had argued that it had been doing its best in the circumstances, that the recurrent scandals had been isolated and unrepresentative incidents, that the adoption of different procedures would have cost much more than any possible savings, and that it had gone a long way to meet criticisms, as the vast expansion of government regulation under the Armed Services Procurement Act had indicated. The Proxmire committee had acknowledged that the Department's staff had been underpaid, overworked, and possibly ill-equipped. Not surprisingly, the first of the key areas that industry and the Department of Defense had declared worthy of joint exploration in 1969 was "achieving higher public and Congressional confidence in [the] integrity and effectiveness of the Defense Procurement Process." The others were "attracting and motivating contractors to accomplish defense requirements," "achieving consistency of field practice with intent of basic DOD policy," and "increasing effectiveness of major weapon system acquisition process." In fairness, it should be noted that military procurement is one of the most difficult areas of government contracting. So too is research and development, where personal evaluations of the contractor and the researcher assume a greater prominence, particularly when decisions are taken rapidly under pressure by a closed circle and tenders include nonprofit organizations (for example, universities, public laboratories, think tanks, voluntary associations, professional societies, technical management corporations). Elsewhere, public authorities rely much more on competitive bidding, fixed price contracts, and frequent retendering.

PUBLIC ENTREPRENEURS

What is not performed by or contracted out to private entrepreneurs is directly performed by public authorities themselves. To this extent, all public administration is public enterprise. Usually the term "public enterprise" is used more restrictively to refer to public entrepreneurs, that is, the part of public administration that sells direct services and goods to the public and whose internal administration is expected to be largely self-contained. These are the public businesses, the oldest of which is probably the post office, and the newest, nuclear-energy power plants and communication satellites. They perform economic activities that could be carried out by private enterprise, or have been carried out by private enterprise in the past, and now include activities that the state has decided to operate in the absence of private initiative. In communist-bloc countries, they cover most business activity. In North America, they include oil and natural-gas pipe lines and multipurpose valley development schemes. In western Europe, they include the Concorde supersonic airplane and the ENI, the Italian state corporation holding company that is an aggressive competitor in the oil industry. In Latin America, Brasilia and the nationalization of foreign-owned companies would qualify. In Africa, the Volta River project and the Aswan Dam complex are public enterprises. In Asia, the birth-control campaign is a marginal public enterprise, but publicly owned industries definitely qualify. In Australasia, the Snowy Mountains Hydro-Electricity scheme is the most notable public enterprise project. At supranational level, the International Bank for Reconstruction and Development is a public entrepreneur. Again, no firm boundary line with private enterprise and noncommercial government activities can be established, simply because the conditions under which the state runs businesses or constructs large-scale developmental projects on behalf of the community vary so greatly.

Rulers have always preferred to run certain businesses themselves. They have wanted to enrich themselves from the profits, diminish political competition, and restrict the growth of autonomous power centers. They have responded to citizens' complaints regarding poor services, extortionate prices, uneven performance, and discrimination in private business. They have sought to meet rising expectations unfulfilled by private initiative. They have abandoned private contractors and have directly assumed the performance of governmental activities. They have believed that they could outperform private enterprise. These motives are as old as civilized society, but in the past century they have been joined by newer motives.

Ideological Imperatives

The institutions of private enterprise and private property have been attacked by communist and socialist theoreticians as being immoral, exploitative, corrupt, bourgeois, parasitic, and wasteful. The communists completely rejected capitalism and insisted on the overthrow of the capitalist state by force. They wanted to abolish private property and the bourgeois class, in whose name the polity was supposedly conducted, and to substitute communal property, egalitarian collectivism, and self-determination in a socialist society that would not need a bureaucratic state apparatus, once the dictatorship of the proletariat rid the community of any trace of bourgeois capitalism. The socialists were prepared to find a place for private property in personal possessions and preferred to work for the gradual replacement of capitalism through existing institutions, including the state bureaucracy. Both seek to enthrone communal values, to eliminate the wastes of competition, and maldistribution of income and wealth, as well as to avoid exploitation of the employee, consumer, and colonial peoples. Whereas one eventually has no place for state enterprise or public entrepreneurs, the other believes in public ownership, nationalized industry, political regulation of economic enterprise, planning, economic democracy, and public initiative.

Public Supports and Correctives

Laissez-faire economists, who favored private initiative the most, recognized that private enterprise could not do everything. Economic exploitation had given rise to intolerable social ills. The solution was not communalism or state socialism, but state paternalism or reform from above. Public initiative should remedy social ills and provide activities that would aid private initiative as its partner. Besides the provision of social welfare, economic regulation, and environmental control functions, the government should ensure the supply of cheap public utilities, promote education and research, and maintain private enterprises that fall on bad times. Further, the government should take the initiative in promoting infant industries, ensuring full employment, widening the economic frontier, and supplying services that private entrepreneurs were not prepared to undertake because of lack of sufficient capital, inadequate profit margins, high risks, and long lead-in time.

Absence, Failure, and Inadequacy of Private Entrepreneurs

Not all societies evidence the Protestant ethic, materialist values, or an inno-vating private sector. There may be no private entrepreneurs or insufficient numbers of them to undertake major economic tasks. They may lack the will to open up new markets or start new industries. They may not have the re-sources, technology, administrative capacity, incentive, or security. The market may be too small, or the rewards may be stolen or otherwise extracted from entrepreneurs. Local enterprise may have been discouraged by colonial rulers, and investment returns may have been exported to absentee owners. Private entrepreneurs may be unable to reach the required standards (in honesty, performance, timing), they may exploit the market, or they may fail to expand their operations. They may be unable to maintain employment, and they may be too parochial, small, numerous, secure, or self-interested.

Concept of Public Interest

The government may feel impelled to nationalize cartels and monopolies, to protect the poor by providing cheap essentials, to confine weapons pro-duction to public authorities, to own essential industries, to rationalize the structure of private enterprise, to embark on prestige projects, to reduce foreign competition and trade deficiencies, to standardize products, to fi-nance noncommercial activities from public enterprise profits, to improve labor relations, to pioneer technological innovations, and to prevent the emigration of qualified people. In pursuit of these political objectives, the government may choose not to become a public entrepreneur, but to subsi-dize private entrepreneurs and join with them in the marginal cases of mixed enterprise and government purchase of stocks and shares. A succeeding government, with different concepts of the public interest, may sell off prof-itable public enterprises to private entrepreneurs or reduce public entre-preneurs to political spoilsmen.

As with private contracting, the extent of public entrepreneurship is dif-ficult to measure accurately. Some public enterprises are indistinguishable from nonentrepreneurial activities conducted by public authorities. As they could never return their costs, no attempt is made to charge a fee or levy a fair market price. For example, public housing is provided free or below cost. Entrepreneurial activities are not separated from other activities by organi-zation, budget, staff, and national-income statistics. They take a variety of forms—ministerial departments, statutory authorities, public corporations, joint stock companies, river-valley authorities, holding companies, inter-governmental agencies, joint enterprises, and representative trusts—some of which are obviously identifiable as public entrepreneurs, others not. Their activities in several areas—public transportation, public utilities, scientific research, mass communications, tourism, banking and insurance, municipal facilities—have direct counterparts in private business, but in others—multipurpose river-valley development, survey and exploration—no direct counterpart may exist and therefore no way of knowing how it might operate or recompense itself.

The most clearly distinguishable form of public enterprise is the public corporation that resembles the private corporation, except that it is incorporated under special statute, and its board of management is appointed by the government. It has been preferred to the ministerial department, whose managerial flexibility has appeared to suffer from rigid central bureaucratic controls, and to the joint stock company, whose management has been too far removed from political control. The public corporation is alleged to combine the advantages of direct political control and managerial flexibility. Its activities are clearly defined in law, and its budget and staff, property, and supplies kept quite distinct. In practice, the matter of form has been determined less by theoretical considerations than by ideology (which has excluded any resemblance to private capitalism), purpose (whether multipurpose or not), area served (local, regional, national, or international), function (operational, regulatory, or holding), past experience, foreign example, personal advocacy of politicians or administrative scholars, and confidentiality of activities. The distinguishing factor is the presence of government in management, directly through representatives or indirectly through instructions and political pressures.

More important than the form are the following operational considerations:

a. *Nature of political controls.* Legislation, policy directions, ministerial supervision, public accounts, judicial review, public inquiries, governmental budgeting, public investment, informal pressures

b. *Degree of political interference.* Political direction, patronage appointments, contribution to party funds, political campaigning, pressure group representation, community participation, imposed legal structure, compensation to past operators, favored treatment

c. *Size and extent of operations.* Place in economy and governmental system, public contracts, area concentration, centralization, nature of market and services, size of finances and staff, internal fragmentation

d. *Monopoly content.* Legal, natural, substitute products, presence of competitors, precariousness of product, market accessibility

e. *Extent of commercialism.* Noneconomic aims, profit criterion, integration with national plans, industry leader, openness, entrepreneurial ability, comsumer representation

f. *Operating efficiency.* Net financial balance, consumer satisfaction, conformity to planning targets, staff morale, pioneering value, attention to social costs, mistakes and shortcomings, mismanagement, goodwill, quality of staff, adaptability

g. *History and experience.* Origins, age, fluctuations in control, form and activities, reputation, political responsiveness, social responsibility
h. *Freedom of action.* Self-contained finances, staff transferability, nature of product, price policy, cost controls, contracting, operating philosophy, internal competition

Public entrepreneurs are *public;* that is, as publicly owned political agencies conducting business activities, they are deeply immersed in the political arena as newsworthy organizations that are expected to satisy the conflicting demands of government and opposition, and consumers and employees.

The public entrepreneur is a different creature from the private entrepreneur. His origin is political; his existence is political; his future is political. He is public property. He is politically guided and, on request, he is expected to subordinate economic considerations to political expediency. At key points—law, management, policy, finance, staff—he is controlled by politicians, and he may find himself part of a Ministry for Public Enterprises or subject to ministerial controls in finance, construction, public relations, investment plans, and structural arrangements. He may find his freedom of action circumscribed by other governmental agencies, representative assemblies, and public inquiries, and his operations conducted in a blaze of publicity. Thus political limitations are comprehensive, certainly well beyond tolerance level for any private entrepreneur. Their presence inhibits entrepreneurial initiative unless special efforts are made to achieve autonomy.

The political limitations are important when considering the profitability of public entrepreneurship. Within any community certain basic needs (for example, bare physical necessities, security, self-expression) have to be met. These basic needs are guaranteed by government whatever the cost, for the alternative is the breakdown of society into chaos and anarchy. Their cost is not to be measured by the volume of resources spent on them, but the social conditions that would prevail if they were not performed at all. Thus the cost of peace is the price of war; of health, illness; of education, ignorance. Financial yardsticks cannot measure the real costs of activities pursued by public authorities in meeting such basic needs; they are incalculable. Once sufficient expenses have been incurred to assure a satisfactory level of performance, the community must choose whether private or societal needs should receive priority. The two cannot be strictly separated, for in meeting one set, the other may also be partly satisfied. Both public and private enterprise serve common ends, but whereas private enterprise concentrates on meeting private needs expressed through the market mechanism, public enterprise concentrates on societal needs expressed through the polity. Whereas private enterprise does not have to reckon the opportunity costs of its activities— that is, the alternative to the society if private entrepreneurs spent their resources in a different way—public enterprise is expected to consider them in responding to political pressures. If private entrepreneurs cannot meet their expenses, they are compulsorily forced out of business. Governments, in contrast, can spend resources above receipts without fear of bankruptcy. Consequently, the evaluation of private enterprise, according to the differences between resources expended and the cash returns, cannot be applied to much public enterprise.

In areas where public entrepreneurs are expected to meet costs from receipts, the profit concept may be applied, providing that its limitations are noted. The excess of receipts over expenditures does not take into account nonfinancial measures, such as the quality of resources or free goods on the input side and social costs on the output side. The profit concept does not confine the surplus to any specific time span, and although an annual budget may be adopted, it may be more meaningful to consider the lifetime of the enterprise, thereby allowing for capital depreciation and trade variations. The profit concept does not reveal how the receipts or expenditures are obtained. The receipts may be influenced by monopoly power (the ability to charge what the traffic will bear), oligopoly (price-fixation agreements), law, planning directives, or perfect competition, and they may be restricted by bad debts, poor management, and self-imposed limitations (on humanitarian grounds or out of sheer laziness). The expenditures may be incurred for noneconomic reasons, and there may be illegal costs (extortion, theft, corruption). The profit concept does not concern itself with the value of the financial unit, which may fluctuate considerably over a lengthy period. Finally, it does not concern itself with the source of profits, at whose expense they are earned, how they are used, and to what purpose they are put.

Applying the profit concept to public entrepreneurs, a likely assumption is that really profitable ventures would be undertaken by private enterprise, and that really unprofitable ventures would, in the absence or failure of private enterprise, have to be assumed by public enterprise. Many public entrepreneurs could never be profitable, but their unprofitability might well result in the profitability of private enterprise through uneconomic provision of public utilities. Those that could be made profitable in the commercial sense may be deliberately run at a loss for political reasons. The government may prefer uniform, national, egalitarian services to discrimination between consumers. It may force public employers to bear the social costs of employing people whom nobody else is willing to employ or to adopt processes, methods, experiments, and innovations that nobody else is willing to undertake. It may deliberately restrict the monopoly power of public entrepreneurs and force them to provide cheap public services, subsidize political ventures, invest in unprofitable areas to provide employment or act as national carriers, and spare foreign currency. The remainder of public entrepreneurs who do make a profit may not reveal their true costs to the community. They may be sheltered by favorable treasury loans, tax exemptions, free land grants, legal monopoly, or higher protective tariffs. Competitors, if allowed, may be able to outperform them. Their social costs may be discounted, even though they may be among the worst offenders in spoiling the environment.

More important than profits is the efficacy of public entrepreneurs, not only from the internal view of productivity and market response, but also from the external view of opportunity costs, societal values, and political responsibility. Entrepreneurial efficacy may detract from communal efficacy in the pursuit of profits, higher productivity, empire building, and prestige. It can be wasteful, divergent from the community's real wishes, and unresponsive to clientele wishes. But efficacy is a much abused word. It has been defined variously as "maximum return with minimum outlay," "ratio of energy output to energy input," "ratio of performance to standard or average performance," "relation between what is accomplished with what could be accomplished," "ratio of means to results," "mimimum opportunity costs." Until national accounting systems are further developed, there is no way of calculating external efficacy. On the other hand, elaborate indices now exist by which the internal efficacy of an enterprise, public or private, can be measured, and new measures are being evolved to gauge objectives, results, and optimum means. If health cannot be measured, it is possible to examine the results of the activities undertaken in pursuit of health, such as the effect of drugs, the reduction of communicable disease, the average duration (in days) of annual sickness per person, and the number of medical examinations per person per doctor. Such measures do not possess much significance in themselves until they are compared with other cultures, past experiences, and planned estimates. They can be used to evaluate the comparative worth of private and public entrepreneurs. Moreover, they could eventually give much needed information concerning the ethics of frugality, the prevention of waste in irreplaceable resources, the elimination of the needless exploitation of human labor (and beasts of burden too), the assessment of the social costs of an acquisitive society and the economic wastes of affluence, the preservation of human life, the gap between rich and poor countries, consumer protection against monopoly exploitation, shoddy workmanship and unethical business practices, better services, and an educated public opinion.

The construction of more sophisticated measures requires much valuable investment in research and development and imposes on all enterprise considerable accounting burdens for problematical results. The search may undermine public confidence in major institutions that are considered solid pillars of respectability and efficiency. Few people are engaged in such work, but the idea is growing that there ought to be a full-time professional unit that would be engaged on the continuous investigation of the organization, administration, and operation of public entrepreneurs and that might also apply itself to private entrepreneurs confident enough to expose their internal affairs to outside scrutiny. In Israel, for instance, the State

Comptroller's Office investigates the performance of all bodies receiving public monies and is evolving norms for public administration.[6] In the United Kingdom, the National Economic Development Council's functions include the examination of economic performance, the consideration of obstacles to quicker growth and improved efficiency, and the search for ways of improving economic performance, competitive performance, and efficiency. Such bodies might eventually give some nonpolitical indicators as to which governmental activities should be contracted to private enterprise or performed by public entrepreneurs. In 1939, Lewis wrote as follows:

> The "basic merits" of private ownership versus public ownership have been debated endlessly, emotionally, and apart from particular factual situations, quite fruitlessly, for many years. . . . One would like to be able to weigh these arguments definitively, or to be able to turn to quantitative data which would settle the public-private ownership controversy beyond question for all times and places. Needless to say, however, such data are not available, and, apart from its settlement as part of some broad program undertaken on general philosophic grounds for at least a major portion of the entire economic system, the problem seems destined to receive only piecemeal answers in particular areas in light largely of particular, local considerations.[7]

Nothing seems to have changed in the meantime. A United Nations survey in 1968 complained about the difficulty of quantification, definition, categorization, and comparability, and pointed out that the most important measure would be the strategic role played by public enterprise in economic development, even though its actual extent "measured by direct contribution to the GNP or amount of employment generated or some other index, may be very modest."[8] In some countries, public and private enterprises are encouraged to compete against one another; in other countries, they complement one another, and competition is discouraged. The situation is further complicated by transitional and temporary mixed enterprises, which have assumed the characteristics of permanency; the nationalization and denationalization of industries with changes in government; and the growth of exotic forms of economic enterprise in developmental regimes.

The danger in public contracting and public enterprises is that, instead of getting the best of both private and public worlds, the fusion of entrepreneurial incentives and public controls, a community may find itself with the worst, namely, private exploitation by partisan bureau-paths. The form is less important than the spirit in which contracts and enterprises are administered. Much depends on the quality and motivation of contractors and public entrepreneurs, the expectations and norms of public authorities

---

[6] M. Gilon, ed., *Norms for Public Administration.* Jerusalem: State Comptroller's Office, 1969.

[7] B. W. Lewis, in L. S. Lyon and V. Abramson, *Government and Economic Life,* Vol. II. Washington, D.C.: The Brookings Institution, 1939, pp. 734–735.

[8] United Nations, *Organization and Administration of Public Enterprises.* New York, ST/TAO/M/36, 1968, p. 3.

that let contracts and supervise public entrepreneurs, and the conceptions and evaluations of the political leaders and the community at large. If contractors and public entrepreneurs disappoint expectations, the fault may not be theirs alone. Expectations may be too high, the functions may be too difficult to perform, or public self-images may bear no relation to actual behavior. Countries that have grappled with the real problems as to where to draw the line between public control and private initiative have encountered considerable difficulty in striking the right balance from business to business. Those that have oversimplified the issue have made their contractors and public entrepreneurs convenient scapegoats for political irresponsibility and communal apathy.

8

Public Finance

Although the structure and processes of public finance may resemble those of private finance, they work in a vastly different environment and with different objectives. For a start, public finances are public documents and public knowledge, at least in nondictatorial regimes. The public, if it desires, can obtain financial details about every public position, contract, purchase, and sale outside security areas, and it may demand a public inquiry into the financial administration of any public authority when dissatisfied with the conduct of its affairs. Although in practice few people understand public budgets, and fewer still realize their powers in seeking explanations, many private bodies would never disclose any details if they were not obliged to by law, and, unlike public bodies, they can deny access where not required by law. The bulk of public expenditures not incurred by self-contained public enterprises is spent on nonmeasurable communal goods and services according to political directives. Most public income is raised by compulsory taxes or forced loans to match expenditures, not to accumulate a surplus. On the contrary, most governments incur large debts and take only token action to reduce them. To ensure that public monies are properly spent, numerous checks are imposed at every stage, and public officials may be obliged to replace missing sums. Receipts are issued for every transaction. These receipts are checked and counterchecked, recorded and stored, examined and audited. The red tape of financial administration, the rigid procedures, the inflexible guidelines, and the strict attention to detail may be largely responsible for projected bureau-pathologic images of public administration (see Chap. 1).

Public finance is considered dull, a province for accounting experts. But for anyone who can master simple arithmetic, public finance is an exciting area for study and is far from revealing its secrets. Under review is a significant portion of the national income, from a low of about 5 percent in low income countries to a high of 95 percent in wartime communist regimes, and between 25 percent and 40 percent in western democracies. Public finance encompasses major blocs of public spending on defense, social welfare, public works, and subsidization of private efforts. It is a major determinant of equality through income redistribution and the provision of freely accessible communal products. It is the principal tool of economic policy and national development. It is a laboratory for experiments in measuring the seemingly immeasurable. It is an area in which outsiders have the greatest potential opportunity within public administration for aiding insiders and in which they have shown the least inclination to assist.

Proportionately more financial resources are flowing through the hands of public authorities the world over now than at any other point in human history. More significantly, public expenditures are increasing at a faster rate than the total available resources of a community in most developing countries. In the United States of America, the world's largest economy, per capita government (federal, state, and local) public expenditures have increased from $21 in 1902 to exceed $1500 in 1969, while per capita tax receipts have risen from $18 to over $1150, and the public debt has accumulated from about $3.25 billion ($41 per capita) to top $500 billion (over $2480 per capita) in the same period.[1] In 1950, the gross national product amounted to $256.5 billion, of which government expenditures accounted for about $61 billion (21.3 percent). Less than twenty years later, the gross national product had topped $850 billion, of which the public sector's share had increased to over 30 percent. In the 1950s, the gross national product grew at an annual average rate of 7.7 percent, compared with 6.4 percent in the private sector and 16.3 percent in the public sector. In the 1960s, the figures for the gross national product and the private sector were about the same, but the public sector had dropped to about 10 percent, still a significantly higher rate.

Within the American public sector, at the opening of the twentieth century, local governments accounted for over 55 percent of government costs, compared with about 11 percent by the states and 33 percent by the federal government. In the 1930s, the federal government's share had risen to about 50 percent, local governments had fallen to 28 percent, but state governments had risen to 22 percent. Since 1950, the figures have stabilized at 63 to 65

---

[1] *Facts and Figures on Government Finance.* New York: Tax Foundation, Inc., 1970.

percent for the federal government, 17 to 19 percent for local governments, and 16 to 17 percent for the states. In functional terms, taking 1967 as a sample year, in which public finances reached $259 billion, $75 billion was spent on defense (all federal), $41 billion on education ($29 billion by local governments, $9 billion by states), $19 billion on health and welfare ($7 billion by states, $7 billion by local governments), $14 billion on highways ($9 billion by states, $5 billion by local governments), $13 billion on debt interest ($10 billion federal), and $10 billion on natural resources ($8 billion federal). Out of $59 billion spent by the states, $19 billion was granted to local governments, compared with $2 billion by the federal government, which granted $13 billion to the states from its $167 billion budget. In addition, $33 billion was spent on government insurance schemes, $24 billion on social security alone. Large though these sums are, a considerable portion receives little open scrutiny (for example, defense, insurance funds, grants, public enterprises), or it is so presented by formidable bureaucratic experts to amateur politicians in packaged budgets that only cursory attention is given to the details. Yet these are not random figures; they constitute a map of public spending to ensure the safety, well-being, and progress of the American community.

The recital of imposing statistics shows how easy it is to slip into elaborate descriptions of government budgets in detail, piling figure after figure on minds used to dealing in far smaller amounts. That the Department of Defense rounds off estimates to the nearest $50 million is barely comprehensible to people who will never handle more than a fiftieth of that sum in the whole of their lives. These huge sums in public finance represent thousands of fully equipped military personnel stationed abroad and scattered across the country, hundreds of new schools fully staffed and equipped, miles of new highways and bridges, thousands of poverty-stricken welfare recipients, acres of parks and woodlands, round-the-clock police patrols, hundreds of research laboratories searching for solutions to contemporary problems, and no doubt some political graft and a few official boondoggles. Behind all this are indignant taxpayers who are being unfairly assessed or paying too high a portion of their incomes, while others avoid their rightful share; harassed officials who are seeking to prevent tax loopholes and to improve public services; shrewd manipulators who amass scarce resources for their pet projects, while more needy programs go short; careful accountants and auditors who search for illegality, waste, imprudence, and extravagance; and confused politicians who are trying to decide on priorities and to assess how the limited public budget can be stretched to meet all demands equitably. Stockbrokers watch for shifts in public finance. So do bankers, entrepreneurs, traders, investors, and trade unionists. Welfare recipients hope for pension increases. Small savers hope for higher interest rates on government bonds. Shoppers hope for a reduction in the sales tax. Motorists hope for lower license and registration fees. Whether they know it or not, all are engrossed in public finance.

THE VORACIOUS GOVERNMENT

Governments invariably complain they are short of money; they never have enough to accomplish all that they wish. Defense is a bottomless pit. A country can acquire more and more of the latest-model missiles, airplanes, ships, and tanks without ever using any of them. Likewise, the needy can never be satisfied. The extent of world poverty makes existing redistributive efforts through international aid, social welfare payments, and progressive direct taxation seem rather puny. Urban renewal, highways, environmental health, leisure facilities, price supports, and airports are random samples of inexhaustible public expenditures. All are needed. All are universally supported. All should be increased—if only resources were sufficient to satisfy these and all other societal demands, but they are not. It is a matter of the highest political significance which societal demands receive priority and how available resources are distributed. In the Soviet Union in the 1920s private consumption was deliberately restricted to build up heavy industries. In the 1950s Galbraith drew attention to private affluence and public poverty in the United States. In the 1960s, low income countries were faced with a grim choice between alleviating rural starvation or urban starvation, or sacrificing population to invest resources elsewhere. Relative affluence does not diminish competition for resources or choice between alternatives; it enables more demands to be met and reduces the emotional strain in choosing.

Over the past century, a definite trend toward increased public expenditures has been experienced, more markedly in high- than low-income countries, for the following reasons.

Economic Growth

Continuous and stable economic growth requires more investment in the economic infrastructure areas such as education, technology, social welfare, and public utilities, as a prerequisite to expansion. Economic growth enables prospering communities to divert more resources away from personal consumption to communal investment and public goods, and to tolerate compulsory income redistribution through government. High public investment and increased propensity to consume, brought about by income redistribution, promote economic growth in a process of circular causation that makes the high-income countries richer, while the spin-off effects in low-income countries are absorbed by population growth itself, partly induced by poverty and paucity of public goods.

Population Growth

Public goods have to be provided to more people, and public expenditures must increase if the same (let alone better) quality service is expected. More children must be taught. More literate citizens must have access to the postal system. More people must be provided shelter and employment, policed, taxed, defended, medically treated, and vaccinated. Once a public service is provided, after heated political struggles, it is rarely discontinued. More likely, beneficiaries demand more and better services, and nonbeneficiaries demand that existing services be extended to them.

Technological Growth

Improved techniques enable the community to do things that individuals could not attempt. Technology requires improved public safeguards against malfunctioning and environmental destruction. Within each public function, technological transformations demand higher public investments. Technological advancement gives rise to new demands that may be satisfied only by the public sector.

War

Rarely has the planet been completely free of warfare between men. Wherever fighting has taken place, the people affected have been prepared to make almost any sacrifices, financial and otherwise, to ensure survival. At the time, their political valuations have been transformed to favor public expenditures, and they have never quite returned to previous patterns of expenditure. War in itself reminds people of the need for public goods and promotes greater community awareness, which permits the higher level of taxation incurred in wartime to stick, or at least to remain above prewar levels. New forms of taxation are not easily abandoned, and the debts accumulated in war have to be serviced afterward. War is a great equalizer, and it is during crisis that societal ills cannot be denied. In this sense war is a principal cause of social progress. It reveals intolerable social deficiencies and strengthens the resolve of all those making sacrifices for the common effort to change things when peace is restored. Small-scale crises—riots, natural disasters, horrifying accidents, revolts—have much the same effect, but on a local scale.

Political Demands

Increased political participation and the spread of mass political movements have steered the nature of the demands placed on the political system toward public goods, rather than subsidization of private interests. The most significant development has been the pressure for social services, particularly education, health and welfare, extending into redeployment, public housing, slum clearance, and leisure facilities. The ability to meet new political demands has been aided by economic growth, stable taxation rates (which automatically return a share of private economic growth to the government), vastly improved revenue administration, increased concessions by the wealthy to the public weal, and more efficient disbursement of govern-mental resources, that is, better value for public money.

None of these reasons is likely to diminish in effect sufficiently to bring about a dramatic reversal in public-expenditure trends. Peace would re-lease sizable resources for other purposes, and world security might reduce taxation needs, in which case private consumption would increase if govern-ments did not divert saved resources into other public goods. Population growth, too, may be halted or at least controlled, particularly in poor coun-tries, and resources used for the extension of existing public services could be used for improving their quality or for other purposes. On the other hand, the revolution of rising expectations sooner or later will be reflected in political demands that will aid economic and technological growth. War neurosis is aided by instant news relayed by mass media and the ineffec-tiveness of disarmament treaties and world councils to diminish national rivalries, international power plays, arms production and distribution, and terrorism. Economic recessions, which only temporarily reduce public finances, will provoke a swing away from private enterprise. Rulers also like to keep something in hand to protect their position. On balance, public expenditures will continue to increase at a faster rate than private expen-ditures and national income, and public revenues will experience increas-ingly centralized administration.

The rate of increase is limited by political opposition to rising public ex-penditures and taxes, and by political and administrative checks on public disbursements. Within western democracies, a hard core of laissez-faire anti-statists survives in positions of considerable influence in the business world, property, club land, and high society. A natural ally is new capital seeking to preserve newly found riches from the tax collector. Both old and new capital have much to lose from high taxation, although in fact thay are wealthy and experienced enough not only to know the loopholes, but also to benefit from increased public expenditures on contracts and subsidies. Their opposition is based on principle. Middle-class resistance is a matter of tax incidence. While the very rich can in some degree escape the tax collector, the middle classes bear a disproportionate share of the tax burden. Few relate what they contribute to government to what they receive from government. Many would prefer to spend their own money their own way, rather than have the state decide for them. Their willingness to permit further taxation constitutes the psychological measure of tolerable taxation. Their hostility to further taxation determines the ceiling or the limit of reasonable taxation, beyond which the politician risks his political future as the middle classes tend to switch to those who promise to curb taxation rates or return taxes. The taxpayers' revolt, however, rarely expresses itself in open refusal to pay taxes (impossible where taxes are deducted at source) or violent protest demonstrations, as organized, for instance, by the French farmers and rural bourgeois. It shows itself at the ballot box and in the correspondence columns of the press, in less publicized curt notes to tax collectors and politicians, and through a greater propensity to tax evasion and white-collar crime. The low-income classes resent all taxes, which they claim they can ill afford, compared to richer folk. In short, nobody enjoys paying taxes, but most people have little choice other than to express their resentment in petty ways or through the ballot. While theoretically there may be no limit to what the traffic can bear, a psychological barrier must be overcome to increase taxation rates.

The other major limitation to public finance is the existence of numerous checks built into the public finance system to ensure that public authorities are not extravagant with public monies. Politically, the most important is the principle of "no taxation without representation," that is, the raising of taxes requires authorization by representative assemblies. In many countries, legislative control is only a formality. Elected representatives cannot alter the government's budget by as much as a cent and have no part in determining expenditures. They can decide taxation rates, but in practice they vote on proposals formulated and submitted by the executive, which is assured of majority support beforehand. In some countries, particularly the United States of America, the legislature takes its financial powers seriously. It can alter the executive's budget and vote monies independently of executive demands. It can question public officials and scrutinize all budget items, either directly through subcommittees or indirectly through agents such as the State Comptroller or Comptroller-General. It can alter all taxation proposals and decide taxation rates of its own. The executive branch may have to tailor its expenditures to match legislative enactment, unless it can bypass legal controls through back-door credits. Moreover, legislatures are not usually noted for their generosity. They want economical government, paring expenditures to a minimum (where voters are hostile to high taxes), or to a minimum consistent with good performance (where voters want value for their money). They demand responsible financial management in the executive. In practice, they are not keen on effective executive management that threatens to cut away their political supports and personal gains.

In the executive, the key position is the finance portfolio, which overviews the magnitude, scope, and quality of public services. In an organizational society, voluntarism can achieve little. Nobody can do much without funds. No contracts can be let, no staff hired, no supplies purchased, no accommodation rented, no communications sent. Power of the purse gives financial administration a whip hand over all other aspects of executive management. Financial administrators realize their power. They are reputed to be rather conservative, if not parsimonious. Scrupulous regard for public property is drilled into them by their political masters and their code of professional ethics. They are among the most honest of public officials, and their job is to ensure that others follow their example or forfeit their trust. They stand little nonsense, and when in doubt, they play for safety by refusing requests. To the rest of government, they appear negative, always suspicious of new proposals and radical departures from set patterns, always revising, over-hauling, checking, changing, and generally interfering in matters beyond their functional expertise. In fact, the severe image is somewhat overdrawn. Nonetheless, the fact that it exists testifies to the internal limitations on public expenditures enforced by financial administrators.

Actually, most public officials share the same outlook as the financial administrators. They are honest, law-abiding, prudent, and moderate in financial matters. Naturally there are some individuals who fall below ex-pected standards, as there are everywhere. But as the financial system is constructed on the assumption that public officials cannot be trusted, few slip through the net, and when they do, the whole public service suffers from the moral opprobrium. So careful are public officials that the public they serve has long trusted their accuracy and honesty in financial matters and come to rely on public records in private business.

None of this applies, however, where corruption is a way of life and where the whole governmental apparatus is rotten from top to bottom and where public office is looked upon as a means for exploiting public power for per-sonal profit. Public services are deliberately neglected to save expenses. Public revenues are diverted to private pockets. The rich find it cheaper to pay bribes than taxes, while the poor are deprived of anything they cannot hide from the tax collectors. Public records are make-believe, and no figures can be trusted. In such circumstances, controls are meaningless. Effective financial administration would need a considerable prior improvement in public morality, accompanied by stringent sanctions against violations of financial legislation and professional ethics.

MEETING GOVERNMENTAL COSTS

Reluctant to pay taxes, people may find themselves paying for public admin-istration in other ways far less convenient or effective, as the following tech-niques for meeting governmental costs indicate.

Debasement of Currency

When the government runs short of money, all it needs to do is to make it. In medieval days, monarchs did just that. They gained a monopoly over currency, and whenever they needed to pay off debts, they manufactured more money or altered the balance of precious metals in the coinage. Just after World War I, the German government printed money at such a rate that the resulting inflation was one of the most spectacular of its kind. No-body could trust the currency, and bank notes were waste paper. The debase-ment of currency remains a significant feature of low-income countries, where internally the citizens hoard the international currency of precious metals instead, and externally, the country frequently devalues its foreign-exchange rates. In developed countries, inflation has the same effect. The government overcommits the economy, incurs persistent budget deficits, and injects money and credit into the banking system through central bank operations. The prime indicators of currency debasement are the net release of income (the government's direct contribution to purchasing power and the multiplier effects therefrom), the net absorption of capital funds (the government's withdrawals from the money and capital markets), and the conversion of capital into income (the excess of income released over capital absorption without changes in the government's cash balance and currency debasement).

Borrowing Credit

Often medieval monarchs found themselves in the debt of merchant bankers and money lenders from whom they had borrowed. Today, poor countries find themselves similarly in debt to rich countries or international bankers (both public and private) and hope to extricate themselves without the dire consequences that befell the medieval monarchs. In poor countries, revolutionaries have threatened to renounce all foreign debts, and some have done so on taking office, only to find that their nonexistent credit rating has virtually ruled them out of international money markets, except upon terms that undermined the country's sovereignty. Repudiating foreign debts turns out to be a short-sighted policy.

More importantly, every country borrows from its citizens by floating loans and generally obtaining credit to the extent indicated by public debts. The great bulk of the national debt in most developed countries represents the costs of wars, the remainder being incurred on large capital projects, weapons procurement, and the slow accumulation of peacetime deficits. Huge as it is, the national debt should be compared with the debt incurred by private business and individuals. In the United States of America, for example, the gross public debt amounted to $441 billion for an average of $2228 per capita in 1967. The net public debt (the gross debt, less duplicated public and private debts) was $411 billion, compared with $1008 billion private debt incurred by business ($534 billion), on private mortgages ($291 billion) and other private debts ($183 billion).[2] In 1929, on the eve of the Great Depression, public debt had been $30 billion, compared with $161 billion in the private sector, incurred by business ($89 billion), mortgages ($41 billion), and other debts ($31 billion), while in 1945, after the conclusion of World War II, public debt was $266 billion, and private debt was $140 billion. Thus, while public debt had increased between 1929 and 1967 nearly fourteen-fold, private debt had increased six-fold, but after 1945 public debt had increased by about 51 percent (the congressionally controlled national debt rising by 14 percent compared to a 727 percent rise in local and state government debt), and private debt had grown by 620 percent. To pay off all these sums would absorb approximately two years of national income at

[2] *Facts and Figures on Government Finance,* p. 64.

current rates, about the same as it would have done in 1929 and 1945. Debts rise proportionately with economic growth.

The public debt is often thought of as a wild extravagance by past generations, to be paid for by future generations. Actually much of it represents savings obtained at the time that are repayable at a future date on which an interest is paid. Like private businesses and individuals, governments continue to borrow as long as they can meet the interest payments from taxation. Governments could repay the public debt by printing money (and creating economic havoc) or by raising taxes (and creating political furor). The former policy would only result in transfer payments between bond holders and would reduce the purchasing power of non-bond holders. The latter policy would only result in the transfer of money from taxpayers to bond holders and would probably deny the poor for the sake of the rich, as the principal bond holders are composed of banks, insurance houses, and wealthier individuals, unlikely to make free presents to non-bond holders or other taxpayers. Not only would some people be giving themselves back money, but the government would also be giving itself money back, because public authorities hold significant portions of public debt, and taxation would automatically return a good proportion of increased private income. In fact, there is a stronger case for increasing the public debt during inflation to reduce liquidity and private consumption, and at other times to increase the supply of public products in place of the private products that might otherwise result from private investment. Either way, preference is given to long-term maturity rather than short-term debt, depending on current interest rates and the outflow of domestic capital to foreign countries.

The sheer volume of public loans to finance capital projects and to keep public authorities liquid during the course of the budget year, when receipts and expenditures are unlikely to match, has an important, if not predominant, influence on money and capital markets. Public loans are secure. As little risk of default is involved, they are attractive to the less speculative investors. In size, they tower over the loans raised by private businesses and inhibit the capacity of private enterprise in raising new capital on the open market. Most large businesses tend to finance their growth from receipts, that is, excess profit margins paid by the consumer, or to seek government loans and subsidies at below-market rates. Thus, public debt management is not a simple matter of attending to the issue and redemption of public loans, but a complicated business of managing economic growth, capital markets, liquidity, credit facilities, forced savings, and advance refundings.

Taxation

Except for forced loans, which are a form of taxation (even when repayable at a later date), contribution to public loans are voluntary and remunerative. Taxation is compulsory ("nothing is certain but death and taxes") and without monetary incentives to contribute, apart from small rebates for swift payment.

The payments are individual; the returns are communal. Everyone knows how much he has to pay and what percentage of his income and wealth is extracted annually, but nobody really knows how much he receives back in nonmeasurable public products, how much he personally benefits from government, or whether he would live a better life by contributiong more or less in taxes to public authorities. For instance, do people receive more value from what they buy from a local store, compared with the equivalent in taxes provided by public authorities? The very rich claim they do, the very poor claim they do not. But how long would the rich last if there were no police force to prevent poor people from expropriating their wealth for themselves, or no military force to ward off external invaders who would burn or steal their property and enslave them? Would the very poor, if deprived of social-welfare payments, seek employment and pull themselves up by their own bootstraps (assuming they could work and that sufficient employment were available), or would they perish or, with nothing to lose, simply revolt? Is the state a tool of the capitalist class to protect property and support labor exploitation, as communists maintain, or is it a tool of the dispossessed to extract from the able that which does not rightfully belong to them, as ultra-conservatives claim? However the issue is seen, the fact remains that most people want more from government, but few people are prepared to meet the costs. While searching to avoid tax payments, taxpayers complain about inadequate public services. "The only good tax is one that is paid by someone else."[3]

The perfect tax would raise maximum revenue at lowest administrative costs, would be simple to understand and operate but difficult to evade, would be just to the taxpayers without adversely affecting their propensity to save, invest, and work, and would act an as economic stabilizer. No such tax exists. Instead, governments adopt a variety of taxes, combining different virtues, but also possessing dysfunctions. The ingenuity of tax collectors in devising new sources of revenue is matched only by the ingenuity of tax evaders. At the present time, taxes are imposed on property, imports and exports, retail sales, business profits, personal income, capital appreciation, land-value appreciation, harmful products, leisure pursuits and entertainment, pets, vehicles and gasoline, luxuries, wealth at death, presents, trust funds, royalties, mines, patents, air transportation, public-utility services, telephone calls, foreign travel, foreign currency, canal users, port and harbor facilities, pensions, insurance premiums, club dues and initiation fees, wagers and bets, coin-operated machines, foodstuffs, safe-deposit boxes, and stock-exchange transactions. Several tax administrators and economists have advocated tax simplification and consolidation. Among the most popular proposals are a wealth or net-worth tax that would be imposed annually, not just at death, on the citizen's taxable assets less his indebtedness, and an expenditure (or

---

[3] J. P. Wernette, *Government and Business.* New York: Crowell Collier & Macmillan, 1964, p. 123.

spendings) tax, which, it is claimed, would be a step toward egalitarianism, while improving the efficiency of operation and rate of progress of the economy.[4] The simplification of tax administration would reduce the amount of overlapping that occurs when different levels of government tax the same source, much to the annoyance of the taxpayer who has to duplicate his records and pay for double administration. On the other hand, it would vastly complicate the distribution of tax revenue between levels of government, already complicated by the growth of intergovernmental loans and grants to reduce local disparities between taxable capacity and public expenditure.

In tax policy, a theoretical distinction is drawn between direct taxes levied on persons or businesses on the basis of income or wealth, which, through progressive rates, are egalitarian, and indirect taxes, levied on transactions involving expenditure, which usually do not discriminate between buyers and sellers and are not considered to be egalitarian. The distinction is difficult to apply. Whereas income taxes and estate taxes are obviously direct, and purchase taxes, sales taxes, and excise taxes are obviously indirect, property taxes can be considered a tax on the consumption of immovable property and therefore direct, although they have the characteristics of indirect taxes. Legal payers should be distinguished from economic payers. The taxes are levied on the former, but they are actually paid by the latter. Thus, landlords pass on their property taxes to tenants, and corporations shift their tax burdens to consumers, though the economic payers may not be conscious that they are paying someone else's tax bill. In comparing tax systems, the respective proportions of direct and indirect taxes, even allowing for inaccurate and imprecise classification, are no real indicators of tax incidence without a further comparison of rates, exemptions, evasion, nature of the economy, employment rate, and political system. In an underemployed economy, direct taxes will be preferred to indirect taxes in order to promote economic growth, whereas in full-employment economies, indirect taxes rather than direct taxes will achieve the same objective. In trade cycles, indirect taxes are more volatile than direct taxes, which act as economic stabilizers. Both kinds tend to be rigid instruments, and tax systems as a whole are difficult to alter, partly because they are so complex, partly because they are so integrated with economic policy, and partly because nobody really can agree what should be done and to whom the tax burden should be shifted.

Surpluses Made on the Sale of Public Products

Self-contained public enterprises may be obliged to contribute their surpluses to the treasury for redistribution to needy public authorities. Indeed, governments may deliberately encourage public entrepreneurs to divert profitable

---

[4] N. Kaldor, *An Expenditure Tax.* London: G. Allen and Unwin, 1955, p. 17.

business away from private enterprise to subsidize public services without increasing taxes or loans. The same objective is obtained by the sale of public lands or the leasing of public domain to private entrepreneurs. The Alaskan government raised nearly a billion dollars in this way in 1969, by leasing land to oil companies. Other sales of public products, though useful contributions, do not cover expenses.

It is becoming rarer to separate these four major sources of public revenues, except for classification purposes, as they are usually handled by the same public authority, namely, the treasury, directly or through subordinate agencies. The close operation of all revenue sources promotes the budget concept.

THE BUDGET

The relatively simple notion that all revenues should be placed into a centrally managed fund, from which all expenditures would be drawn, has gradually been adopted by bureaucratic states as the most advantageous method of organizing public finance. The aim is to present a clear picture not only of all revenues, expenditures and reserves, but also a coordinated map of public policy. It assumes that legislatures do not create autonomous revenue funds designated for specific purposes, that public authorities do not insist on self-financing, that adequate central staff are competent to design meaningful budget maps and maintain control of the whole system through a decentralized network of subordinates, and that political overseers prefer to deal with a consolidated budget, rather than many smaller budgets designed to serve special purposes. These assumptions are not fulfilled in local government, where financial officers may be elected, certain taxes may be maintained in a separate fund for use only on designated functions, standard definitions and classifications may not be used in the separate budgets, financial administration may be loosely coordinated, and budget approval may be obtained directly from the voters or taxpayers. In contrast, the budget concept envisages that the budget is planned by the career officials; assembled, coordinated, and standardized by a budget agency; submitted to the political overseers for approval; and relayed to the legislature for concurrence and official execution supervised by the budget agency. The central position of the budget agency enables it to perform economic-policy functions, budget planning, purchasing, taxation, accounting, efficiency audit, and personnel control in a super-housekeeping organization.

To simplify any description of the budgetary process, the institutional environment—the nature of the economy, the size of the public sector, the political and constitutional arrangements, the location and powers of the budget agency, and the number and functions of operating agencies—is assumed as given. In practice, the budgetary process is open, and environmental changes will continually influence the behavior of participants.

Estimates

Operating agencies review their current programs and projects, scrutinize continuing functions, and map in detail likely possible changes in the forth-coming financial year. Regional and local offices submit their financial plans, while the head office anticipates work load, policy changes, new legislation, executive reorganization, price movements, contract terms, and staffing needs. In routine activities, the short-run future can be planned quite accu-rately, and major construction projects can be mapped out in great detail. In other areas, forecasting is mostly guesswork based on hunch, political trends, public opinion, professional shoptalk, and wishful thinking. Expe-rienced administrators have a shrewd idea of how much they can request without too many questions being asked, and they make assessments beyond that about the political feasibility of anything extra having regard to govern-ment policy, budget directives, political supports and obstacles, pressure group influences, budgeting strategies, and personalities in the budgetary process.

Budget Planning

Before the estimates are submitted by operating agencies, the budgeting authority prepares a preliminary model of its expectations of the final out-come based on past performance, knowledge of government thinking, eco-nomic trends, and fiscal policy. The model is tentative and is altered as more precise intelligence comes to hand. The submitted estimates are compared against the preliminary plan, and where they differ widely, the parties discuss contrasting estimates, while budgeting officers search for possible padding and carry-over. The operating agency may be informed that its estimates must be reduced, or the budget agency, on checking the figures and the political directives, may revise its plan upward and search for adjustments elsewhere. The process of reconciliation may be extended as the final budget plan takes shape, but outstanding issues may be left open for political author-ization.

Political Authorization

The budget plan is debated by the political overseers, with the assistance of operating agencies, budget agency, and any other party the politicians want to consult. It may be radically altered, and much work may have to be redone by operating agencies and budget agency to readjust plans and estimates according to political directives. Much depends on the polity. In Britain, the Chancellor of the Exchequer has a free hand in constructing the budget, and until recently showed it to Cabinet more as a courtesy gesture on his part than as a deliberative council on its part. His plan is submitted to Parliament for formal approval and, to prevent speculation, many measures have instant effect. In western European coalition governments, the budget is hotly disputed in the Cabinet, and there is no guarantee that the plan submitted to Parliament will be accepted in detail. In the United States, at federal level, the budget is framed within the executive and submitted by the President to Congress without any guarantee that it will be accepted in whole or part by both chambers.

Budget Management

Before consolidated funds existed, revenue collectors maintained their own funds, often with personal gain and risks to public money. Now the consolidated funds are placed in safekeeping and earn a return of their own. The management of the consolidated funds, involving receipt of funds and authorization of expenditures according to the Appropriations Act, may be separated from budget preparation, but usually it is not. Budget management involves elaborate accounting and audit, governed by detailed financial laws, elaborate instruction manuals, complex filing procedures, and a great detail of *paperasserie*. The budget-management authority employs a large army, both at the central office and in the field, where each operating agency has an even larger staff of financial officers—bookkeepers, auditors, inspectors, analysts, programmers—to keep track of every financial transaction, from receipt of funds from clientele fees and purchases, leases, taxes, and so on, to disbursement of funds to contractors, suppliers, welfare recipients, and staff. The magnitude of the task can be illustrated by impressive statistics, but it suffices to say that central government budgets account for a sizable portion of the community's financial transactions in value if not volume, and they probably exceed capacity for thorough annual review of every item. Correspondingly, the opportunities for abuse are great, and the elaborate precautions to minimize fraud, misappropriation, illegal expenditures, theft, and genuine mistakes add even further to the complexity. Tolerable seepage varies from country to country, public authority to public authority, administrative unit to administrative unit, even supervisor to supervisor. In most countries, the public and the public officials have reason to be proud of the little that does escape attention, compared with nongovernmental institutions, even where appropriations are not itemized in detail.

Budget management is more than appropriation control. The Appropriations Act authorizes expenditures, it does not compel expenditures, and budget managers ensure that only necessary expenditures are incurred. Their job is not merely to follow standard procedure, but to go behind form and evaluate expenditures. To certify that correct procedures have been followed is different from ascertaining whether inspected bodies have done their proper homework and from making recommendations for the rectification of defects and reforms in the administration of inspected bodies. Unfortunately, the training of budget managers still accentuates the negative, control side of the job, rather than the constructive, management side, and too few governmental accountants have sufficient experience in real estate, property management, social administration, scientific and technological research and development, and community relations work to enable them to see financial administration in context. Ripe for simplification and reform in many countries is budget management itself, where calculated risks would probably reduce the whole operation and speed the work flow, particularly in handling postal services, accounts, direct taxes, and social-welfare payments.

Post-Audit

The size, scope, and complexity of financial administration in the modern bureaucratic state exclude the likelihood of complete control. Thorough as the system is, better results would entail an even larger force of inspectors and a more elaborate checking system. Instead, greater reliance is placed on independent outside audit, which covers major items and spot-checks the remainder. How accurate were estimates, compared with final expenditures? How much waste was incurred? Where did irregularities occur? Was criminal negligence involved? The independent report is usually made public, and because it focuses on past failings, it is an indictment further distorted by mass media, which usually ignore the compliments also contained in it and the corrected procedures currently in effect.

In reviewing the budgetary process, several points deserve consideration. First, the budget serves a variety of purposes, which have to be combined in a political compromise that may serve none of them well. The budget is the principal instrument of managing a mixed-enterprise economy through fiscal policy and national economic planning. It constitutes a plan of public products and a design for income redistribution. It reflects dominant political ideologies, party compromises, and electoral promises. It is a management device for improving administration and public-policy making. Lastly, it provides the public with information about the economy, new governmental programs, debt management, economic objectives, and resource allocation between public and private sectors.

Second, in contrast to law making, budget making is a confidential process. Whereas one can discover the origins of a bill and trace different amendments to their source, outsiders do not know who frames the estimates or why they are constructed as they are. The in-fighting is not conducted in the legal draftsman's office or on the floor of the legislature, but in numerous closed meetings between budget agency and operating agencies.

It would be useful to know to what extent the United States Bureau of the Budget influences substantive policy, if at all; to what extent it overrules, curtails or amplifies agency programs; in what cases it operates without consulting the President; when an agency feels warranted in appealing Bureau decisions to the President (and why and with what success); to what extent the initial recommendations of a budget examiner against a department prevail; what strategy the departments employ to protect their estimates in the Bureau of the Budget and before the appropriations committees; and what means a President employs to protect his budget against attack or sabotage. Those who know these mysteries do not reveal them.[5]

The same sentiments are echoed around the world. In the United States, some light has been thrown on the political aspects of budgeting in A. Wildavsky, *The Politics of the Budgetary Process* (Boston: Little Brown, 1964), which attempts to uncover what really goes on behind the scenes. It is successful as far as it goes, but much ground has still to be covered.

Third, the budget is by no means a revealing document. Omitted altogether or disguised are secret funds, defense expenditures, intergovernmental transfers, capital commitments, mixed enterprises, and the operating budgets of public enterprises. Even where they are included in the budget statement, their details are not, so there is no way of telling how the proposed expenditures will be disbursed and whether they are necessary at all. The form in which the budget is presented may not distinguish between continuing and new activities, capital and working expenses, and once-and-for-all payments and long-term commitments. The headings and subheadings may be meaningless for evaluative purposes. Public authorities may manage large trust funds free of annual budget review, and they may borrow what they cannot obtain from the legislature. Back-door spending—the ability to expend from public debt receipts and revolving funds—has grown significantly in recent decades, to finance large public services in insurance, housing, credit, foreign loans, and public international banking. At local government levels, matching grants, grants-in-aid, block grants, and other intergovernmental transfers compensate for lack of public debt funding. Finally, public service salaries, pension schemes, social-welfare reimbursement formulae, and other expenditures related to cost-of-living adjustments or executive discretion are not subject to budget controls. The President's Commission on Budget Concepts in the United States in 1967 faulted the federal budget on many of these points and recommended that more information be detailed in a unified summary budget, which would include all government programs and trust funds, provide greater consistency throughout the budget in the treatment of receipts and expenditures on an accrual basis, and identify the budgetary effects of lending programs.

Fourth, the budget itself is becoming outdated in certain ways. The yearly review is too short for long-range developments and too long for fiscal adjustments in rapidly fluctuating economies. To be effective, it requires large staffs in four different areas, namely, operating agencies, budget agency, legislature, and audit office, many of whom are doing identical work on the assumption that the others cannot be trusted. Budget overheads are inflated. Classification of expenditures according to means tells little, if anything, about the purposes for which they are being employed. Estimates constructed

---

[5] L. D. White, *Introduction to the Study of Public Administration.* New York: Crowell Collier & Macmillan, 1955, p. 266.

according to means promote padding and bargaining, rather than planning, economy, and rational measures of functional performance. The budget tends to be too rigid for the administrative flexibility required in a turbulent environment. It has already been surpassed by administrative and financial devices that exclude from outside review and control many important budget items—government by contract, trust funds, debt management, defense expenditures, back-door spending, intergovernmental financing, and capital projects.

For these reasons, the search began after World War II for alternatives to the annual budget system and improvements in the budget statement. The most important outcome has been the adoption of planning-programming-budgeting systems by the United States federal government, first embryonically in the War Production Board in 1942, more elaborately in the Department of Defense in 1961, and then generally by presidential direction in 1966, despite warnings that it might not prove transferable and that it would inflate budget overheads and complicate budgetary politics. The President was persuaded that these dysfunctions would be offset by meaningful budgets and better policy making.

PLANNING-PROGRAMMING-BUDGETING SYSTEMS (PPBS)

The most important aspect of budgeting is not the marginal alternations made by legislatures or the political bargaining over total figures, but the way the budget is put together by the operating agencies in conjunction with the budget agency. Under the annual means system, officials calculate their resource requirements over a forthcoming twelve-month period in carrying out continuing and new activities. Before World War I, such calculations were rather crude rule-of-thumb affairs. Scientific managers between the world wars began to concentrate on the end product, the program, for which the resources were needed and to work backwards through an elementary systems approach. In this way they could plan a program from the very beginning. Once they had a plan, they could experiment with prediction methods such as trend lines, synoptic narratives, and econometric graphs, to review methods such as cost-benefit analysis, and to incorporate new techniques for designing, testing, and implementing new systems in operations research. By the end of World War II, it was possible to think in terms of objectives, plan different ways of achieving the objectives, cost the plans, and arrange the costs into fairly accurate multiyear budget forecasts by program and program components, not line items.

Program budgeting was advanced by three postwar developments. The first was the enhanced role of macroeconomists in fiscal policy and budget preparation. They demanded longer-range projections of government expenditures, distinctions between current outlays and new investments, and the classification of expenditures according to major functions (or programs).

The second was the evolution of computers, whose vast storage data banks and fast retrieval systems enabled more information to be processed quickly. They speeded calculations in traditional input analysis and prompted exploration in output analysis and productivity measures. The third was the application of performance budgeting as a management tool. Following various prewar experiments, notably by C. E. Ridley and H. A. Simon (*Measuring Municipal Activities* [Chicago: International City Managers' Association, 1938], cost accounting and work measurement had been applied to governmental activities, and in 1949 the Hoover Commission recommended that work-cost measurements should be generally applied as appraisals of administrative performance. Performance budgets necessitated the reconstruction of budgets from line items to functions, activities, and programs with the emphasis on measuring input-output performance within given objectives.

The next step was to transfer attention from incremental changes in inputs and outputs to radical changes in programs still within incremental budgeting, and to search for ways of measuring the efficacy of programs in meeting governmental objectives. These, in turn, raised problems in defining objectives, framing alternative programs to satisfy objectives better, evaluating alternative programs, designing multiyear budget forecasts for each, and choosing the most feasible priority program capable of being altered for budget purposes in the light of changing circumstances. Whereas performance budgets concentrated on how things were being done, program budgets wanted to know why they were being done at all and whether they best promoted their ultimate objectives. The budget became a statement of policy, indicating choices made between competing claims (between objectives, programs, and program components) and a flexible instrument in public-policy making without replacing judgment, wisdom, and political leadership.

Planning-programming-budgeting systems are still experimental. Enthusiasts have exaggerated their revolutionary impact on governmental decision making, without convincing conservative politicans and administrators to abandon more traditional budgetary processes. They are not standardized, but they do contain common elements.

Planning

The aim is to reduce uncertainty by replacing intuition and nonrational forecasting with sustained intelligence and rational methods. PPBS attempts to broaden horizons by a continual process of preparing sets of decisions for future action, directed at achieving goals by optimum means.[6] Budget makers are encouraged to become ends-means oriented, comprehensive and future minded, and to conceive budgets in five-, even ten-year terms, allowing for changes in activities and lengthy lead-in times for new programs. They are

---

[6] Y. Dror, "The Planning Process: A Facet Design," *Internation Review of Administrative Services,* 29, No. 1 (1963), pp. 46–48.

made conscious of the continuing need for resources and the relationship between planned activities and resource competition. Multiyear budgets are constructed to show what resources will be needed five years ahead, given the anticipated level of activity with existing techniques at current costs. The danger is that the planners may be so mesmerized by their own plans that they overlook the risks and assumptions in constructing the plans, that they idolize the plans and substitute them for rethinking, that they concentrate too much on quantifiable measures and ignore qualitative measures, and that they forget that they live in a political environment in which plans are viewed as political documents, not as an embodiment of justice and wisdom. Plans are not commitments.

Clarification of Objectives

Before plans can be translated into feasible action programs, PPBS attempts to define objectives or at least to clarify what the government is attempting to do or should be doing in terms of societal objectives. Often it is found that administrators and their political masters have never thought about the ultimate purposes, and on some occasions objectives are found to be contradictory, meaningless generalizations or unattainable perfection. Otherwise, the redefinition of goals may be a useful exercise in itself in confirming current policies and reassuring staff that what they do is worthwhile and the best yet conceived by man. The budget is framed in terms of defined objectives, and programs are classified accordingly. The danger is that clarification may become a semantic exercise, or worse still, usurpation of political processes in the name of rationality and scientism. While it may point to new ways of looking at things and stimulate new approaches, it may also become a reformulation of the status quo, a check to innovation, and a search for currently acceptable objectives unrelated to future societal needs. Many governmental objectives cannot be defined, simply because no political agreement exists, or because, by their very nature, they are abstract concepts. Clarification may suggest redistribution of functions, consolidation of activities, and reorganization, such as the centralization of all health functions, but it may be cheaper, administratively more efficient, and more convenient to keep them where they are.

Suboptimization

PPBS has not yet devised techniques for optimization of the whole budget. It concentrates on maximizing benefits within stated objectives or programs, not between them. To this purpose, heavy reliance is placed on (a) systems analysis, (b) operations research, and (c) cost-benefit analysis.

Systems analysis is directed at zero-based budgeting (which assumes that it is possible to begin completely anew), by providing "decision makers with a full, accurate, and meaningful summary of the information relevant to clearly defined issues and alternatives."[7] Thinking is not confined within boundaries of existing programs and objectives, but may redefine objectives and suggest new programs.

> The essence of the method is to construct and operate within a "model," a simplified abstraction of the real situation appropriate to the question. Such a model, which may take such varied forms as computer simulation, an operational game, or even a purely verbal "scenario," introduces a precise structure and terminology that serve primarily as an effective means of communication, enabling the participants in the study to exercise their judgment and intuition in a concrete context and in proper relation to others. Moreover, through feedback from the model (the results of computation, the counter moves in the game, or the critique of the scenario), the experts have a chance to revise early judgments and thus arrive at a clearer understanding of the problem and its context, and perhaps of their subject matter.[8]

According to Quade, it is a circular process of collecting data, building models, weighing cost against effectiveness, testing for sensitivity, questioning assumptions, reexamining objectives, opening new alternatives, formulating the problem, selecting objectives, designing alternatives, collecting data, and so on, around again.[9] In this way the relevant is separated from the irrelevant, and the importance of the relevant weighed.

Operations research is similar to systems analysis, but is confined within boundaries of existing programs and objectives, and it analyzes in detail the implications of a single set of assumptions.

Cost-benefit analysis concentrates on economic measures, allowing where possible for noneconomic measures. The aim is to enable decision makers to know the cost-benefit results of alternative programs and to allow them to allocate resources between competing programs, so that the estimated marginal returns would be equal on all programs. Cost-benefit analysis identifies relevant alternatives and clarifies their respective implications. Budget makers choose the program or objective that maximizes returns.

The danger in suboptimization through these techniques is that the experts tend to forget that their analysis is always incomplete, that their measures of effectiveness are only approximate, and that their future predictions are highly suspect. They give too much weight to the measurable and neglect income redistribution, welfare, quality, and political feasibility. Too often, they measure costs and benefits from the bureaucratic standpoint, not the political, societal, cultural, or clientele viewpoints, which may be quite different.

---

[7] A. Enthoven, "Systems Analysis and the Navy," United States Naval Institute, reproduced in F. J. Lyden and E. G. Miller, eds., *Planning, Programming, Budgeting.* Chicago: Markham, 1968, p. 265.

[8] E. S. Quade, "Systems Analysis Techniques for Planning-Programming-Budgeting," Rand Corporation; reproduced in Lyden and Miller, *Planning, Programming, Budgeting,* p. 295.

[9] Lyden and Miller, *Planning, Programming, Budgeting,* p. 298.

Allocation of Resources between Competing Program Demands

Because of the similarity of the budget problem to the economic problem, economists believe they have the keys to budget analysis. At this point they run up against the noneconomic dimensions of budget making enshrined in more traditional processes—legislative control, political evaluations and compromises, political ideology, pressure group and clientele interests, bureaucratic defense mechanisms and survival ploys, personal charisma and leadership, public opinion, and so forth. Resource requirements cannot be decided according to market models or economic criteria. PPBS will recommend resource allocation according to the predominant influences in the PPBS network of experts, probably accentuating overall public interests, bureaucratic centralism, economic efficiency, and political incrementalism. How well the recommendations fare depends on political leadership, nonbureaucratic pressures, the quality of PPBS work and the status of its practitioners, and the complexity of the real-world situation in which the budget operates.

Program Budgeting

The final form of the budget shows multiyear expenditures on major objectives broken down into program structures (programs, subprograms, and program elements), indicating last year's actual costs, this year's current estimates, next year's budget estimates, program estimates for successive years, and total costs for the planning period. It identifies future-year implications. It focuses on activities as they relate to the fundamental objectives of government, regardless of organizational placement, that is, on what is right rather than who is right. It is based presumably on the best choice of alternative ways of carrying out objectives, backed by the most modern scientific tools, the finest available research talent, and the widest range of relevant data. The end product, however, may be inferior to traditional budget processes. Program budgeting does not guarantee any better decisions, particularly in rapidly changing circumstances and in unsettled policy areas. It may involve a great deal of paper work in proving the obvious or measuring the immeasurable. It probably stresses bureaucratic centralism over partisan mutual adjustment and other diffused bargaining patterns.

Is it worth while to formulate (a) program memoranda, outlining the objectives, broad strategy, major choices, and tentative recommendations with respect to all programs; (b) multiyear programs and financial plans, showing the present and future budgetary and output consequences of the current year's decisions; and (c) special studies, providing analytic basis for decisions on program issues in the memoranda? PPBS involves considerable pioneer work, new types of budget staff, reorganization of budget processes, dislocation of existing arrangements, changes in bargaining strengths in the budget process, challenge to sacred cows in budgeting, conservative staff resistance, expansion of statistical services, and diversion from other pursuits. It does not add to action capabilities (but may reduce them in the transition period), reduce political risk taking, or improve optimization (except through suboptimization, which may detract from overall objectives). Controversy rages as to whether it (a) has improved military decision making and reduced military waste (where it was first applied); (b) can be applied beyond the limited areas of military hardware and economic goods; (c) can be extended meaningfully to low-income countries; (d) implies wholesale changes in the political system away from community participation, political representation, political consensus, and politics toward rule by experts, insensitive statistocracy, and bureaucratic dictatorship, thereby provoking anti-institutional political movements that could threaten the whole fabric of society by polarizing the population into conformists and nonconformists; and (e) works at all or is just a passing fad, oversimplified, unproved, oversold, unpolitical, and maybe not much different in practice from traditional budgetary processes.[10] As with all new developments in public administration, after one generation it is too early to judge. PPBS in certain areas widens the range of choice, provides realistic and balanced plans, evaluates policy as well as performance, and provides a new way of looking at public finance. In other areas, however, it is not operational or, more accurately, no one has been able to make it work.

[10] See the symposium entitled "P. P. B. S. Reexamined," *Public Administration Review,* 29 (1969), pp. 111–202.

9

Public Service

Most public finance is spent on paying people to carry out public functions, either indirectly through contracts or directly through public service. Again, large figures are involved. At least 5 percent of the gainfully occupied work force is employed in the public service, a proportion that rises to between 15 and 30 percent in the western democracies, and over 60 percent in communist regimes. Every legitimate occupation, trade, craft, and skill can be found somewhere in the public sector. The government is the fastest growing employer; public employment expands at a higher rate than the private sector and the population as a whole, as existing activities grow and new activities are undertaken. Every year, increasing numbers of new employees can find employment only in the public sector. So far, the expansion of the public service has not resulted in any radical questioning of administrative approaches, comparable to PPBS in public finance. Behaviorally, the expansion is having an impact as the public and private sectors merge, public authorities cannot exclude potential problem cases (that is, bureaucratic nonconformists), bureaucratic power countermands effective controls, and career officials seek to improve their employment conditions. Much of the formal apparatus of public-personnel administration is based on assumptions about societal conditions that are becoming increasingly outmoded. Thus, operating agencies are devising their own informal techniques for dealing with the gap between form and reality.

Most public servants do not work at office desks. Instead, they are more likely to be found in supply and repair depots, military camps, scientific laboratories, schools, ports and harbors, and post offices. There is no typical public servant. The false image of the bureaucrat is based largely on hearsay or on a relatively small part of the public sector with which the public comes into daily contact — usually appointed, regulatory career officials, whose job it is to enforce standard laws in diverse and swiftly changing conditions. The image concentrates on those whose function is to control public actions and to prevent people from doing as they please where the repercussions have harmful community effects. Misrepresentation persists because of mass media concentration on this area of the public sector, more particularly on counter staff, that is, those directly meeting with the general public, and bureaucratic elites, often portrayed as power-hungry usurpers of political decision making. But these constitute the tip of the iceberg. The great mass of technically proficient services, public business enterprises, and orderly routine operations is overlooked or ignored, simply because it gives no cause for comment or is inaccessible to outsiders.

Academic studies of the public service also tend to be disjointed. They concentrate on the unique features of public-personnel administration, not the large areas of public administration staffing, which are conducted in much the same way as their counterparts in the private sector. More particularly, they are concerned with high-level career officials in government service, who influence political decision making. These are quite important people in the community, as attested by their social standing, occupational prestige, and remuneration. They are a relatively immobile occupational group, prone to inbreeding through specialized career channels based on functional expertise, largely self-governing in internal housekeeping functions, and subject to codes of personal conduct suitable to the public bureaucratic frameworks in which they work. They are treated differently from any other group of employees in the community. They are also subject to political direction. Their conditions of employment are governed by public laws, embodying certain basic principles such as openness, equal opportunity, just treatment, and fair geographical representation. They are expected to preserve public secrets and to show loyalty to the polity, in return for which they may be denied the political, industrial, and economic rights of other employees so as to achieve a higher level of business morality than obtained elsewhere in the community. These are good reasons for singling out the tip of the iceberg for special treatment, for despite overconcentration on this group, coverage has not been comprehensive. For instance, only insiders really know how effective training is or how promotion is conducted. Public authorities preserve their staffing secrets, and academic studies are faced with a choice of relaying information about formal rules, without revealing the practice, or omitting such topics altogether. Even so, less secrecy exists in the public sector than in private institutions, where two employees performing identical work alongside each other may not know what remuneration the other receives or how they can prepare themselves for advancement.

OFFICIALDOM

A common question asked of the public bureaucrat is "What is it like to work for the government?" No simple answer is possible. Much depends on the polity, the public authority, the function performed by the public authority, the level of the public employee in the bureaucratic hierarchy, his place of work, and the kind of work that he does. No two administrative units operate identically, even where the same routine activities are performed. No two groups are identically composed. The working atmosphere of two adjacent rooms may be quite different. The variety in public employment cannot be overstressed. Even where surface similarities in formal conditions pertain, they may conceal diametrically opposing work attitudes and perceptions of role, which prevent the presentation of a uniform picture. For instance, one person may be enthusiastic about his job because he was recently promoted; another may paint a horrifying picture of the same situation because he has been denied promotion and is working off a personal grudge. To find out what it is like to work for the government, the inquirer would have to work in the government and gain experience in different work environments. There should be sufficient variety to satisfy most wants; it is a matter of finding the right slot.

Apart from their variety, governmental organizations share certain features with all large-scale organizations. They are collections of people cooperating for specific purposes, located in the same or related buildings, subject to common rules, satisfying external interests, using resources, and producing goods and services. Remove the people, and all that remains is an empty shell, useless capital, wasting stocks, a desert. Organizations are people — what they do, think, behave, act — and how good they are depends on the quality of the people. Without them, the rest does not make sense. Even with them, the rest will not make sense unless certain basic requirements are satisfied.

First, the individuals who compose the organization must cooperate with one another, each subordinating his personal interests and sinking his differences to that extent. Cooperation, however, is not always easy to achieve even among bureaucratic peoples.

Second, the purpose of the organization must be acceptable to its members and the community, but since organizations have more than one purpose, members may differ over what they consider to be preferential purposes. To the top level manager, the purpose may be the efficient production of societal goods. To the low-level performer, it may be an escape from domestic drudgery or a means of gaining a livelihood in a monetary economy.

Third, the members must sense a common identification and belonging to develop a group spirit or differentiating in-group attitude.

Fourth, the organization must be able to command resources in addition to members.

Fifth, the transformatory process from resources to end products entails division of labor, specialization, and differential ownership. Different roles mean different contributions from different talents, for different rewards. Members must accept the existence of differences and reconcile themselves with their lot. This does not mean, however, that they will be satisfied with these arrangements or that they will accept the distribution of power embodied in the arrangements or that those with power, formal or informal, will exercise their power responsibly.

These basic conditions are achieved by bureaucratic means. The purposes are set by legislation and political directive and are further spelled out in detailed subordinate legislation and official memoranda. Each member is assigned his place in the hierarchy of command and knows what he can and cannot do, leaving a small margin unaccounted for. His formal links to his superiors and subordinates are clear, as are those with his peers. His channel of advancement is defined. His external relations are controlled by instructions. The arrangements are orderly, set to a pattern required by the nature of the activities being performed. To the newcomer, things feel very strange at first, but as he finds his feet, they become familiar and routine, and the part begins to relate to the whole. In the meantime, the member has been introduced to the informal relationships that make life easier and smoother. He learns things from the grape vine before they are confirmed in official communications. He accepts group norms and conforms to them. He cuts across formal structures by searching for informal leaders and making informal contacts during and after work. Eventually, he learns how to get around the formalities altogether.

Not all individuals can adapt themselves to the requirements of the public organization. Some people cannot adjust themselves to any organization and remain misfits in the organizational society. Where once they might have been farmers or artisans, now they drift from one organization to another, never identifying, never accepting organizational behavior, never conforming to rules and procedures, and always arguing about rights and obligations. Others put personal interests first. Having satisfied their immediate money needs, they drop out or move on to something else. Their jobs may not satisfy them or suit their talents. They may have no opportunity to develop themselves for other jobs. They may feel frustrated, search for outlets in other organizations, and eventually desert the public organization. Members may be baffled by the sheer complexity of the public organization and shield behind group defenses, resign themselves to being a pawn (so that they do not have to make the effort to understand), or strive to overcome their difficulties through self-improvement (perhaps to discover better returns elsewhere). In short, the human personality may find itself at odds with bureaucratic expectations. The conflict may eventually exceed tolerance level, and the individual may show his resentment in aggressive, regressive, or repetitive behavior.

Public bureaucracies are not always equipped to deal with such inner stresses and strains. They cannot easily transfer staff between jobs, match talents to vacancies, tolerate deviants and nonconformists, satisfy expectations, develop potential, uncover latent talents, provide adequate compensations, or discover in time an individual's threshold of intolerance. Their managers prefer to cope with the problems emanating from inner stress as they arise rather than anticipate them. They pass problem cases on to others, no better equipped. They tolerate passengers, employees who do not pull their full weight, yet keep out of mischief and escape a formal enquiry into individual work performance. They try to minimize conflicts between the organization and the individual by erecting numerous barriers to public employment to ensure that new recruits will accept the organization and conform to its requirements. However, the sheer size of the public bureaucracy, its formality, routine, and anonymity, may induce stress symptoms after entry, and in areas where staff turnover is high, vacancies exceed applicants, and formal barriers are relaxed, a significant number of organizational misfits is bound to occur.

The possible conflict between the public organization and the public servant raises many questions, which have yet to be answered satisfactorily. Why do people become public servants? Why do they remain public servants? Does the public organization make greater demands on its staff than the private organization? How does the individual personality adjust itself to the requirements of public office? Is the division of labor in public organizations too rigid for healthy personnel management? How different are group norms in public service than in private concerns? Is the individual adequately recognized, and are his personal needs catered to adequately? These questions take on added significance as more and more people enter public service, as public organizations grow in size, as administration becomes more bureaucratized, as the public service embraces increasingly diverse occupations, as the individual as such matters even less, and as the possibility of treating all public servants fairly diminishes. Automated records and decentralization, together with greater flexibility in organizational arrangements and more emphasis on positive personnel management, should aid the public bureaucracy in coping with the internal dimensions of the conflict by conveying to the individual that he is needed, that his work is important to the community, that others depend on his fine performance, that the rewards will be commensurate with the job, that his future prospects are not being overlooked, and that he is still respected as an individual, and is not just a cog in an insensitive machine.

CONTROLS

The world of the official is full of controls. He is restricted on all sides, and his official discretion is limited. But his personal initiative and ingenuity are by no means denied. They are channeled into work problems, though no regulatory system prevents them being used for personal advantage. Fear that officials might exploit the governmental apparatus for their own selfish ambitions is largely responsible for the persistence of so many controls over individual action. No one else is prepared to trust the public servant always to place the public first. The living constitution commands too much power, too many resources, too much functional expertise and information, and it is one step removed from direct public control. Officials are too powerful a political force in their own right. Their performance affects political reputations. Their costs are a significant portion of the community's resources. Their multifarious roles are too important for autonomy. They can make and break governments and usurp governmental power. They must be controlled by the community, on whose behalf they act, to minimize individual misdemeanor, group aggrandizement, and usurpation of political power.

Political Controls

The nature of political controls depends on the polity and constitutional structure. Except in totally bureaucratic polities, public bureaucracies are subordinate to their political masters. In politicized bureaucracies, any departure from political directives is likely to provoke instant retaliation. In depoliticized bureaucracies, political leaders maintain constant vigil and retain power over key points and the ability to intervene at all times. Public officials may be given the opportunity of protesting against political orders on grounds of conscience, but rarely can they disobey or disregard political orders without the imposition of sanctions.

Legal Controls

Absolute discretion is fettered by public law. Public servants cannot act in most cases without legal authorization. If they do, their actions can be challenged in the courts and nullified if found *ultra vires*. The law applies equally to all citizens and all institutions. Until the law is changed according to established procedures, it must be followed at least formally. The nature of government, however, gives the public bureaucracy exceptional privileges, particularly in emergencies.

Judicial Controls

Where the judiciary is independent of both political and bureaucratic institutions, it may be a strong limiting factor on both. The government itself may be overruled for misinterpreting or disobeying constitutional law, and official rulings may be reversed.

Public Controls

The community has certain expectations regarding the behavior of the public bureaucracy. These expectations may be expressed by elected representatives, mass media, independent expert inquiries, trade unions, pressure groups, and citizen associations, which remind public servants of their public obligations.

Internal Controls

Apart from hierarchical controls and central administrative agency controls (over finance, personnel, supplies, contracts, public works, advertising, and so on), public servants find themselves controlled by competing agencies and special watchdogs. The public bureaucracy is no monolith; it is fragmented by function, organization, professional interest, and law. No part is completely self-sufficient or monopolistic. Activities overlap, and policy issues and problem areas recognize no organizational boundaries. Internal competition encourages partisan mutual adjustment, a self-regulatory system of checks and balances. In addition, certain bodies exist solely to check (or spy) on other bodies and to report their findings to bureaucratic and/or political elites.

Self-Controls

On the whole, public servants are not unscrupulous men who stop at nothing to achieve their personal or organizational goals, although such types exist in all organizations. Most public servants acknowledge the self-controls embodied in professional ethics and group norms governing personal conduct, not only on the job, but also in domestic life.

Increased bureaucratic power has raised questions about the effectiveness of these controls singly and in combination. The politicians cannot know everything that is done in their name by public servants. The laws cannot cover every conceivable situation, and they must not inhibit executive action in crisis. The judiciary may be unable to intervene, and when it does intervene, it may be far too late. Public controls work only insofar as outsiders have access to the public bureaucracy and can influence official conduct. Internal controls and self-imposed controls may not work where bureaucratic self-interest is dominant. A possible solution, apart of course from strengthening existing forms of control, is to make the public bureaucracy representative of the community that it is supposed to serve, to prevent monopoly by any section and undue weight being given in the exercise of bureaucratic power to limited perspectives. Public servants would presumably safeguard the interests of the groups from which they were drawn or with whom they consorted outside of working hours. Each group would have fair representation in the bureaucracy relative to its strength in the community, and its very presence would be a limiting or controlling factor in public administration. Advocates of this solution support the division of public offices on a geographical basis in federations and on a party basis in a spoils system or coalition situation. Such proposals are well received in multiracial communities, particularly by underrepresented minorities, which want a greater say in public affairs.

While there can be little dispute with the idea that somewhere within the public bureaucracy diverse views and unpopular opinions should be aired and considered, it does not follow that the public bureaucracy could or should be a mirror of the social structure. First, a public servant's social background is no clue to the views and opinions he holds. The very fact of his public employment may change his whole outlook on life (see Chap. 4). It is unlikely that his views will remain unchanged throughout his public service career. He may make a most undesirable advocate for his class of origin.

Second, appointment according to social-structure quotas subordinates other considerations, such as political affiliation, educational qualifications, and job aptitude, and ignores nepotism within the social group. If anything, it hardens the social structure by denying minorities access to social mobility within the public sector. It may limit their opportunities in the few areas where they are not discriminated against and where they may need to develop career opportunities denied to them elsewhere.

Third, public service is not proportionately attractive to all social groups. Quotas may go unfilled simply because few may be interested in a public-service career.

Fourth, those offering themselves are not likely to be an exact mirror of the social structure. For a start, the very young and the very old do not work, nor do those still completing their education or excluded from the labor market as a result of deformity, incapacity, or social custom. For instance, self-sufficient rural communities are not likely to contribute many applicants, and women may be precluded from public life.

Fifth, the requirements of the public bureaucracy may be very selective in terms of nationality, residence, locality, health, literacy, mobility, loyalty, job qualifications, training, comparative rewards, and competitive entry. In a country where illiteracy is high and disease rampant, selection is automatically confined to the educated healthy, and the public sector may even have to attract qualified immigrants to fill vacancies.

Sixth, even if it were possible to recruit an approximate reflection of the social structure, it is unlikely that every public authority or every administrative unit would be so staffed. In many routine jobs, it does not matter who is employed, what his political opinions are, and with whom and in what manner he spends his leisure time, as long as he can do the work. The number of sensitive positions, where social group background might be important, is relatively small in public employment. Only here may social representativeness be important, and then more for show than any juxtaposition of different attitudes.

Finally, bureaucratic power is only one of many influences shaping society. It is important, but not necessarily the most important. Social representativeness may be more crucial in representative assemblies, coalition governments, mass political parties, trade unions, business enterprises, and the military forces. Better control over the public bureaucracy may be achieved by strengthening these other institutions, rather than devising quota systems for the public service.

CAREER SERVICE

The public service is staffed in many different ways. The great majority of middle and higher level public officials are appointed on the assumption that, providing they behave themselves and the work lasts, they will be employed for as long as they desire to serve, until they reach statutory retirement age. Before considering this career-service concept, alternative methods are briefly reviewed.

Voluntary Service

People offer their services free of charge to the government and undertake a variety of work without compensation or for token remuneration. Voluntary service is most frequently found at local government level and in public welfare agencies, but in wartime many people offer their help in any capacity. Volunteers may make up in enthusiasm what they lack in experience and skills.

Contracted Work

In addition to contracting out large areas of public work, public authorities employ individuals on a contract basis, either because they can offer more money than under normal public employment conditions, or because they or the individuals want to be bound only for a limited period. Quality performance varies considerably between contractors.

Compulsory Service

The only way to staff public services may be to compel citizens to serve, which is a device used to maintain large standing armies and sizable military reserves in preparation for war. Jury service in legal systems is viewed by citizens in the same light, although the theory is quite different. Doctors and teachers, on qualifying, may be compelled to serve in isolated areas or fill public vacancies before they can practice in wealthy suburbs.

Election

Besides filling representative assemblies by election, citizens may be called upon to elect senior executive officials and legal officers. Politicization is virtually unavoidable.

Appointment is preferred to these alternatives, as there is no implied sense of obligation on either side. The individual offers himself freely and accepts the conditions of employment offered to him. If dissatisfied, he is not obliged to continue his employment, and once he has left, the employing authority has no further obligations, except a continuing pension for past service. The employing authority can determine whom it will employ from rival applicants and is not obliged to accept anyone at all or anyone who is not sufficiently qualified. The successful applicant is guaranteed set conditions of employment and does not have to campaign publicly for reappointment. Nevertheless, the alternatives have their place, and bureaucratization has not eclipsed them altogether. In some areas, they could well be revived.

The career-service concept in contemporary bureaucratic states is derived from the feudal concept of service. The master not only gave employment, but also provided living conditions, education, and welfare services, and he also tended to the moral welfare of his charges, even to picking a spouse. The servant, in return, gave faithful service and looked after his master's interests as his own. Their mutual bond was for life; it could not be broken unless the master failed to provide a livelihood or the servant was unfaithful. Absolute monarchs applied the same notions to their servants and passed them on to the bureaucratic state in modified form. The state provides the livelihood and looks after its faithful servants for life, in return for their forgone opportunities when they devote themselves to public service. The state expects absolute loyalty, and the public servants subordinate all other interests in serving the state.

The concept of career service is not confined to public employment. Increasing numbers of private employers of sizable work forces are offering career-service conditions—guaranteed life-long employment, uniform conditions of employment, and safeguards against arbitrary treatment. They want to retain experienced staff and reduce the costs of retraining and dislocation. They want to foster a good public image and gain a reputation as a good employer. They want to accommodate trade-union demands for equity and fair employment practices. They want to take advantage of good personnel practices. For all this, they still possess considerably more discretion in personnel administration than a public authority within a career-service framework. They can hire and fire at will. They can discriminate between employees and treat each individual differently. They can promote whom they want without fear of public reaction, trade-union pressure, or legal action. Public-service systems, in contrast, permit only limited discretion. They are obliged to adopt standardized conditions of employment; and they cannot compete with one another. The standardized conditions are embodied in law, and exemptions are made sparingly. They are policed by a central personnel agency, with full powers of inquiry and ability to impose sanctions. Recruitment is open to all qualified citizens whenever practicable, and personnel procedures endeavor to give all employees fair consideration. Public-service systems must go through the motions, no matter how cumbrous and slow, to preserve public confidence in their impartiality. Despite the uninviting prospect that their upper reaches might present to the outsider— the comparatively low rewards, strain, overwork, questionable prestige— they expect their staffs to be totally committed and to make sacrifices for the public weal that few private employers would demand.

Public-service systems are not uniform; each has its own peculiarities as well as similarities. Simplified, their differences can be tabulated and compared with two extreme types, the open career system and the closed career system (see Table 1). The open career system, which bears some resemblance to the pre-1939 United States Civil Service, allows for considerable mobility between public and private sectors. It assumes that all new recruits will be qualified for their jobs before they are appointed. Further advancement depends on individual self-initiative in spotting the openings and in self-preparation. The closed system, resembling the pre-1939 British Civil Service, separates the career service from the rest of the community, by recruiting at fairly young age directly from the education system and training the young-sters on the job. Higher positions are not thrown open to all comers, but confined to promotion from the lower ranks of the same division.

Table 1
OPEN AND CLOSED CAREER SYSTEMS IN THE PUBLIC SERVICE

	Open Career System	Closed Career System
Tenure	Discretionary	Guaranteed
Structure	Integrated	Differentiated
Classification	Position	Rank
Recruitment	All levels	Base level only
Entry qualifications	Job performance	General education
Salary scales	Short, overlapping	Long, separated
Training	External	Internal on-the-job
Promotion	Open	Closed
Promotion criterion	Most competent	Senior competent
Staff relations	Business like	Paternal
Retirement	Contributory pension	Non-contributory pension

In contemporary, complex public bureaucracies, both models can be found. The closed model suits occupational categories confined to public employment (departmental classes), such as postal work, tax collection, foreign service, and customs inspection, which have no counterpart in the public sector. No recruit could have obtained prior experience and training. Incumbents are dependent on internal advancement in their chosen specialty. The open model suits occupational categories common to both private and public sectors (general classes), such as machine operators, professionals, and craftsmen. Recruits can be expected to have been trained outside in the education system or with private employers and to be experienced on entry. Similarly, internal trainees might well leave public service for private employment. Traffic will flow both ways. In practice, the open system has been applied to departmental classes that have not been able to obtain sufficient recruits to fill higher levels from within, because of poor image, over-full employment, and high turnover. The closed system has been applied to general classes to isolate the public service, to develop group loyalty among a permanent staff corps, and to create an elite image.

The confusion of open and closed career systems had led to distorted notions of the career-service concept. The first is that public servants should not share the same rights as other employees. Public servants are supposed to be different simply because they work for public authorities, not private employers, although it is not always clear how they are different. They are supposed to enjoy superior employment conditions such as tenure and pensions. They are supposed to be faithful servants to the absolute master. They are supposed to have special responsibilities to the community, government, clientele, and their chosen profession. These suppositions ignore the rapid advancement of employment conditions outside the public service and the relative deterioration of those inside the public service, plus the obligations of the community, government, clientele, and their chosen profession to see that, if public servants cannot share the same rights as any other employees, special machinery should be established to minimize their inconvenience. This distorted notion is largely an excuse to economize on government costs at the expense of silenced public employees, who are expected to continue with their faithful service regardless of personal sacrifice.

The second is that public servants should be prohibited from striking, whatever other employee rights they may enjoy. The same notion is not applied to private counterparts performing similar work or to private employees, who may be performing more important functions in communal life. Even self-employed professions have been known to strike.

The third is that the government cannot dismiss public servants. While governments endeavor to employ public servants for life, they reserve the right to dismiss anyone for misconduct, and they often use it. They retrench staff whenever work is insufficient to justify continued employment.

The fourth is that entry should be confined to youth at lower levels. Young people are deemed to be easier to train, for they do not bring foreign ideas to public service. Consequently, some public services have an age limit as low as twenty-one years or twenty-five years, although they also make special entry provisions for retired military staff, post-graduates, and others unable to meet age qualifications. Few positions, let alone whole occupational groups, require such limitations. For most, an upper age limit to recoup on training costs and pension schemes would seem all that is required. A ceiling set so much lower would indicate a large surplus of qualified candidates.

The fifth is that security, prestige, and superannuation should compensate for low remuneration. The job itself is supposed to be its own satisfaction and sufficient justification to exploit relatively weak groups such as nurses, teachers, and clerks.

The sixth is that the career-service concept should cover all public servants, that is, that the closed system apply to all government workers, irrespective of the work they perform. Far from being applicable to the general classes, it may have to be limited even in application to the departmental classes if too much inbreeding, isolation, and parochialism occur.

PUBLIC-PERSONNEL ADMINISTRATION

Justifiably or not, the career-service concept is applied to most appointed public servants in white-collar positions and to considerable numbers of blue-collar public employees also. The expectation of permanency reduces the volume of staffing work that would otherwise prevail if the career service concept were not applied. As every public employee has to be recruited, paid, trained, supplied with proper tools and suitable working space, and generally serviced, personnel administration involves much more than routine salary administration. It spreads over into manpower planning, image building, motivation and morale, staff development, performance evaluation, conflict resolution, productivity, safety standards, work-place environment, health facilities, and collective bargaining.

The full ramifications of positive personnel administration are still not realized in many public services. Particularly is this true of underdeveloped countries, where there are many more qualified candidates than there are openings. Competition solves many problems. Elsewhere, public-service systems have lived on borrowed time and the good will generated before the rapid expansion of public employment in recent decades. They have accepted the routine of negative personnel administration embodied in detailed laws and regulations. They have scrimped and saved on nonessentials, including work accommodation, welfare services, and many facilities (for example, canteens, pleasant surroundings, house journals), which private employers now regard as imperative in retaining their staffs. Public-service systems believe that they have a captive work force. They have not tried as hard to please, especially if it meant battling with the treasury, politicians, and self-appointed guardians of the public purse outside, who view anything above strict economy as pampering public employees at the taxpayer's expense. Parsimony, combined with rapid staff expansion, has usually resulted in overcrowding, unsuitable temporary accommodation (that remains permanent in fact), makeshift work arrangements, depressing work conditions, and much unnecessary dissatisfaction that has readily sparked into anger. The real picture is distorted by constant harping on the few show-pieces in the public sector or by persistent reiteration of conditions at the top, both of which are untypical, as far as the average career grades are concerned.

The central personnel agency is responsible for the general conditions governing public-service employment. It polices public-personnel legislation, advises governments on personnel policy, coordinates operating agency programs, bargains collectively with employee organizations, and conducts centralized personnel services such as recruiting and training. Its *raison d'être* is the reduction of departmentalism and politicization. In its absence, operating agencies would go their own ways; they would choose those practices that best suit their own needs without reference to what any other public authority in the same public service system may be doing. Consequently, operating agencies within the same system would employ diverse standards, severely restricting interagency transfer. Uniform rules and procedures maintained by a central personnel agency limit interagency competition, reduce the possibility of injustice between employees in the same system, and extend opportunities for transfer. Even where such rules are not enforced by a central personnel agency, experience has proved the value of a central clearing house for uniform interpretation.

Political patronage also results in injustice arising from diverse standards and has the additional handicap of overdependence on patrons. Transfer of patronage to operating agencies is no remedy, as political leaders may still interfere wtih selection. Depoliticization is entrusted to the autonomous central personnel agency, independent of political leaders and operating agencies. It stands outside the political arena and above agency in-fighting. It does not have to conduct personnel activities itself, merely ensure that the operating agencies are conducting themselves correctly. In practice, it has preferred to carry out recruitment and promotion activities itself until sure that the operating agencies could be trusted to prevent politicization.

The existence of a central personnel agency encourages the centralization of other personnel activities. Governments and employee organizations prefer to deal with one body, not several splinter operating agencies. Uniform classification, to ensure that all public employees are fairly treated, is an obvious candidate for central control. Gradually the central personnel agency finds itself taking on additional personnel functions, partly because of its centrality, and partly because of economies of scale. Its intimate knowledge of the public service may be utilized in management audits and administrative reform. Its concern with a sizable proportion of the public sector and the labor force as a whole may be enlarged into general employment and labor policies for the government.

No matter what form the central personnel agency takes, the major portion of public-personnel administration is conducted by the operating agencies. It performs all those personnel activities not undertaken by the central personnel agency, joint management bodies, and all delegated personnel activities—recruitment (attraction, selection, placement, induction), training and education, promotion, classification, work arrangements, employment conditions, discipline, counseling, and staff relations. As far as the public employee is concerned, the employing organ is his boss. It provides his job, and the job is his daily preoccupation. It provides his work situation—facilities, accommodation, traveling demands, hours of work, location. It provides his colleagues—the number, composition, interrelationships, and perhaps even marriage prospects. It determines his access to people on the job and his opportunities for advancement and improved living standards. Although the central personnel agency may obtain the staff, the operating agency is responsible for keeping them. It is closer to the people concerned and knows the peculiarities. It can make quick decisions informally and can compromise in ways that the central personnel agency cannot. It is more flexible and avoids delays that occur when personnel decisions are centralized.

The organization of personnel administration within employing organs depends on their size, geographical distribution, functions, occupational categories, and volume of personnel work. In small organizations, personnel administration is integrated with general administration and finance, although there might be a designated personnel officer to handle staff grievances, welfare, and training. Other personnel activities are conducted in the general course of events. In larger organizations, personnel work is performed by specialized personnel staff, who divide the work between them by area. The largest organizations have large personnel sections with elaborate internal arrangements. Even so, personnel officers in public-personnel administration do not have the same discretion as their private counterparts. Instead, they are glorified technicians in work study and salary administration, or training, recruitment and classification specialists. Rarely are they rounded personnel administrators capable of instigating new programs, heading off labor troubles, or developing creative relationships. Too often, they are not organized for positive action, only for routine administration of set laws and procedures. Positive personnel administration goes by default, unless the vacuum is filled by the central personnel agency staff, the general operating staff, or low-level supervisors.

The brunt of positive personnel work is borne by supervisors, although job descriptions may give no hint of their importance in public-personnel administration. The supervisors are the key links between the supervised and personnel administrators, and the main instigators of action. They may be aided by instruction books, in-service training courses, or advice from the personnel specialists, but often they have no formal training or relevant experience in handling people. Thus they have to learn as they go along. Yet their actions have a profound effect on staff retention, working atmosphere, organizational morale, productivity, and the prospects of their charges. In establishment work, they recommend which jobs should be continued or stopped, which vacancies should be abolished or filled, and how the work should be arranged. In classfication work, they comment on job descriptions and sift demands for reclassification. In recruitment and promotion, they advise in selection. They conduct training and they discipline charges. Their sins of omission will sooner or later appear in staff representations. They bend formal instructions to fit circumstances. They can make or break personnel sections. They can heap work on the central personnel agency or prevent it by taking personal responsibility. Investment at supervisory level pays handsome dividends in lessening the load on top management and personnel administrators.

STAFF RELATIONS

Public-personnel administration is no longer a monopoly of the official side, that is, management, as it was before the nineteenth century. Until then the official side decided how a public servant should behave and what rights and obligations he had, and it determined all staffing questions. Public servants were prepared to accept unilateral action, for they had guaranteed employment in prestige jobs. Their conditions of employment were good, and the pace of work was slow. They enjoyed perquisites. Moreover, they feared giving offence to their patrons. During the nineteenth century, however, their attitude shifted, as alternative channels of prestige employment became available to them. Economy and efficiency reduced employment conditions and increased the work load. Patronage was replaced by various forms of depoliticized merit systems. The expansion of public services brought in new classes of unskilled and semiskilled public servants who began to demand the same rights to organize as private employees, much to the chagrin of white-collar, middle-class public servants. The official attitude was hostile. The government was a good employer, the official side argued, and public servants had no need to organize. The senior officials were kind and paternalistic to their charges, whose best interests they safeguarded. Since public services had to be maintained at all times, public officials could not share the same rights as private employees. Besides, their boss was the community, not some grasping capitalist exploiter. If public servants were allowed to organize, they would be exposed to dual loyalties. On these grounds, the official side resisted unionization.

The industrial public servants in the post office, telegraph and telephone services, and railroads fought an open war with their supervisors, with the labor movement behind them. Outside trade unions sought members in the public sector and made no distinction between public and private employees. In western Europe and the British Commonwealth, and later North America, the low-level public servants did obtain industrial rights. First they gained the right to organize, that is, to collect subscriptions and to help members over hard times. Next they gained the right of recognition—to be consulted in advance on all matters affecting their members and to advise on members' employment conditions. Finally, they gained the right to negotiate through collective bargaining and arbitration tribunals.

White-collar public servants did not follow their example until much later, for they did not wish to associate with blue-collar workers. They were educated and had alternatives to public employment. They were also obsessed with middle-class norms, even though they were losing ground, compared with white-collar employees in the private sector and with industrial blue-collar workers generally. Eventually they discovered that they were actually worse off. They organized first in social clubs, which arranged annual dinners and weekly outings, then in educational societies, which published technical journals whose subject matter extended into employment conditions, and finally in protest meetings, where grievances were aired and complaints voiced. They too formed associations and unions to remedy grievances, promote better employment conditions, and obtain the rights to organize and to negotiate with their public employers.

Wherever public servants have been accorded industrial rights in democratic polities, they have shown a greater readiness to join employee organizations than private employees, and at a higher rate than comparable occupational categories in the private sector. They recognized that they could do nothing as individuals and that their only strength was in unity and the collective threat of passive resistance or withdrawal of labor. The employee organization was their only defense.

The employee organization institutionalized individual grievances and complaints, and protected the individual from victimization. It sifted grievances and demands, and pursued only those that seem justified. In this, it acted as a clearinghouse and performed much work that supervisors and personnel sections in operating agencies had neglected. It had equal status with the official side, something that no public servant by himself had. It possessed collective rights, political as well as industrial, that were denied to individuals. It also furnished other services, such as legal aid, loans, discounts, and training facilities, which members could not provide for themselves.

Why do career public servants join employee organizations? First, because they are vulnerable, possibly among the most vulnerable employees in the community. Their mobility is restricted. Their prospects are limited. Their civil rights may be curbed. Their employer is the government, which is always tempted to exploit public servants to keep costs or taxes down and to increase the quantity and quality of public services. Second, public servants work closely together, and social pressures to join are high, particularly after union successes. Third, the government may encourage unionism and may make it easy for public servants to join. Governments favorable to the labor movement may compel unionization as a condition of employment. Fourth, formal arbitration tribunals may confine awards to union members. But not all public servants join. Higher-level public servants consider themselves more akin to managers than employees. Female public servants, like females generally, show less disposition to join. Young people, too, are less willing to commit themselves: some are undecided about a public-service career, others are ambitious or want to show their individuality or cannot appreciate union functions. Other public servants have political and religious objections to unionization.

Unionization has brought the staff side into public-personnel administration. The official side has something pushing against it, challenging its decisions and practices, demanding explanations and justifications, exposing its blind spots, confronting it in public. It must keep looking over its shoulder, trying to anticipate the moves of the employee organizations. As opponents, the official and staff sides can defeat each other's purposes, but as allies, they can mutually benefit. They have many things in common and seek many of the same objectives, namely, a contented efficient public service, fairly treated and well regarded in the polity. If the political masters reject officials' representations, the staff can enter the political arena and fight for the officials' proposals, such as changes in legislation and improvements in working conditions. If the official side runs out of ideas, it can tap the staff side, and vice versa. The two sides may work together to quell staff discontent, head off strikes, and quash unofficial staff actions and member revolts. In decisions affecting an individual's career, it may be desirable to have the staff side formally represented to ensure justice and the appearance of fairness. Thus, relations between staff and officials are complicated; they are not usually characterized by continual hostility and conflict, and where these exist, it is more for the sake of public posture than effective action.

The overriding advantage of unionization is the ability of public servants to appear in the political arena as a separate pressure group. Realistically, the official side can only participate in the political arena as the mouthpiece of the government. Individual public servants are not inclined to participate actively in politics (even where permitted to do so), and rarely against the government. Employee organizations, however, are not as inhibited. They have little option if they want to be effective. Political parties are not neutral to public services or employee organizations. Some parties are more favorably disposed than others toward public servants, just as employee organizations are more favorably disposed to certain political parties than others. Governments use the public service politically. In depressions, in response to public demand, they reduce employment conditions, and during inflation, they curb pay increases as a signal to private employers to do likewise. They employ women, disabled persons, minority groups, and other persons discriminated against in the labor market, to set an example to all employers. More importantly, only they can grant many of the demands made by public servants and their unions. In response, employee organizations try to influence the votes of their members and to convince political parties that they command the "public service vote." The concern of political parties may be assessed from the promises made to public servants before elections and the tendency of governments to grant pay increases in election year (and to retrench and economize in the year following elections).

To reduce the political pressure of public-service organizations and to keep the public service out of the political arena, governments provide alternative channels through which public servants and their unions can obtain redress of their grievances. Formal councils, composed equally of representatives from official and staff sides, may be established to discuss all matters of common interest, except perhaps salary increases, and to make recommendations to the government. Simple majority vote may suffice, or unanimity may be required before any proposals are put to the government for action. As the government will have already made its views known through the official side, recommendations and proposals are likely to be implemented. Such joint management bodies may be found at any level of government, and councils at different levels may be formally linked. For salary and other matters involving considerable sums of money, the government may provide a formal collective bargaining apparatus, replete with mediators and conciliators. It may also agree to resolve outstanding issues through independent arbitration, both official and staff sides being willing to accept the decision of the arbitrator. For matters of crucial concern to individual public servants, their representatives may be formal participants in decision-making processes and on appeal boards.

EMPLOYMENT CONDITIONS

Employment conditions between public and private sectors are growing much closer to each other as public authorities extend their occupational coverage and private organizations grow in size and bureaucratize. Staff mobility and interchange are more common. Trade unions insist on uniformity for all members, irrespective of their employer. The principle of comparability, whereby governments seek to maintain parity with private employers, is being extended as quickly as suitable research and negotiating machinery can be established. Yet, public services retain several peculiar features that distinguish them from private employment.

Classification

Every public employee is classified in an elaborate structure of divisions and grades, horizontally based on job importance, quality of intelligence required in the performance of the work, and the administrative content of the job; and vertically based on occupational categories, training requirements, functional specialization, and organizational differentiation. Since too many people are employed to be dealt with individually, it is easier administratively to handle a small number of classes instead. Age, sex, nature of work, qualifications possessed, and seniority (or length of service) have all been employed as criteria for class differentiation, and are still employed within major groupings based on salary or occupation. Classification by salary is fairly simple and presumably reflects the importance of the work and the person. But salary may be more a reflection of social class (and/or personal influence with patrons), unrelated to the work performed or competence in performing the work. More sophisticated measures are needed to measure work value and to base salary on work value. For this reason, classifiers prefer occupational categories as defined by professional associations, trade unions, and employee organizations and job evaluators. The structuring of classes usually embodies the following concepts: (a) that the public service structure should reflect the education system, which in many countries reflects the social structure; (b) that administrative generalists should head specialized professionals, or that an elite corps of administrators be superimposed at the apex; (c) that occupational classes also found outside the public service should reflect community valuation, as ascertained by pay research data, and that noncomparable occupational classes should be integrated according to comparable job qualifications; and (d) that to prevent abuse, temporary employees should receive only the minimum rates accorded to permanent employees. These concepts assume a greater importance where the divisions, horizontal and vertical, are rigid and separate, for the individual is typed from the very beginning and may be unable to switch jobs or occupational channels after entry.

Recruitment

Public employers are obliged to follow certain principles in recruitment that are not incumbent on private employers.

Open entry   Public authorities are expected to open their jobs to all qualified citizens. For this purpose, they are obliged to notify any potential applicants of vacancies. They may have to advertise vacancies widely throughout the country, undertake extensive recruitment propaganda to offset adverse public images, and maintain close contacts with educational establishments and other potential sources of applicants.

Fair consideration   Public employers must assume that all who apply really want the job, even though the formalities may be so complicated and time-consuming that the best applicants may already have obtained alternative employment. All applicants are expected to receive fair consideration. All must be processed, and the results notified to them. Appeal provisions may also be provided to guarantee fairness.

Legal and other restrictions   Public services are restrictive in their choice. Apart from legal requirements relating to age, sex, nationality, character, education, health and residence, there are job requirements, such as technical qualifications, physical characteristics, and competence, and there are also public-service requirements, such as security, behavior pattern, and personal appearance. Elaborate application forms and examinations have to be completed, and behind the scenes much checking of personal records and references takes place before an offer of permanent employment can be made.

Probation   The probationary period gives time to complete formal checking and to see whether the probationer measures up to the job. The recruit's educational qualifications may be no indication of his practical competence. He may not be suitable as a public servant because of defects in work habits and personality. The information on his application form may prove to be false. He may not like the public service at all, or he may dislike his first placement.

Promotion

Promotion mania is not confined to public services; it is characteristic of every bureaucracy. For most public employees, advancement is the only way they can improve their living standards, social status, and self-esteem. But promotion opportunities are not uniform. The horizontal structure of occupational categories prevents more than a very small proportion from gaining promotion beyond the first few steps. The vertical divisional structure may prevent any career switch between occupational categories. Public authorities do not grow at the same rate, and some even decline. Staff known to promoting authorities are likely to receive more favorable consideration than unknown staff, which means that head office staff usually receive preference over field staff. Finally, in many areas of the public service, it is virtually impossible to demonstrate on-the-job qualities required in higher positions. Equal opportunity will not apply throughout a public service; at best, it will apply within occupational categories. Objectivity will not apply throughout a public service; at best, it will apply within individual organizations.

As a public servant moves through the ranks, two considerations are likely to increase in importance. First, how many mistakes has he made? Politicians are wary about public servants who have made embarrassing mistakes in the past and could make mistakes with worse implications in the future. In other words, a public servant is usually measured by his freedom from mistakes, not the number of his successes. Second, how politically acceptable is he? Politicians do not want public servants at the top whom they cannot trust. This does not mean that officials must be partisan supporters of the political leaders, only that they can be relied on to give of their utmost and act in the best interests of the political leaders without publicly embarrassing them. Otherwise, promotion criteria should satisfy public servants and secure group consensus, and they should be publicly available, general enough to permit flexibility and the exercise of human judgement, but specifically detailed to assure a sense of justice among those involved.

Rewards

Before the nineteenth century, the public service was a highly regarded profession. Not only was remuneration at upper levels high even by modern standards, but the opportunities for extra rewards were extensive. In low-income countries and totalitarian regimes, public service is similarly profitable. Elsewhere, egalitarianism, democratization, and scientific management have considerably reduced the comparative rewards of public service, and opportunities for extra rewards have been greatly curtailed, if not ended altogether. Where social status and occupational prestige are measured in terms of material rewards, the public service has declined with the fall in comparative rewards. The public service remains attractive to (a) wealthy persons who find public service its own reward, (b) poor persons who find public service rewarding materially, particularly groups who are discriminated against in other professions, (c) nonwealthy public-service-minded persons who would work for the government whatever the rewards, because they like the work and the public service, and (d) those qualified persons who cannot find employment elsewhere or have failed on their own or in private enterprise. Once they have gotten used to public service, they are reluctant to leave it. They care less about alternative employment and more about their work as a vocation. In time, their loyalty to their colleagues strengthens, even though they may become personally embittered as prospects for advancement recede.

On the whole, the working atmosphere in public service is pleasant, at least among equals. As everyone is receiving the same as everyone else, there is little pretension. Everyone realizes that most of his colleagues will not change, so people can relax their guard and cover for one another, knowing that they can rely on others to reciprocate. On the other hand, nonmaterial rewards—the separate room, a carpet on the floor, a window with a view—take on added significance far beyond their intrinsic worth. Normally tolerant and rational public servants can be turned into spiteful sulks when deprived of small privileges they had come to expect as their right. When no other channels are available, pettiness becomes an expression of self-importance. Nonmaterial rewards seem the most important to middle ranks and women. Top ranks have too much else to occupy them and have other compensations, such as nearness to political leaders, privilege of rank, and sense of power. The lowest ranks are preoccupied with making ends meet domestically and prefer material compensation to work privileges. Women seem more possessive about the extras and need to bolster their own sense of importance in a male-dominated environment.

The exceptional demands imposed on public servants in the course of their employment are compensated for in various ways. First, although absolute lifetime security cannot be guaranteed, the expansion of public services guarantees security to increasing numbers of permanent public employees for whom work is assured even in recessions. Secure employment and fair employment practices are values the world over, less so perhaps in full-employment economies, where jobs are freely available and employers compete for scarce labor.

Second, any expenses incurred on the job are reimbursed. The public employee does not suffer economic hardship or risk his own capital. Only at top levels may public servants be penalized. They may receive no credit for excessive hours worked, and their standard of living on government business may not compare with their counterparts in the private sector. The unscrupulous may defraud the government by illegitimate claims for expenses, but undetected profits are usually small, compared with private business practices.

> The ethical behavior of public servants . . . is higher than in most sectors of American society, but it can never rise much above the standard of its environment. It is rather difficult to build and maintain integrity in the administrative agencies of government when legislators and private interests connive to commit far greater damage to the general welfare than any bureaucrat has ever been accused of. As long as millionaires can get by without paying income taxes, as long as depletion allowances can help to create a culturally shabby "nouveau riche" in the oil states,

as long as factories can get away with shoddy or unsafe products and pollute our streams and our air with impurity—as long as these big thefts within the public weal are permitted, I cannot get too excited about the relatively minor graft that may occasionally crop up in the bowels of the bureaucracy.[1]

The scrupulous public servant has little cause for complaint; he is fairly compensated for legitimate expenses.

Third, pensions are esteemed where social services are poorly developed and private employers ungenerous. The loss of livelihood is probably the worst blow that confronts most employees, but governments look after their own. Their generosity is offset by compulsory retirement, which forces many able-bodied, competent, and keen public servants to cease public employment while still capable.

Finally, the sense of satisfaction of a job well done cannot be measured. Public servants know that they will never be rich legally, but they will make an adequate living. Their compensation cannot be wholly material, nor do they expect it to be; otherwise, they would seek their fortunes elsewhere. They gain inner contentment by performing socially useful work, contributing what they can toward the good society, helping their fellow men, realizing political objectives, enjoying the company of like-minded people, and leaving the world a better place for their efforts. These constitute the real meaning of public service.

[1] O. G. Stahl, "Summary and Prospects," in Public Personnel Association, *Personnel Dialogue for the Seventies,* Personnel Report No. 712, Chicago, 1971, p. 31.

IV

Theory and Comparison Administration

10

Administrative Theory

One of the most compelling reasons why public administration is denied the status of an academic discipline in the older seats of higher learning is that it has yet to develop a systematic body of theory. There are theories *in* public administration, but there are no general theories *of* public administration. Rarely is the term "public-administration theory" employed in the literature of public administration, as it evokes memories of the simplistic normative slogans of administrative reformers against politicization and of the naïve administrative proverbs of the scientific management approach to public administration before World War II. The disillusionment with public-administration theory following the publication of Simon's *Administrative Behavior* and Waldo's *The Administrative State,* neither of which were intended to destroy public-administration theory per se, but to reaffirm its importance by jettisoning inadequate theory and by redirecting theorists to set their sights higher, lasted two decades, and it may take a similar period to restore faith in a new generation of theorists. Meanwhile, public adminstrators have gone outside traditional confines to borrow ideas, methods, techniques, and approaches from other disciplines and have applied them, with varying degrees of success, to public administration. People trained in other disciplines have applied their ideas to the largest and most obvious organizations in society, namely, the military, the civil bureaucracy, social-service agencies, and public businesses, which are conceptually, institutionally, and functionally within the discipline of public administration. Thus, theory in public administration has been expanding. The new body of theory tries to avoid the criticisms of pre-World War II classical theory, neatly summarized by Waldo as "crude, presumptuous, incomplete—wrong in some of its conclusions, naïve in its scientific methodology, parochial in its outlook."[1]

The abundant theories in public administration deal with things bigger and smaller than public administration, but not with public administration itself. On the one hand, they deal with all administration, all organized cooperative effort, all decision making, all societal organizations, all human behavior, of which public administration is part; on the other, they deal with unique practices, specific organizations, special administrative case studies, and particular administrative subprocesses that constitute parts of public administration. But few deal with the meaning of public administration. Instead, they accept public administration as a given of the polity or culture. Although public administration serves interests and ends beneficent to all members of the community, the theorists rarely attempt to explain what should compose the interests and ends, or how public administration might maximize those interests and ends. The good life, the good individual, the good community—these the theorists leave to political philosophers. Normative overtones are directed at maximizing the interests and ends of individual public authorities, bureaucratic elites, and upwardly mobile public administrators, which are not at all the same. At public-administration level, the theories are mainly descriptive and analytical, and studiously objective in that, following behavioralism, they stick to the facts and describe public administration as it really is, not what it purports to be or should be.

In the organizational society, all but the most intimate personal needs are met through organizations. Its members can do little for themselves unless they accept the demands of the organizational society. First, they must accommodate themselves to organizational discipline and subordinate their individuality accordingly. They are committed to social organisms from which there is no escape. Second, the organizations enable them to attain things that they could not achieve by themselves. Organizations supply fellowship and provide avenues by which the individual can fulfill himself through group activity. The individual transcends his limitations, and collectively men overcome their individual shortcomings. Organizations harness cooperative human effort, draw on all community resources, utilize all members' expertise, and direct combined energies toward common goals. In this way, they master their environment. Different organizations, however, compete and may use their power to annihilate one other. The same capacity for good can be used for bad. Third, organizations centralize power. The masses

---

[1] D. Waldo, "Organization Theory: An Elephantine Problem," *Public Administration Review,* 11 (Autumn 1961), p. 220.

are directed by elites with a vested interest in the status quo, an ordered world, a managed environment, unquestioned authority, low mobility, stability, and other props to elitism. Elites have a disproportionate say in what should be done. On the other hand, centralized power makes revolution easier through the capture of strategic key points. To limit the possible abuse of centralized power, power centers are separated and compete against one another, and elites are subordinated to the depersonalized authority of universal laws and are screened to ensure representativeness and responsibility. Fourth, elites prefer rationality, as against the uncertainty and disorder of irrationality. Choice is restricted, and more givens can be assumed. Outcomes can be predicted with greater assurance. Similarly, they prefer the measurable concrete to the immeasurable abstract. Their ideal is a military model, with everything in its place, guaranteed submissiveness, and little romanticism or sentimentality. The end is survival; the means, autocracy of objectivity. But a society cannot be run like a military camp. Instead of ordaining strict obedience, the elite engineer loyal cooperation through warm personal relationships, mutual self-interest, spontaneous cooperation, and concessions to the sentiments and emotions of the masses. Thus, the organizational society tends to be conformist, powerful, elitist, rational, and paternal, and theories about the organizational society tend to justify its principal features and exaggerate the organizational solution to the human predicament.

Most public-administration theorists have consciously or unconsciously subsumed the philosophy of the organizational society, with the exception of comparative-administration theorists, who will be dealt with separately in Chapter 11. Either they are members and aspiring members of elites in organizational societies, or they are advocates of the organizational society in other cultures. Few question the assumptions of the organizational society or make the assumptions explicit in their writings. Aware of the political implications, they tend to pull back from the deeper philosophical, moral, and political issues involved in theorizing about public activities and public institutions. Instead, they take refuge behind behavioral administrative science. They are prepared to theorize about the internal technical aspects of public administration, which closely parallel the internal technical aspects of any organization, but not about the external nontechnical aspects, for which they believe themselves illequipped. Thus, the practitioners have been grappling with a transformed external world without much relevant theoretical guidance, and they have become sceptical about any possible value of theory in internal housekeeping functions when the (unstated) premises are foreign to their political environment. The practitioners appreciate theories that rationalize what is currently happening in public administration and what they want to happen, such as the human-relations approach in democratic administration to overcome excessive formality, and the challenge to the specialist-generalist dichotomy at the apex of bureaucratic structures. They also appreciate theories that idealize administrative practices, such as budgeting theory, service orientation, professional values, and concern for individual liberty. They do not believe, however, that the public-administration theorists have provided the basic ideas about public administration.

The major thrust of the practitioners, when they care about theory at all, is directed against the bland application of theories from other disciplines, particularly business administration, without sufficient appreciation of the public nature of public administration. With some justification, they claim that public-administration theorists have not contributed much of their own, apart from "illustrative case materials" and "supplementary model-building."[2] In short, the theorists have made no appreciable advance in public-administration theory. Worse still, in borrowing so much, they have projected inapplicable presuppositions. Efficient productivity is not the only objective in public administration. Rational decisions are not necessarily good decisions in a political environment. What the practitioners want is relevant public administration theory, but very little exists.

The paucity of public-administration theory, as opposed to advice, is readily explainable. First, there must be something distinctive to theorize about. Historically, the study of public adminstration has been part of something else—political science, law, government, history, cameralism—and controversy still rages whether it can exist on its own. If there is no such thing as public administration, then there can be no public-administration theory. Second, that there was something to theorize about only became apparent in some cultures with the recent rise of big government and with the proliferation of public authorities, public laws, and public services. Third, people must be prepared to theorize about public administration, an action area that has not attracted philosophers. It is a practical man's field—to get things done without fuss and without drawing attention to oneself. Administration should be unobtrusive; it should appear as natural as sleeping or walking; practical administrators are not very interested in philosophizing about what they do, nor are they keen to reveal the tricks of the trade and undermine the mystique of the profession. Fourth, while there has never been any shortage of people prepared to tell others what to do and how to do it better, only with the development of social science has systematic thought and research been applied to their assumptions, recommendations, projections, generalizations, and idealizations. Fifth, when things are going smoothly, there seems no reason to speculate about practices. Crisis provokes self-inquiry and an examination of apparently insoluble problems, but by this time the urgency of the moment permits little time for contemplation. Sixth, American public-administration theory has been too culture-bound to be of much use elsewhere, and comparatively little theorizing has occurred outside the United States. Attempts to export foreign concepts have been disastrous, thus reinforcing predilections toward pragmatic empiricism and improvisation. Much

---

[2] A. Lepawsky, in J. C. Charlesworth, ed., *Theory and Practice of Public Administration,* Monograph 8, American Academy of Political and Social Science, 1968, p. 150.

theory has been ill-conceived, ineffectual, or confined to theorists. Until a larger body of public-administration theory exists, public-administration students have to be satisfied with exhortations to theorize, borrowed theories, and guidelines to a possible theory of public administration.

WHY THEORY?

Practitioners claim they have no use for theory. They can perform just as well, and perhaps even better, without their heads being filled with theory, conceptual frameworks, ideal models, unverifiable hypotheses. Theirs is the real world—of crucial problems that cannot wait, of important societal activities that must be carried out without interruption, of political power plays between rival ideologies, values and interests that cannot be ignored, of large-scale organizations, large sums of money and large bodies of people that have to be managed, of administrative in-fighting that permits no relaxation, of ceaseless movement that cannot be stopped. Thus they are extremely busy people, married to the job of administration, mixing business with pleasure and work with leisure. Rarely do they have a moment to call their own let alone time to pause, reflect, philosophize. Yet, unconsciously, they are employing theory, making assumptions, testing concepts, verifying hypotheses, and evaluating ideas. Man is a thinking animal, with exceptional capacity to abstract and to absorb and learn from abstractions. An ounce of such applicable theory has been worth tons of needless labor, and to ignore theory altogether, as many practitioners pride themselves on doing, is to reject man's intellectuality and his ability to make shortcuts via abstraction. Theory is "the shortest way of saying something important. . . . From the chaos of observation and experience, man abstracts patterns of regularity and probability and gives these patterns symbolic expression and logical connection."[3]

Men cannot help thinking; they intellectualize problems, drawing upon the accumulated wisdom of the past. Thus, there will always be theorists and theories, some of which will be better than others. In administration, theorists engage in unstructured research. They experiment. As in the physical sciences, nothing may result—no new discoveries, no feasible solutions, nothing that can be verified, nothing tangible to show for so much effort. On the other hand, a certain percentage will be good theory, eminently applicable and rewarding, and a small fraction will be so far ahead of its time that its true worth will not be recognized for decades, perhaps centuries, afterward. But bad theory may drive out good theory until further proof is available to test veracity. Men are wise not to embrace every new theory, just because it appeals to common-sense notions and direct observation, or because it is new and people are dissatisfied with the theory they have. Thus, the coolness of

[3] S. K. Bailey, quoting E. Schattschneider, in J. C. Charlesworth, ed., *Theory and Practice of Public Administration,* p. 128.

practitioners to public administration theorists may be sensible, given that many theories are experimental, suggestive, confining, and unverifiable, and not in accord with the facts as known to practitioners. However, the existence of bad theory is no excuse for rejecting all theory or the good theory that does exist.

Theory is an essential tool for the progress of civilized man. As the symbolic representation of the real, it enables people to communicate quickly and effectively. It is intellectual shorthand, which saves each generation having to relearn all that has already been discovered. As man learns more and more, his vocabulary expands and his theories change considerably. Theorists who have mixed up their facts or misinterpreted and distorted them are eventually ignored. Their unreal and untenable theories are abandoned as pure tautology or specialized jargon, dressed up to say the obvious. In contrast, verifiable theories—stated relationships ordering observable data or experience—have much to offer. First, they tell something meaningful about the real world that can be applied to real-life situations. Second, by ordering otherwise disjointed or overwhelming data, they give perspective to the real world and convey something important to the observer. Third, by revealing a reality that may not be readily self-evident from the facts themselves, they stimulate new ways of looking at familiar things and different actions. This may be expecially helpful in problem solving. Fourth, they form a solid base from which further theorizing can take place. Fifth, definite relationships imply the possibility of controlled relationships and prediction. For these reasons, the value of administrative theory cannot be underrated in the organizational society.

The value of theory is further enhanced by examining the constituents of theory. (a) *Postulates* are assumption that are not directly demonstrable. They are inspirational movers of men; they drive administrative reformers; they set ideal targets; they indicate possibilities. But if too presumptive, they may frustrate and disappoint when people fail to live up to them. (b) *Definitions* describe terms used in postulates. They may direct attention to the complexity of administration and the need for clarification of terms used in normal speech. Extended, the definitional techniques become theoretical frameworks, typologies, and classifications for empirical study. (c) *Propositions* indicate logical relationships between concepts derived from postulates and definitions. They indicate what will happen should a certain requirement be met. Much administrative theory is propositional. "If a public authority adopts the merit system, then the quality of its staff will improve" is a typical example. Unfortunately, too few variables may be considered, or, more frequently, what is intended as instrumental is normative, that is, rationalized, wishful thinking, based on superficial observation. (d) *Hypotheses,* measurable propositional statements about the relationships between variables, are operational and the most useful of all theory in administration.

Stephen Bailey has reshuffled these constituents into four categories of theory: (i) descriptive-explanatory, concerned with "what" and "why"; (ii) normative, concerned with "should" and "good"; (iii) assumption, concerned with "pre-conditions" and "possibilities"; and (iv) instrumental, concerned with "how" and "when."[4] He believes the following:

> The objectives of public administration theory are to draw together the insights of the humanities and the validated propositions of the social and behaviorial sciences and to apply these insights and propositions to the task of improving the processes of government aimed at achieving politically legitimated goals by constitutionally mandated means.[5]

He does not envisage a general theory of man derived from a theory of administrative man, of which public administration theory would be part. He would work the other way round, that is, draw from theories about the nature of man in constructing public administration theory.

Theorizing about public administration from the outside has its drawbacks. The theorist, as outsider, is denied access to crucial areas. He is forced to theorize about only part of the whole. This part may be the less important one, and if no insiders theorize about the remainder, it may be given exaggerated attention. The outsider is likely to be affected by general trends in theorizing. There are fashions, fads, and fancies and at one particular moment, one way may be more popular than another. For instance, in the past two decades, the Scandinavian institution of citizen's defender against the public bureaucracy—the ombudsman—has become a temporary fad. Behavioralism was (and remains) fashionable. The concept of system replaced the machine and the organism images that were previously used. Community development was revived. "Think tanks" became more popular, but reorganization faded. The notion that theorizing could be a group activity, copying business "buzz" sessions, also took hold, although key breakthrough in theory have always been achieved by individuals around whom disciples have flocked and new schools of thought built. At present, there are no distinctive schools of public administration theory. Theoretical work in public administration take place within the general field of administration.

SCHOOLS OF ADMINISTRATIVE THEORY

The rapid expansion of administrative theory in recent decades precludes the possibility that all theories and theorists can be fully described. One way of handling the bulk and complexity is to classify theories and theorists according to their major premises. It is important to note at the outset that they do share certain things. The terms "administration" and "management" are used interchangeably to denote the same kinds of activity and people

---

[4] S. K. Bailey, "Objectives of the Theory of Public Administration," in J. C. Charlesworth, ed., *Theory and Practice of Public Administration,* p. 129.
[5] Bailey, "Objectives of the Theory of Public Administration," p. 129.

found at the apex of bureaucracies in organizational societies. Management is the term preferred in business to separate the activities of the bureaucratic elite from those of the owners or directors of private companies and the subordinate submanagerial classes. Administration is the term preferred in public administration to refer to similar activities performed by officials sandwiched between the political executive and subordinate submanagerial classes, with the accent more on external responsibilities than internal controls. Both terms refer to a process—the way people get things done through other people in an organizational setting. Certain generalizations are made about this process, as follows:

a. The process consists of a number of interrelated and interdependent subprocesses, which are means to an end, not ends in themselves. They are habitual institutionalized actions.
b. The subprocesses are employed by a formally orgainzed group of people working together to attain common goals normally beyond individual accomplishment. Generalizations about the subprocesses are valid for all organizations.
c. The success of the process is measured in terms of accomplishing common goals, which may be subject to change.
d. The ability to work through other people is a specialized skill that can be observed, studied, and possibly taught, and is transferable between organizations.
e. Although the process is intangible and invisible, it is concerned with the ordering of resources, more especially human resources, throughout the organization. It is largely a mental activity.
f. The process is conditioned by the culture in which it operates, and the skill is shaped by social factors such as education, technical knowledge, law, and communications.

These six propositions are the starting point of most writing about the nature of administrative activity. They are not universally accepted, least of all by public administrators. In reviewing the different schools of administrative theory, following Koontz's classification,[6] one must keep in mind the story of the six blind men and the elephant. Although all attempt to describe the same object, by touching different aspects they appear to be describing different things.

Administrative-Process School

The administrative-process school analyzes the nature of administrative activities and seeks to identify common operating principles that can be generally applied to improve administrative practice. Whereas F. W. Taylor started with the individual worker at the bottom of the hierarchy and moved upward and outward to cover all factors that might affect the capacity of the worker to give of his best, Henri Fayol, a successful French industrialist,

[6] H. Koontz, "The Management Theory Jungle," *Journal of the Academy of Management,* 4, No. 3 (1961), 174–188.

started at the top with the general manager. Fayol insisted that his success was not due to his personal qualities, but to the methods he employed. He classified the functions of major business operations and defined the administrative group as organizing, coordinating, commanding, controlling, and *prévoyance* (a mixture of forecasting and planning). Drawing on his experience, he listed fourteen administrative principles and sixteen administrative rules for the guidance of administrators, which he taught at the Paris Institute of Administration, established in 1918. In the United States, Taylorism had been transformed into a similar approach at senior levels, but it was not until the 1930s that Gulick reinterpreted Fayol and spelt out the POSDCORB formula. The administrative process consisted of planning, organizing, staffing, directing, coordinating, reporting, and budgeting, the study of which could reveal universal principles with predictive value based on verifiable experience, applicable in all administration. The principles could be built into a framework from which a general theory of administration would emerge.

Despite Simon's attack in the mid 1940s, the principles approach has, if anything, been strengthened. The subprocesses of administration are studied in meticulous detail. On the basis of observation, model building, experimentation, and validation, general propositions are formulated about each subprocess. Although descriptive-explanatory, they are used normatively to tell the administrator how he should act. The administrator's own experience should indicate which guiding principles he should adopt in his peculiar circumstances. The administrative-process school does not usually go beyond the confines of identifiable administrative processes, nor does it attempt to relate administrative behavior to other aspects of human behavior. Even so, the number of propositions and principles expands annually. Some are later disproved; others are found to be culture-bound.

The main criticisms of the administrative-porcess school are that its principles are either too generalized to be useful or too elaborate and too couched in jargon to be readily understood; that too little testing of propositions and their assumptions is undertaken; that there are too many principles that need consolidating; and that the scope of administrative activity is defined too narrowly, being too inward-looking and too conscious of the elite. From the public-administration viewpoint, considerable doubt exists whether the principles are valid in a political setting, whether administrative problems can be treated purely in process terms, whether the discipline should be wholly concerned with the solution of practical problems and guidelines to administrators and politicans, and whether the principles are related to actual behavior in real-life situations. The administrative-process model may be too rational, too formal, too authoritarian, too conformist, too dependent on cosmic constitutionalism (that is, that "oughts" can be derived from facts). At least, it has become more rigorous, more intellectually demanding, closer to the facts, and more meaningful than the naïve principles approach between the world wars.

The Empirical School

The empirical school resembles the administrative-process school in conceiving that general theories can emerge from the study of practical experience. The principles evolved are verifiable propositions based on actual case studies in the real world, not hypothetical constructs or idealizations of current practices. By studying experience or grappling with administrative problems, the student learns to appreciate the most effective techniques and which principles to apply under what circumstances. The empirical school may be more relevant to public administration in that public authorities are fairly permanent and stable organizations, their environments have not radically changed in the past, and their staffs are career public servants. In quickly changing circumstances, past experience may be no guide to coping with new conditions and novel problems.

Human-Behavior School

As administration is getting things done through other people, the human-behavior school concentrates on interpersonal relationships. Studies, heavily dependent on psychology and social psychology, range from individual personality to transcultural influences, and as the title implies, they represent the new wave of behavioralism in the social sciences. Their aim is to describe administration as it really is. They are not very concerned about normative implications of their discoveries, which contrasts with the emphasis between the world wars on the application of human relations to democratize administration and to make the work location a more inviting prospect in the hope that happier employees would increase productivity. The human-relations approach that spread through Elton Mayo and his associates following the Hawthorne experiments (1927–1932) has remained important, largely through popularization in the United States, where it satisfied egalitarian drives to cloak the elitist assumptions of the bureaucratic organization. However, the simple idea of treating employees as human beings, rather than work hands or human appendages of machinery, has been superseded by sophisticated studies of morale, leadership, communications, and informal relationships in an organizational setting. How to get the best out of workers through the manipulation of human psychology has been put aside by academic theorists, who have begun to explore the implications of cultural heritage, the impact of bureaucratization on the individual personality, deviation and conformity in group behavior, generational and sex differences in work roles, breakdowns in communications, personal reactions in crisis situations, organizational structures, value systems, learning patterns, and participative management. Gradually the scope of the human-behavior school has extended from work norms and incentives to applied behavioral science.

The contribution of the human-behavior school to public administration has been less than the administrative process and empirical schools, partly because researchers have not been able to penetrate the bureaucratic mask of officialdom, and partly because practitioners in public administration have been sceptical toward general theories of human behavior. Official reaction has been cool, describing the latest theories as already known to good administrators, who pick them up intuitively. Where researchers have been able to explore public bureaucracies, they have found officials to be human, after all, and the organization to possess a soul. The main impact has been revelations of the informal workings of government and personalization of working conditions at lower levels. The human-behavior theories are criticized for their vagueness, psychological jargon, distortion of the organizational environment, and unwillingness to distinguish the administrative aspects. There is more to administration than human relations, and less of human behavior relevant to administrative theory.

Social-System School

The social-system school concentrates on the organizational setting of administrative activity and institutionalized patterns of behavior. At the one end, it concentrates on formal bureaucratic structures. At the other, it overlaps with the human-behavior school, but differs in that it is sociologically rather than psychologically oriented. The breadth of the social-system school necessitates a subclassification for convenience.

Bureaucratic theory Bureaucratic theory begins with Max Weber's ideal model, brought to the United States in the 1930s by refugee academics, but not widely circulated until translations were freely available after World War II. Weber distinguished between power, which might involve coercion, and authority, which was voluntary obedience, based on custom (traditional), personal leadership (charismatic), or impersonal rules (legal-rational or bureaucratic). The legal-rational orginization, the most effective form of social combination, was hierarchically staffed by specialists administering impersonal rules in the most efficient manner to attain objectives. Ideally, the staff should be disinterested career employees, appointed on the basis of competency, who should record their decisions for continuity in interpreting impersonal rules. Discounting criticisms and refinements emanating from mistranslation and misinterpretation, post-Weberian bureaucratic theory has explored the characteristics of the ideal type in the real world, the functional and dysfunctional aspects of bureaucratic administration, bureaucratic behavior, the cultural environment of bureaucracy, bureaucratic power, bureaucratic displacement of goals (de-bureaucratization), categories of bureaucracy, and the bureaucratization of the administrative culture. The obvious relationship between bureaucratic theory and public administration needs little elaboration, as in many low-income countries public authorities may be the only bureaucracies, and in all societies they are the largest and most important bureaucratic organizations.

Nonbureaucratic organizational theory   Bureaucratic theory dominates organizational theory, but not all formal organizations are bureaucratic, and not all organizations are formal. Chester Barnard, in *The Functions of the Executuve* (Cambridge, Mass.: Harvard University Press, 1938), first outlined a theory of cooperative systems—that organizations were elaborate systems of mutual cooperation to overcome individual limitations and master the natural environment for a better life. Sociologists, in exploring the administrative aspects of informal organizations, find themselves in the territory of the human-behavior school, when they explore informal relationships in formal organizations. Much of the theory in this area concerns alternatives to bureaucracy such as cooperatives, communes, voluntary associations, professional societies, and temporary and unstructured organizations.

Systems theory   Systems theory directs attention to the relationships between component parts in the administrative system. At one level, the relationships between the administrative system and other systems are explored in terms of input-output energy transformation models. At another, the same relationships are described in structural-functional terms, that is, the objectives of the administrative process or societal functions and their institutionalized forms. Alternatively, administration and organization are viewed as closed systems with authority structures, status symbols, common working rules, differently composed groups, conflicts, self-correcting mechanisms, and internal dynamics.

Administrative roles   In contrast to administrative process and bureaucratic characteristics, theories about administration and philosophies of administration analyze the role of administration in society. They focus on the ends— the well-ordered society, the good life, the fully realized individual—and on the part that the administrative system could play in achieving those ends as stabilizer, initiator, unifier, appeaser, and entrepreneur.

Because public administration, however defined, is a social system, these different approaches have been valuable, some more than others. They have broken the barriers of the administrative process and empirical schools and brought a wider perspective to xenophobic public authorities and inward-looking public administrators. They have helped to place the subject in its social milieu and set its location within social science, without being swallowed by sociology. However, administration cannot be equated with organization, nor organizational behavior with administrative behavior, although they are intimately related. The danger is that the social-systems school may obliterate the distinction altogether.

Decision-Making School

The universalistic implications of the social-systems school have been carried further by the decision-making school, originating in Herbert Simon's *Administrative Behavior* (New York: Crowell-Collier-Macmillan, 1947), in which he pointed out that there was no connection between the perfection of administrative processes, as then conceived in the POSDCORB formula, and the attainment of objectives. The missing factor was correct decision making, by which he meant the optimum rational choice between alternative courses of action. Thus began Simon's search for rational decision-making models, from which guides to real-world decision making might be derived. It led him into mathematical theory and cybernetics, and later still to recording the process of thinking itself. The search for rational decision making was joined early by economic theorists, whose techniques of rational economic analysis seemed eminently suitable, and economic practitioners in governmental business who were seeking better ways of economic forecasting and decision making.

Rational model building, based on economic data, dominated the decision-making school until behavioralism gained ground and theorists began to study how decisions were actually made in different situations. The decision-making school has since widened its horizons to include the circumstances giving rise to the need for decisions, decision makers, the processes of decision making, fact-value controversies, practical aids to better decision making, and the ramifications of decisions. By the time theorists have taken into consideration everything that decision makers do and may or should take into account when making decisions, they may find themselves considering all human knowledge, providing that some connection can be traced. It is debatable whether decision making deserves a school of its own. It may be just another administrative subprocess to add to the POSDCORB formula. As the importance of good decisions grows while man increases his capacity for self-destruction, public administration seeks leads to better decision making (which is not the same as rational decision making or economic rationality) and will look increasingly to the decision-making school for help.

Mathematics School

As general theories deal with the abstract, mathematical physics can be employed, as Simon quickly discovered. The mathematics school, tracing its origins to the pioneer scientific-management movement at the close of the nineteenth century, believes that administration is a logical process and can be "expressed in terms of mathematical symbols and relationships."[7] Mathematical models simulate reality. As real-life data replaces mathematical symbols, the models approximate what should happen. They are indispensable in handling complexity, prediction, and tangibles. On a limited scale, they have been employed with success in decision making, organizational design, budgeting, construction projects, research and development, and supplies and storage. But as the other administrative-theory schools indicate, its basic premises are wrong. Administration is not logical, nor can it be reduced to

[7] Koontz, "The Management Theory Jungle," p. 185.

mathematical symbols. Mathematical physics—ranging from systems analysis and operations research to cybernetics and probability theory—is a useful tool for administrative practitioners, particularly in planning, policy making, management controls, and data collection, but it can only be applied to quantifiable data.

Integration School

Koontz's classification can be reduced to two major schools, the reductionist administrative-process school that would incorporate the empirical, decision-making, and mathematic schools, and a holistic administrative-system school that would incorporate the human-behavior and social-systems schools. The former would examine the components of administrative activity, while the latter would place administrative activity in context. Perhaps the two schools could be further integrated, as the integration school believes they can be. The differences between them are not so wide to justify the paper warfare being conducted between administrative theorists. The integrationalists follow two broad strategies. The first is amalgamation through standard definitions, cross reference, indexing, and analysis of existing theories. In this way overlapping and duplication would be eliminated, contradictions reconciled, differences patched up, and the whole field reduced considerably in size to basic propositions, both tested and untested. A start is made within the different schools, and then the operation is extended to the whole field. In 1958, J. G. March and H. A. Simon made an attempt in *Organizations* (New York: Wiley, 1958) to consolidate theories of economic organization, and later, J. G. March reviewed the state of organizational theory in encyclopedical form in *Handbook of Organizations* (Chicago: Rand McNally, 1965).

The second strategy is fusion within a broad framework of an all-embracive administrative or organizational theory. The *Administrative Science Quarterly* began with this idea probably in mind when it published E. H. Litchfield's "Notes on a General Theory of Administration" (1., No. 1. [June 1956], 3–29), and later, A. de Grazia's "The Science and Values of Administration" (5., No. 1. [Dec. 1960], 363–398 and No. 2. [March 1961], 557–583). More ambitious than these attempts at defining the field of administrative theory was B. Gross, in *The Managing of Organizations* (New York: Free Press, 1964), who endeavored to encompass all theories and theorists within a general framework of administrative theory. The intellectual feat has not been rewarding. Administrative theorists have shown no inclination to accept the framework of Litchfield, de Grazia, or Gross, or to coordinate their approaches. Instead, they have continued to go their respective ways and fly off at tangents, to the utter confusion of fellow theorists and newcomers to administrative theory. As Waldo remarks, "There is no reason to believe that agreement, unification, simplification, and systematization lie in the immediate future."[8]

[8] Waldo, "Organization Theory," p. 223.

Administrative theory may be richer in theories than public administration theory, but it finds itself in a similar quandary. What are the theories trying to describe? Is there something identifiable as administration, administrative activity, administrative skill, administrative science? Can that something be isolated, studied in isolation, and abstracted into general theories in isolation? Would a concentrated attack on the central issue profit more than a ragged assault on different aspects according to individual fancy? Could the creative theorists forget their personal rivalries and their conceptual differences long enough to coordinate their efforts into a concerted drive on major methodological and philosophical issues? Are breakthroughs made in this way in other fields of study? Variety and competition have their merits. They stimulate exploration and act as self-correcting devices when either anarchy or monopoly threaten. Administrative theory is comparatively new, and early mistakes must be expected. Much effort will be spent at the beginning chasing unfruitful leads. Progress is not uniform; plateaus and reverses are encountered, as well as breakthroughs, but sufficient progress has been made in the last two decades to warrent patience.

> Administrative science is still in its pre-paradigmatic stage marked by a plethora of competing schools, a polyglot of languages, and, accordingly, a confusion of logics. There is neither a common research tradition nor the necessary consensus for a common field of inquiry. Each of the competing schools questions the others, adventurism is rampant, and commonly accepted standards of control do not exist.[9]

The evolving "normal science" of administration has yet to accept a common paradigm that will provide the necessary consensus for a common field of inquiry (that is, a discipline) and generate a distinctive and coherent research tradition. It is still open to novelty and innovation. Once it reaches the stage of a normal science, efforts will be directed almost exclusively to the problems that arise in the context of the paradigm.

> Creativity in normal science is creative problem-solving within the terms and conditions of the paradigm. Innovation means finding ingenious solutions to the problems that it generates. What is sought is not surprise, not the unexpected, not new theories and models, but findings that will lend greater clarity and precision to the paradigm and extend its range of application.[10]

At the paradigmatic stage, the babble will cease, and the schools will unite, but administrative theory will lose much of its originality and novelty. It will be less receptive to new ideas until the agreed paradigm is challenged by new phenomena, the appearance of anomalies and the search for a new conceptual framework. A common paradigm has its disadvantages. It may be preferable at this time to keep administrative theory open-ended, ambiguous,

[9] M. Landau, "The Study of Organizational Behavior," Papers in Comparative Public Administration, Special Series No. 3, American Society for Public Administration, Dec. 1966, pp. 38–39, following T. S. Kuhn, *The Structure of Scientific Revolution.* Chicago: International Encyclopedia of Unified Sciences, Vol. II, No. 2.

[10] Landau, "The Study of Organizational Behavior," p. 39.

and receptive to structural phenomena and behavioral characteristics, both of which are constantly changing. Nevertheless, the need remains for appropriate boundaries for administrative theory, not only to distinguish it from social-action theories, general theories of human behavior, and organizational theory, but to prevent theorists from studying all knowledge.

PROBLEMS IN PUBLIC-ADMINISTRATION THEORY

Public-administration theory shares some problems with administrative theory and has additional problems of its own. First, the theorists fritter away scarce resources on internecine warfare, instead of pushing ahead with their mutual task of seeking an acceptable paradigm. The battles scare off the practitioners and destroy the practical worth of much theory. Independence has its place, but reluctance to follow somebody else's definitions and usages results in semantic confusion, which produces a mass of terminologies that pass as new theories. Too much theory is produced for theory's sake. The remedy lies in the hands of the theorists themselves; they must put their own house in order if they want to influence a wider audience and attract the practitioners to their cause. After all, the ultimate test of theory is in practice. Not only should theorists reduce their attacks, recalling that the very heart of administrative endeavor is mutual cooperation, but they should try to develop stronger links with practitioners. Professional societies that cater to practitioners and theorists have to ensure that they do meet and exchange ideas and experiences, but not in random fashion at infrequent conferences that are too large in size and too short in time to allow cross-fertilization. The theorists need to offer their wares more actively in the practitioner's domain; the practitioners need to maintain close permanent contact with theorists and invade the latter's domain occasionally. Above all, the practitioners need to be encouraged to theorize before retirement, and the theorists need to be given a grounding in practice beyond the halls of academe apart from national crises.

Second, there is an overabundance of untested theory, for very little theory is abandoned. But the solution is not to call a moratorium on all further theory until existing theories have been tested and verified. More practicable would be the establishment of laboratories for theory validation. At present, the gap between pure theory and practice is not filled by applied theory. Thus PPBS is generalized before it is adequately tested in the areas in which it is supposed to be successful and without adequate feasibility tests. In new areas, nobody really knows whether a theory will work, and nobody is capable of translating it into practice. Laboratories would make excellent training grounds for theorists and practitioners to learn something of each other's skills, and they might liberate both from unnecessary jargon.

Third, the whole field is confused. The core concepts need clarification. Where does administrative theory stop and organization theory start? Can "administration" and "organization" be defined accurately? Does administrative man exist? How do administrative subprocesses differ between organizational and nonorganizational settings? Can administrative subprocesses be considered apart from administrative objectives? It is not always clear that the theorists themselves recognize that they need to answer these kinds of questions satisfactorily to themselves before they begin. They only succeed in adding to the confusion. Perhaps less excusable is failure to explore previous attempts at theory in the same or related areas. Some theories begin anew and recreate what has already been discovered elsewhere or further back in time. Systematic administrative theory may only have developed in the twentieth century, but this is no reason for ignoring or rejecting the random theory that has been accumulated over the centuries, either as folklore or as the wisdom of past sages. Circumstances may have been transformed, but the administrative predicament seems perennial from generation to generation, unless man himself too has been transformed. Perhaps a sorting house is required, or simply more vigorous scientific standards.

Fourth, much theory seems obsessed with bureacracy's search for rationality, legitimacy, stability, order, security, conformity, and much appears as advice to bureaucratic elites on how to maintain their position and still get the most out of the subordinate masses. The theorists tend to look downward and inward, rather than upward and outward, mesmerized with bureaucratic organization and reluctantly conceding that society could be administered in other ways. For the same reason, they tend to look backward rather than forward and to rest on past achievements, not dwell on future challenges, to assume a stable environment in equilibrium, not a turbulent environment in the grip of uncontrollable forces. Their approach tends to be static, not dynamic, and consequently increasingly outmoded and irrelevant to practitioners in contemporary society. The historical sense is largely missing; the parameters are drawn too narrowly; too many givens are assumed. The agreed paradigm is not bureaucracy.

Fifth, some place, distinctive or otherwise, has to be found for public-administration theory. While public administrators borrow much from administrative theory, administrative theorists borrow little from public administration. Until administrative theory takes public administration more fully into account, it cannot justify its claim of universality. Public-administration theory, in contrast, does not claim universality, but if it borrows so much and neglects its own field, it cannot claim distinctiveness. In any case, theory should remain relevant. By neglecting its own province, public-administration theory is in danger of becoming irrelevant. This has been a theme in Waldo's editorship of *Public Administration Review* and of younger scholars who believe in more socially oriented theory. In particular, public-administration theory is criticized on the following grounds: (a) that in overreacting to behavioralist attacks, public-administration theorists have virtually contracted out of normative theory and value considerations; (b) that in overreacting to academic attacks on the classical scientific-principles approach, public-administration theory has overcommitted itself to a priori thinking and neglected to pursue generalizations based on accumulated practical experience; (c) that public-administration theorists have tended to play down their political and public context; (d) that public-administration theory has concentrated too much on process and too little on objectives and results; (e) that public administration theory has ignored interorganizational relationships and behavior, in contrast to intraorganizational techniques and mores; (f) that public-administration theory has failed to cope with the radical transformation taking place in the role of public administration in contemporary society in conditions of turbulence; (g) that public-administration theory relies too heavily on static equilibrium analysis, rather than dynamic change analysis; and (h) that public-administration theorists have not assimilated the new provinces of public administration, such as environmental control, research and development, limited warfare, and civil liberties, into public administration theory.

The growing list of charges against public-administration theory is likely to provoke a reaction among theorists and to attract newcomers willing to meet the challenge. The most important needs are to update theory and to increase awareness of the philosophical issues behind the contemporary problem solving in public administration, particularly in the mixed-enterprise democratic states. Bailey neatly summarizes the problem:

> For if history teaches anything, it is that neither Plato's philosopher kings nor Jackson's untutored citizenry can safely manage a free society. Something besides natural or divine law must contain the propensities of the powerful: something beyond the transient prejudices and groupings of the demos must determine the end and means of society. Within this framework, public administration theory must attempt to fashion descriptions of reality, postulates of betterment, sophisticated assumptions about the capacities of men and institutions, and workable tenets of instrumentation which can improve both the ends and means of democratic government.[11]

Among those who have responded to the challenge is Todd La Porte, who proposes that the normative premise of public administration "should be that *the purpose of public organization is the reduction of economic, social and psychic suffering and the enhancement of life opportunities for those within and outside the organization.*"[12] The premise could guide efforts to select and integrate theories applicable to public organizations. He suggests further investigation into factors accounting for variations in (a) the power of public organizations in the polity, (b) their administrative productivity, (c) their internal authority structures, and (d) the role behavior of their executives, and the reciprocal consequences of various administrative actions for the

---

[11] S. K. Bailey, in Charlesworth, ed., *Theory and Practice of Public Administration*, p. 139.
[12] T. La Porte, "The Recovery of Relevance in the Study of Public Organizations," in F. Marini, ed., *Toward a New Public Administration*, San Francisco: Chandler, 1971, p. 32. Author's italics.

culture. If theorists follow his recommendation, he proposes that they *"write theory in such a way that if it is false it can be verified to be so"* and that they frame problems in ways which enable choice between alternative explanations.

> Empirical research without theory is barren; theory without normative awareness is pernicious; normative awareness without conceptual analysis and research is a denial of intellectual responsibility.[13]

His ideas are likely to influence the current search for a theory of public administration (see Chap. 12).

[13] La Porte, "The Recovery of Relevance in the Study of Public Organizations," p. 47.

11

Administrative Systems

Every society has a political system, an economic system, a social system, and an administrative system, and different societies have different administrative systems. None are identical, although similar societies, sharing cultural traits, may have similar administrative systems, that is, similar ways of getting things done. For example, the way things are done in France is quite different from the way they are done in Iraq or Indonesia or Iceland. The way things are done in affluent, middle-class suburbs is different from that in poor working-class slums or self-sufficient rural communes. There are private administrative systems, public administrative systems, and various mixtures of the two. The public-administrative systems may be highly bureaucratized in distinct public organizations, or they may be highly personal and rely on nonpublic organizations to perform their functions. Moreover, the same society may have many different public administration systems, and the same public authority may be part of many different administration systems.

Although each administrative system is unique, administrative systems can be compared according to their (a) processes, (b) purposes, (c) structures, and (d) environmental interaction. Transcultural administrative processes—that is, how different cultures get things done—can be examined at many different levels, from individuals to international arrangements, and according to race, sex, and other ascriptive criteria. The processes can be approached from different angles, namely, administrative ideology, methods, relations, actions, and results. Administrative purposes can also be examined at different levels, in terms of objectives, power plays, decision making, and behavioral norms. Administrative structures, through which the processes operate and the purposes are defined, can be divided into formal arrangements and behavioral networks, including organizational frameworks, nonbureaucratic systems and grapevines, or informal communications systems. The interaction between the administrative system and its environment can be approached in two ways: first, the environmental influences on the administrative system (for example, geography, history, culture, social structure, economic system, polity, religious doctrines, technology), and second, the administrative system's influence on its environment (for example, task fulfillment, rational cooperation, material progress, and transformation of environmental factors). The same comparative schema can be employed for nonpublic administrative systems and mixed systems.

Before World War II, the study of public administration, reflecting the preoccupation of every country with its own problems, was introverted. If studies of foreign systems were undertaken at all, they were directed at discovering what might be borrowed to help solve domestic administrative problems. They constituted little more than checklists of possible transnational reforms. Otherwise, comparative studies were country-by-country descriptions of the governmental systems of the major powers, with little analysis of their similarities and differences according to a conceptual framework. Each country was caught up in its own ideological strife, political crisis, economic upheavals, and social clashes. Great powers, which might have overcome cultural barriers, showed no inclination. They superimposed their peculiar administrative systems on other peoples through various forms of colonialism and trusteeship. The white man assumed natural superiority and could not conceive that he could learn anything from other peoples. On the contrary, his mission was to teach the natives to be good subjects. He did not have to be sensitive to international feeling, for there was no meaningful international community. Hardly any permanent international bodies existed, and their scope was strictly limited.

World War II transformed the situation by generating a continuing interest in foreign administrative systems. The war altered the political shape of the world. It destroyed the political regimes of the defeated powers and crippled the economies of most of the combatants. Few imperial powers could afford to maintain colonies. They could not resist militant national movements boosted by the war and the rivalry between the United States and the Soviet Union to champion subject peoples. War mobilization took many people into strange lands and forced them to work together in temporary international administrations. Prewar parochialism was challenged by war trauma and the ideological controversy that accompanied the peace. Internationalism assumed a new meaning as the world shrank in size and distance, with technological progress in transportation, communications, and weapons systems.

During the war, new, permanent international bodies were created to function after hostilities ended. Thus, the postwar world promised to be significantly different.

From the administrative standpoint, it has been different. First, the administrative systems of war-stricken countries were reconstructed or recreated according to foreign models, with the active support of local peoples. The western allies supported democratization. The Soviet Union assisted communist countries. In both cases, apparently successful formulas were later exported in modified form elsewhere in technical assistance programs, sometimes with unexpected results. Second, the Cold War and other postwar crises questioned assumptions held about administrative systems. As no system proved obviously superior to any other, much more information about the real workings of established administrative systems was needed. Third, as colonialism waned, and newly independent states came to outnumber the old, colonial administrative systems were revamped by indigenous peoples or abandoned altogether for something novel. Almost without exception, the new administrative systems soon ran into difficulties and needed external assistance. They were inappropriate, lacked the necessary infrastructures and resources, were overburdened, or collapsed in chaos. Fourth, a new international order came into being. In addition to the United Nations complex, a large number of international, regional, and multinational bodies was established, ranging from defense-treaty organizations, such as the North Atlantic Treaty Organization, with permanent headquarters, to economic unions, such as the European Economic Commission; from political associations, such as the Organization of African States, to regulatory bodies, such as the International Civil Aviation Organization. Finally, academics recognized that public administration had to be truly universal. Each administrative system had to be studied according to a common conceptual framework. Theorists therefore turned their attention to the virgin territory of comparative public administration.

The most important outcome in the postwar decades has been the recognition of many different public administration systems at different levels of public concern, with different functions and widely varying boundaries at different stages of development. To reduce the complexity, several classifications have been attempted; most follow the classification of their parent political system. Thus, there is a separate category for communist regimes, another for western democracies, perhaps separated into common-law Anglo-American systems and administrative-law western European systems, and various categories for newly independent and traditional states that fall into neither camp—either by region, such as Latin America, or the Middle East, or by polity, such as bureaucratic, autocratic, and dominant party. Other classifications prefer distinction by parent cultural pattern, such as fused agraria, diffracted industria, and prismatic societies that are moving from fusion to differentiation.[1]

[1] F. W. Riggs, *Administration in Developing Countries.* Boston: Houghton Mifflin, 1964.

For simplification, only three major types of public administration system will be considered here—new multicultural international systems, well-established national administrative systems within relatively homogeneous cultures, and newly established national developmental systems with heterogeneous cultures.

INTERNATIONAL SYSTEMS

International systems are very new. As they are still evolving distinctive patterns of their own, it is difficult to identify typical characteristics. The task grows easier as more international systems evolve and establish permanency, in contrast to what were formerly extensions of foreign diplomacy, temporary ad hoc arrangements, and international bodies without autonomy, powers, sanctions, or structures. The new permanent systems have autonomous organizational structures at a settled location, command independent resources, possess sanctions (including expulsion), and employ independent professional staffs, although their governing bodies may meet infrequently. They are likely to increase in number, scope, and activity as sovereign states find themselves incapable of coping with international problems and as notions of world government spread. They constitute a new province for law and order in human relationships. They demand more international public servants and extend international administrative law.

What is most distinctive about international systems is their ideology of internationalism—one world, human unity, and an ideal that all men are brothers responsible for one another. Their ideals are those of mankind—peace, security, safety, well-being, cultural integrity, equality, humanitarianism. They are deeply concerned about man and his environment, particularly (a) the planet and the solar system and the problems of space exploration; (b) the unexplored areas of the planet, including the seas, ice caps, mountain chains, and deserts; (c) the plant and animal world, especially the protection of rare species and the control of pests; and (d) the relations between men that threaten destruction, violence, pain, disease, and genocide. But the world is not ready to accept the ideology of internationalism: international systems find themselves isolated whenever member states place domestic and national considerations above internationalism. They are subject to bitter criticism for failing to live up to their projected ideals and to fulfill expectations. They are convenient scapegoats for the human predicament, about which they can do little without member support and adequate resources.

The purposes of international systems await classification. They are engaged in conflict resolution, scientific research, international social services, law and order, economic planning, rescue work, postal integration, and cultural enrichment, to mention but a few of the functions they perform. A whole discipline—international relations—is concerned with policy making in the international arena, international institutions, power plays, and many other aspects of international administrative systems. Rather than repeat what is extensively covered elsewhere, selected administrative concerns of international systems are briefly outlined to illuminate their evolving dynamics.

International systems have been slow to develop distinctive administrative techniques, for they can only progress as fast as member states permit. In addition, they have little formal power—no standing militia or police force, no prison system, and only a marginal system of rewards and punishments. Thus they rely on moral authority and appeal to human ideals. They also employ persuasion, example, influence, and appeals to emotion, rationality, and self-interest. They can depend on the idealism and devotion of their staffs, and above all, they are great improvisers, for they have to be. They have few guidelines, little experience, and scant resources. More importantly, they are working in novel areas. Before this century, nobody had attempted to disarm, control population growth voluntarily, improve health and education standards of people who could not help themselves, create enterprise where none existed, police international crime, or keep the peace between hostile neighbors, without adequate powers, sanctions, resources, and cooperation. International systems have to experiment, improvise, and make their own rules as they progress. Their work is both exciting and frustrating. The challenge is attractive, but environmental handicaps, such as having to work within member state limitations and bureaucratic boundaries, is frustrating. In some areas, international effort is so puny, compared with the task, that those involved are tempted to abandon what they do. They feel insignificant. They do not wish to act as face savers for man's inhumanity to man. They cannot abide the hypocrisy that allows their mentors to mouth pious ideals while acting in a contrary manner. Similar traits are found in all administrative systems where administrators feel that they are pushing against the mainstream.

If international public servants are to continue to perform in the face of overwhelming odds, they really must believe in what they do. Their loyalty is to internationalism. They are citizens of the world dealing with a public interest of world dimensions. Yet their background is nationalist, they remain state nationals (with exceptional privileges), and if they want to change careers, they must return to a national setting. Their national governments are not above subordinating international interests or exploiting nationals working for international bodies. The international organization can guard against subversives, but the problem of dual loyalty for the international civil servant persists. The United Nations insists on a loyalty oath that precludes rival instructions to its own and the International Civil Service Advisory Board has formulated an ethical code that stresses organizational loyalty, cooperation with all colleagues, international mindedness, and restraint in personal and political expression likely to offend. The air of impermanence or temporariness that surrounds international systems, whose functions can be abandoned at any time and whose resources are precarious at best, undermines official sanctions against staff with ready career alternatives.

International systems have other peculiar problems. International organizations have no real control over their future. They cannot plan meaningfully. They cannot choose their own staffs without offending member states in some way. If they institute merit systems, member states with superior education systems are favored. Unless the permanent headquarters is rotated, the host state benefits from the capital inflows and generated employment in positions for which foreign recruitment is too expensive or fair representation is not required. Quota systems break down if demand exceeds supply. Fluency in common languages is an automatic self-selecting device. Foreign location, frequent moves, constant travel, social isolation, and cultural shock, which may be part of international work, are other handicaps of international employment, although the status and prestige of international jobs and the excitement and mystery of foreign lands exploited by the tourist and travel industries remain powerful magnets. Foreign services in domestic systems face similar problems, but without the career handicaps.

International systems are the wave of the future. Some contemporary difficulties will disappear as increasingly international systems become accepted, permanent, resourceful, and adaptive. Their existence will be less precarious, their base secured, their reputation enhanced, and their appeal more attractive. Public and private systems will probably draw close together in association, function, and staff interchange, and possibly greater uniformity in adminstrative principles and methods will develop. It may then be possible to study their inner workings and to discover whether their operations are significantly different from other administrative systems. In the meantime, their influence over national administrative systems will continue to grow.

COMPARATIVE POLITICAL SYSTEMS

Contemporary analysis of national and developmental administrative systems is derived largely from comparative political analysis. Discussion of national and developmental systems is therefore prefaced by analysis of national systems in political science. Political scientists see public administration as part of the political system: "the patterned interaction of roles affecting decisions backed up by the threat of physical compulsion."[2] Public administration has been identified for most of its history with the formal apparatus of the public bureaucracy used as a political instrument by the rulers to implement their decisions. This tradition, reaching back beyond Aristotle, continues. Political scientists consider that no description of any polity or governmental system is complete without some reference to the public bureaucracy and an account of the administrative apparatus of the polity. As governmental systems are being formed and reformed continuously, and as

[2] G. A. Almond, "Comparative Political Systems," *The Journal of Politics,* 18 (Aug. 1956), 395.

their parts and relationships change ceaselessly, there is a constant demand for descriptions of national systems.

Since World War II, the demand for studies of national political and administrative systems has risen immeasurably. National systems are more important than ever before, and there are more of them. Besides natural curiosity and the endless search for new knowledge, more has to be known about foreign systems to anticipate and provide for international repercussions of domestic happenings. More people are traveling beyond their own countries and want to know about conditions pertaining elsewhere. More information is needed to prepare people for foreign and international service. Domestic problems are forcing more administrators to search for solutions in foreign experience and to enlist the aid of foreign administrators. Academic scholars are no longer content with formal descriptions of institutions; they want to go beyond the form to discover what really transpires and how administrative systems really work. They want to explain observed variables and construct models from which they can appraise actions and policies, identify problems and trends, hypothesize about the real world, and build general theories of society with predictive value.

Dissatisfaction with traditional descriptive approaches first came to a head at a conference of political scientists held under the auspices of the Social Science Research Council at Northwestern University in 1952. Virtually no studies of political systems outside the western democratic framework had been undertaken. The descriptions of western democracies had been too formal, too concerned with history and law and not enough with social science. These descriptions were divorced from their total cultures and did not demonstrate the linkages between the polity and its environment. They ignored the substance of politics—issues, problems, power, ideology, values, decisions, legitimate force. They were idiographic descriptions of unique governmental systems, according to internal peculiarities: they were not based on a common conceptual framework from which similarities and differences would be readily discernable. Comparative study had to be truly comparative; it had to consider substance as well as form, universals as well as idiosyncracies, dynamics as well as statics. What was wanted was "an emphasis on dynamic processes, coupled with a rediscovery of the discipline's forgotten responsibility for policy decisions: a desire for integration of the social sciences, dictated by a prevailing multi-causal approach to an entangled, intricate, reality; and a new summons to a theoretical reorientation of the whole field."[3]

The conference participants proceeded to map some guidelines for future comparative studies. Some, like the exhortation to study nonwestern polities, were obvious. Others were directed at grappling with the problems of scope, depth, purpose, and subjection in determining criteria for the definition and

[3] S. Neumann, "Comparative Politics: A Half-Century Appraisal," *Journal of Politics*, 19 (1957), pp. 369–390.

adequate representation of variables. As comparison against identical backgrounds was impossible, comparison should take place at different levels of complexity and abstraction, from simple elements in fairly homogeneous systems to whole systems, using categories and concepts either within the framework of a general theory or ad hoc according to the problem, process, or institution under study. Working from low-level tested hypotheses, a general theory of politics would emerge from a conceptual scheme. The immediate need was the search for a suitable classificatory scheme that would aid conceptualization at various levels of abstraction.

Four possible classificatory schemes were suggested—international relations, area, problem, and decision making. The decision-making schema envisaged politics as providing enforceable legitimate decisions. The political process was a struggle between power aspiration and policy aspiration for legitimacy. The outcome was determined by the effective power structure, and the end condition, legitimacy, reflected societal values. Comparative political analysis should be concerned with exploring the basis of legitimacy, political aspirations and processes, effective power factors, the decision-making system, and a theory of change that would account for tensions between formal and informal processes.[4]

Despite open hostility to the theoretical bent of the Northwestern Conference and sharp criticism of its classificatory scheme, even by those who applauded its challenge to tradition, political scientists concerned with comparative analysis continued their search for more suitable classificatory schemes on two major lines; (a) general system theories and (b) political culture theories.

General-System Theories

General-system theories follow the Northwestern Conference support for a general theory of politics based on a conceptual scheme of a political system, with political actors and political relationships between them. The system is considered a convenient analytical device to separate the political aspects of society from the rest of social activity.

Easton's input-output model conceived the political system ("how authoritative decisions are made and executed for a society") as an energy model, in which systems management processes maintain a steady flow of inputs to be converted into outputs.[5] In the political system the inputs were demands (political issues) and supports ("energy in the form of actions or orientations promoting and resisting a political system, the demands arising in it, and the decisions issuing from it") relating to the community, regime, and government.

---

[4] "Research in Comparative Politics: Report of the Inter-University Summer Seminar on Comparative Politics, Social Science Research Council," *American Political Science Review,* 47 (1953) pp. 641–657.

[5] D. Easton, *The Political System.* New York: Alfred A. Knopf, 1953; and "An Approach to the Analysis of Political Systems," *World Politics,* IX (Apr. 1957), pp. 383–400.

The outputs were decisions and policies. Comparative analysis should concentrate on how demands arose and were transformed into issues and outputs, and on how systems maintain a steady flow of inputs.

Snyder's decision-making model had two fundamental purposes: "to help identify and isolate the 'crucial structures' in the political realm where change takes place—where action is initiated and carried out, where decisions must be made; and to help analyze systematically the decision-making behavior which leads to action and which sustains action."[6] Comparative analysis should concentrate on decisions within the governmental organization (thus using a narrower definition of politics than Easton) and authoritative decision makers.

Macridis tried to combine the traditional approach with the decision-making emphasis of Easton and Snyder by constructing a model[7] based on four categories—decision making, power, ideology, and institutions—which he later[8] reduced to three—authority and purpose, deliberation and decision making, and interest configuration. The political system was an action system, in which individuals and groups acted to translate their objectives into binding decisions. Comparative analysis should concentrate on the structure of authority and purposes, interest configuration, and the decision-making system.

Apter preferred the following categories in comparative analysis: social stratification, political groups, and government[9]—which are broader political categories than those used by Snyder. At least Apter's model had some empirical backing;[10] it also stressed the role of government in systems maintenance.

> The crucial concerns of government are those which threaten the existence of the unit of which it is part. With its practical monopoly of coercive powers, government has an indivisible responsibility for protecting the system. Government handles its responsibilities in terms of certain minimal structures. If any of these structures should fail to operate, government itself must undergo drastic modification, and/or the system itself will undergo drastic modification. Therefore, important threats to the system are, first, threats to the ability of government to work in terms of its structural requisites. Second, they can derive from inadequate performance of government within the structural requisites from the point of view of the system as a whole, i.e. bad policy, inadequate action etc. . . . A tentative set of goals can be listed for any government as follows: (1) The structure of authoritative decision making; (2) the structure of accountability and consent; (3) the

[6] R. C. Snyder, "Decision-Making Approach to the Study of Political Phenomena," in R. Young, ed., *Approaches to the Study of Politics.* Evanston, Ill.: Northwestern University Press, 1958, p. 15.

[7] R. Macridis, *The Study of Comparative Government.* New York: Random House, 1955.

[8] R. Macridis, "Interest Groups and the Political System in Comparative Analysis," Southern Political Science Association, Nov. 1959.

[9] D. Apter, "A Comparative Method for the Study of Politics," *American Journal of Sociology,* 9 (Nov. 1958), 221–237.

[10] D. Apter, *The Gold Coast in Transition.* Princeton: Princeton University Press, 1955.

structure of coercion and punishment; (4) the structure of resource determination and allocation; and (5) the structure of political recruitment and role assignment.[11]

Comparative analysis should concentrate on structural requisites (goals) and format (dictatorial, oligarchical, indirect or direct representation), as related to the setting and the manner in which the three categories interact and change.

The importance of these general systems theories in public administration is the obvious temptation to replace the word "politics" with "administration" and to reframe the models with administrative systems in mind. In this way, a general theory of (public) administration, universal to all administrative systems, might emerge. The models of Easton and Snyder would need little alteration, whereas those of Macridis and Apter would involve a search for equivalents in the administrative system. All have obvious advantage in breaking away from the traditional descriptions of formal institutions to direct attention to the administrative system in context, the administrative transformation of resources (inputs) into societal products (outputs), the structure and functions of the administrative system, administrative behavior, administrative stratification, and administrative recruitment. They escape from the bureaucratic paradigm and are especially helpful in reorienting the western mind to nonbureaucratic administrative systems.

Political-Culture Theories

Political-culture theories do not begin with universals, but acknowledge the existence of variety. They seek to reduce diversity by classifying the different systems according to common criteria, from which narrow-range and middle-range hypotheses can be formulated, and from which, in turn, general theories may eventually emerge. They are grounded in Talcott Parson's interpretation of the concept of systems in sociology, particularly his systems problems of pattern maintenance, integration, adaptation, and goal adaptation, and his pattern variables: universalism—particularism, achievement—ascription, specificity—diffuseness, emotion—reason. They discern different political cultures, each molded in its environment so that the political system cannot be meaningfully abstracted. They draw attention to the complex interrelationships between the political system and its parent culture. They are prepared to accept nonwestern cultures at face value, rather than conceive them in the western terms built into general systems models.

Political roles   Almond objected to the particularistic, regional, and structural-institutional classifications of the traditional approach because of their irrelevancy to the substance of politics, particularly in the nonwestern world. He turned to sociological concepts to highlight the essential differences

[11] D. Apter, "A Comparative Method for the Study of Politics," *American Journal of Sociology,* 9 (Nov. 1958) 225.

between the political systems of Anglo-America, continental Europe, totalitarianism, and pre-industrial or partially industrial systems. He combined Parson's idea of patterned interaction (or roles), based on empirically observable behavior, with Weber's definition of the political system (the legitimate monopoly of physical coercion over a given territory or population), and saw the task of comparative analysis as characterizing all the patterned interactions or interdependent roles within a political system.[12] A political culture was the peculiar pattern of orientations to political action in which the political system was embedded. It did not coincide either with the political system or the whole culture. Thus, the Anglo-American countries shared a political culture, but not political systems. They were characterized by a homogeneous, secular political culture, "a multi-varied political culture, a rational-calculating, bargaining and experimental political culture." Their role structure was "(1) highly differentiated, (2) manifest, organized and bureaucratized, (3) characterized by a high degree of stability in the functions of the roles, and (4) likely to have a diffusion of power and influence." In contrast, the nonconsensual totalitarian political systems had synthetically homogeneous political cultures, in which the characteristic orientation to authority tended to be a combination of conformity and apathy. They were tyrannies, characterized by the predominance of coercive roles and the functional instability of the power roles to prevent stable delegation of power and possible creation of other power centers. Pre-industrial political systems were embedded in mixed political cultures, an unstable and unpredictable amalgam of western and indigenous cultures, characterized by a relatively low degree of structural differentiation, a high degree of substitutive possibility of roles, and mixed political role structures.

Political functions   Almond continued to explore the possibilities of a structural-functional classification of political systems, first with Coleman[13] in a static model, and then with Powell[14] in a dynamic model. Again political systems were treated as whole entities, shaping and being shaped by their environments, grounded in political cultures—that is, their psychological dimensions (consisting of attitudes, beliefs, values, and skills). Analysis concentrated on their activities or functions.

First, a system's capabilities denoted its performance in its environment— its ability to extract resources from its environment, its ability to regulate the behavior of its constituents, its ability to maintain a flow of effective symbols, its ability to distribute benefits to constituents, and its ability to respond to demands and pressures, both domestically and internationally.

Second, the system's conversion processes referred to the ways a system transformed inputs into outputs: interest articulation—the way demands

[12] G. A. Almond, "Comparative Political Systems," pp. 391–409.

[13] G. A. Almond and J. S. Coleman, eds., *The Politics of the Developing Areas.* Princeton: Princeton University Press, 1960.

[14] G. A. Almond and G. Bingham Powell, *Comparative Politics.* Boston: Little, Brown, 1966.

were formulated; interest aggregation—the ways demands were combined in the form of alternative courses of action; rule making—the ways authoritative rules were formulated; rule application—the way the rules were applied and enforced; rule adjudication—the way individual cases were decided in rule application; and communication—the way these activities were communicated within the system and between the system and its environment.

Third, system maintenance and adaptation described how the system survived through political recruitment (how political roles were filled) and socialization (how political cultures were maintained and changed). Almond and Powell proceeded to classify political systems according to the degree of structural differentiation and cultural secularization. Primitive systems had intermittent political structures, in which there was a minimum of structural differentiation and a concommitant diffuse, parochial culture. Traditional systems had differentiated governmental-political structures. Modern systems had differentiated political infrastructures. Within the major classes, further distinction could be made according to degree of structural differentiation, structural autonomy, secularization, and other factors.

Modernizing regimes   Dynamic models had already been applied to developmental polities that brought relatively backward societies to modernity. Shils, reviewing newly independent states, classified them into five major types; (a) political democracy, (b) tutelary democracy, (c) modernizing oligarchies, (d) totalitarian oligarchy, and (e) traditional oligarchy, according to the nature of their preconditions (ruling elite, opposition, machinery of authority, public opinion, civil order) and their characteristic structural conditions and behavioral patterns (or components).[15] Apter, also combining structural and functional characteristics, reduced these categories to (a) mobilization (aristocratic) regimes, (b) reconciliation (representative) regimes, and (c) neomercantilist (autocratic) regimes.[16]

Political institutions   Riggs[17] believed that functionalism has been taken too far, that it had been interpreted too narrowly in terms of an organizational society and too widely in terms of behavioral characteristics, and that it distinguished too sharply between public politics and private politics. The mistake was in rejecting institutionalism altogether, instead of overhauling it to omit its ethnocentric bias and value loading. He proposed redefining functionalism in terms of structural rather than behavioral relevance, and returning to structural rather than functional identification of political systems. He began by identifying the most important kinds of governmental institutions, which he designated as executives, bureaucracies, legislatures, and parties. He identified six basic types of polity (cephaly): acephaly (folk), which lacked all four institutions; procephaly (classical), which contained

[15] E. Shils, *Political Development in the New States.* The Hague: 1962.

[16] D. Apter, *The Politics of Modernization.* Chicago: University of Chicago Press, 1965.

[17] F. W. Riggs, "The Comparison of Whole Political Systems," in R. T. Holt and J. E. Turner, eds., *The Methodology of Comparative Research.* New York: Free Press, 1970.

only an executive; orthocephaly (traditional), which included a bureaucracy as well; heterocephaly (premodern), which contained a legislature too; metacephaly (contemporary), which contained all four institutions; and supracephaly, which contained more political institutions still. Each category contained a cluster of epitypes, ranging from the right, which emphasized conservatism, order, stability, *capacity;* to the left, which emphasized change, justice, reform and *equality;* with a transitional center form representing a dialectical stage of synthesis. At metacephaly level and above both left and right, polities had to be subdivided to allow for the complexity of modern political systems. At metacephaly level, Riggs identified hypotonic (movement) regimes and atonic (inclusive) regimes on the left (syntonic) and heterotonic (dyarchic) regimes and autotonic (stratocratic) regimes on the right (hypertonic). At supracephaly level, he identified anatonic (soviet) regimes, isotonic (presidential) regimes, and monotonic (coalitional and noncoalitional) regimes.

Whereas the general-systems approach emphasizes universals, that is, similarities, the political-culture approach emphasizes peculiarities, that is, differences, although again the transition from political culture to administrative culture is tempting. More so than the general-systems approach, the political-cultures approach challenges western egocentrism by directing attention to the divergences both in space and time. Political systems are different because their environments are different, and the environments are different because to some extent their political systems are different. Yet, political systems with a similar political culture may be studied together to advantage, as can apparently similar political systems (from the institutional viewpoint) with different political cultures. New concepts are needed for political systems that are both institutionally and functionally different, and that have diverse political cultures; old concepts based on homogeneous political cultures do not apply. Finally, performance of the system is related to the underlying culture, the nature of the environment, the volume and diversity of demand not met through other systems, and the ability of the system to change and adapt. These ideas were needed imports for comparative public administration.

COMPARATIVE ADMINISTRATIVE SYSTEMS

Work in comparative public administration has closely followed comparative political analysis. The same people have been involved, moving from one to the other without any difficulty. Whereas the comparative political scientists have worked within the American Political Science Association, the comparative public-administration scholars have worked within the Comparative Administration Group of the American Society for Public Administration and have developed closer links with counterparts throughout the world on an individual basis, and collectively, through the International Institute of

Administrative Sciences. Their postwar criticisms of comparative analysis were almost identical, namely, that descriptions of formal institutions, legal norms, and administrative regulations were not comparative, but unreal, narrow, egocentric, subjective, and static. In 1947 Dahl, for instance, bemoaned the absence of a universal public administration.[18] In 1952, moved by the need for better training in comparative administration to meet practical problems posed by America's new role in world affairs, the Public Administration Clearing House hosted a conference on comparative administration at Princeton. It was agreed first, that a distinction should be drawn between policy values in government programs and academic values in understanding administration; second, that focused research would be more rewarding than reclassifying existing data; and third, that criteria of relevance were indispensable. A subcommittee of the Committee on Public Administration of the American Political Science Association was formed to develop "criteria of relevance" and to prepare a research guide.

A summary frame of reference had been prepared by Sayre and Kaufman for the Princeton Conference. It contained a series of questions concerning the organization of the administrative system, its control, and its ability to secure compliance. Kaufman had revised the original draft to include proposals for more hypotheses and for criteria of adequate performance as a guide to practitioners. The subcommittee bypassed the Sayre-Kaufman design (which would have absorbed large research funds for what now seem somewhat simplistic and culture-bound assumptions) and proposed instead an investigation of the administrative systems of three emerging countries with similar backgrounds, on the assumption that if they did not have similar public administration systems, other factors were at work. The American Political Science Association asked Sayre, Kaufman, Sharp (the chairman of the subcommittee), and Riggs to develop the research design. The revised Sayre-Kaufman draft was further reworked into a conceptual scheme to be applied to three similar cultures on a general ecological approach advocated by Riggs. But it could attract no financial support. This early setback, however, did not discourage the new comparative administration movement, which soon became the most prolific area of research and publication in the discipline.

Slowly but surely, information gaps about national administrative systems have been filled, particularly for countries where research could be conducted in English. The most serious deficiencies have remained in communist and totalitarian regimes, Latin America, and the newest of the newly independent states. Idiographic studies have tried to meet Dahl's 1947 criticism by hypothesizing at narrow- and middle-range theory level, although much idiographic research has followed traditional lines. These studies have borrowed extensively from other social sciences, and they have incorporated,

---

[18] R. A. Dahl, "The Science of Public Administration: Three Problems," *Public Administration Review,* 7, No. 1 (1947), 8.

both consciously and unconsciously, the theoretical models and conceptions of comparative politics. They have become so ecologically oriented that no idiographic study lacks its introductory cultural perspective, even if the relations between the environment and the administrative system or subsystem are not properly linked in the rest of the text. They are less prescriptive, exhibit less self-assurance that the western model is superior, and are less normative than previous idiographic studies. Institutionalism is being overtaken by behavioralism. Above all, the studies are truly comparative and attempt to fulfill the purposes of comparison:

> . . . to learn the distinctive characteristics of a particular administrative system or cluster of systems; to find out what makes certain administrative features work well in one country or era while they fail dismally in another; to identify the factors—cultural, political, and social—that are involved in success or failure; to explain the differences in behavior of bureaucrats and bureaucracies in different countries and cultures; and, finally to discern what changes, if any, ought to be introduced and how they can be introduced to improve the performance of a bureaucracy . . . to arrive at a conceptual knowledge rather than a knowledge of details.[19]

They also reflect the two major concerns of comparative administration as envisaged at the Princeton Conference, namely, the search for a conceptual framework, or a nomothetic approach (which "seeks generalizations, 'laws,' hypotheses that assert regularities of behavior, [and] correlations between variables"),[20] and practical improvements in governmental programs, or a developmental approach.

The nomothetic approach shares its theory, conceptualization, and methodology with comparative politics, which is hardly surprising, given the breakdown of the politics-administration dichotomy, common concern with whole cultures in time and space, fusion in less-developed countries, and dependence on behavioralism, model building, and structural-functional theories. Two important departures deserve special attention.

Bureaucratic Theory

Because the public bureaucracy has been the central concern of public administration, comparative public administration has been equated largely with comparative public bureaucracies. The comparative-administration movement killed the instrumentality thesis, which had been the core of the traditional institutional approach derived from western neutrality norms. The bureaucracy is now portrayed as a political actor, an essential ingredient of the political system, a consumer and producer of societal products, a power center, a pressure group, a systems stabilizer, a change agent, a polit-

---

[19] N. Raphaeli, "Comparative Public Administration: An Overview," in N. Raphaeli, ed., *Readings in Comparative Public Administration.* Boston: Allyn & Bacon, 1967, p. 4.

[20] F. W. Riggs, "Trends in the Comparative Study of Public Administration," *International Review of Administrative Sciences.* 28, No. 1 (1962), pp. 9–15.

ical symbol, a political socializer, a social elite, an interest articulator, a political, social and economic system, a source of political recruitment, a decision broker, and an environmental determinant. As a result, bureaucratic theory has been transformed; bureaucratic theories now take into account these new dimensions:

a. *Bureaucratic typologies.* Structural characteristics, functional roles, recruitment systems, political system, general culture, and behavioral characteristics
b. *Bureaucratic ideologies.* Role of the bureaucracy in the political system and self-perceived roles of the bureaucrat
c. *Bureaucratic power base.* Control and dependence, functions, resources, enterprise, status, alliances and rivals, and expectations
d. *Bureaucratic decision making.* Scope, extent, direction, quality, locus, style, composition of decision makers, and suitability.
e. *Bureaucratic actions.* Processes, communications, public relations, administrative behavior, and rationality
f. *Bureaucratic performance.* Conversion processes, political socialization and recruitment, systems maintenance and adaptation, administrative capacity and the satisfaction of societal needs
g. *Bureaucratic setting.* International and domestic hazards, resource mobility, cultural ambivalence, political culture, social stratification, economic system, political regime, organizational scale and other ecological variables
h. *Bureaucratic models.* Input-output, information-energy, decision making, policy making, social system, and development
i. *Bureaucratic dynamics.* Attitudes, values, external relations, internal mobility, objectives, adaptability, and dysfunctions

The province of bureaucratic theory grows increasingly complex as theorists become aware that they must get outside their own culture, values, conceptions, and approaches to appreciate how different other people are and how many different ways exist of achieving the same objectives. The functionalists warn that the structural emphasis of bureaucracy makes it an inadequate tool. The bureaucratic theorists respond that, inadequate or not, it is the best available, certainly better than a functional tool that involves searching for the structures through which functions are performed or wrestling with behavior boundaries.

Model Building

A spate of model building has characterized the comparative-administration movement. To structure the mass of data accumulated in comparative studies, a model of some kind has been indispensable. Researchers have not gone into the field without preconceived notions about what they were looking for and which facts would be relevant. To do otherwise would leave them swamped with undigested and unrelated information. The new comparative-administration movement has not only made its models explicit, but has been prepared to debate the models and to risk professional criticism. Hence, the

Weberian ideal type of bureaucratic model has been subject to rigorous examination and reformulation. No theorist maintains that the models coincide with reality, but models do highlight general characteristics and important relationships; facilitate instruction, research, and analysis; point to factors that may escape empirical observation; illustrate variables, and guide proposition building. Among the models in use are law, machine, organ, system, business, militia, science, art, ethnics, cybernetics, and mathematics.[21] They are inductive and deductive, structurally and functionally oriented, parochially and universally oriented, prescriptive and descriptive, static and dynamic.[22]

Probably the most creative and ambitious model builder is Fred Riggs. His empirical research has been conducted mainly in Southeast Asia, from which he constructed a model of Thailand's bureaucratic polity.[23] His dissatisfaction with traditional and modified traditional approaches to the study of administrative systems in the Third World has been expressed in a series of models designed to challenge culture-bound assumptions implicit, for instance, in the bureaucratic model.

Agraria-industria   In 1955 Sutton constructed two idea models, agraria and industria, to illustrate the relationship between societal structures and whole cultures.

Agraria	*Industria*
1. Predominance of ascriptive, particularistic, diffuse patterns.	1. Predominance of universalistic, specific and achievement norms.
2. Stable local groups and limited spatial mobility.	2. High degree of social mobility.
3. Relatively simple and stable "occupational" differentiation.	3. Well-developed occupational system, insulated from other social structures.
4. A "deferential" stratification system of diffuse impact.	4. "Egalitarian" class system based on generalized patterns of occupational achievement.
	5. Prevalence of "associations," that is, functionally specific nonascriptive structures.[24]

[21] D. Waldo, *Perspectives on Administration.* University, Ala.: University of Alabama Press, 1956, pp. 26–49.

[22] F. W. Riggs, "Models in the Comparative Study of Public Administration," in F. W. Riggs and E. W. Weidner, *Models and Priorities in the Comparative Study of Public Administration.* Papers in Comparative Public Administration. Special Series No. 1, Comparative Administration Group, American Society for Public Administration, 1963, pp. 6–43.

[23] F. Heady, "Comparative Public Administration: Concerns and Priorities," in F. Heady and S. L. Stokes, eds., *Papers in Comparative Public Administration.* Ann Arbor, Mich.: Institute of Public Administration, University of Michigan, 1962.

[24] F. X. Sutton, "Social Theory and Comparative Politics," in H. Eckstein and D. E. Apter, eds., *Comparative Politics.* New York: Free Press, 1963.

Riggs suggested an inductive typology of administrative systems[25] along a continuum between agraria and industria. Every society comprised a vast network of interrelated parts, each one of which could only be understood in relation to the others and to the whole. Administrative behavior constituted an integral, interacting part of the total society and government and could only be understood in terms of a broad range of categories that characterized the whole social system. He illustrated two ideal types of public administration systems in agraria and industria and claimed that similar ideal types could be constructed at various transitional stages between agraria and industria, with similar categories illustrating the interdependence of administrative systems and societies. As his conceptualization proved too abstract to apply, he turned away from general-systems models to middle-range theory, based on his empirical research in Southeast Asia.

Prismatic-sala model   Riggs again constructed two ideal opposite types— a refracted society, in which every function has a corresponding structure that specializes in its performance, and a fused society, in which a single structure performs all functions.[26] Just as a prism refracts white (fused) light into the colors of the spectrum, the prismatic society was a midpoint or intermediary form of transitional society between the two ideal types. The prismatic society combines fused and refracted traits, which are characterized by heterogeneity ("the simultaneous presence, side by side, of quite different kinds of systems, practices and viewpoints"); formalism ("the extent to which discrepancy exists between the prescriptive and descriptive, between formal and effective power", between impressions and actual practices); and overlapping ("the extent to which what is described as 'administrative' behavior is actually determined by non-administrative criteria"). Thus, the economic system combines the pure barter and market traits in a "bazaar-canteen," whose equivalent in the administrative system is the "sala," which combines the pure (fused) chamber and (refracted) office traits. The "sala men" recognize both administrative rationality and nonadministrative considerations. Riggs justified his prismatic-sala model on the grounds that "it enables us to cope with many problems of transitional societies that slip through the net of established social sciences. . . . Whereas it is possible, for example, to speak with some meaningfulness of 'public administration' as a separate institutional sphere and academic discipline in the American setting, it becomes highly misleading to take such an approach in Iran, Indonesia or Malagasy."[27]

[25] F. W. Riggs, "Agraria and Industria—Toward a Typology of Public Administration," in W. J. Siffin, ed., *Toward the Comparative Study of Public Administration.* Bloomington, Ind.: Department of Government, Indiana University, 1957, pp. 23–116.

[26] F. W. Riggs, "An Ecological Approach: The 'Sala Model,'" in F. Heady and S. L. Stokes, *Papers in Comparative Public Administration,* pp. 19–36. See also F. W. Riggs, *The Ecology of Public Administration.* New York: Asia Publishing House, 1961; and F. W. Riggs, *Administration in Developing Countries.* Boston: Houghton Mifflin, 1964.

[27] F. W. Riggs, *Administration in Developing Countries.* pp. 50–51.

Brady found considerable difficulty in applying the prismatic-sala model to Japan,[28] particularly in trying to maintain manageable boundaries for the administrative system and in assessing the variables.

Administrative-polities classification   Following his excursion into political-cultures theory, Riggs explored the relationships between tonic polities, which have constitutional systems, and complex public bureaucracies.[29] He distinguished three major categories: (a) orthotonic polities have an elective, constitutive system and a responsible, career-oriented, complex (balanced) bureaucracy; (b) syntonic polities have an elective, nonreciprocative, constitutive system and a responsible, but not career-oriented, complex (unbalanced) bureaucracy; and (c) hypertonic polities have a nonelective, constitutive system and an irresponsible, career-oriented, complex (unbalanced) bureaucracy. Within the orthotonic category, anatonic polities have an elective, nonreciprocative, constitutive system; monotonic polities have an elective, reciprocative, parliamentary, constitutive system; and isotonic polities have an elective, reciprocative, nonparliamentary, constitutive system. Within the syntonic category, hypotonic polities have an elective, noncompetitive, constitutive system; and atonic polities have an elective, competitive, but nonreciprocative, constitutive system. Within the hypertonic polities, autotonic polities have executives recruited from bureaucratic careers, and heterotonic polities have executives recruited from outside the bureaucracy and outside the constitutive system. While the classification continues Rigg's ecological approach to administrative systems, it replaces the functional base used in his other models with a structural base.

Nomothetic theory (a Riggsian term) is experimental. As a new venture, it suffers all the deficiencies of novelty, and may not be successful. As Riggs has argued, models with built-in bureaucratic assumptions cannot be applied to nonbureaucratic or semibureaucratic administrative systems, and the very attempt to approach all societies with a single conception is intellectually self-destructive. Universal theory should be built on the basis of tested narrow-range and middle-range theory. Otherwise, it may be excessively abstract and nonoperational, that is, theory for theory's sake, and classification for classification's sake. Much nomothetic theory is nonoperational and even stultifying. The new vocabulary is handled ambiguously by its creators.[30] The terms are too general; they do not permit their basic com-

[28] J. R. Brady, "Japanese Administrative Behavior and the 'Sala Model'" *Philippine Journal of Public Administration,* 8, No. 4 (Oct. 1964), 314–324.

[29] F. W. Riggs, "The Political Structures of Administrative Development," Comparative Administration Group, American Society for Public Administration, 1968; and "The Structures of Government and Administrative Reform," in R. Braibanti, ed., *Political and Administrative Development.* Durham, N. C. : Duke University Press, 1969, pp. 220–324.

[30] R. A. Chapman, "Prismatic Theory in Public Administration: A Review of the Theories of Fred W. Riggs," *Public Administration* (London), 43 (Winter 1966), pp. 423–425.

ponents to be managed. The classifications are unwieldy. Elegant and logically self-consistent models are constructed without concern for implementation or connection with derived case studies. On the other hand, they have reshaped thinking about national administrative systems and given new insights into the way administrative systems really work. The practitioners' task is to rescue operational concepts from the mass of largely indigestible academic theory. Most do not know where to begin or how to go about exploration, without ploughing through a voluminous literature for which they have neither time nor inclination. Thus, nomothetic theory is ignored by those to whom presumably it was originally addressed.

More serious are the attacks against nomothetic theory as such, not just as bad or inoperable theory. First, the attempt to make administration a science—objective, value-free, quantitative where possible, freed of terms and categories with variant meanings built upon a verifiable theory of meaning, and capable of universal application—will not succeed until theoretical work is also conducted outside the United States by scholars not trained in the American tradition. Riggs, at least, tried to shrug off his culture-bound socialization, but other theorists are still projecting their American values as objective theory.

Second, as Riggs has argued, there is not one universe, but several coexistent universes. "Propositions drawn from one universe are communicable to individuals living in another, but are not reducible to those of another in a useful fashion."[31] Only raw history can encompass all events within a single framework. Integration of insights can only take place at the level of an empirically defined problem, in which case it is not their validity that is important, but their relevance and utility within a particular context.

Third, the conceptual framework has become an article of faith without questioning the basic assumptions of the idea, justification of the need, and proper understanding of the nature of its scientific and philosophical inquiry.

To the extent which the idea of the conceptual framework has been provided with philosophical support, it has been in terms of certain obsolescent doctrines of logical empiricism such as instrumentalism and operationalism and the conception of the relation between theory language and observation language which these doctrines entail. Apart from the burden of being grounded in an outmoded philosophy of science, the belief in the symmetry of explanation in natural and social science, the idea that the conceptual framework corresponds to some logical structure in natural science, and the assumption that its use is largely what makes possible objective empirical explanation and comparison and differentiates contemporary social science from traditional social and political theory are mistaken. The conceptual framework offers a parallel neither to theory in natural science nor the regulative paradigmatic assumptions which inform this enterprise, and rather than differentiating social science from a past intellectual tradition, it is a

[31] V. C. Ferkiss, "The Coexistent Universes of Comparative Administration," paper presented to the American Political Science Association Conference, Washington, D.C.: Sept. 1968.

legacy of that tradition and creates the very problem of objectivity which it seeks to solve.[32]

Fourth, the theories are merely updated and revamped versions of comprehensive models that can be found in other disciplines or in political philosophy of previous ages. They are not new, and they might be improved if their "creators" had widened their reading. Finally, nomothetic theory has not fulfilled its original purpose, namely, helping administrators in the Third World, both indigenous and foreign, to solve their practical problems or cope with new environments, which is the foundation of development administration.

DEVELOPMENTAL SYSTEMS

While nomothetic theory struggles, another offshoot of comparative national systems since the early 1950s, development administration, has become a multidisciplinary field in its own right. In the past two decades development has evoked images of economic well-being, social harmony, universal political participation, mass literacy, cultural freedom, and other desirable objectives for mankind. It has held out hope for the poor, starving, diseased, and downtrodden and has promised accelerated progress for everyone else. Development administration, as an indispensable tool in the attainment of the good society, has attracted the mainstream of comparative administrators seeking ways to improve administrative performance and strengthen the planning and execution of development programs. It is grounded in normative concepts—that development is desirable; that development can be planned, directed, or controlled in some way by administrative systems; that improvements in the quality and quantity of societal products is desirable; that obstacles to development can be overcome, and that macroproblems handicapping societal progress can be solved. Because the conditions of mankind are so obvious, so real, and so compelling, development administration is also grounded in reality—the practical solution of human problems, the nitty-gritty of public administration, the real world of people, the practitioners' domain. Theory has a place, but only insofar as it really helps the practitioner in his everyday confrontation with life. It is further grounded in a more questionable assumption:

> Development is not a "natural" process which need only be let free to evolve, nor a series of bottlenecks which enlightened policy makers, like production expediters, can break successively to permit restrained energies to flow freely. It is a series of humdrum tasks for which the physical, social, psychological, and institutional resources are seldom available in sufficient quantity in the proper combina-

[32] J. G. Gunnell, "Administrative Structure and Administrative Action: Comparison and Explanation," paper presented to the American Political Science Association Conference, Washington, D.C.: 1968, Abstract.

tions. The obstacles to achievement are so often over powering, and time is a relentless enemy to those who hope to realize results in decades rather than centuries.[33]

Furthermore, it rejects any distinction between countries that appear to be generating their own changes, where growth is spontaneous, needing no artificial stimulus, and where the capacity to cope with accelerating change is self-adjusting, and those countries that seem to lack the requisite components of self-development, and where change has to be induced externally or through governmental action. All countries are developing, some at a faster pace than others, and in different directions. Each has different development problems. The most serious problem of all, however, is the persistent gap between rich and poor countries, quickly developing and slowly developing regions, and the possibility that the gap between them is widening or that some countries may actually be regressing.

Development administration had its origins in the desire of the richer countries to aid the poorer countries, and more especially in the obvious needs of newly emerging states to transform their colonial bureaucracies into more responsible instruments of societal change. The simple underlying conception was that the transfer of resources and know-how would hasten the modernization process from agraria to industria, using government and public-sponsored bodies as change agents. The transfer of resources would be conducted through international bodies, mutual aid programs, and bilateral agreements, and the recipients would channel their new resources into areas that would generate change of their own accord, such as education, health, capital investment, communications, science and research, and administrative capability. Development, however, proved to be much more complex. Which countries needed most help? Which countries should receive priority? Who could best advise on the specific needs of individual countries? Could domestic governments handle their aid wisely, or would it be better to channel aid through foreign experts stationed in the country? Where would aid produce the best results, for whom, in which way, at what price, from whose viewpoint? Before long, technical assistance and foreign-aid bureaucracies sprouted in the United Nations complex and in the foreign services of the major powers, and international experts with the requisite know-how became globe-trotters. Within assisted countries or potential recipients, other bureaucracies sprang up to assist foreign experts, to devise ways and means of extracting additional international aid, to plan where to use foreign contributions, and to manage technical-assistance programs, including how to disguise the use of external assistance for purposes for which they were not originally or ostensibly intended, for only a small part of foreign aid was free from obligations and commitments on the part of the recipient. Moreover, not all was donated in a useful form. Quite a bit was squandered

[33] M. J. Esman, "The Politics of Development Administration," in J. D. Montgomery and W. J. Siffin, eds., *Approaches to Development: Politics, Administration and Change.* New York: McGraw-Hill, 1966, p. 71.

on show places, white elephants, nonproductive investment, and conspicuous consumption of elites.

Foreign aid did not turn out to be a universal stimulant. In western Europe and Japan, where war had temporarily reduced development capacity, it was successful, but elsewhere its effects were mixed. Some countries used their aid wisely, others frittered it away. For most newly emerging countries, it was a drop in the ocean, compared with requirements. Domestic sources would have to be mobilized for development. An inventory of available domestic resources was required. Programs, projects, and plans had to be devised for their most effective use, and these practical schemes had to be activated through existing institutions and new creations. Then, once activated, they had to be properly managed. Thus, development administration spread its interest from foreign-aid programs to the domestic, public-policy problems of recipients. At the time, it was largely virgin territory. Many colonial administrators showed no interest or were too absorbed in evacuation problems. New political leaders had no experience in statecraft and very little technical competence. Few recipient countries had the benefit of a highly qualified indigenous public bureaucracy, business community, trade-union movement, or militia. As no one had tried before to accelerate development artificially, there were no guidelines. At first everything had to be improvised before any kind of base could be established from which coherent public policies could be formulated and practical programs implemented. Usually, the developmental network had to be superimposed on a traditional law-and-order frame or placed alongside the existing structure. At any event, it was something completely new and untried. But it was innovative, challenging, and very attractive to humanitarian professionals and normative social scientists, who joined those already engrossed in foreign-aid administration.

Proficient specialists, however, soon found their efforts frustrated by poor administration. They were no longer working in organizational societies with bureaucratic peoples; theirs was a new world. Nothing seemed to work properly. Time was perceived differently. Cooperation was half-hearted. Business was more personal. The society lacked proper institutions. The organizations lacked proper methods. The people lacked proper skills. What was needed, said the administrative experts, was the accumulated wisdom of the western administrative systems; the new world had to be made in the image of the old. So bureaucratization was essential, institution-building unavoidable, and western administrative folklore indispensable. Westernized elites accepted the prescription and quickly learned the right things to do, at least according to the book. The rest of society was unmoved and would not abandon traditional ways. Western administrative precepts, however, were not universal; there was no one best way, and something different had to be tried. Development administrators thus began to look closely at the material with which they had to deal, that is, indigenous administrative systems, to discover what might be useful for development purposes. In this endeavor, the ecological approach of Riggs and much narrow- and middle-range theory proved very useful.

Still, the academic world was not content. If development was universal, and if modernized societies had already experienced the problems confronting modernizing or transitional societies, there had to be universals. Perhaps they could be derived from historical models of the great powers, which in any case might prove useful to practitioners in the field groping for guidelines. With development becoming a more magical word every moment, and with more resources available for the study of anything about development, development administration became a catch-all for idiographic, applied social scientists and nomothetic theorists. Development administration took off into modernization, nation building, social change, industrialization, cultural anthropology, urbanization, political ecology, and anything else that seemed to promise help for policy makers in developing countries. By now, the recipients of foreign aid had been pushed further and further into the background, as the new wave of development theorists discovered that their own societies faced identical problems at a different level of complexity. Perhaps by studying the simpler processes of the so-called underdeveloped countries, the so-called developed countries might learn something to their advantage.

The wheel has traveled almost full circle, and the result is absolute confusion. Nobody really knows what the word development really stands for any more. Economists identify it with economic productivity, sociologists with social change or social differentiation; political scientists with democratization, political capacity, or expanded government; administrators with bureaucratization, optimum efficiency, performance, or capacity to assume all burdens. Not surprisingly, nomothetic theorists are seeking a universal frame of reference and a conceptual scheme.

Development administration is not administrative development. It is the aspect of public administration that focuses on government-influenced change toward progressive political, economic, and social objectives, once confined to recipients of foreign aid, but now universally applied.

> Development administration thus encompasses the organization of new agencies such as planning organizations and development corporations; the reorientation of established agencies such as departments of agriculture; the delegation of administrative powers to development agencies; and the creation of a cadre of administrators who can provide leadership in stimulating and supporting programs of social and economic improvement.It has the purpose of making change attractive and possible.[34]

It consists of efficient management of public development programs and the stimulation of private development programs. Esman defines the tasks

[34] G. F. Grant, "A Note on Applications of Development Administration," *Public Policy,* XV (1966), pp. 200–201.

of nation building and socioeconomic development in broad political rather than administrative terms, as follows:

1. Achieving security against external aggression and ensuring internal order
2. Establishing and maintaining consensus on the legitimacy of the regime
3. Integrating diverse ethnic, religious, communal, and regional elements into a national political community
4. Organizing and distributing formal powers and functions among organs of central, regional, and local governments and between public authority and the private sector
5. Displacement of vested traditional social and economic interests
6. Development of modernizing skills and institutions
7. Fostering of psychological and material security
8. Mobilization of savings and of current financial resources
9. Rational programming of investment
10. Efficient management of facilities and services
11. Activating participation in modernizing activities, especially in decision-making roles
12. Achieving a secure position in the international community[35]

Though Esman has the Third World in mind, his developmental tasks are universal. Unlike others, he does not recommend anything for the underdeveloped countries that he would not recommend for the developed countries. The range of interests is wide, from philosophical speculation about the nature of development administration objectives to techniques for inducing peasants to adopt improved seeds, fertilizers, and mechanical tools. The view of the administrator in a developmental system is not only that of program formulator, manager, and implementer, but, following Almond, also of policy maker and adviser, interest aggregator and articulator, political communicator, adjudicator, and socializer.[36] A brief review of the major concerns of development administration should make this clear.

Development Theory

Why develop? What is development? What are (or should be) the objectives of development? What are the assumptions behind development? What is the impact of development on society? These are some of the questions that development theorists try to answer. While others rush headlong into development, the theorists want to know where they are rushing, for what reasons, and with which motivations. The answers are by no means obvious. Development may destroy humanity and the planet. Development may keep more people longer in the same object state of poverty, disease, and pain. Develop-

[35] M. J. Esman, "The Politics of Development Administration," in Montgomery and Siffin, *Approaches to Development,* pp. 61–64.

[36] R. L. Harris, "The Role of the Administrator under Conditions of Systematic Political Change," paper presented to the National Conference on Public Administration, San Francisco, March 1967, and reproduced by the Comparative Administration Group in May 1967.

ment may create intellectual tyrannies, military and bureaucratic polities, and technological enslavement. Common-sense meanings may not be fulfilled in the postindustrial world, particularly if national development, rather than international or human development receives priority.

Development Ideology

The goal of development is not westernization or modernization into industria, but the employment of modern techniques, both technical and social, in the pursuit of societal objectives. It is the attainment of results, not rationality, form, or ritual. To achieve this end, an ideology of development is essential, something Weidner has described as a "state of mind," which fosters a belief in equitable progress. Esman sees it as a doctrine incorporating (a) reliance on ideology for decision criteria, (b) priority to fundamental social reform (c) political and social mobilization, (d) latitude for competitive political action and interest articulation, (e) ethnic, religious, and regional integration, (f) governmental guidance of economic and social policy, and (g) commitment to the future.

Development Politics

Within society, people have different ideas about the future and different abilities to realize their ideas. Development is controversial simply because it reflects the clash of ideas and power. Elites do not voluntarily preside over their dissolution, nor are they united in everything they do. Further, they work within ecological restraints and cannot achieve all that they seek to do. Their priorities may not coincide with the values of the masses, and compromises have to be struck. Development is political. It depends on government action. It reflects the political culture. It is carried out by the living constitution. It is affected by changes in the political regime, party composition of government, and personality of political leaders. Here development administration is fused with political science.

Technical Cooperation

Technical cooperation has become big business. The United States has continued substantial aid programs, although the size of funds and the direction of their use have altered since the Marshall Aid program of the late 1940s. The United Nations complex has cajoled member states into increasing their international assistance contributions under its auspices. Private foundations, particularly in the United States, have assumed voluntary obligations to aid technical cooperation, which has involved more than the lending of experts and the gift or loan of resources. It has had far-reaching repercussions on recipient countries and donors. The recipients have experienced unexpected spin-offs in nontechnical areas. The donors have been deprived of resources that they could have used for their domestic problems, rather than in questionable foreign ventures. One disappointing area of technical cooperation has been in public administration itself, largely because the transformation of the discipline since World War II was not reflected in aid missions, which relied largely on pre-World War II notions that had already been challenged at home. The transfer of know-how was not enough, and had to be related to the environment of the recipient, the nature of the polity and indigenous administrative styles, the kinds of practical programs being undertaken, and the whole circumstances surrounding the need for and the use of the required know-how.

Institution Building

Technical cooperation has resisted the temptation to perform development activities on behalf of recipients, although in some cases there has been no alternative, simply because the recipient had no means of carrying out the contemplated activities itself. Instead, the emphasis has been on helping recipients to carry out continuing activities themselves by concentrating on institution building, that is, the ability to routinize innovative activities. In some cases, this meant constructing bureaucracies; framing laws; building storehouses, ports, roads, and other physical requirements; and expanding education and health services. In other cases, it meant encouraging political action, private entrepreneurship, and community development. In public administration, it largely took the form of establishing institutes of public administration for research, education, and training throughout the world, plus student exchange programs.

Administrative Reform

Much work in public administration undertaken in newly emerging states simply imitated the great powers or exaggerated the administrative traits of the former imperial power. In the absence of any indigenous administrative tradition, the adoption of foreign patterns was accepted and performed to expectations, until expectations changed and foreign patterns could not meet the challenge. According to performance standards in developed countries, the administrative systems of the Third World are grossly deficient. Maladministration is blamed. The emphasis is on improvement through transnational reform and internal multiplier effects. Gone are early simplistic notions of the "one best way," except in United Nations circles, where the traditional universal-principles approach have been codified in handbooks and manuals. In their place are various strategies that Ilchman has classified as (a) administrative-systems approach, which supports transnational administrative reform in balanced across-the-board form or unbalanced key segment form; (b) balanced, social-growth approach, which does not advocate administrative improvement for its own sake but in close harmony with other societal improvement, lest the public bureaucracy swamps other institutions; and

(c) unbalanced, social-growth approach, which permits autonomous administrative improvement whatever the consequences, with or without reference to the polity and local political support.[37] Again, development administration is fused with political science.

National Planning and Budgeting

National planning is now accepted as an essential element in economic development. Donor countries have insisted on plans to reassure themselves that recipients really know what they are doing, while recipients have produced plans, not merely to attract foreign aid, but as symbols of development ideology and guidelines to possible action in accelerating the rate of economic and social progress. Everyone plans, but whether anything practical results from the process is a different matter. Macroplanning is comparable to nomothetic theorizing, in that no one has been able to activate the conceptual framework or translate the general objectives into practical programs and projects. Microplanning, which combines existing and contemplated projects and programs and frames budgets on that basis, is more successful, but constitutes budget making rather than planning, a process that has fixed objectives in mind and decides on values and priorities. The preoccupation of economists with grand designs and project planning and implementation, econometrics and budget administration, public initiatives and cooperative ventures, has lessened their appreciation of the politics of planning, particularly in the Third World, where expedient political considerations override rational economic precepts, where the statistical infrastructure is inadequate, and where instability undermines projections.

Technical Administration

Development is centered on action programs in a wide range of technical fields—medicine, environmental health, school systems, higher education, sanitary engineering, traffic control, public housing, forestry, agricultural cooperatives, product design, and so forth. Professional results are diminished by poor administrative arrangements in the technical sphere. The technicians have to be sensitized to their administrative environment, and administrators have to be trained to work in a technical environment. In short, it is not enough to know *what* to do. It is more important to use effectively the knowledge at one's disposal.

Nonbureaucratic Mechanisms

The bureaucratic mechanisms of the developed countries may be inapplicable in a nonbureaucratized society, or undesirable where they threaten a nonbureaucratic polity. In both cases, development administration seeks to use

---

[37] W. F. Ilchman, "Rising Expectations and the Revolution in Development Administration," *Public Administration Review,* 25 (1965), pp. 314–328.

nonbureaucratic mechanisms in the administrative system. As alternatives to public authorities, development projects are administered by political parties, trade unions, private enterprise, religious bodies, and other nonpublic institutions. As effective controls of the public bureaucracy, development programs may be directed at strengthening a legal system, mass media, or political cadres. Bureaucratic power may be fragmented by local government systems, regionalism, communes, rural government, and community development. Development administrators may prefer to use existing nonbureaucratic mechanisms, such as corruption (as a taxing device on the rich), unattached middlemen, and traditional folkways, rather than to impose administrative reform. Studies of such mechanisms have helped developed countries in dealing with their nonbureaucratized minorities and problems of turbulence not susceptible to bureaucratic solutions. In this, the Third World may return something tangible on donor investment.

The study of developmental systems has revealed many ways to achieve the same objectives. To measure the performance of an administrative system—international, national, or developmental—the whole environment, the demands made on the system, and its available resources have to be taken into account. None of these is susceptible to precise qualification or, at this stage, complete identification. Although evaluation is likely to remain impressionistic for some time, much more is known about foreign administrative systems than ever before, and considerably more is known about relationships both within and without them. The earlier naïvité has been shed, although perhaps not completely, and in its place more sophisticated multidisciplinary tools are available, along with a respect for complexity and an appreciation of human ingenuity. The whole study of administrative systems has added a new dimension to the study of human behavior, and many stimulating ideas have resulted. Admittedly, basic concepts have been challenged and the validity of cherished principles doubted. The whole field is confused and confusing; conceptual frameworks crumble when put to the test of universality; existing methods are unsatisfactory; new operational techniques are needed. To conclude with Ilchman that the comparative administration movement has failed to make any significant theoretical breakthrough beyond conventional wisdom and discover empirically useful developmental methods and approaches[38] is to ignore the higher quality of theoretical work and its increased value to practitioners which shows that people are aware of the shortcomings. This awareness may in time generate the impetus to break through existing barriers that handicap human development, just as man has succeeded in his other endeavors, such as climbing the highest mountains, exploring the deepest underwater chasms, traveling beyond the stratosphere, and discovering the secret of life itself. When he eventually succeeds, the returns to mankind will be equally if not more, impressive.

[38] W. F. Ilchman, "Comparative Wisdom and Conventional Administration: The Comparative Administration Group and Its Contribution," paper presented to the Comparative Administration Group Conference, Syracuse, April 1971.

V

Administration
in the Seventies

12

New Patterns in Public Administration

Practitioners who learned their public administration between the world wars and have had no opportunity since to return to their studies would barely recognize the discipline today. As in other disciplines, it may be necessary to insist on frequent refresher courses to enable practitioners and teachers to keep abreast of current developments before they find themselves unable to understand new trends. Textbooks cannot be revised quickly enough to incorporate new knowledge. Journals, which concentrate on new knowledge, optimistically assume that their readers need no personal guidance to relate the contents to what is already known. Conferences and training courses designed to fill the gap may fail to stress the continuity between old and new and to link the central core with new offshoots. The danger is that, in tracing the tortuous evolution of the discipline, too much stress may be placed on the past and too little on current developments, and conversely, that, in incorporating new knowledge, too much emphasis may be placed on innovation and too little on tradition. Somewhere room must be found for the overview, that is, a general stock-taking of the discipline to discover what is obsolete and should be excised and what has become established and should be incorporated. Between overviews, some way must be found to inject consolidated summaries of new patterns into the mainstream of public-administration literature.

Anyone unfamiliar with either historical tradition or contemporary trends would find the present scene quite confusing. Yet, there is order in the apparent disarray, and reason in the controversies. The field of public administration has exploded since World War II, and the discipline has yet to subsume new developments in practice and theory. The traditionalists, trained before World War II, have been slow to react to innovations, preferring to wait and see before committing themselves to new directions. In response, the avant-garde administrators have gone their own ways and worked within their own conceptions and ideas, unmindful of tradition, critical of the conservative establishment, and hopeful that the discipline will follow them eventually. In other words, extremists in both camps have not shown tolerance or patience, the reactionaries blasting the more radical departures that they have not been prepared to consider, and the radicals lampooning the traditionalists for failing to understand them. While the in-fighting has been enjoyed by the onlooking moderates, occasionally the casualties on both sides have been heavy. Some outstanding contributors to the development of the discipline have had their reputations irreparably and perhaps unfairly tarnished. Some outstanding original thinkers have been forced to leave the field and develop their ideas under another rubric. Others have spent years in the wilderness until they regained favor. Perhaps this is inevitable if a discipline is to keep healthy and develop along new lines uncomfortable to past sages.

Several times since World War II the discipline has been subject to splits that have threatened to demolish it as a field of study. Each time the animosities have been smoothed over and competing ideas reconciled by restructuring the central core to accommodate new departures. As a result, public administration is healthier today than it has been at any time since the Great Depression. While once it was dull, it is now exciting; while once it appeared to be dying for lack of invention, it is now very much alive and bursting with new research designs. It appears to have recovered from a period of crisis involving considerable self-doubt, introspective questioning, and loss of of faith. Paradoxically, while the field was exploding in all directions, the discipline was depressed. Theorists worried whether there was a discipline of public administration at all. They were caught in an endless debate over the so-called basic issues, which were false dichotomies and questionable, culture-bound norms that were stultifying the discipline with ill-conceived approaches, wrong questions, and obsolete frameworks and assumptions. They began to resemble obtuse clerics debating the number of angels who could dance on the head of a pin. No wonder the practitioners were frightened off. No wonder too that students thought the discipline deadly dull, the textbooks unreal, the debates pointless, the controversies meaningless, the theories incomprehensible, and the practical training worthless. The subject consisted of intellectual game playing, that is, trying to find the right answer or the right principle from the material presented. It never seemed to be going anywhere.

The crisis in confidence was most evident in the United States, to which intellectual leadership had passed. Elsewhere, concepts of community, social awareness, publicness, and collectivism were stronger, and governmental intervention and initative were more firmly established. Public administration had firmer roots in the society, even if it had not achieved the academic standing of a discipline, as it had in the United States. Outside the communist bloc, scholars were content to continue with what they had been doing for decades, only much better. The worldwide improvement in standards was largely due to the import of American ideas, methods, and approaches. Foreign scholars could select what seemed to them most applicable to their own circumstances, while shielding themselves from the internal rivalries and animosities of the United States. They were saved the revolt that broke out toward the end of the postwar crisis in confidence just as the discipline was recovering its sense of purpose. Young American scholars, intolerant of the malaise and impatient for guidance, were strong in their criticisms of what they felt was aimless wandering.

> An increasing crisis of meaning seems to underlie much in the study and actions of public organizations: a loss of confidence in traditional, stabilizing values; a loss of conceptual direction; foreshortened vision and a failure of nerve in exploring the consequences for public organization and politics occasioned by new conditions, new aspirations and new anger with the underfulfilled promises of abundance.[1]

> Some regard public administration as "the stepchild of political science." As with real children of the times, public administration suffers from many of the same confusions and dilemmas, from identity crises to parental rejection, from a critical confusion in basic values to a halfhearted acceptance of value-neutral scientism, from a propensity for hyperactive activism to an inclination towards frustration, cynicism, and inaction resulting from unsuccessful attempts to get the quick results desired.[2]

The new wave, best represented in F. Marini, ed., *The New Public Administration* (San Francisco: Chandler 1970), was not prepared to desert the field. Its members wanted to reformulate it according to the real world around them and to assume leadership in the discipline, if the establishment—chief office holders in public administration societies, leading contributors to public-administration literature, principal beneficiaries of research foundations— ignored their challenge. However, members of the establishment recognized their own image in the new wave. They recalled their own challenge to the principles orthodoxy of their youth for its intellectual stagnation and its distance from the real world of the New Deal and extremist ideologies. Between them, the establishment and the new wave are seeking a modus vivendi by shaping new patterns in public administration. Basically, they agree on aims—the implementation of the ideals and goals contained in the American

[1] Todd La Porte, "The Recovery of Relevance in the Study of Public Organizations," in F. Marini, ed., *Toward a New Public Administration.* San Francisco: Chandler, 1971.

[2] P. Gordon, "A Decisive Direction for a New Public Administration—Some Basic Considerations," Berkeley: Graduate School of Public Affairs, University of California, Spring 1969, p. 1.

constitution, the revitalization of public administration to meet contemporary challenges and to anticipate incipient revolutions, the further democratization of public organizations at service delivery points, and the restoration of public confidence in public institutions—but they disagree on time schedules, the complexity of methods and procedures, and interpretations of contemporary happenings in America. Their joint reformulation may be too late for the more radical students now passing through graduate schools in public affairs.

PUBLIC ADMINISTRATION IN FERMENT

The restructuring of public administration in the United States reflects fundamental changes in the American scene. Government intervention is no longer viewed as a tragedy, something to be avoided by alternative political strategies, and the American people have assimilated the ideological and practical repercussions of big government. In many new areas of the postindustrial age, government intervention is recognized as unavoidable and generally welcome. Public administration is no longer on the defensive, although deep-seated resentment of government remains in conservative suburbs and country areas. Private business has realized that, rather than fight governmental intervention, cooperation and infiltration are more advantageous in the long run. The naïve notion that all that was needed to improve public administration was the application of business methods has been dropped. Government *is* different from business; and so are public-policy making and the public administration system. As recognition grows that the most important problems of American society can only be tackled by public authorities, some of the glamor of well financed business administration is beginning to rub off on its poor relation, public administration. Socially aware younger generations, rebelling against the acquistive society, racial intolerance, urban sprawl, the industrial-military complex, and so on, reject egocentric social sciences for public-oriented social sciences such as public health, public education, social welfare, criminology, public law, and public administration. Renewed interest paves the way to foundation grants, public-authority response, graduate-school extensions, motivated students, practitioner interest, higher rewards and status for teachers and researchers, and hopefully higher quality work.

Had the discipline of public administration continued as it was during the 1950s, it is doubtful whether it would have attained this new lease of life. The most exciting advances were derived outside the discipline itself. Sociologists, psychologists, behavioralists, and administrative scientists developed administrative theory. Economists, urban planners, and public engineers explored decision making, fiscal policy, budgeting, and planning. Political scientists and anthropologists examined comparative administrative systems. Scientists, technical experts, and professionals drew attention to new areas of public life requiring political action and governmental intervention. Labor economists, industrialists, and trade unionists pointed to the revaluation of public-service occupations and government-employee militancy. The old boundaries were collapsing, and if the public administration establishment was not willing to acknowledge the fact, others were. Public administration as subject matter in search of a discipline was open to invasion and susceptible to take-over bids.

For the practitioners, the academic study was increasingly irrelevant. Public administrators were grappling with new problems and entering new functional areas. They searched vainly in public-administration literature for guidance. They were forced to improvise and resort to pragmatism in dealing with the private-public coalition in military matters, the rise of social democracy reflected in civil-rights movements and social welfare programs, the management of the richest economy the world had ever seen, and the defense of American interests around the globe. In coping with the critical public issues of the day, political leaders sought help where they could. The public-administration establishment proved unresponsive, being reluctant to enter the political arena or explore uncharted public territory, content to follow well defined, well trodden paths and to revamp old ideas. The vacuum was partially filled by interest groups in problem areas, newly established research bodies serving the new market for public-oriented social sciences, and public-policy-oriented specialists from border disciplines who were prepared to experiment. While public-administration practitioners enhanced their role in public-policy making, public-administration consultants were confined largely to their narrow, specialist concerns, where they were not very successful. Their proposals for executive reorganization, a senior civil-service or bureaucratic elite corps, local government reform, regionalism, ombudsman, and decentralization were politically resisted. The discipline of public administration was "regarded as a somewhat secondary subject of study, characterized by a rather narrow emphasis upon technique and arid structural detail rather than a more elevated intellectual content."[3]

In these circumstances, political science tried to disown public administration, but could not shake it off, as no other discipline wanted to take it over. Floating in a no-man's land and unable to increase its share of enlarged university and foundation money for social sciences, public administration declined in status and morale. Frustration welled within, and dissatisfaction flourished. Scapegoats were found, and the blame was attributed to factors beyond control. Researchers looked to other disciplines for leads and pursued their own interests on the frontiers. Despite several pleas for reformulation of the central core, no group or individual took the task in hand. Yet, beneath the surface, progress was being made, and the crisis in confidence was opening the way to the ready acceptance of reformulation, something that Simon had failed to achieve in 1946. Obviously, the discipline would have to incorporate the new world of the practical administrator and prove its worth to

---

[3] W. J. Siffin, "The New Public Administration—Its Study in the United States," *Public Administration* (London), XXXIV (Winter 1956), p. 362.

him. It would have to review the whole foundation of public-policy making and the environmental context of public administration. It would have to recover its relevance to society and reestablish its place in the world of theory. It would have to design new guidelines and frameworks. It would have to acknowledge, in the words of a pamphlet circulated at the 1970 ASPA Conference, the following circumstances:

Contemporary public administration is

—imbedded in a turbulent environment resulting from inequity in the distribution of public and private goods. Modern public administrators must attempt to redress these inequities. If not, the turbulence will increase and public servants will be asked to repress the deprived.

—more fundamentally concerned with the *results* (who gets what) of public programs and less concerned with "how to administer" this or that kind of program.

—far more concerned with organizational change and devolution and less concerned with institutional maintenance and preservation.

—concerned about ways of accommodating widespread citizen participation (not just influence by established elite groups). . . .

—far more interested in a decentralization and autonomous and semi-autonomous sub-units than in centralization and central control.

—more concerned with the importance and dignity of each individual in the organization and concerned with searching for means to accommodate the needs of the individual within the broader purposes of the organization.

—very concerned with discrimination against women, blacks, and others (often through the use of "merit" techniques) in organizational hiring and promotion.

—concerned with pathologies of our society—poverty, racial discrimination, the environment, and the city.

Without public fanfare, the discipline set about putting its house in order. The restructuring was not a conscious effort of working parties, but a general rethinking and assimilation of new patterns. Several landmarks are readily identifiable. The Comparative Administration Group, backed by the establishment and foundation grants, breached the cultural barrier and, in a series of annual conferences, reshaped comparative public administration. Next, leading members of the academic establishment were invited to a reformulation meeting under the auspices of the American Academy of Political and Social Science at the end of 1967. In the summer of 1968, Syracuse University hosted a lengthy seminar of leading members of the new wave. By the end of the 1960s, several leading textbooks had been revised to incorporate new knowledge. In many respects, teachers had already anticipated new trends. They had redesigned their courses and found their own teaching materials in new collections, government publications, case studies, and background papers. While they might not agree on what should consitute the discipline's core, they were positive that (a) no ends-means separation was possible, (b) no strict boundary existed between what was public and private, (c) a stable law and order environment had been replaced by unstable turbulence demanding public innovation, (d) no one best way existed, and no absolute principles were universally applicable, (e) bureaucratic solutions were not universally valid, (f) interorganizational or communal problems were more important than intraorganizational problems, and (g) no general profession of public administration could be identified, although many public professions with high administrative content existed. It was not the administrative aspects that were distinctive about public administration, but the public aspects.

In the search for new conceptualization, the obvious analogy was medicine. Like public administration, medicine had a broad social purpose indispensable to modern civilization, was expanding in many different directions in a booming field of study, and incidentally was becoming more public. It was founded on an oath of allegiance to public service, backed by a stringent code of professional ethics enforced by sanctions, which was itself rooted in a philosophy of the public interest. It was professional in every respect—special training, unique skills, dedicated career service, distinct body of knowledge—and covered proliferating professions concerned with public health. Its practice was an art; its study was a science. It distinguished between theory and practice, and between study and application. It borrowed from and lent to other disciplines, some of which overlapped in subject matter. These parallels between the disciplines had led some scholars and practitioners to fashion public administration in the image of medical science.[4] But they have been handicapped by the lack of established status for public administration, the difficulty of defining its body of knowledge, the failure to agree over an enforceable common code of public ethics, and the threat of other disciplines to swallow it.

The most likely candidates to swallow public administration are political science and administrative science. Political science has moved in a different direction, but a reaction against behavioralism and a social-awareness revolt could radically alter the situation in a relatively short time. Administrative science has greater affinity to public administration at the present time than political science. Administrators' skills are transferable. Policy makers and decision makers move from institution to institution, and from problem to problem. Management-science techniques are employed by all administrations. Automation and computers are transforming administrative styles. Bureaucratic and organization theories apply equally to public and nonpublic administrations. Human relations approaches are employed wherever people work in collectivities.

Undoubtedly, public administration belongs to the family of administrative

[4] See D. Waldo, "Scope of the Theory of Public Administration," in J. C. Charlesworth, ed., *Theory and Practice of Public Administration,* Monograph 8, American Academy of Political and Social Science, 1968, p. 10.

systems, and its way of getting things done can be compared and contrasted to the way nonpublic administration systems get things done, just as different public administration systems and mixed public-private systems can be compared and contrasted. Simplified, the distinguishing features stem from differences in the ultimate objectives, which define the administrative system (policy making or functional analysis), the nature of the parts that constitute the system (structural analysis), the relationships between the system's parts (behavioral analysis), and the system and its environment (ecological analysis). The case for treating public-administration systems separately rests on the possibility of distinguishing them from other administrative systems by function, structure, behavior, and ecology. If the crisis in confidence did nothing else, it proved conclusively that public administration could be distinguished in these respects and could claim autonomy at least as a subdiscipline, and perhaps as a full discipline, in view of the extent and scope of its subject matter. Present efforts are devoted to redrawing the map of public administration along these lines.

EVOLVING CONCEPTIONS

In the mid-1950s, when the crisis in confidence was most widespread, Siffin wrote as follows:

> The study of public administration in the United States is currently characterized by vitality and diversity of development reflected in a constantly widening scope and deepening content. The absence of any closed frame of reference has had its blessings as well as its disadvantages. Indeed, the field has become so vast and sprawling in its dishabille that merely keeping track of current developments presents a challenge. An attempt to delineate major lines of evolution is not easy and may provoke controversy on one or both of two grounds—the omission of some sacrosanct province altogether, or at least the failure to pay due respect to one or another important contribution. After all, what you include or exclude does depend to some extent upon how you set the boundaries; and in public administration the current boundaries resemble tracings in the sand.[5]

No longer is the evolving shape of the discipline of public administration so unstructured. It follows certain clearly defined paths, mainly extensions of trends in both theory and practice since World War II. As yet, it is not possible to fit them within a logical, comprehensive framework of public action. They center on the public political arena, community ideals, and societal problems, and they share a concern with contemporary events—philosophical movements, ideological revisions, scientific discoveries, political revolutions, moral issues—that require collective communal action through the political system. Entirely rejected is public administration as solely a law-and-order, inward-looking, housekeeping function of governmental institutions.

[5] W. J. Siffin, "The New Public Administration," p. 367.

A General Theory or Philosophy of Public Administration

An accurate definition of publicness requires the backing of a general theory or philosophy of public administration, the need for which has long been realized.[6] None has proved generally acceptable outside the specific culture from which it was derived. The closest to date has been the extension of the general concepts of the French Revolution to democratization, creative human relations, public initiative, developmental goals, and internationalism, to which lip service has been paid by international bodies, professional societies, political parties, and governments. Further synthesis is impeded by differences in political values and academic controversy over normative or behavioral stress. Any theory of public administration presupposes a general theory of politics or social action or living. For democrats, it would have to concern liberty, equality, constitutionalism, political accountability, community representation, and majority rule. For elitists, it would have to incorporate notions of political leadership, public interest, rational order, societal responsibility, and mass loyalty. The utopian nature of a theory is recognized by those who have sought to provide a lead.

> The qualities of the public service required . . . are almost self-evident. High competence in administration, integrity, stability and reliability in performance; and most significantly, the capacity for innovation and creativity are needed to envision and attain national goals. . . . These virtues must be achieved within the norms of a democratic society which demand that the public service be representative in its composition, responsive in its behavior, and responsible to popular institutions in its exercise of power.[7]

---

[6] See D. Waldo, "The Administrative State Revisited," *Public Administration Review,* 25 (March 1965) pp. 24–26; and L. K. Caldwell, "Methodology in the Theory of Public Administration," in J. C. Charlesworth, *Theory and Practice of Public Administration,* pp. 208–210. Siffin had made the same point ten years previously.

> If public administration has become the heart of the modern State, the pertinency of its study surely penetrates below the surface realm of technique and methodology, of how-to courses and prescriptive slogans. Process and techniques are vital, but their significance and even their applicability are not inherent. They can be broadly understood only in terms of some framework; and this framework has pertinence for the practitioner who would know the answers to such questions as "why?" and "how come?" as well as "how to?" The most profound problems of public administration are not problems of skill, or at least manipulative skill. They are problems of comprehension. As Goethe observed, "There is nothing more frightful than ignorance in action." In view of world-wide demands for more and better administration, there has never been a greater need for wise and penetrating approaches to the subject—nor any greater opportunity for misfortune in politically young and ambitious nations with vast governmental obligations which seek their administrative salvations chiefly in the realms of cant and gimmick.

Siffin, "The New Public Administration," pp. 369–370.

[7] W. S. Sayre, "The Public Service," in The American Assembly, *Goals for Americans.* Englewood, N.J.: Prentice-Hall, 1960, p. 285.

What makes a man a public executive is . . . his consciousness of a responsibility to the public interest. . . . Since the public interest in social situations is, paradoxically, so intimately personal a decision, I cannot give you a series of universal ethical principles . . . only . . . the frame that I use in making moral and political judgments about public affairs . . . welfare, equity, achievment, and participation . . . "feelings" or "senses" based on vague judgments about the relationship of the individual to the society in which he finds himself.[8]

The heart of the modern managerial task is to close the gap between man's goals and the fulfillment of those goals; to make practical in men's daily lives the discoveries of the scientist and the techniques of the engineer; to translate into reality the visions and dreams of poets and artists; to bring to actual fruition in men's lives the aspirations of social reformers, the theories and concepts of scholars and economists, the stirrings in the hearts of the compassionate, the desperate need of the hungry, the shelterless, the sick and the heavy laden. . . . Management requires a humanist outlook on life rather than merely mastery of technique. It is based on the capacity for understanding of individuals and their motivations, their fears, their hopes, what they love and what they hate, the ugly and the good side of human nature. It is an ability to move these individuals, to help them define their wants, to help them discover, step by step, how to achieve them. . . . The newer concept of the manager is the expression in another form of democracy's basic concept of man himself, of man as the center, the object of all our efforts; our belief in his capacity for growth, the measure of our faith in man in his future.[9]

The public administration of the future, whatever its *form,* will in *function* be the coordination, nurture, protection, and direction of *res publica,* the public affairs of society. . . . This challenge goes far beyond maintenance of the viability of a political constitution. . . . It now becomes maintenance of the viability of the greater society itself, in which government and citizen, science and technology, enterprise and philanthropy are interrelated in a new form of political order. . . . An ultimate task of public administration . . . is maintaining the viability of spaceship Earth and giving its evolution a direction beneficial to humanity.[10]

The challenge for public administration is to determine what is needed most now and in the future and then to gear actions and efforts toward implementing human needs and objectives. . . . At this point in human history, it is imperative that we devote our energies both to maintaining life, survival, and to enhancing the quality of life.[11]

As long as men differ over the ultimate objectives of society and ways to achieve them, their philosophies of public administration will differ.

[8] H. Cleveland, "A Philosophy for the Public Executive," in U. S. Department of Agriculture, *The Influences of Social, Scientific, and Economic Trends on Government Administration.* Washington, D.C.: 1960, pp. 14–16.

[9] D. E. Lillienthal, *Management: A Humanist Art.* New York: Columbia University Press, 1967, pp. 15, 16, 23.

[10] L. K. Caldwell, "Methodology in the Theory of Public Administration," pp. 216, 222.

[11] P. Gordon, "A Decisive Direction for a New Public Administration," pp. 3, 5, 6.

Turbulent Environment

The pace of change in human development has sharply accelerated since the eighteenth century. Stability has virtually disappeared, except in isolated cultures and low-income countries unable to reach take-off point in development. It has been replaced by turbulence, a permanently unstable environment in which human activities are conducted with fewer familiar landmarks. Correspondingly, in the study of public administration, static analysis based on placid order is being replaced by dynamic analysis based on ceaseless movement. In the practice of public administration, tradition and precedent are less relevant, but adaptation, assimilation, and predictive capacity more relevant. As the environment grows more complex and activities become increasingly interrelated through accelerating but uneven change rates, attention switches from single-purpose to multipurpose activities. Certainty gives way to uncertainty. Societal problems subsume lesser problems. Social organizations, public and private, enter into closer relations. Planning and futurizing assume greater importance. Public administration enlarges its scope and intervenes in previously nonpublic concerns. It becomes proactive, as opposed to reactive;[12] that is, it anticipates crisis rather than responds to crisis. The notion of turbulent environment thus overturns many established conceptions in public administration, as do explorations of the transitional impact of the postindustrial society on public affairs. The emphasis shifts from internal dynamics of public organizations to "the interactions between public organizations and their environments, with internal dynamics viewed as an *aspect* of this process".[13]

Public-Policy Problems

The turbulent environment has internationalized national problems and nationalized lesser problems. The level of decision making has been pushed upward, and the distance between decision makers and citizens has grown. Not only has the public problem-solving process changed, but the nature of public problems has radically altered too, perhaps beyond present capabilities of assimilation and solution. Public administration has begun to rediscover public problems to which nobody has any answers. That it is willing to tackle them by drawing on historical and comparative analysis and public-policy making science constitutes a new conception of a practical and socially relevant discipline. Some of the more compelling problems include the following:

Military strength   Throughout the world, the professional soldier has become more powerful. He has new weapons, a stable and disciplined organi-

---

[12] Gordon, "A Decisive Direction for a New Public Administration," p. 8.

[13] O. White, "The Problem of Urban Administration and Environmental Turbulence: A Case Study," paper presented at the 1970 conference on "Public Administration and Neighborhood Control," Boulder, Colorado, p. 3.

zation, and greater access to the political system. In both stagnating and turbulent regimes, the people may look to the military for government in preference to civilian politicians. Elsewhere, the industrial-military complex gives cause for concern, and the whole world is worried by arms races and the extension of thermonuclear capacity. How can military strength be contained? How can military resources be diverted to peaceful purposes? How can arms and thermonuclear capacity be policed? How can total war be prevented? What replacements can be found for military virtues?

Galloping technology Scientific discovery is largely responsible for man's turbulent environment. If new knowledge ceased, a greater measure of stability would probably exist. Such a possibility diminishes in time as galloping technology becomes a fact of life. Unfortunately, man's technology has outstripped his capacity to control the consequences. Only recently have advanced countries come to realize the problems associated with accelerated material development and science as a prime mover in modern civilization — insensitive technocrats, waste disposal, built-in obsolescence, ecological imbalance, inadequately tested products, expensive research and development, and badly managed creative organizations. How can governments ensure that experts remain on tap, not on top? How can scientists be sensitized to community repercussions of new knowledge? What criteria are needed to devise meaningful cost-benefit indicators in research and development? Is competition or cooperation preferable in scientific discovery?

Urbanism Outside self-sufficient communities, population growth means urban overcrowding or metropolitan spill-over. The world balance is shifting to urbanism. Most people of the future will know only an urban civilization, as is already the case in advanced countries. Like members of self-sufficient communities, they will not have to go far to fulfill their needs, but with the crucial difference that they will be dependent on the reasonable performance of highly sophisticated administrative systems. The dramatic transformation of cities as a result of population growth, rapid transit systems, and economic integration has overtaken municipal administration and local government. Urbanism has become a national and international problem. How are increasingly sophisticated urban administrative systems to be maintained? How can cities provide more and better public service in a confined space? How can the quality of city life be improved? How can the rest of the population share the benefits of urban civilization?

Civil rights Throughout the world, discrimination based on prejudice is abhorred. Safeguards are being sought to protect individuals from persecution based on sex, religion, race, color, age, ethnic background, mental and physical incapacity, ignorance, poverty, and nationality. Similarly, protection is being sought against the abuse of power by governments, militia, monopolies, elites, bureaucracies, and organized crime. How can international aid be made more effective? How can individual choice and personal freedom be extended? How can the individual participate in community decisions that affect him personally? How can justice be ensured in the maintenance of law and order? How can sophisticated crime be combated? What redress does the citizen have against public maladministration?

Development Development is the new catch-word of the era. Public administration contributes to development, bolsters development, ensures development, personifies development. But what exactly is development? Whose development? For what purpose? How can different aspects of development be reconciled?

In this way the list of new concepts in public administration emanating from new public policy problems could be extended. The total effect has been to bring public administration into the mainstream of public life, grounded in "concern for human welfare, for the maintenance and improvement of the human condition, for the improvement in the quality of life, and for the development of a more human civilization."[14] Legal-rational bureaucracy has been replaced by productive-rational bureaucracy.[15]

New Functional Areas

Just as public administration cannot ignore public-policy problems, it cannot ignore the new functional areas of government. What limits forays outside the housekeeping areas is the existence of other disciplines that have already staked claims in public health, public education, criminology, international relations, industrial relations, librarianship, and military science. Public administration no longer stops at the housekeeping end of these and other public activities, such as forestry, laboratory administration, gallery administration, archives, and engineering. It concerns itself with public-policy issues in which public authorities are involved. The following are examples of new functional areas:

a. Population growth and control; family planning; sex education and hygiene; contraception
b. Drugs; harmful substances; intoxicants; smoking; antisocial products; disease-inducing products
c. Space law; reentry problems; cosmonaut quarantine; radiation hazards
d. Police-community relations; court administration; legal processes; rights of criminals and victims
e. University administration; academic research; student government; curricula
f. Administration of foreign affairs; technical assistance; secret services; cultural exchange; immigration
g. Public morals; censorship; spying, corruption; crime

[14] P. Gordon, "A Decisive Direction for a New Public Administration," p. 2.

[15] W. F. Ilchman, "Productivity, Administrative Reform and Antipolitics: Dilemmas for Developing States," in R. Braibanti, ed., *Political and Administrative Development.* Durham N.C.: Duke University Press, 1969, pp. 478–480.

    h. Medical ethics; prolongation of life; genetics; euthanasia; fertility; control of mortality

    i. Electoral administration; community participation; campaign controls; mass-media distortion

In each, the research frontier is wide open, as it remains in well established functional areas such as postal services, employment bureaus, quarantine stations, and navigation aids, which are less glamorous but equally important public activities.

New Organizations and Structures

Some disenchantment with bureaucracy has sent people scurrying for alternative structures in the administration of public affairs. Nonbureaucratic devices are receiving more attention, and several attempts are being made to anticipate the organizational form that may replace bureaucracy in public affairs. In the meantime, the bureaucratic form has not been exhausted. Indeed, several exotic designs have appeared in international and developmental systems. National planning organizations and ombudsmen have received special attention. Likely forms to receive similar treatment in the future include mixed public-private enterprises, research organizations, policy councils, training agencies, intergovernmental bodies, advisory and consulting staff mechanisms, nonprofit contractors, and various forms of neighborhood and community self-government.

New Techniques and Processes

Public administration does not stand still. As progressive entrepreneurs, public authorities adopt the most effective techniques and processes, and they rank among leading innovators in computer technology, information systems, T-groups, and PPBS. Public ethics are also under active reconsideration.

New Approaches

Most contemporary textbooks still follow the successful prewar administrative-process formula (see Bibliographical Guide), with modifications to accommodate Simon's decision-making approach; Simon, Smithburg, and Thompson's behavioral approach; Riggs' ecological approach; and Lasswell's public-policy approach. It is likely that the 1970s will witness several radical attempts to reformulate the whole field from a completely new perspective, which will be more suitable for the postindustrial era, or to reshape existing (and new) material according to models drawn from other disciplines. The shape of things to come was previewed in I. Sharkansky's *Public Administration* (Chicago: Markham, 1970), where the outlines of an input-output conversion-system approach, relying heavily on the political systems models of Easton and Almond, were sketched. The post-behavioral shift from description, explanation, and verification (which never caught on in public administration, as they did in political science) to prescription, ethical enquiry, and action; from methodology, technique, and pure research to real societal problems, urgent needs, and applied research; and from passivity to commitment will be accompanied by increased participation by scholars in the political arena in the role of advocates, consultants, political candidates, bureaucratic advisers, and it will also be accompanied by a significant upsurge in students seeking a subject relevant to the contemporary predicament.

Possibly no reorientation, whether on these or other lines, will be adequate to cope with the challenge of the times. For over a century, a revitalized public administration alone has been unable to deal with contemporary problems. Radical changes will be needed in all societal institutions, perhaps in societal goals and community values too, if man is to survive in the face of thermonuclear threats, overpopulation, environmental destruction, and technological acceleration. In the immediate future, public administration will be called upon to aid in a peaceful transition to the postindustrial era being urged by humane anti-technocrats to halt further technological enslavement and to decentralize, democratize, and humanize itself. On the one hand, public administration intervenes more in the life of the community through political direction, economic management, social engineering, and increased bureaucratization and mechanization. On the other, opposition grows to its increased intervention, and political forces push for decentralization in governmental functions and greater community self-control, involving meaningful citizenship, individual participation in decision making, and job variety. Alienated groups in the postindustrial society reject the rules of the game and play havoc with institutionalized values and processes. They refuse to assimilate, and attempts to make them conform produce autocracy and a repressive officialdom. Public administration, as Orion White points out, has to be revamped to cope with the confrontation between technological and social imperatives, to cope with the organizational demands of the technological imperative, and to cope with the necessities of the social imperative.[16]

A NEW IMAGE FOR THE PUBLIC ADMINISTRATOR

An impediment to the restructuring of the discipline of public administration is the dismal portrayal of the public official in mass media and folklore. To some extent, the portrayal is accurate of the conservative, bureaucratic politicians, who have reached the apex and reshape their organizations in their own image. They are found in every public activity. They are indispensable in consolidating new policies. They are the stabilizers of public policy

[16] O. White, "Organization and Administration for New Technological and Social Imperatives," paper presented at the 1969 Conference of the American Political Science Association, New York.

and the supervisors of large-scale public services. They excel at conflict resolution, consensus formation, mediation, and bargaining. On the whole, they are not original thinkers and innovators, although they are creative in in guiding public policies through political shoals, and innovative in devising defenses and loopholes both for their organizations and themselves. They are competent and hold their own in any company. They are not very concerned about what others think of them, as long as they feel that they are doing a good job and that the people who really count, their political masters, know their true worth.

But the public service embraces a much wider sample of a country's talent, and public activities demand more than safe, consolidating bureaucrats. At the top are to be found inventive scientists, able professionals, maverick geniuses, inspirational policy formulators, able entrepreneurs, tough politicians, quicksilver academics, rebels with a cause, religious fanatics, public idols, clever publicists, outstanding authors and speakers, consummate artists, and skilled actors. By no shred of the imagination could these be identified with the greatly exaggerated stereotype of public officials. Outstanding public servants are known to the public. Indeed, their names may be better known generally than their political masters. All manner of people try to seduce them away from public service, and though many are tempted, far fewer leave than might be expected from folklore descriptions of life within a leviathan and of disparate rewards. When they do leave, they often regret their decision, and, where permitted, return. Why? No accurate survey has been made, but it is likely that they miss the excitement of government, the aura of historical impact, the thrill of public power and authority, the sense of public mission, and the ability to command vast resources, in addition to familiar faces and routines, old friends, and reminders of past achievements.

The image of the public administrator has long needed a face-lifting. In the reconstruction of public administration, the task cannot be delayed further if public policy is to attract the people that it needs both now and in the future. In a turbulent environment, with familiar features of public administration disappearing, the role of the consolidating bureaucrat diminishes. It is replaced by other roles requiring different talents, as follows:

a. Crusading reformer, intent on transforming some aspect of community life according to preconceived notions of the ideal society
b. Proactive policy formulator, ready with possible strategies to meet the unknown
c. Social-change agent, ready to accept new ideas and to push others into accepting them also
d. Crisis manager, slow to burn but quick to act, and brilliant at immediate improvisation
e. Dynamic program manager, able to shape new courses and adapt ongoing arrangements
f. Humanitarian employer, treating staff with respect and meting out even-handed justice
g. Political campaigner, responsive to public needs and champion of public causes

h. Competent administrator, ensuring effective performance with minimum political embarrassment
i. Interest broker, choosing among competing interests and reconciling all parties to the outcome
j. Public-relations expert, adept at building up support and showing his area to advantage
k. Speedy decision maker, prepared to assume responsibility and give clear instructions
l. Constructive thinker, not easily lead astray by others who would want to make up his mind for him
m. Optimistic leader, not easily discouraged in adversity, but able to command attention and stimulate subordinates

It would appear that the evolving conception of public administration requires a race of supermen in public office. In these circumstances, fortunate indeed is the administration that satisfies a fraction of its needs and commands its fair share of community talent.

Obviously, the ideal is unrealizable, even if it does point to a target to which training, education, and recruitment systems should aim. In practice, the ideal public executive will only perform as well as he is permitted by environmental constraints, political feasibility, communal expectations, and operational limitations. The least that can be hoped for is a rejection by the new breed of public administrators of such damning traits of the conservative consolidators as (a) reluctance to combat adverse images of public service and public misconceptions about public work, (b) bureaucratic complacency and ineptitude in response to public demands and changing circumstances, (c) tolerance of mediocrity or something less than quality performance, (d) lack of concern with developing staff potential and tapping latent talent, (e) undue reliance on improvisation and trial-and-error methods, even when better alternatives are available, (f) conformist patterns of behavior exacted, and (g) safety-first style of decision making. The new breed is expected to be more innovative, to keep abreast of current research and new techniques, to encourage staff initiative and develop employee potential, to demand quality performance, to encourage new ideas and experimentation, to respond to public demands, to act quickly and courageously, and to combat adverse images and unfounded criticism. Above all, the new breed is expected to cope with the failure of conventional political processes to head off militant groups which take to coercion and lawlessness to get what they want, sometimes in the hope that repression will contribute to chaos, anarchy or revolution. The new breed is supposed to ensure that militancy does not pay and "to enforce continued respect for established institutions and political processes by demonstrating that they can be—and are—responsive without illegal pressure."[17] How is something for the new academies to puzzle out.

---

[17] A. H. Raskin, "The Administrator's Role in Intense Social Conflict," presentation to the American Academy of Political and Social Science, Philadelphia, April 1970.

NEW ACADEMIES

Revitalized public administration, recapturing its self confidence and sense of purpose, is in a better position to retain its disciplinary autonomy. Supported by the political arena, public bureaucracy and community at large, its professional and academic status will rise. Public services will enlarge their training and education facilities and, where they have not done so already, establish institutes for higher education and independent research. They will put more money into academic research and consultancy and will seek assistance from universities in solving their staffing problems. The need to enlarge the public administration area will be appreciated by political leaders, and foundations and university authorities will adjust their policies accordingly, particularly the public vocational university supported by public funds, "directed by political decisions, and dedicated to the production of applied knowledge useful to the leaders of our political order."[18] As a reflection of new public awareness, students and faculty will be attracted to public administration, particularly if money and positions become freely available. Business schools will accept new Public Administration schools but Political Science and Administrative Science faculties will probably resist. To overcome academic opposition, and to denote a break with past approaches, public administration scholars may change its title to public affairs or public policy, and temporarily drop the housekeeping aspects to concentrate on policy analysis. These trends are already identifiable in North America and to a lesser extent in Western Europe.

In the new academies catering for public administration, the nature of instruction will change in several important respects. The emphasis will shift from content skills and learning about what exists to interactional skills and learning personal techniques for coping with new situations. Description will be superseded by analysis, and formal instruction will give way to peer interaction and role playing in model case studies. The public side will be stressed more than the administrative side by an outward-looking view of the world. Moral philosophy will temper behavioral philosophy, with renewed stress on judgment, sensitivity, wisdom, balance, relativity, creativity, and personal initiative. Students will be impressed with the political framework of public administration, the value premises of public action, the societal consequences of public policies and decisions, and the intricate power play in the public arena between cultures, ideologies, institutions, and people. The kinds of questions posed will not vary, although the answers will differ according to circumstances. Why is public intervention necessary? At what political level is public action suitable? What needs to be done? What resources should be expended, and from where should they be drawn? How can the community obtain maximum value? Who benefits and who suffers? Who

[18] E. Litt, *The Public Vocational University.* New York: Holt, Rinehart and Winston, 1969, p. 9.

chooses what is to be done? How do the people most affected know what is about to happen, and how are their feelings represented in decision making? Answers to such questions can be classified into distinct problem areas, as follows:

a. Public interest, general will, community mobilization, modernization, societal objectives
b. Information, knowledge, research, comprehension, analysis, education
c. Anticipation, prediction, mobilization
d. Participation, elitism, social engineering, oversimplification, decision making, and policy formulation
e. Responsiveness, responsibility, leadership, bureaucratism
f. Apathy, egocentricism, reaction, backlash, violence
g. Social adaptation, change, movement, adjustment, reform, revolution
h. Allocation, size, complexity, centralization, organization, budgeting
i. Performance, accountability, control
j. Measurement, assessment, evaluation
k. Instability, turbulence, crisis, problem circles, frustration

Inevitably, the student will be forced to explore the frontiers of public administration and to know something about other disciplines. He will not be able to study public administration in isolation. It will give him no answers by itself, only the equipment to find answers by himself. It cannot ensure that the equipment will be properly used, if at all, or whether it will always be relevant. The student will find out for himself that the art of administration

> . . . consists of issuing orders based on inaccurate, incomplete and archaic data, to meet a situation which is dimly understood, and which will not be what the issuer visualizes, orders which will frequently be misinterpreted and often ignored, to accomplish a purpose about which many of the personnel are not enthusiastic.[19]

The new academies will bring practitioners and theorists closer together. The practitioners will begin to appreciate the relevance of theories, frameworks, and intellectual tools in their work, personal prospects for advancement, and professional image. The theorists will be grounded in practice, and although they may be tempted into flights of fancy, their intellectual efforts will be relevant to contemporary problems and strategies. Together they could work out administrative indicators, just as the economists have evolved economic indicators and social scientists are evolving social indicators to measure the quality of life. An administrative accounting system would determine the effectiveness of administrative systems in transforming available resources into societal objectives with the minimum dysfunction and in satisfying shared needs that can only be met through joint action. At the present time, nobody can assess administrative performance with any appreciable degree of objectivity. If we could, the universal adverse images

---

[19] General W. Reeder, quoted by H. Cleveland, "A Philosophy for the Public Executive," p. 6, and also in Charlesworth, *Theory and Practice of Public Administration,* p. 175.

of public-administration systems might be reversed. This may turn out to be the theorist's major contribution to society. Perhaps more important at this stage in history is the administrator's confrontation with turbulence and his need for new guidelines in coping with its societal ramifications.

COPING WITH TURBULENCE

The loss of confidence in public institutions and growing disrespect for authority or democratic elitism by young activists, particularly in the United States, may indicate that the restructuring of public administration currently taking place may be too little, too late. Compared with the challenge of the times, something more drastic may be required. The current societal malaise may be one of the first symptoms of the failure of organizational societies to cope with the relatively new societal experience of turbulence, characterized by self-induced dynamism, insatiable rising expectations, and accelerating interrelated and reinforcing changes. Increasing strain is placed on the adaptive capacity of administrative cultures. Unless societal institutions keep pace with cultural transformation, breakdowns will threaten the social fabric, permanent imbalances will generate discontent, alienation, escapism, violence and fear, and eventually the society will face disintegration and will collapse. In this situation, rarely experienced by civilized society before the modern era, the administrative culture performs a crucial role in maintaining social harmony and keeping reasonably tolerable order in human affairs.

In turbulence, a continual stream of societal problems that threaten civilized harmony and order demands immediate action without adequate time for contemplation. Administratively, the society has to be able to recognize emerging problems, settle them close to the point of action, inform affected parties and involve them in the decision-making process, minimize formality and irrelevant information, and absorb decisions in institutional frameworks geared to quick responses. Because of inability to divert resources to create new institutional frameworks for new problems at short notice, solutions have to be grafted on what already exists. Administrations must be capable of ready improvisation and willingness to assume new responsibilities. Vacuums must be avoided; as soon as one administration moves out of a problem area or fails, another must step in. Resources must be freely available for emergency mobilization (for example, unused capacity), or already committed resources must be capable of swift transfer and able to satisfy different needs at the same time. Thus, the administrative requirements of a turbulent society run counter to much orthodox administrative rationality currently incorporated in both the practice and theory of public administration.

Neat, logical, consistent rational classifications of autonomous, unifunctional or single purpose bureaucracies are societally dysfunctional. They divert attention from organizational or administrative interface with environment and the actual delivery of services at the point of impact to sterile, egocentric, internecine warfare over policy or problem boundaries and organizational aggrandizement. Legal, disciplinary, financial, social, and psychological distinctions become less significant so long as there are administrations—public, private, or mixed—willing to fill policy and problem vacuums as they arise. Impact, not form, is what really counts.

The multiplication of single-purpose organizations is increasingly hazardous to societal welfare. The chances of breakdown are enhanced by overdependence on the performance of individual specialized parts. The risk is diminished in each problem or policy area by the presence of numerous overlapping, multifunctional institutions, which provide numerous checks and counterchecks on each other. Such built-in societal redundance[20] is indispensable in turbulent societies. While underemployed capacity and duplication of effort constitute waste in terms of administrative rationality, they are essential safety valves and self-correcting devices in crisis and emergency situations, which are persistent features of a turbulent society.

Bureaucratic elites can tackle only a small proportion of societal problems. Centralization only serves to overload them even more and threatens to diminish their effectiveness. A turbulent society has to learn to live with its problems. Only high-priority problems can be tackled by bureaucratic elites, and they will concentrate only on those problems that *have* to be tackled, that is, where action is unavoidable. They will not get a breathing space to enable them to deal with lesser problems. They should not, therefore, promise to tackle all problems or profess that solutions exist to all problems. Such comforting sentiments and false assurances will eventually rebound as disillusionment grows and as it becomes obvious that a turbulent society is chained to a problem treadmill—the faster the action, the more furious the problem rate, with no end in sight. Temporary relief would be possible if everyone were encouraged to solve his own particular problems, without relying on higher authorities for decision and action; if low-priority problem solving were decentralized to local initiative, at some cost in uniformity and completeness; and if people learned to avoid creating unnecessary societal problems, such as forcing bureaucratization on nonbureaucratic groups or deliberately antagonizing nonconformists in trivial matters.

Little reliance can be placed on bureaucratic macroplanning, even assuming that the necessary technical facilities exist. Within the rapid change of turbulence, it is impossible to predict the future or to anticipate the effects of change. It is meaningless to extrapolate a noncomparable past. It cannot be assumed that a broad consensus on aims and means exists in the polity, that stable conditions will return, or that planning directives are acceptable. Apart from feasible, indispensable, and meaningful microplanning in technical areas, preference should be given to decentralized facet planning and

---

[20] M. Landau, "Redundancy, Rationality and the Problem of Duplication and Overlap," *Public Administration Review,* 29 (July/Aug. 1969), pp. 346–358.

partisan mutual adjustment, which is nonbureaucratic, decentralized, quickly amenable to changing values and sudden societal changes, and able to work within established institutional frameworks.

Bureaucratic politics in egocentric and introverted administrations discourage the free flow of information that is crucial for complex problem solving in turbulent societies. There is a tendency to suppress grievances, cover up mistakes, and ridicule complaints. Legitimate problems may escalate because of an initial reluctance to take complaints seriously or to acknowledge that grievances may be symptomatic of deeper malaise. Nobody's business ends up by being everybody's business. Administrations in turbulent societies have to accommodate themselves to openness and the existence of multiple, societal busybodies looking for trouble and ready to interfere at any time with the internal affairs of any societal institution that may be having adverse societal repercussion.

A fast flow of action requires minimal formality and short communication routes. The elaboration of administrative infrastructures, the multiplication of top positions, complicated networks of formal committees, and lengthy chains of authority, while giving the appearance of action and movement, actually lengthen delays and impede operations at service delivery points.

Administrative preparation for the turbulent society would seem to involve a radical change in outlook. In disciplinary terms, the focus of study needs to shift from the formal, static elements in the administrative situation—such as institutional forms, methods, processes, laws, formal behavioral codes, and organizational propaganda—to the behavioral, dynamic elements that enable administrations to retain their flexibility and adapt themselves to new circumstances—such as organizational strategies, administrative politics, administrative reform, bureaucratic change processes, informal behavior, grape vines, and self-corrective devices. Likewise, the emphasis of normative theory needs to shift from bureaucratization, professionalization, political consensus, power elites, standardization, and sugared coercion to self-activation, voluntarism, participative administration, conflict management, service delivery systems, heterogeneity, open-ended problems, and uncertainty. In professional training, the teaching emphasis needs to be shifted from the accumulation of information to the development of interactional skills. The production of conforming organization men needs to be leavened by a sprinkling of creative activists able to anticipate problems, mobilize resources in advance, devise appropriate solutions, adopt self-corrective devices, and assess results—prepared, if necessary, to fill political as well as administrative vacuums. The present restructuring of public administration in the United States is moving in this direction, but there is considerable opposition among public administrators to abandoning secure bureaucratic territory for the uncertainties of the public political arena. Turbulent societies will need both types of public administrator—the consolidating bureaucrat and the crusading administrative reformer—in complementary roles.

In the meantime, something must be done to improve administrative capacity in dealing with societal problems. In particular, attention needs to be directed at developing certain sets of ability to learn from past and present experience in problem solving that may stand public administration in good stead in coping with turbulence:

a.   The ability to recognize new problems that require new solutions rather than modifications of old solutions
b.   The ability to reformulate problems in new terms in order to elicit new responses and initiatives
c.   The ability to turn crisis to advantage; to use deviation and conflict in problem solving to generate self-transformation with minimum alienation
d.   The ability to deal with uncertainty and fluidity and to absorb change, instability, and interdependence
e.   The ability to tolerate deviation, conflict, and confrontation without overreaching or losing sense of proportion
f.   The ability to mobilize resources to meet problems and to engage in interdisciplinary problem solving
g.   The ability to encourage error-correction initiative and creativity, and to learn from mistakes
h.   The ability to learn from experience and uncertainty
i.   The ability to remain human and humane under stress

Nobody knows how to develop these sets of ability. Present formal methods employed in training and education for public life are quite inadequate, although T-groups, case studies, role playing, and policy analysis undoubtedly help. This is one area where practitioners and theorists, teachers and students, insiders and outsiders could assist one another in making the discipline of public administration truly operational, hopefully based on a metaphysic of social justice than aristocratic utilitarianism, but at least creative, adaptive, sensitive, realistic, and contributory to a higher quality of living.

Bibliographical
Guide

This selected bibliography is meant for the reader who has been sufficiently stimulated by this introductory survey of current trends in public administration to search out source material for himself and to read more deeply in the subject, beyond the references mentioned directly in the text and accompanying footnotes.

A specialized library at a renowned research university or a public professional organization contains tens of thousands of references in many languages. To read them all is a lifetime's work. As the output of relevant material is accelerating, the nonprofessional reader—that is, someone who is not required to review new sources as part of his daily work—has to confine himself to a fraction of available information. Fortunately for him, a great deal is not important or worthwhile from his viewpoint; much is repetitious, highly specialized, or purely technical, and can thus be skimmed. He ought to know, however, his way around general source material and the places to look for new developments. Since he will find only a few fleeting references in his daily newspaper, monthly reviews, and publishers' best-selling lists, he must rely mostly on advertisements and book notes in professional journals, usually some months after publication date. There he will find what were considered to be the most relevant sources at the beginning of the 1970s.

The following selection, directed at newcomers, is confined to materials written in English that are generally accessible according to sales and circulation figures, original in content, and relevant to the contemporary world. It is not complete and cannot be tailored to individual requirements. Nevertheless, it should be sufficiently comprehensive to meet most needs.

GENERAL BIBLIOGRAPHIES

No complete bibliography of all published material in public administration exists. In individual countries, where general copyright laws apply and where a national library or archives is legally empowered to receive a copy of all copyright material, fairly complete lists could be compiled if the need arose and the costs were not prohibitive. Only large international research foundations and governments could undertake the task, providing some agreement were reached on the scope of public administration and the status of official publications. Keeping such a bibliography up to date requires a large continuing investment. Any bibliography compiled before 1950 is of historical interest only, and the further back in time a bibliography, the less relevant it is. Still useful are the following:

Cornell University, Graduate School of Business and Public Administration, *Basic Library in Public Administration* (Ithaca, N.Y.: Cornell University Press, June 1956), 59 pp.

Mars, D., and Frederickson, G.H., *Suggested Library in Public Administration* (Los Angeles: School of Public Administration, University of Southern California, 1964), 203 pp.

Seckler-Hudson, C., *Bibliography on Public Administration: Annotated,* fourth ed. (Washington, D.C.: American University Press, 1953), 131 pp.

United Nations, *International Bibliography of Public Administration* (New York: Technical Assistance Program, 1957).

Wasserman, P., *Information for Administrators: A Guide to Publications and Services for Management in Business and Government* (Ithaca, N.Y.: Cornell University Press, 1956), 375 pp.

More specialized publications:

Caldwell, L.K., *Science, Technology and Public Policy: A Selective and Annotated Bibliography, 1945–1965* (Indianapolis: Institute of Public Administration, Indiana University, 1966), 128 pp.

Heady, F., and Stokes, S., *Comparative Public Administration: A Selected Annotated Bibliography* (Ann Arbor, Mich.: Institute of Public Administration, University of Michigan, 1960), 98 pp.

Jones, G. N., and Giordano, R. N., *Planned Organizational Change: A Working Bibliography* (Los Angeles: School of Public Administration, University of Southern California, 1964), 58 pp.

Spitz, A. A., and Weidner, E. W., *Development Administration: An Annotated Bibliography* (Honolulu: East-West Center Press, 1963), 116 pp.

Spitz, A. A., *Developmental Change: An Annotated Bibliography* (Lexington, Ky.: University of Kentucky Press, 1969).

More generalized publications:

American Behavioral Scientist, *The ABS Guide to Recent Publications in the Social and Behavioral Sciences* (New York: Hermitage Press, 1965), 781 pp.

International Committee for Social Science Documentation, *International Bibliography of Political Science* (Chicago: Aldine, 1963), 273 pp.

None of these adequately serves current purposes. More reliance should be placed on professional journals, which review current publications and running bibliographies, or lists of new accessions in public administration maintained by the Library of Congress, Washington, D.C.; Public Administration Service, Chicago; International Institute of Administrative Sciences, Brussels; Royal Institute of Public Administration, London; and similar national libraries, research institutes of public administration, and universities. For this purpose, R. P. Haro, *A Directory of Governmental, Public and Urban Affairs Research Centers in the United States* (Davis, Calif.: Institute of Governmental Affairs, University of California, September 1969) is most helpful. Most major universities and schools of public administration and public affairs publish monthly accession lists or running bibliographies on all materials obtained for their libraries.

The Joint Reference Library of Chicago publishes a weekly list, indicating pertinent books, official reports, periodical articles, journal articles, and pamphlets dealing with governmental topics. Such lists are mailed to all American colleges and universities that request them. Address: 1313 60 St., Chicago, Ill. 60637.

The Government Printing Office of the United States publishes a monthly catalog of virtually all publications issued by government agencies during the preceding month. Another running bibliography, *Selected United States Government Publications,* printed semi-monthly, is available to the student at no cost and may be received on request to the Superintendent of Documents, Government Printing Office, Washington, D.C.

The Library of Congress publishes a monthly *Checklist of State Publications,* which comes close to being a complete list of publications published by all departments in all fifty states. The entries are compiled in an annual index, which is sent to all college and university libraries on request.

Public Affairs Information Service Bulletin, published weekly, is a selective list of the latest books, pamphlets, government publications, reports of public and private agencies, and periodical articles relating to economic and social conditions, public administration, and international relations.

Various state libraries, government-related and intergovernmental agencies, such as the Regional Government Association, also publish weekly or monthly acquisition lists, which can usually be found in most university and government research libraries.

PROFESSIONAL JOURNALS

The frontiers of a discipline are usually presented in the latest issues of professional journals, providing editors remain receptive to new ideas and trends. In these journals, controversial articles provoke debate. Current research findings are summarized. Book reviews and notes inform specialists of recent worthy publications. Conference reports, staff news, and employment services promote professional intercourse. Currently, over one thousand journals have some bearing on public administration, of which about fifty have been selected for review here. In addition, there are high-quality professional journals devoted to public administration published in languages other than English in France, Western Germany, Sweden, Poland, the U.S.S.R., Yugoslavia, Italy, Brazil, Chile, Egypt, Turkey, the Sudan, Iran, Israel, Thailand, Pakistan, India, Japan, China, South Vietnam, South Korea, Malaysia, and Ceylon. Although available on request, few circulate outside their countries of publication or highly specialized international libraries.

Administration (Dublin). Published quarterly by the Institute of Public Administration of Ireland. Devoted almost exclusively to Irish administration, with an occasional article on western-European administration. A brief book-review section.

Administrative Science Quarterly (Ithaca, N.Y.). Published quarterly by the Graduate School of Business and Public Administration, Cornell University. Reputed to be the foremost journal in administrative theory, rich in organizational theory of special relevance to public administration. Précis of articles supplied. Extensive book-review section of high quality. Indispensable reading for the serious student.

American Behavioral Scientist (Beverly Hills, Calif.). Published bimonthly by Sage Publications, California. An advanced journal in social science, difficult for new students unfamiliar with behavioralism and intermediary statistics. Contains book notes, with extensive coverage of the social sciences.

American Journal of Public Health (New York). Published monthly by the American Public Health Association. Devoted to policy and administration aspects of public health in the USA. Professional notes; book notes.

American Journal of Sociology (Chicago). Published bimonthly by the University of Chicago. Contains occasional articles relevant to public-administration theory and public policy. An extensive book-review section of high quality.

American Political Science Review (Washington, D.C.). Published quarterly by the American Political Science Association. Until 1968 contained articles and book reviews relevant to all facets of public administration, but since then has concentrated on public-policy making and the political aspects of public organizations. High-quality book reviews on boundary topics. Reports of graduate theses and of academic and staff news.

American Sociological Review (New York). Published bimonthly by the American Sociological Association. Contains frequent articles relevant to administrative behavior, bureaucracy, organization theory, and social issues. Quality book reviews.

Annals of the American Academy of Political and Social Science (Philadelphia). Each issue concentrates on a specific problem area in the social sciences. Under a general editor, expert contributions are collected to explore a problem area in detail. Unrelated to the problem is the extensive quality book-review and notes section covering the social sciences and related disciplines.

Canadian Public Administration (Toronto). Published by the Institute of Public Administration of Canada. Devoted to Canadian public administration and comparative analysis. Book-review section. Articles in English and French.

Chinese Journal of Administration (Taipei). Published by the Center for Public and Business Education, National Chengchi University. Devoted to Taiwanese and development administration. Selected book reviews. Articles in English and Chinese.

Economic Development and Cultural Change (Chicago). Published quarterly by the Center in Economic Development and Cultural Change, University of Chicago. Devoted to preliminary research findings in development.

Federal Accountant (Washington, D.C.) Published quarterly by the Federal Government Accountants Association. Devoted to public finance and budgeting.

Federal Bar Journal (Washington, D.C.). Published quarterly by the Federal Bar Association. Devoted to public law and legal aspects of public policy. Book reviews of quality.

Foreign Affairs (New York). Published quarterly by Council on Foreign Relations. Devoted to United States foreign policy, with occasional articles on the administration of foreign affairs, technical assistance, and international organizations. Extensive book notes.

Harvard Business Review (Boston). Published bimonthly by the Graduate School of Business Administration, Harvard University. Useful for comparative administration and administrative processes. Selected book reviews.

Indian Administrative and Management Review (New Delhi). Published quarterly. Devoted to the administrative aspects of public policy and development. Selected book reviews.

Indian Journal of Public Administration (New Delhi). Published quarterly by the Indian Institute of Public Administration. Devoted to Indian administration, comparative analysis, and development administration. Selected book reviews.

Industrial and Labor Relations Review (Ithaca, N.Y.). Published quarterly by the New York State School of Industrial Labor Relations, Cornell University. Devoted to industrial relations in both public and private sectors. Research notes. Extensive book-review section of quality.

International Development Review (Washington, D.C.). Published quarterly by the Society for International Development. Short articles devoted to development. Comprehensive book review section. Research notes.

International Organization (Boston). Published quarterly by the World Peace Foundation. Devoted to the theoretical aspects of international studies, with an occasional article on international administration. Survey of United Nations affairs. Book-review articles.

International Review of Administrative Sciences (Brussels). Published quarterly by the International Institute of Administrative Sciences. Devoted exclusively to comparative public administration and international administration. Extensive book notes. Reports of Institutes of Public Administration, international conferences, international exchange schemes, and staff news. Articles in English, French, and Spanish.

International Social Science Journal (Paris). Published quarterly by the United Nations Educational, Scientific, and Cultural Organization. Issues devoted to social-science themes, including comparative and development administration. Selected book notes and reports of international conferences, exchange schemes, and technical assistance vacancies. Articles in English and French.

Journal of Administration Overseas (London). Published quarterly by the Ministry of Overseas Development. Concerned with pre-independence administration and developmental administration. Selected book notes.

Journal of the American Institute of Planners (Baltimore). Published bimonthly by the American Institute of Planners. Devoted to public planning. Quality book reviews.

Journal of Applied Behavioral Science (Washington, D.C.). Published quarterly by the Institute for Applied Behavioral Science. Devoted to applied behavioralism, particularly social psychology in administration.

Journal of Comparative Administration (Beverly Hills, Calif.). Published quarterly by Sage Publications, California, for the Comparative Administration Group. Devoted to comparative administration. Review articles.

Journal of Criminal Law, Criminology and Police Science (Baltimore). Published quarterly by the Northwestern University School of Law. Devoted to policy and administration of law enforcement. Case notes. Book notes.

Journal of Politics (Gainesville, Fla.). Published quarterly by the Southern Political Science Association. Occasional public-administration articles. Comprehensive quality book reviews.

Management International Review (Munich). Published quarterly by The International University Contact for Management Education *et al.* Devoted to comparative administrative theory, mostly private administration. Book notes. Articles in English, French, and German.

Management Science (Providence). Published monthly by the Institute of Management Sciences. Heavily oriented to mathematics, systems, and scientific method in administration for advanced specialists. Occasional philosophical articles. Extensive book notes.

Midwest Journal of Political Science (Detroit). Published quarterly by the Midwest Political Science Association. Occasional public administration articles. Comprehensive quality book reviews.

New Zealand Journal of Public Administration (Wellington). Published biannually by the New Zealand Institute of Public Administration. Devoted to New Zealand administration and comparative analysis. Selected book reviews.

Personnel (New York). Published bimonthly by the American Management Association. Short articles on staffing. Book notes.

Personnel Administration (Washington, D.C.). Published bimonthly by The Society for Personnel Administration. Useful for public-personnel administration and comparative analysis. Selected book reviews.

Philippine Journal of Public Administration (Manila). Published quarterly by the College of Public Administration, University of the Philippines. Devoted to Southeast Asia administration, comparative analysis, and development administration. Selected book reviews of quality and reports on academic news.

Policy Sciences (New York). Published quarterly by American Elsevier. Devoted to public-policy theory. Quality book reviews.

Political Quarterly (London). Published quarterly. Devoted to public-policy issues, administrative law, and public administration in Britain. Comprehensive quality book reviews.

Public Administration (London). Published quarterly by the Royal Institute of Public Administration. Devoted to British administration and comparative analysis. Extensive book reviews and notes of quality. Lists recent British Government publications. Very readable.

Public Administration (Sydney). Published quarterly by the Australian Group of the Royal Institute of Public Administration. Devoted exclusively to Australian administration. Selected book reviews.

Public Administration in Israel and Abroad (Jerusalem). Published annually by the Institute of Public Administration. Selected articles on Israeli administration and comparative administration. Book notes.

Public Administration Review (Washington, D.C.). Published bimonthly by the American Society for Public Administration. The most important American journal concerned with the study of public administration. Its varied articles are contributed by leading scholars. Review articles of high quality. Controversial letter column. Research notes. Indispensable reading. Selected articles published by C. E. Hawley and R. G. Weintraub eds., *Administrative Questions and Political Answers* (Princeton, N.J.: Van Nostrand, 1967).

Public Finance (The Hague). Published quarterly by the Foundation Journal Public Finance. Devoted to comparative public finance, budgeting, and taxation. Book-review section. Articles in English, French, and German.

Public Management (Chicago). Published monthly by the International City Manager's Association. Short articles devoted exclusively to urban administration. Book notes.

Public Personnel Review (Chicago). Published quarterly by the Public Personnel Association. Short articles devoted to public-personnel administration. Extensive book notes.

Public Policy (Boston). Published annually by the Graduate School of Public Administration, Harvard University. Comprehensive articles on public policy and administrative aspects of public affairs by leading contributors.

Public Welfare (Chicago). Published quarterly by the American Public Welfare Association. Devoted to policy and administration of public welfare in the USA. Book-review section. Research notes.

State Government (Chicago). Published quarterly by the Council of State Governments. Devoted to state and local government problems in the USA.

The Public Interest (New York). Published quarterly by National Affairs, Inc. Controversial quality articles on public-policy issues by leading academic contributors. Indispensable for students and practitioners.

Transaction (New Brunswick, N.J.). Published monthly by private group of concerned social scientists to publicize the relevance of social-science research to contemporary social issues and public policy. Short articles. Quality book-review section. Lively reading.

Western Political Quarterly (Salt Lake City). Published quarterly by the Western Political Science Association *et al.* Occasional articles on public administration. Extensive book-review section of quality.

World Politics (Princeton). Published quarterly by the Center of International Studies, Princeton University. Devoted to international politics, but occasional articles on international organizations. Review articles.

GENERAL TEXTS

In presenting a general overview of public administration, general texts sacrifice depth to coverage and need to be supplemented with specialized texts. As consistency in covering all facets of the subject is rarely attained, it is often wise to compare general texts and select those that best meet the personal needs of the reader, retain his unflagging interest, and lend themselves to easy reference. On the whole, they usually cover much the same ground from a similar management-process viewpoint and divide the subject matter in much the same way under similar chapter headings arranged in similar sequence. Otherwise, each has its own special characteristics in style, treatment, sources, values, emphasis and linkages. There are still too few to permit the reader to choose among them solely on the basis of such secondary characteristics as size, cost, and so on.

Introductory Texts

Beginners' manuals are largely produced as short, cheap paperbacks in bright jackets. Their quality varies considerably. Some are badly written, superficial, and pedagogically dogmatic. Others are pieces of literature in their own right, thorough in treatment and scope, and masterful in their treatment of complexity and controversy. The following are recommended:

Buechner, J. C., *Public Administration,* (Belmont, Calif.: Dickenson, 1968), 114 pp., including annotated bibliography and index. A bird's-eye view of public administration as a study, process, and vocation. Commences with a survey of different approaches to the discipline and takes the reader through organization theory, bureaucratic theory, public finance, and comparative administration; ends with a summary of the discipline's problems and challenges.

Corson, J. J., and Harris, J. P., *Public Administration in Modern Society* (New York: McGraw-Hill, 1963), 155 pp., including short reading list and index. A review of

American public administration within its political and societal context. Part One traces the rise and implications of big government, problems in constructing the machinery of government, and staffing public authorities. Part Two describes federal government administration according to institutional arrangements and functions, American defense administration, and economic regulation by fiscal methods and regulatory agencies. Needs revising as the practitioner's introduction.

Emmerich, H. A., *A Handbook of Public Administration* (New York: United Nations Technical Assistance Programme, 1961), 126 pp. A report on concepts and practices for improving public administration in underdeveloped countries, urged by technical experts employed by the United Nations on public officials engaged in developmental administration. Basically a primer of somewhat dogmatic management norms for public authorities covering organization, methods, merit systems, decentralization, public enterprises, public finance, planning, decision making, and public relations. Concludes with a review of U.N. Technical Assistance facilities.

Marx, F. M., *The Administrative State* (Chicago: University of Chicago Press, 1957), 202 pp., including bibliography and index. An examination of the public bureaucracy, its place in different societies, its role in the modern state, and its basic essentials. Reviews problems of bureaucratic self-perception, responsibility and control, representativeness, merit systems, and working atmosphere and norms. Comparative public-service approach, now dated by advances in comparative political and administrative systems.

Molitor, A., *The University Teaching of Social Sciences: Public Administration* (Paris: UNESCO, 1959), 192 pp. A report of a survey conducted in the mid-1950s by the International Institute of Administrative Sciences of the study of public administration in institutes of higher education in twenty-seven countries around the world. Covers the history of the discipline, trends in academic approaches, status in the academic world, teachers and trainers, methods and facilities, and research centers. Appendix illustrates typical curricula. Survey now outdated.

Waldo, D., *The Study of Public Administration* (New York: Random House, 1955), 72 pp., including bibliographical note. Still the most competent analysis of the methodological issues in the study of public administration, which does not ignore or skim the intellectual difficulties of definition, scope, relation with related disciplines, and objectivity. Describes the historical development of the discipline, different approaches, and contemporary challenges. The academic's introduction.

Basic Texts

Basic course material is contained in large hard-cover textbooks, considerably more expensive than the introductory texts, but well below the cost of textbooks in the physical sciences, and within the reach of most students. The better textbooks trace their first editions before 1945, and a comparison of successive editions would provide the basis for a history of the discipline. While their basic structures may not have changed that much, their contents, approaches, and views have been transformed. Nevertheless, the management-process approach still dominates, indicated by sections on organization, staffing, financing, rules, laws and norms, executive leadership, and controls. To these have been added policy making, decision making, political participation, administrative behavior, administrative theory, and comparative analysis. They are still largely lacking considerations of nonbureaucratic administration, community participation, measurement of policy and functional performance, and nondemocratic systems. All are extensively footnoted and indexed.

Dimock, M. E., and Dimock, G. O., *Public Administration,* fourth ed. (New York: Holt, Rinehart and Winston, 1969), 623 pp., including name and general indices. Divided into four parts, three of which—Forces, Institutions and Environment, The Vocational Appeal, and Finance and Economic Policy—have seven chapters each; Program Management contains eleven chapters. All chapters completed with a bibliography and cross-indexed with a companion case book. In the fourth edition, management processes have been relegated to considerations of the ends of government, political behavior, comparative systems, fiscal policy, and administrative ecology, although the emphasis remains on the federal government of the United States. Probably directed at students who intend to enter public service, for administrative theory is not well represented. Copious references in text and bibliographies. Well written, up-to-date; text much improved for the revision. Liberal outlook.

Marx, F. M., ed., *Elements of Public Administration,* second ed. (Englewood Cliffs, N.J.: Prentice-Hall, 1959), 572 pp., including index. No bibliography. The first revised postwar textbook that rejects the politics-administration dichotomy, being written by a team of fourteen contributors, all then employed in public administration. Continuous exchange between them, plus strong editorship, has reduced duplication and has produced a systematic and integrated text more generalized than American books at the time. In the revision, the structure has been retained, but the content updated. Part One, entitled the Role of Public Administration, covers its growth, study, bureaucratic nature, place in democracy, and societal functions. Part Two, Organization and Management, contains ten chapters on both the formal and informal machinery of American government. Part Three, Working Methods, deals with policy formulation and application, management and supervision, research, and administrative behavior. Part Four, Responsibility and Accountability, discusses political, judicial, staff, and financial controls. Administrative theory, comparative analysis, development administration, and other postwar developments are missing. Unlikely to be revised. Outdated.

Millett, J. D., *Management in the Public Service: The Quest for Effective Performance* (New York: McGraw-Hill, 1954), 417 pp., including index; and *Government and Public Administration: The Quest for Responsible Performance* (New York: McGraw-Hill, 1959), 484 pp., including index. Selected footnotes. No bibliography. This two-volume text looks at public administration from the management perspective and, separately, from the political perspective of American federalism. The first volume resembles a government management manual; it is divided into three parts, concerned with work direction (leadership, planning, communication, supervision, public relations), work operation (organization, human relations, finance, personnel, legality), and internal services (capital plant, supplies). The second volume concentrates on the administrative aspects of the American system of government or the American public bureaucracy as a responsible political institution. It is divided into four parts, concerned with the constitutional framework of American public administration and the tripartite division of powers, with emphasis on political control over a professionally managed public bureaucracy. Whereas the first volume tends to be prescriptive, the second veers toward the descriptive and has been overtaken by events. Both volumes should have been integrated, reduced by shortening historical discussions, and extended beyond institutional analysis. They contain much sensible advice for the American official, still relevant today.

Nigro, F. A., *Modern Public Administration,* second ed. (New York: Harper & Row, 1970), 490 pp., including index. Bibliographies at end of each of the twenty-two chapters; footnotes in the side margins. The second edition is a considerable improvement in appearance and presentation on the first, as it has been extensively rewritten and updated. The structure of seven parts remains basically unchanged—Nature and Scope of the Field, Administrative Organism, Basic Problems of Management, Personnel Administration, Financial Administration, Administrative Responsibility, and International Administration—with strengthened chapters on organizational theory, budgeting, and industrial relations. Covers a wider perspective than other texts and incorporates events of the late 1960s, but still neglects comparative and development administration, although it draws on examples from American state and local government.

Pfiffner, J. M., and Presthus, R., *Public Administration,* fifth ed. (New York: Ronald Press, 1967), 567 pp., including name and subject indices and a selected bibliography. A prewar book that has gone through several editions and complete rewritings to become possibly the leading text in the discipline, intended as a balanced and realistic appraisal of the American public bureaucracy. Combines behavioralism and institutional-managerial process. Thirty-one chapters are divided among seven parts concerned with general disciplinary aspects, administrative roles, organization, staffing, financing, administrative law and regulation, and administrative responsibility. Widest coverage of any text, including discussions of administrative theory, computer application, comparative systems, bureaucratic political power, behavioral research, and administrative reform. Weak on state and local administration, policy formulation, international systems, and functional content; bibliography could be improved. Conservatively inclined.

Sharkansky, I., *Public Administration: Policy-Making in Government Agencies* (Chicago: Markham, 1970), 307 pp., including index. Selected footnotes only. No bibliography. An experimental-systems approach to American public administration, built around a conversion model of high-level bureaucratic policy makers. Following a general description of the model, successive parts concentrate on the environment of the system, the conversion processes of decision making, machinery of government and bureaucratic leaders, the inputs of the system such as the status of public administration, political pressures and governmental processes, and the outputs of the system such as intergovernmental relations. A good idea badly executed, lacking comprehensiveness, depth, and precision. A contrast with management-process approach. For the academically inclined.

Simon, H. A., Smithburg, D. W., and Thompson, V. A., *Public Administration* (New York: Alfred A. Knopf, 1950), 600 pp., including index and bibliographical notes. Constitutes a challenge to the formalistic institutional approach by stressing the behavioral aspects of public authorities within a management-process framework in an attempt to bring the subject to life for prospective public servants. Conveys the working atmosphere of large public organizations from the employee's viewpoint and avoids sterile formalism and dogmatism. Essentially, applied administrative theory in real situations, drawing on actual experience, social psychology, and managerial politics. Concentrates on the executive function in American government; the twenty-five chapters cover public authorities as organisms and social systems, human relations, group behavior, leadership, adaptation and survival, informal relations, and administrative evaluation. While it was refreshing in its day, it badly needs updating and revision in the light of more recent research in behavioralism; also, less importantly, it needs to take into account the transformation of American public administration.

White, L. D., *Introduction to the Study of Public Administration,* fourth ed. (New York: Crowell Collier & Macmillan, 1955), 531 pp., including index. No bibliography. Probably the most influential textbook before the 1960s. Originally a management-process approach as a challenge to legalistic descriptions and dogmatic scientific management before the Great Depression; later expanded to cover fiscal management and administrative action as well as organization, staffing and financing; then overhauled to include policy orientation, behavioral aspects, and clientele relations; finally, completely revised to take into account postwar organization, finance, personnel, and administrative control. Largely descriptive—analytical of the federal government; weak on administrative theory, policy making, nondemocratic and nonbureaucratic processes, functions, and comparative systems. Outdated, but a badly needed revision is unlikely.

B. Gournay *et al., Administration Publique,* (Paris: Presses Universitaires de France, 1967), 516 pp., might be consulted for comparison. H. L. Blum and A. R. Leonard, *Public Administration—A Public Health Viewpoint* (New York: Crowell Collier & Macmillan, 1963), is highly recommended to public-health administrators.

Symposia on Basic Methodological Issues

Charlesworth, J. C., ed., *Theory and Practice of Public Administration: Scope, Objectives, and Methods* (Philadelphia: The American Academy of Political and Social Science, 1968), 336 pp. Papers and proceedings of a conference held 28-29 December 1967 in Philadelphia to appraise the discipline and discuss whether a new synthesis was emerging. Major papers were presented by D. Waldo, F. W. Riggs, H. Emmerich, S. K. Bailey, H. Cleveland, L. K. Caldwell, and H. Sherman, representing the key figures of the 1960s in the study of public administration in the United States; J. C. Charlesworth has analyzed the papers and discussions. A methodological state of the discipline as it headed into the 1970s from the establishment viewpoint.

Marini, F., *Toward A New Public Administration* (San Francisco: Chandler, 1971), 372 pp. Revised papers of a workshop of younger scholars, held September 1968 at the Minnowbrook Conference Center under the auspices of Syracuse University, to appraise the state of the discipline as it headed into the 1970s. The papers and comments are somewhat critical of the establishment viewpoint and advocate a reorientation of the discipline away from static management-process approaches to policy content, socially relevant normative administrative theory, and administrative dynamics.

General Readers

The basic text is usually written by one or two persons who undertake the arduous task of covering the field systematically. In contrast, a general reader is a collection of articles specially written for an anthology or reprinted from professional journals, where much of the highest-quality work is to be found. It serves different purposes. It may be a convenient handbook of the classic writings in the discipline that may be otherwise inaccessible. It may be an illustrative manual to accompany a basic text. It may be a special collection designed for experimental courses in new frontiers of the discipline. It may be a colloquium of disparate and controversial views and approaches to the discipline. It may also be a way for the editor to become widely known academically without contributing anything original himself. The following are considered to be worthwhile student companions, to aid his intellectual development beyond textbook descriptions and analyses.

Altshuler, A. A., *The Politics of the Federal Bureaucracy* (New York: Dodd, Mead, 1968). Contains about forty selections of article length on the borders of politics and administration in the United States government, concerned with the reconciliation of bureaucracy with democracy, the adequacy of control devices, and the nature of administrative conflict and accommodation.

Banfield, E. C., *Urban Government: A Reader in Politics and Administration* (New York: Free Press, 1969). Includes a glossary, bibliography, and index. Over sixty selections concerned with the running of the American metropolis, with much space devoted to intergovernmental relations, local self-government, administrative reform, city-manager concept, management problems, planning, and policy formulation. Concentrates on process, not technique; analysis, not description; real problems, not ideal solutions.

Gawthrop, L. C., *The Administrative Process and Democratic Theory* (Boston: Houghton Mifflin, 1970). Contains thirty-two readings tracing the historical development of American administrative concepts from the beginning of the republic to the present, covering administration as policy determinent, management science, politics, interpersonal behavior, incrementalism, analytic methods, and turbulence.

Golembiewski, R. T., Gibson, R., and Cornog, G. Y., *Public Administration: Readings in Institutions, Processes, Behavior* (Chicago: Rand McNally, 1966). Fifty-three selections arranged in alphabetical order ranging over the whole gamut of public administration, including extracts from specialized texts, as well as articles and annotated official reports, to illustrate the various worlds—behavioral, institutional, functional and procedural—in which the public official operates. Various plans are presented to coordinate the selections in a systematic instructional framework.

Golembiewski, R. T., *Public Budgeting and Finance: Readings in Theory and Practice* (Itasca, Ill.: F. E. Peacock, 1968). Forty-seven selections deal with institutional, technical, and behavioral aspects of public budgeting.

Lepawsky, A., *Administration: The Art and Science of Organization and Management* (New York: Alfred A. Knopf, 1949). The first administrative reader, ranging back into ancient history and across administrative science, including public administration. A large number of selections from diverse sources, including extracts from the classic works. Now dated and overtaken, but still includes valuable sources neglected elsewhere.

Martin, R. C., *Public Administration and Democracy* (Syracuse, N.Y.: Syracuse University Press, 1965). A rich collection of commemorative essays by leading scholars to honor the memory of Paul H. Appleby, covering the whole field of public administration, including comparative and development administration and administrative reform.

Merton, R. K., Gray, A. P., Hockey, B., and Selvin, H. C., *Reader in Bureaucracy* (New York: Free Press, 1952). Over fifty selections of articles and book extracts on the nature of bureaucracy, including public authorities, treated sociologically. Dated, but sections on theory, power, structure, status, and pathology still relevant. Bibliography was extensive for the time. Not confined to the United States.

Nigro, F. A., *Public Administration: Readings and Documents* (New York: Holt, Rinehart and Winston, 1951). The first public administration reader, containing a wide selection of articles, official reports, newspaper comment, and book extracts, within the narrower definition of the discipline then prevalent.

O'Donnell, M. E., *Readings in Public Administration* (Boston: Houghton Mifflin, 1966). Contains the pick of the postwar methodological articles, together with some classics in the orthodox tradition.

Rourke, F. E., *Bureaucratic Power in National Politics* (Boston: Little, Brown, 1965). Sixteen articles concerning the meeting of politics and administration, such as bureaucratic power, official-clientele relations, political controls, administrative politics, and administrative responsibility.

Rowat, D. C., *Basic Issues in Public Administration* (New York: Crowell Collier & Macmillan, 1961). Presents selected controversial views of methodological and ideological issues to stimulate the student into thinking out his personal position and to challenge the written word. Follows the general pattern of basic textbooks— disciplinary problems, organizational arrangements, methods, merit systems, employee rights, budgeting, and accountability and responsibility. Unfortunately, contains false dichotomies and misplaced questions, which can divert the student's attention from the real issues.

Waldo, D., *Ideas and Issues in Public Administration* (New York: McGraw-Hill, 1953). A popular reader of the 1950s, containing a wide selection of stimulating source material ranging across the public-administration spectrum. Overtaken by events.

Woll, P., *Public Administration and Policy: Selected Essays* (New York: Harper & Row, 1966). Reflects the meeting of politics and administration, with similar content to Rourke, *Bureaucratic Power in National Politics.*

Case Studies

Case studies are designed to give the student a feel of the real thing and to acquaint those without any practical experience or knowledge in public administration with the public official's world. They may take him through a complete episode or present a suggestive scenario to be acted out in different roles. At one time, they were be-lieved to constitute the new educational wave, but they have not been used widely, compared with business administration. All make engrossing reading. Explanations of the use of case studies usually introduce each book.

Bock, E. A., *State and Local Government: A Case Book* (University, Ala.: University of Alabama Press, 1963) is a collection of case studies about various problems confronting state and local government. Emphasis is on the sensitivity of local officials to local pressures and interests.

Golembiewski, R. T., *Perspectives on Public Management: Cases and Learning Designs* (Itasca, Ill.: F. E. Peacock, 1968) contains thirteen cases largely concerned with management process in public authorities, each preceded by a learning design.

Inter-University Case Program Series. Studies of government administration and policy formation, published by Bobbs-Merrill for the Inter-University Case Program, Inc. (131 Stadium Ave., Syracuse, N.Y. 12310). Over one hundred individual case studies in political science and public administration of diverse interest, varying length and quality, at different prices. Index and summary available from the publishers or the president, Professor E. A. Bock, whose *Essays on the Case Method in Public Administration and Political Science* are obtainable from the International Institute of Administrative Sciences and the Public Administration Service (1313 East 60 St., Chicago, Ill. 60637).

Mosher, F. C., *Governmental Reorganizations: Cases and Commentary* (Indianapolis: Bobbs-Merrill, 1967) is concerned with intra-organizational reforms of considerable variety, with special emphasis on the concepts of participation and reorganization. The editor has laid down guidelines for the contributors and provides an extensive general commentary on the nature of the reorganizations. Good bibliography on organizational participation. The cases themselves are lengthy and detailed, perhaps too elaborate to hold the attention of nonspecialized students.

Novogrod, R. J., Dimock, M. E., and Dimock, G. O., *Casebook in Public Administration* (New York: Holt, Rinehart and Winston, 1969). Intended to illustrate any basic text, including Dimock and Dimock, *Public Administration*. The cases are short and varied, ranging widely around American public administration. They concentrate on the actors in confronting daily problems. Some cases are based on extensive depth interviewing, and the transcribed interviews are reproduced. Study questions are provided after each case study.

Stein, H., *Public Administration and Policy Development* (New York: Harcourt Brace Jovanovich, 1952). The first case book in public administration; still relevant, even though the cases are now past rather than recent administrative history. The editor's introductory essay is not only a declaration of intent and faith, but a methodological essay that finally collapsed the administration-politics dichotomy. The emphasis is on decision making in policy issues, not technicalities.

SPECIALIZED TEXTS

In pruning many hundreds of worthwhile references, some difficult decisions had to be made. Obviously, it was impossible to include every reference or to give more than a curt comment about those chosen. The aim is not completeness, but a fair presentation of the richness and variety of sources in the major concerns of this book as a guide to the interested reader. For every reference quoted, two or three others would have served equally, and their partisans, like their irate authors and publishers, may object strongly to their exclusion. More importantly, only books have been listed (in alphabetical order to facilitate ordering). The task of listing articles appearing in the journals listed earlier is beyond current resources. Every journal, however, maintains an annual index for easy reference, and attention is drawn to the Bobbs-Merrill Reprint Series in the Social Sciences, which reproduces contemporary journal articles that have become classics.

The Study of Public Administration

The scope and nature of public administration has been extensively debated at different times since the publication of Woodrow Wilson's 1887 essay, "The Study of Public Administration," which was reproduced in the *Political Science Quarterly,* LVI (December 1941), 481–506. A recent summary of the debate is contained in W. J. M. Mackenzie, *Politics and Social Science* (Middlesex, England: Penguin, 1967).

Still relevant are P. H. Appleby, *Public Administration in a Welfare State* (New York: Asia Publishing House, 1961); M. E. Dimock, *The Philosophy of Administration* (New York: Harper & Row, 1958); J. M. Gaus, *Reflections on Public Administration* (University, Ala.: University of Alabama Press, 1947); H. Lasswell, *The Future of Political Science* (New York: Atherton Press, 1963); R. Presthus, *Behavioral Approaches to Public Administration* (University, Ala.: University of Alabama Press, 1965); E. S. Redford, *Ideal and Practice in Public Administration* (University, Ala.: University of Alabama Press, 1958); E. S. Redford, *Democracy in the Administrative State* (New York: Oxford University Press, 1969); W. A. Robson, *Politics and Government at Home and Abroad* (London: G. Allen and Unwin, 1967); D. Waldo, *The Administrative State* (New York: Ronald Press, 1948); D. Waldo, *Perspectives on Administration* (University, Ala.: University of Alabama Press, 1956); and L. D. White, *New Horizons in Public Administration* (University, Ala.: University of Alabama Press, 1945). A survey of trends in the mid-1960s was presented in the Silver Anniversary issue of the *Public Administration Review,* XXV, No. 1 (March 1965), which could be profitably compared with early postwar hopes, represented in articles by G. A. Graham, J. M. Gaus, C. S. Ascher, and W. S. Sayre in the *Public Administration Review* from Spring 1950 to Spring 1951 and in W. Anderson and J. M. Gaus, *Research in Public Administration* (Chicago: Social Science Research Council, 1945). A recapitulation of new developments in the postwar era has been given by D. Waldo, "Public Administration, 1948–1968," *Journal of Politics,* 30 (May 1968), reproduced in M. D. Irish, ed., *Political Science* (Englewood Cliffs, N.J.: Prentice-Hall, 1968), 153–189.

A history of the discipline of public administration has yet to be written, and few references can be found in A. Somit and J. Tanenhaus, *The Development of American Political Science* (Boston: Allyn & Bacon, 1967). Sketches are included in the major texts and in the histories of research institutions concerned with public administration (such as The Brookings Institution and the Rand Corporation) and research foundations (such as the Rockefeller Foundation and the Ford Foundation), which can be obtained directly from them unless published independently, such as B. L. R. Smith, *The Rand Corporation* (Cambridge, Mass.: Harvard University Press, 1966). Increased recognition of the use of public-administration studies in public-policy making is outlined in G. M. Lyons, *The Uneasy Partnership* (New York: Russell Sage Foundation, 1969), and their general significance is highlighted by M. F. Millikan, "Inquiry and Policy: The Relation of Knowledge to Action," in D. Lerner, ed., *Human Meaning of the Social Sciences* (New York: Meridian, 1959); and R. K. Merton, "Role of the Intellectual in Public Bureaucracy," in R. K. Merton, *Social Theory and Social Structure* (New York: Free Press, 1957), 207–224. Its place within the social sciences, especially administrative science and the contemporary scene, is the concern of P. M. Blau, *Bureaucracy in Modern Society* (New York: Random House, 1956); A. Downs, *Inside Bureaucracy* (Boston: Little, Brown, 1967); A. Etzioni, *Modern Organizations* (Englewood Cliffs, N.J.: Prentice-Hall, 1964); J. K. Galbraith, *The New Industrial State* (London: Hamish Hamilton, 1967); J. Gould, ed., *Penguin Survey of the Social Sciences* (Middlesex, England: Penguin, 1965); O. Helmer, *Social Technology* (New York: Basic Books, 1966); P. Meyer, *Administrative Organization* (London: Stevens, 1957); C. N. Parkinson, *Parkinson's Law* (Boston: Houghton Mifflin, 1957); R. Presthus, *The Organizational Society* (New York: Vintage Books, 1965); H. A. Simon, *Research Frontiers in Politics and Government* (Washington, D.C.: The Brookings Institution, 1955); O. Tead, *Democratic Administration* (New York: Association Press, 1945); O. Tead, *The Art of Administration* (New York: McGraw-Hill, 1951);

and R. Young, ed., *Approaches to the Study of Politics* (Evanston, Ill.: Northwestern University Press, 1958). Unsympathetic reaction is described by T. Roszak, *The Making of a Counter Culture* (New York: Doubleday, 1969).

Teaching and research methods in public administration have not received special attention in recent years. Long since dated are G. A. Graham, *Education for Public Administration* (Chicago: Social Science Research Council, 1941) and J. McLean, *Public Service and University Education* (Princeton: Princeton University Press, 1954). More recent are F. P. Sherwood and W. B. Storm, *Teaching in Public Administration* (Los Angeles: School of Public Administration, University of Southern California, 1962); D. C. Stone, ed., *Education in Public Administration* (Brussels: International Institute of Administrative Sciences, 1963); and G. J. Mangone, ed., *Public Affairs Education and the University* (Syracuse: Maxwell Graduate School, 1963). Much more has been published on the establishment of schools or institutes of public administration as institution building in underdeveloped countries, one of the most comprehensive being The Graduate School of Public and International Affairs, *Organizing Schools and Institutes of Administration* (Pittsburgh: The Graduate School of Public and International Affairs, 1969). On research, J. M. Pfiffner, *Research Method in Public Administration* (New York: Ronald Press, 1940) is dated but has not been replaced, though supplemented by K. C. Davis, "Instruction and Research in Public Administration: Reflections of a Law Professor," *American Political Science Review,* XLVII, No. 3 (September 1953), 728–752. The student has to turn to more general studies, such as A. Kaplan, *The Concept of Enquiry* (San Francisco: Chandler, 1964); J. R. Lawrence, *Operations Research and the Social Sciences* (New York: Tavistock, 1966); and P. Lazarfield *et al.,* eds., *The Uses of Sociology* (New York: Basic Books, 1967); or two useful papers in the Comparative Public Administration Special Series: F. W. Riggs and E. W. Weidner, *Models and Priorities in the Comparative Study of Public Administration* (1963) and G. D. Paige, *Proposition Building in the Study of Comparative Administration* (1968). Contrasting research methods into the same general area— public images and attitudes toward public bureaucracy—can be ascertained from A. P. Barnabas, S. J. Eldersveld, and V. Jagarnadham, *The Citizen and the Administrator in a Developing Democracy* (Glenview, Ill.: Scott, Foresman, 1968); G. E. Caiden and N. Raphaeli, *Student Perception of Public Administration in Israel* (Jerusalem: Kaplan School, Hebrew University, 1968); Civil Service Commission of Canada, *High School "Image" Survey of the Canadian Civil Service* (Ottawa: Personnel Research Section, 1964); and F. P. Kilpatrick *et al., The Image of the Federal Service* (Washington, D.C.: The Brookings Institution, 1964).

Administrative history is usually a byproduct of other historical research. An extensive bibliography of administrative systems before the modern bureaucratic state has been compiled by the Graduate School of Public Administration at New York University, and extensive references can be found in G. E. Caiden, *Administrative Reform* (Chicago: Aldine, 1969); S. N. Eisenstadt, *The Political System of Empires* (New York: Free Press, 1963); and K. A. Wittfogel, *Oriental Despotism* (New Haven: Yale University Press, 1957). Among notable sources can be included E. Barker, *The Development of the Public Service in Western Europe 1660–1930* (London: Oxford University Press, 1944); G. E. Caiden, *Career Service* (Melbourne, Australia: Melbourne University Press, 1965); B. Chapman, *The Profession of Government* (London: G. Allen and Unwin, 1959); E. Cohen, *The Growth of the British Civil Service 1780– 1939* (London: G. Allen and Unwin, 1941); J. D. Kingsley, *Representative Bureaucracy* (Yellow Springs, Ohio: Antioch Press, 1944); L. S. S. O'Malley, *The Indian Civil Ser-*

vice 1901–1930 (London: J. Murray, 1931); H. Rosenberg, *Bureaucracy, Aristocracy and Autocracy: The Prussian Experience 1660–1815* (Cambridge, Mass.: Harvard University Press, 1958); P. Van Riper, *History of the United States Civil Service* (New York: Harper & Row, 1958); and the L. D. White Series: *The Jeffersonians* (1951); *The Jacksonians* (1954); *The Federalists* (1956); and *The Republican Era* (1958) — all published in New York by Macmillan. In the United States, the pre-1945 publications of the New York Municipal Research Bureau, National Civil Service Reform League, National Institute of Public Administration, the Brookings Institution, and the Public Administration Clearing House now constitute administrative history, as do the institutional or organizational histories of federal and state government bodies. As interest grows in this area, more publications, like A. Hoogenboom, *Outlawing the Spoils* (Urbana, Ill.: University of Illinois, 1968), can be expected.

Public-Policy Making

An extensive bibliography can be found in Y. Dror, *Public Policy Making Reexamined* (San Francisco: Chandler, 1968) and continued in Y. Dror, "Recent Literature in Policy Sciences," *Policy Sciences* 1, No. 2 (1970). Also helpful, if somewhat restricted in scope and time, is P. Wasserman and F. S. Silander, *Decision-Making: An Annotated Bibliography* (Ithaca, N.Y.: Graduate School of Business and Public Administration, Cornell University, 1958) and supplement (1964). Recommended readers are R. A. Bauer and K. J. Gergen, eds., *The Study of Policy Formation* (New York: Free Press, 1968); T. E. Cronin and S. D. Greenberg, eds., *The Presidential Advisory System* (New York: Harper & Row, 1969); F. J. Lyden *et al.,* eds., *Policies, Decisions and Organization* (New York: Appleton, 1969); A. Ranney, ed., *Political Science and Public Policy* (Chicago: Markham, 1968); M. Reagan, ed., *The Administration of Public Policy* (Glenview, Ill.: Scott, Foresman, 1969); R. R. Ripley, ed., *Public Policies and Their Politics* (New York: W. W. Norton, 1966); and I. Sharkansky, ed., *Policy Analysis in Political Science* (Chicago: Markham, 1969). Students should also note the public-policy making series of Markham Publishing Co. (Chicago), The Brookings Institution (Washington, D.C.), and The Rand Corporation (Santa Monica). Two good introductions are C. E. Lindblom, *The Policy Making Process* (Englewood Cliffs, N.J.: Prentice-Hall, 1968); and F. E. Rourke, *Bureaucracy, Politics and Public Policy* (Boston: Little, Brown, 1969).

Case studies in public-policy making are growing more popular. Apart from the Inter-University Case Program, several collections of case studies are available, including E. S. Redford, ed., *Public Administration and Policy Formation* (Austin: University of Texas Press, 1958); A. P. Sindler, ed., *American Political Institutions and Public Policy* (Boston: Little, Brown, 1969); H. Stein, ed., *American Civil-Military Decisions* (University, Ala.: University of Alabama Press, 1963); F. M. G. Wilson, *Administrators in Action,* Vol. I (London: G. Allen and Unwin, 1961); and G. Rhodes, *Administrators in Action,* Vol. II (London: G. Allen and Unwin, 1965); and D. Corbett and B. Schaffer, eds., *Decisions* (Melbourne, Australia: Cheshire, 1965). Individual case studies related to their environment are recorded in A. A. Altshuler, *The City Planning Process: A Political Analysis* (Ithaca, N.Y.: Cornell University Press, 1965); R. J. Art, *The TFX Decision* (Boston: Little, Brown, 1968); E. C. Banfield, *Political Influence* (New York: Free Press, 1961); R. A. Bauer, I. de Sola Pool, and L. A. Dexter, *American Business and Public Policy* (New York: Atherton, 1963); R. A. Dahl, *Who Governs?* (New Haven: Yale University Press, 1961); M. Mayerson and E. G. Banfield,

Politics, Planning, and the Public Interest: The Case of Public Housing in Chicago (New York: Free Press, 1955); S. I. Ploss, *Conflict and Decision-Making in Soviet Russia: A Case Study of Agricultural Policy 1913–1963* (Princeton: Princeton University Press, 1965); W. S. Sayre and H. Kaufman, *Governing New York City* (New York: Russell Sage Foundation. 1960); and J. H. Sundquist, *Politics and Policy: The Eisenhower, Kennedy and Johnson Years* (Washington, D.C.: The Brookings Institution, 1968). These should be read in the light of A. Etzioni, *The Active Society* (New York: Free Press, 1968); and T. J. Lowi, *The End of Liberalism* (New York: W. W. Norton, 1969); and different conceptions of the public interest examined in R. E. Flathman, *The Public Interest* (New York: John Wiley & Sons, 1966); C. J. Friedrich, ed., *The Public Interest* (New York, Atherton, 1962); and G. Schubert, *The Public Interest* (New York: Free Press, 1960); balanced by T. R. Dye, *Politics, Economics and the Public* (Chicago: Rand McNally, 1966).

Policy studies are particularly well developed in certain strategic areas.

Defense. K. E. Boulding: *Conflict and Defense: A General Theory* (New York: Harper & Row, 1962); S. Enke, ed., *Defense Management* (Englewood Cliffs, N.J.: Prentice-Hall, 1967); C.J. Hitch, *Decision-Making for Defense* (Berkeley: University of California Press, 1965); C. J. Hitch and R. N. McKean, *The Economics of Defense in a Nuclear Age* (Cambridge, Mass.: Harvard University Press, 1960); H. Kahn, *On Thermonuclear War* (Princeton: Princeton University Press, 1960); H. Kahn, *Thinking About the Unthinkable* (New York: Horizon Press, Inc., 1962); H. Kahn, *On Escalation, Metaphors and Scenarios* (New York: Frederick A. Praeger, 1965); E. S. Quade, ed., *Analysis for Military Decisions* (Chicago: Rand McNally, 1964); E. S. Quade and W. I. Boucher, eds., *Systems Analysis and Policy Planning: Applications in Defense* (New York: American Elsevier, 1968); T. C. Schelling, *The Strategy of Conflict* (Cambridge, Mass.: Harvard University Press, 1960).

Foreign Affairs. H. A. Kissinger, *Nuclear Weapons and Foreign Policy* (New York: Harper & Row, 1957); A. Rappaport, *Fights, Games, and Debates* (Ann Arbor, Mich.: The University of Michigan Press, 1960); B. M. Sapin, *The Making of United States Foreign Policy* (Washington, D.C.: The Brookings Institution, 1966); R. C. Snyder *et al., Foreign Policy Decision-Making* (New York: Free Press, 1962).

Science. R. Gilpin, *American Scientists and Nuclear Weapons Policy* (Princeton: Princeton University Press, 1962); R. Gilpin and C. Wright, eds., *Scientists and National Policy Making* (New York: Columbia University Press, 1964); A. Griffith, *The National Aeronautics and Space Act: A Study of the Development of Public Policy* (Washington, D.C.: Public Affairs Press, 1962); S. A. Lakoff, ed., *Knowledge and Power: Essays on Science and Government* (New York: Free Press, 1966); D. K. Price, *Government and Science* (New York: New York University Press, 1954); D. K. Price, *The Scientific Estate* (Cambridge, Mass.: Harvard University Press, 1965).

Transportation. D. Corbett, *Politics and the Airlines* (London: G. Allen and Unwin, 1965); L. C. Fitch *et al., Urban Transportation and Public Policy* (San Francisco: Chandler, 1964); S. A. Lawrence, *U.S. Merchant Shipping Policies and Politics* (Washington, D.C.: The Brookings Institution, 1966); F. C. Thayer, *Air Transport Policy and National Security* (Chapel Hill, N.C.: University of North Carolina Press, 1965.

Urbanization. A. K. Campbell and S. Sacks, *Metropolitan America: Fiscal Patterns and Governmental Systems* (New York: Free Press, 1967); M. Davis and M. G. Weinbaum, *Metropolitan Decision Processes* (Chicago: Rand McNally, 1969); O. P. Williams and C. R. Adrian, *Four Cities: A Study in Comparative Policy Making* (Philadelphia: University of Pennsylvania Press, 1963); J. Q. Wilson, ed., *City Problems and Public Policy: A Reader* (New York: John Wiley & Sons, 1963). See also J. V. Lindsay, *The City* (New York: Norton, 1969).

Water. T. H. Campbell and R. O. Sylvester, *Water Resources Management and Public Policy* (Seattle: University of Washington Press, 1968); A. Maass *et al., Design of Water Resource Systems* (Cambridge, Mass.: Harvard University Press, 1962).

Contemporary policy issues are surveyed in K. Gordon, ed., *Agenda for the Nation* (Washington, D.C.: The Brookings Institution, 1968).

Besides the classic works of Herbert Simon, decision making has other seminal works. A useful reader is W. J. Gore and J. W. Dyson, eds., *The Making of Decisions: A Reader in Administrative Behavior* (New York: Free Press, 1964); and further collections can be found in C. J. Friedrich, ed., *Nomos VII. Rational Decision* (New York: Atherton, 1964); and G. Tullock, ed., *Papers on Non-Market Decision-Making* (Charlottesville, Va.: University of Virginia Press, 1966). Extensive bibliographies accompany the survey essays of D. W. Taylor, "Decision-Making and Problem Solving" (pp. 48–86) and J. Feldman and H. E. Kantor, "Organizational Decision-Making" (pp. 614–644), in J. G. March, ed., *Handbook of Organizations* (Chicago: Rand McNally, 1965). Other seminal works include M. Alexis and C. Z. Wilson, *Organization Decision-Making* (Englewood Cliffs, N.J.: Prentice-Hall, 1967); D. Braybrooke and C. E. Lindblom, *A Strategy of Decision* (New York: Free Press, 1963); R. M. Cyert and J. G. March, *A Behavioral Theory of the Firm* (Englewood Cliffs, N.J.: Prentice-Hall, 1964); A. Downs, *Bureaucratic Structure and Decision-Making* (Santa Monica: The Rand Corporation, 1966); W. Edwards and A. Tversky, eds., *Decision-Making* (Middlesex, England: Penguin, 1967); T. A. Goldman, *Cost Effectiveness Analysis* (New York: Frederick A. Praeger, 1967); W. J. Gore, *Administrative Decision-Making: A Heuristic Model* (New York: John Wiley & Sons, 1964); C. E. Lindblom, "The Science of Muddling Through," *Public Administration Review,* XIX (1959), 79–88; D. W. Miller and M. K. Starr, *The Structure of Human Decisions* (Englewood Cliffs, N.J.: Prentice-Hall, 1967); J. D. Millett, *Decision-Making and Administration in Higher Education* (Kent, Ohio: Kent State University Press, 1968); T. C. Sorenson, *Decision-Making in the White House* (New York: Columbia University Press, 1963); G. Vickers, *The Art of Judgment: A Theory of Policy Making* (London: Chapman and Hall, 1965). For futurizing influences, see S. Chase, *The Most Probable World* (New York: Harper & Row, 1968); R. Jungh and J. Galtong, eds., *Mankind 2000* (Oslo: Norwegian University Press, 1968); and H. Kahn and A. J. Weiner, *The Year 2000* (New York: Crowell Collier & Macmillan, 1967).

Much policy and decision analysis is based on systems theory, expounded in L. von Bertalanffy, *General Systems Theory: Foundations, Development, Application* (New York: George Braziller, 1968); F. K. Berrien, *General and Social Systems* (New Brunswick, N.J.: Rutgers University Press, 1968); W. Buckley, ed., *Modern Systems Research for the Behavioral Scientist* (Chicago: Aldine, 1968); C. W. Churchman, *The Systems Approach* (New York: Delacorte, 1968); A. D. Hall, *A Methodology for Systems Engineering* (Princeton: Van Nostrand, 1962); and in the continuing series of the Society for General Systems Research, *General Systems* (Ann Arbor, Mich.). On a more general level, systems theory gave rise to R. A. Dahl, *A Preface to Democratic Theory* (Chicago: University of Chicago Press, 1956); R. A. Dahl and C. E. Lindblom,

Politics, Economics and Welfare (New York: Harper & Row, 1953); K. W. Deutsch, *The Nerves of Government* (New York: Free Press, 1966); D. Easton, *A Systems Analysis of Political Life* (New York: John Wiley & Sons, 1965); C. E. Lindblom, *The Intelligence of Democracy: Decision-Making Through Mutual Adjustment* (New York: Free Press, 1965). At the management-service level, it produced R. L. Ackoff and P. Rivett, *A Manager's Guide to Operations Research* (New York: John Wiley & Sons, 1966); E. C. Bursk and J. F. Chapman, eds., *New Decision-Making Tools for Managers* (Cambridge, Mass.: Harvard University Press, 1963); and D. Novick, ed., *Program Budgeting: Program Analysis and the Federal Government* (Cambridge, Mass.: Harvard University Press, 1965). Other aids to policy making can be found in R. D. Luce and H. Raiffa, *Games and Decisions* (New York: John Wiley & Sons, 1958), and A. Rappaport, *Strategy and Conscience* (New York: Harper & Row, 1964).

Politics and Administration

The history of the politics-administration controversy has been traced in an unpublished draft monograph, G. E. Caiden, "Politics and Administration—The Rise and Fall of an Untenable Dichotomy" (Berkeley: Department of Political Science, University of California, 1969). On the low status of politics in the United States, see J. H. Bunzel, *Anti-Politics in America* (New York: Alfred A. Knopf, 1967). Leading the reintegration movement were P. H. Appleby, *Big Democracy* (New York: Knopf, 1945); P. H. Appleby, *Policy and Administration* (University, Ala.: University of Alabama Press, 1949); C. A. Beard, *Public Policy and General Welfare* (New Haven: Yale University Press, 1941); F. F. Blachley and M. E. Oatman, *Federal Regulatory Action and Control* (Washington, D.C.: The Brookings Institution, 1940); C. S. Hyneman, *Bureaucracy in a Democracy* (New York: Harper & Row, 1950); A. Leighton, *The Governing of Men* (Princeton: Princeton University Press, 1946); A. Leiserson, *Administrative Regulation* (Chicago: University of Chicago Press, 1942); and D. E. Lilenthal, *T. V.A.: Democracy on the March* (New York: Harper & Row, 1944). Since then, the reintegration has been consolidated in P. H. Appleby, *Morality and Administration in Democratic Government* (Baton Rouge, La.: Louisiana State University Press, 1952); W. W. Boyer, *Bureaucracy on Trial* (Indianapolis: Bobbs-Merrill, 1964); W. L. Cary, *Politics and the Regulatory Agencies* (New York: McGraw-Hill, 1967); L. C. Gawthrop, *Bureaucratic Behavior in the Executive Branch* (New York: Free Press, 1969); N. Long, *The Polity* (Chicago: Rand McNally, 1962); F. C. Mosher, *Democracy and the Public Service* (New York: Oxford University Press, 1968); N. J. Powell, *Responsible Public Bureaucracy in the United States* (Boston: Allyn & Bacon, 1967); and P. Woll, *American Bureaucracy* (New York: W. W. Norton, 1963). The political nature of public administration has long been demonstrated by numerous case studies and depth reports, such as H. Kaufman, *The Forest Ranger* (Baltimore: Johns Hopkins Press, 1960), and more recently, S. K. Bailey and E. K. Mosher, *E. S. E. A.: The Office of Education Administers a Law* (Syracuse: Syracuse University Press, 1968); D. Rogers, *110 Livingston St.: Politics and Bureaucracy in the New York City Schools* (New York: Random House, 1968); and P. Woll, *Administrative Law: The Informal Process* (Berkeley: University of California Press, 1963).

The bureaucratic exercise of power is considered in analyzing current concepts of power in A. S. McFarland, *Power and Leadership in Pluralist Systems* (Stanford, Calif.: Stanford University Press, 1969), which could well be read alongside general overviews of American government: C. R. Adrian, *Governing Urban America* (New York:

McGraw-Hill, 1955); D. J. Boorstin, *The Genius of American Politics* (Chicago: University of Chicago Press, 1953); R. A. Dahl, *Pluralist Democracy in the United States* (Chicago: Rand McNally, 1966); W. B. Graves, *American Intergovernmental Relations* (New York: Charles Scribner's Sons, 1964); M. Grodzins, *The American System* (Chicago: Rand McNally, 1966); H. Kariel, *The Decline of American Pluralism* (Stanford, Calif.: Stanford University Press, 1961); and G. McConnell, *Private Power and American Democracy* (New York: Alfred A. Knopf, 1966). The issue of power is debated in J. M. Burns, *Deadlock of Democracy* (Englewood Cliffs, N.J.: Prentice-Hall, 1963); J. S. Coleman, *Community Conflict* (New York: Free Press, 1957); J. Deakin, *The Lobbyist* (Washington, D.C.: Public Affairs Press, 1966); M. Edelman, *The Symbolic Uses of Politics* (Urbana, Ill.: University of Illinois Press, 1967); R. E. Elder, *The Policy Machine* (Syracuse: Syracuse University Press, 1960); J. L. Freeman, *The Political Process* (New York: Random House, 1965); P. Herring, *The Politics of Democracy* (New York: W. W. Norton, 1965); G. C. Homans, *The Human Group* (New York: Harcourt Brace Jovanovich, 1950); H. D. Lasswell and A. Kaplan, *Power and Society* (New Haven: Yale University Press, 1950); L. W. Milbrath, *Political Participation* (Chicago: Rand McNally, 1965); C. W. Mills, *The Power Elite* (New York: Oxford, 1956); T. Parsons, *Structure and Process in Modern Societies* (New York: Free Press, 1960); W. H. Riker, *The Theory of Political Coalitions* (New Haven: Yale University Press, 1962); D. B. Truman, *The Governmental Process* (New York: Alfred A. Knopf, 1951); A. F. Westin, *The Uses of Power* (New York: Harcourt Brace Jovanovich, 1962). Closely allied are W. Bell *et al., Public Leadership* (San Francisco: Chandler, 1961); and A. W. Gouldner, ed., *Studies in Leadership* (New York: Harper & Row, 1950).

The meshing of public officials and politicians in the American governmental system is the concern of C. E. Jacob, *Policy and Bureaucracy* (Princeton: Van Nostrand, 1966); and J. M. Landis, *The Administrative Process* (New Haven: Yale University Press, 1966). For the judicial angle, see H. Jacob, ed., *Law, Politics and the Federal Courts* (Boston: Little, Brown, 1967); R. S. Lorch, *Democratic Process and Administrative Law* (Detroit: Wayne State University Press, 1969); G. Schubert, *The Judicial Mind* (Evanston, Ill.: Northwestern University Press, 1965); and G. Schubert, *Judicial Policy Making* (Glenview, Ill.: Scott, Foresman, 1965). For the legislative angle, see B. M. Gross, *The Legislative Struggle* (New York: McGraw-Hill, 1953); J. P. Harris, *Congressional Control of Administration* (Washington, D.C.: The Brookings Institution, 1964); and M. E. Jewel and S. C. Patterson, *The Legislative Process in the United States* (New York: Random House, 1966). Among the many works concerned with the executive angle, see W. L. Cary, *Politics and the Regulatory Agencies* (New York: McGraw-Hill, 1967); L. W. Koenig, *The Chief Executive* (New York: Harcourt Brace Jovanovich, 1964); L. W. Koenig, *Congress and the President: Official Makers of Public Policy* (Glenview, Ill.: Scott, Foresman, 1965); S. Krislow and L. D. Musolf, eds., *The Politics of Regulation* (Boston: Houghton Mifflin, 1964); D. E. Mann and J. W. Doig, *The Assistant Secretaries* (Washington, D.C.: The Brookings Institution, 1965); G. Tulloch, *The Politics of Bureaucracy* (Washington, D.C.: Public Affairs Press, 1965); and A. Wildavsky, ed., *The Presidency* (Boston: Little, Brown, 1969).

The best source materials remain the published proceedings of public inquiries and legislative committees, official reports and public-relations administration of public authorities, and transcripts and judgments in public and administrative law. No better education exists than an exciting cross exchange between inquiring legislator and defending official, or between a sharp judge and a legal counsel acting on behalf of a public authority. Legislators have all manner of relevant source material inserted in the *Congressional Record*. As the great bulk of the material is public, it is available free or at nominal cost on application, and public authorities generally welcome public inquiries and additions to their mailing lists. Further, most public libraries of any size are depositories of official publications. For a responsible approach to governmental public relations, see M. Ogilvy Webb, *The Government Explains* (London: G. Allen, 1965) and L. F. Schneckebier and R. B. Eastin, *Government Publications and Their Use* (Washington, D.C.: The Brookings Institution, 1969). The issue of suppression is aired in F. E. Rourke, *Secrecy and Publicity* (Baltimore: Johns Hopkins Press, 1961).

Bureaucratic Arrangements

The formal structure of government is usually contained in a Government Manual, Government Directory, or similar compendium, listing all governmental authorities, their functions, laws, locations, and chief administrative and political officers. In turn, each public authority has an elaborate chart of its own organization, detailing every position. Some may possess a list of their most regular or important correspondents. Although the formal side is accessible, the informal side is not, and one has to rely on such unsatisfactory devices as office gossip, public-relations lapses, detailed public inquiries, and newspaper stories. Later—but too late for contemporary analysis—there will be official histories, access to archives, and revealing memoirs. Although no source can be up to date (so fast do changes take place in the formal, let alone informal, structure) in every country, there are handbooks describing the formal constitution and other details concerning the machinery of government. For the student who wants something more, J. D. Millett, *Organization for the Public Service* (Princeton: Van Nostrand, 1966) is a good introduction before he embarks on a wide range of how-to-do-it books in managerial organization, among which J. D. Mooney, *The Principles of Organization* (New York: Harper & Row, 1947); J. A. Litterer, *The Analysis of Organizations* (New York: John Wiley & Sons, 1965); and L. Urwick, *The Elements of Administration* (London: Pitman, 1947) rate as classics of their kind. More relevant to public administration are J. W. Fesler, *Area and Administration* (University, Ala.: University of Alabama Press, 1949); H. J. Friendly, *The Federal Administrative Agencies* (Cambridge, Mass.: Harvard University Press, 1962); R. B. Highshaw and D. L. Bowen, eds., *Communication in Public Administration* (Birmingham: University of Alabama Press, 1965); D. T. Stanley, *Changing Administrations* (Washington, D.C.: The Brookings Institution, 1965); J. M. Pfiffner and F. P. Sherwood, *Administrative Organization* (Englewood Cliffs, N.J.: Prentice-Hall, 1960); and S. C. Wallace, *Federal Departmentalization: A Critique of Theories of Organization* (New York: Columbia University Press, 1941).

Possibly the best sources, from the academic viewpoint, are found in the evidence, working papers, and reports of public inquiries into governmental administration. In the United States, reorganization and reform movements have succeeded in opening public administration to external review at some time in the present century in most states and counties. At federal level, the Taft Commission, Brownlow committee, and Hoover Commission are classics and constitute subjects for investigation in their own right. A recent private foundation enquiry of similar quality is J. L. Sundquist, *Making Federalism Work* (Washington, D.C.: The Brookings Institution, 1969). In Britain, the Royal Commissions into the Civil Service and related matters have similarly stimulated wider interest, particularly the Priestley, Plowden and Fulton Reports, obtainable from H.M.S.O., 49 High Holborn, London, W.C.1, under commissioned numbers, obtained from the H.M.S.O. itself or listed in *Public Administration* (London). In Canada, the Glassco Commission report is obtainable from the Government Printer, and similar arrangements prevail for the McCarthy Commission in New Zealand and the Boyer Committee in the Commonwealth of Australia. In many countries, the reports of such public inquiries are bound in annual volumes of papers presented to the legislature or in annual volumes of governmental reports. The working papers and other evidence may not be available at all, or only to bona fide scholars actually in the country. Failing access to any documents, one must resort to summaries in local newspapers and professional journals.

Studies of individual public authorities are usually published commercially. In Britain, the Whitehall series, published under the auspices of the Royal Institute of Public Administration, traces the history, functions, and organization of the national ministries. In the United States, the Institute of Public Administration issued a similar series in the 1920s, but the venture was not continued after the Great Depression. Individual agencies commission their own studies or cooperate with interested outsiders. At the beginning of the 1960s, Frederick A. Praeger, Inc., decided to launch its Library of U.S. Government Departments and Agencies; by 1970, some dozen studies have been published, including, for example, C. W. Borkland, *The Department of Defense* (New York: Praeger, 1968); and G. Cullinan, *The Post Office Department* (New York: Frederick A. Praeger, 1968). For more exotic forms of government organization, one has to turn to specialized texts. In the 1950s, the European administrative-law system and the French Conseil D'Etat attracted scholars. In the 1960s, the ombudsman received widespread attention in S. V. Anderson, *Ombudsman Papers: American Experiences and Proposals* (Berkeley: Institute of Governmental Studies, 1969); W. Gellhorn, *Ombudsmen and Others: Citizens' Protectors in Nine Countries* (Cambridge, Mass.: Harvard University Press, 1966); and D. C. Rowat, *The Ombudsman: Citizens' Defender* (Toronto: University of Toronto Press, 1965). For other exotic forms, administrative-law texts should be consulted, particularly L. N. Brown and J. F. Garner, *French Administrative Law* (London: Butterworth, 1967); J. A. G. Griffith and H. Street, *Principles of Administrative Law* (London: Pitman, 1967); H. W. R. Wade, *Administrative Law* (New York: Oxford University Press, 1967), for comparative purposes, and K. C. Davis, *Administrative Law in Government* (St. Paul: West, 1960) and W. Gellhorn, ed., *Administrative Law: Cases and Comments* (New York: Foundation Press, 1960) for American conditions.

The impact of automation on the organization of government has not been treated separately from its impact on any other large-scale organization. For example, see E. C. Berkeley, *The Computer Revolution* (New York: Doubleday, 1962). Three notable exceptions are H. H. Fite, *The Computer Challenge to Urban Planners and State Administrators* (New York: Spartan Books, 1965); J. Kanter, *The Computer and the Executive* (Englewood Cliffs, N.J.: Prentice-Hall, 1967); and B. G. Schumacher, *Computer Dynamics in Public Administration* (New York: Spartan Books, 1967). An extensive bibliography on administrative reform is found in G. E. Caiden, *Administrative Reform* (Chicago: Aldine, 1969). A comprehensive bibliography on decentralization is contained in M. Melrood, ed., *A Bibliography on Decentralization* (Milwaukee: Institute of Governmental Affairs, University of Wisconsin, 1970). The issues are discussed in A. A. Altshuler, *Community Control* (New York: Pegasus, 1970); J. W. Fesler, *Area and Administration* (University, Ala.: University of Alabama Press, 1949); and in the papers presented to a conference on "Public Administration and

Neighborhood Control" (Boulder, Colorado, 1970), sponsored by the Center for Governmental Studies, which specializes in community participation.

Functional Expertise

Contemporary functions of public authorities change so rapidly in detail that anything written more than a decade ago is obsolete. For specific functions, the student is recommended to the local branch office of the particular public authority performing those functions, which should be able to supply information or direct him to further information. For many functions, particularly of the traditional kind, the need has been considered so obvious that secondary sources concentrate on how many re- sources should be spent and in which way. For current controversies of this nature, the student is recommended to background papers released by Government Printing Offices or prepared by national newspapers, and to legislative debates and executive statements. To the professional journals, the student should add international weeklies or monthlies, such as *Encounter, Daedalus, Atlantic Monthly, New York Review of Books,* and *New Republic.* Some of the best journal articles are reproduced in the *Congressional Report* and, as appendices, to Congressional Committee reports. Much relevant information is conveniently collected by public agencies in specialized libraries for internal use, but usually accessible to bona fide scholars on application. It is fairly easy to maintain running files of one's own in a selected area at small cost by receiving official publications and photocopying selected articles from less acces- sible sources. Otherwise, source material can be found in other disciplines, such as sociology, social welfare, criminology, police and prison administration, military science, diplomacy, education, public health, industrial relations, economics, and a wide range of physical sciences, from geology to astrophysics.

National-building. Most works are found in development administration. A useful book is R. Bendix, *Nation-Building and Citizenship* (New York: John Wiley & Sons, 1964).

Economic development. The new relationships between the government and the economy in nonsocialist regimes have produced a spate of books, both pro and con governmental direction and interference with the market system. Still relevant are M. E. Dimock, *The New American Political Economy* (New York: Harper & Row, 1962); J. K. Galbraith, *The Affluent Society* (Boston: Houghton Mifflin, 1958); W. Heller, *New Dimensions in Political Economy* (New York: W. W. Norton, 1967); L. D. Musoff, *Government and the Economy* (Glenview, Ill.: Scott, Foresman, 1965); E. S. Redford, *American Government and the Economy* (New York: Crowell Collier & Macmillan, 1965); A. Shonfield, *Modern Capitalism* (New York: Oxford University Press, 1965); M. Weidenbaum, *The Modern Public Sector* (New York: Basic Books, 1969); and J. P. Wernette, *Government and Business* (New York: Crowell Collier & Macmillan, 1964). National economic planning is amply covered in a series entitled National Planning, edited by B. M. Gross and issued by Syracuse University, which covers both developed and undeveloped countries. Over twenty titles are available, each with a select bibliography on national planning in a particular country.

Social services. Much of the theoretical literature has been developed outside the United States, particularly in Scandinavia and western Europe. A good introduction is R. M. Titmuss, *Commitment to Welfare* (London: G. Allen and Unwin, 1968). The collection of extracts in F. Krinsky and J. Boskin, *The Welfare State* (Beverly Hills, Calif.: Glencoe, 1968) guides the American reader. For other British views, see D. V. Donnison, *Social Policy and Administration* (London: G. Allen and Unwin, 1965); J. Parker, *Local Health and Welfare Services* (London: G. Allen and Unwin, 1965); and P. Willmott, *Consumer's Guide to the British Social Services* (Middlesex, England: Penguin, 1967). A short introductory history of social services is in G. Williams, *The Coming of the Welfare State* (London: G. Allen and Unwin, 1967); and of the police, in T. A. Critchley, *A History of Police in England and Wales, 1900–1966* (London: Constable, 1967). There is an extensive literature on the management of social services, particularly hospitals, schools, welfare agencies, and prisons. In education, G. Becker, *Human Capital* (New York: Columbia University Press, 1964) should be required reading, along with W. J. Biddle and L. Biddle, *The Community Development Process* (New York: Holt, Rinehart and Winston, 1965) and C. E. Beeby, *The Quality of Education in Developing Countries* (Cambridge, Mass.: Harvard University Press, 1967). In social welfare, see G. Y. Steiner, *Social Insecurity: The Politics of Welfare* (Chicago: Rand McNally, 1966) and B. Jones, ed., *The Health of Americans* (Englewood Cliffs, N.J.: Prentice-Hall, 1970).

Science and technology   The booming literature on government and the technological era includes readers, such as F. R. Allen *et al.,* eds., *Technology and Social Change* (New York: Appleton-Century-Crofts, 1957); B. Barker and W. Hirsch, eds., *The Sociology of Science* (New York: Free Press, 1962); G. Gilpin and C. Wright, eds., *Scientists and National Policy Making* (New York: Columbia University Press, 1964); A. C. Benjamin, ed., *Science Technology and Human Values* (Columbia, Missouri: University of Missouri Press, 1965); W. R. Nelson, ed., *The Politics of Science* (New York: Oxford University Press, 1968). General background texts include R. Aron *et al.,* *World Technology and Human Destiny* (Ann Arbor, Mich.: The University of Michigan Press, 1963); J. R. Bright, *Research, Development and Technical Innovation* (Homewood, Ill.: Irwin, 1964); Committee on Science and Public Policy, *Basic Research and National Goals* (Washington, D.C.: National Academy of Science, 1965); J. Ellul, *The Technological Society* (New York: Alfred A. Knopf, 1964); M. Grodzins and E. Rabinowitch, eds., *The Atomic Age* (New York: Basic Books, 1963); D. K. Price, *Government and Science* (New York: New York University Press, 1954); D. K. Price, *The Scientific Estate* (Cambridge, Mass.: Harvard University Press, 1965). Closer to the heart of public administration are H. Brooks, *The Government of Science* (Cambridge, Mass.: M. I. T. Press, 1968); J. S. Dupre and S. A. Lakoff, *Science and the Nation* (Englewood Cliffs, N.J.: Prentice-Hall, 1962); J. E. Hodgetts, *Administering the Atom for Peace* (New York: Atherton, 1964); E. W. Lindveit, *Scientism in Government* (Washington, D.C.: Public Affairs Press, 1960); J. L. McCamy, *Science and Public Administration* (University, Ala.: University of Alabama Press, 1961); H. Orlans, *Contracting for Atoms* (Washington, D. C.: The Brookings Institution, 1967); M. D. Reagan, *Science and the Federal Patron* (New York: Oxford University Press, 1969); and C. Stover, *The Government of Science* (Santa Barbara: Center for the Study of Democratic Institutions, 1962).

Ecology   Apart from popular attacks by Rachel Carson and Ralph Nadar, and official responses from the Department of the Interior, a concerted approach to government and environmental control can be found in I. Burton and R. W. Kates, eds., *Readings in Resource Management and Conservation* (Chicago: University of Chicago Press, 1965); L. K. Caldwell, ed., *Environmental Studies* (Bloomington, Ind.: Institute of Public Administration, University of Indiana, 1967); L. K. Caldwell, *Environment*

(Garden City, N.Y.: Natural History Press, 1970); J. C. Davis, *The Politics of Pollution* (New York: Pegasus, 1970); and W. R. Ewald, *Environment and Policy: The Next Fifty Years* (Bloomington, Ind., Indiana University Press, 1968). These should be compared with the empirical evidence in M. Scott, *American City Planning since 1890* (Berkeley: University of California Press, 1970).

The bureaucratic power derived from functional expertise is treated in the general literature on bureaucracy and bureaucratic theory. The transformed role of the public official in the industrial system was recognized by Thorstein Veblen, most pointedly in *The Engineers and the Price System* (New York: Viking, 1933). That was followed by C. I. Barnard, *The Functions of the Executive* (Cambridge, Mass.: Harvard University Press, 1938); and J. Burnham, *The Managerial Revolution* (London: Putnam, 1941). The significance of the technocrat is underscored in J. Ahmed, *The Expert and the Administrator* (Pittsburgh: University of Pittsburgh Press, 1959); K. E. Boulding, *The Skills of the Economist* (Cleveland, Ohio: Howard Allen, 1958); D. Peltz and F. M. Andrews, *Scientists in Organizations* (New York: John Wiley & Sons, 1967); B. Schwartz, *The Professor and the Commissions* (New York: Alfred A. Knopf, 1959); and W. F. Whyte, ed., *Industry and Society* (New York: McGraw-Hill, 1946). The theme that the bureaucrat has, does, or could subvert the politician has been repeated continually since C. K. Allen, *Bureaucracy Triumphant* (New York: Oxford University Press, 1931) and J. M. Beck, *Our Wonderland of Bureaucracy* (New York: Crowell Collier & Macmillan, 1932). It is more than implied in J. H. Crider, *The Bureaucrat* (Philadelphia: Lippincott, 1944); E. Strauss, *The Ruling Servants: Bureaucracy in Russia, France and Britain* (New York: Frederick A. Praeger, 1961); J. D. Williams, *The Compleat Strategyst* (New York: McGraw-Hill, 1966); D. Wise and T. B. Ross, *The Invisible Government* (New York: Random House, 1964); and P. Woodruff, *The Men Who Ruled India* (London: J. Cape, 1954). On the other hand, possible control factors are described in E. Bontecou, *The Federal Loyalty-Security Plan* (Ithaca, N. Y.: Cornell University Press, 1953) and R. S. Brown, *Loyalty and Security: Employment Tests in the United States* (New Haven: Yale University Press, 1958).

Contracts and Public Enterprise

Apart from how-to-do-it treatises on public contracting, few studies have been made of its actual operations, for obvious reasons. Scandals make good newspaper copy, but they are supposedly atypical. Government manuals on contracting are readily available, and in the United States the prime contracting authorities issue numerous publications and handouts for prospective contractors. Law cases concerning public contracts are good source material, but again they are atypical. In general, the facts about contracting, as opposed to gossip, are not well known. The major texts do not even index government contracting, although D. K. Price had a chapter "Federalism by Contract" in *Government and Science* (New York: New York University Press, 1954). Problems of Research and Development contracting are discussed in C. H. Danhof, *Government Contracting and Technological Change* (Washington, D.C.: The Brookings Institution, 1968). The fusion of public and private business is well illustrated in R. B. Ripley, ed., *Public Policies and Their Politics* (New York: W. W. Norton, 1966). Otherwise, the student has to rely on governmental publications relating to contracting and procurement, congressional inquiries into governmental contracting, particularly the Task Force Report of the Hoover Commission (1955), House Committee on Government Operations, Joint Committee on Defense Production,

Joint Economic Committee's Subcommittee on Defense Procurement and Sub-committee on Federal Procurement and Regulation, publications of the General Accounting Office, and articles—H. M. Carlisle, "Incentive Contracts," *Public Administration Review,* 24 (March 1964), 21–28; J. Dupre and W. E. Gustafson, "Contracting for Defense," *Political Science Quarterly,* 77 (June 1962), 161–177; R. B. Hall, "The Annual Service Procurement Act of 1947 Should be Reformed," *Government Accounting Office Review* (Spring 1969), 3–22; R. D. Lyons *et al.,* "Managing Defense Contracts," *The Federal Accountant,* 13 (September 1963), 153–187; and a series of publications of the Department of Economics, Washington University (St. Louis, Missouri), edited by M. L. Weidenbaum.

Although public enterprise has not been well covered in the United States, since most universities classify it under business administration or public finance, it has been extensively dealt with in western Europe (ideologically and analytically) and in the underdeveloped nations and the communist bloc (descriptively). Specifically devoted to public enterprise in the United States is *Public Utilities Fortnightly* (Washington, D.C.), published by Public Utilities Reports, Inc. An extensive bibliography can be found in W. A. Robson, *Nationalized Industry and Public Ownership,* (London: G. Allen and Unwin, 1962), which covers much that has been written up to the 1960s in the British tradition. The ideological perspective is summarized in J. Schumpeter, *Capitalism, Socialism and Democracy* (New York: Harper & Row, 1950), which should be read in conjunction with the classics of Marxism and Fascism, including Mussolini, *Four Speeches on the Corporate State* [1935] and F. Pitigliani, *The Italian Corporate State* [London: King, 1933] and the less extreme debate between P. Shore and T. E. Utley in *Public Law* (London: Vol. 2 1957), pp. 203–230. Although much of the literature is polemical, public-sector initiative has become fairly respectable through the work of liberal economists such as Keynes and Arthur Lewis, and democratic socialists in public administration such as W. A. Robson and G. Myrdal. In the United States, several texts deal with the philosophical and value aspects: C. P. Coiter, *Government and Private Enterprise* (New York: Holt, Rinehart and Winston, 1960); M. E. Dimock, *Business and Government* (New York: Holt, Rinehart and Winston, 1965); E. Ginzberg *et al., The Pluralist Economy* (New York: McGraw-Hill, 1965); V. A. Mund, *Government and Business* (New York: Harper & Row, 1960); D. F. Pegrum, *Public Regulation of Business* (Homewood, Ill.: Irwin, 1965). The ecological problems are discussed in F. P. Sherwood, *The Problem of Public Enterprise* (Bloomington, Ind.: Comparative Administration Group, June 1966).

The issue of nationalization is amply covered in D. Coombs, *The Member of Parliament and the Administration: The Case of the Select Committee on Nationalized Industries* (London: G. Allen and Unwin, 1966); A. H. Hanson, ed., *Nationalization: A Book of Readings* (London: G. Allen and Unwin, 1963); A. H. Hanson, *Parliament and Public Ownership* (London: Cassell, 1961); K. Katzarov, *Theory of Nationalization* (The Hague: Nijhoff, 1965); W. Thornhill, *The Nationalized Industries* (London: Nelson, 1968); L. Tivey, *Nationalization in British Industry* (London: J. Cape, 1966). The principal form of public ownership adopted in western Europe for nationalized industries and the public corporation is described in W. G. Friedmann (ed.), *The Public Corporation: A Comparative Symposium* (Toronto: Carswell, 1954), still not outdated by the United Nations, *Report on the Seminar on Organization and Management of Public Enterprises* (New York: United Nations, 1967); S. D. Goldberg, *The Government Corporation* (Chicago: Public Administration Service, 1953); A. H. Hanson, *Public Enterprise and Economic Development* (London: Routledge and Kegan Paul, 1965); J. Jewkes, *Public and Private Enterprise* (London:

Routledge and Kegan Paul, 1965). For a comparison of different forms of public enterprise, transportation could be taken as an example; see T. E. Kuhn, *Public Enterprise Economics and Transport Problem* (Berkeley: University of California, 1962); and C. F. Phillips, *The Economics of Regulation* (Homewood, Ill.: Irwin, 1965). A comparison could be made with several studies of the Tennessee Valley Authority— J. V. Krutilla and O. Eckstein, *Multi-Purpose Power Development* (Baltimore: Johns Hopkins Press, 1958); D. Lilienthal, *T.V.A.: Democracy on the March* (New York: Harper and Row, 1944); P. Selznick, *T.V.A. and the Grass Roots* (Berkeley: University of California Press, 1949); A. Wildavsky, *Dixon-Yates: A Study in Power Politics* (New Haven: Yale University Press, 1961). Other industries—airlines, defense, electricity, water, postal communications—in which public authorities have a virtual monopoly, have their own literature, much of which is devoted to the technical and managerial aspects, rather than their public nature. Several studies, now dated, exist of public enterprise in individual countries—Sweden, France, Italy, Australia, India, Israel—but the best have yet to be translated into English. For communist-bloc approaches, see *The Role of Public Enterprises in the Formulation and Implementation of Development Plans in Centrally Planned Economies* (New York: United Nations, ST/TAO/M/37, c. 1968).

The merging of public and private sectors in the economy of the United States is best treated in M. Weidenbaum, *The Modern Public Sector* (New York: Basic Books, 1969), the Wadsworth series in Public Policy, and the American Elsener Series in Policy Sciences.

Public Finance

Like public enterprise and private contractors, public finance is found in disciplines other than public administration, particularly accountancy and economics. Good, but now dated, introductions are J. Burkhead, *Government Budgeting* (New York: John Wiley & Sons, 1956); and F. C. Mosher and O. F. Poland, *The Costs of American Government: Facts, Trends, Myths* (New York: Dodd, Mead, 1964). Updated readers are available in R. T. Golembiewski, ed., *Public Budgeting and Finance* (Itasca, Ill.: F. E. Peacock, 1968); and J. Scherer and J. A. Papke, eds., *Public Finance and Fiscal Policy* (Boston: Houghton Mifflin, 1966). It is difficult to choose between several general texts, all with slightly differing emphases, but generally recommended are J. M. Buchanan, *Public Finance in Democratic Process* (Chapel Hill, N.C.: University of North Carolina Press, 1967); O. Eckstein, *Public Finance* (Englewood Cliffs, N.J.: Prentice-Hall, 1967); F. R. Fenno, *The Public Purse* (Boston: Little, Brown, 1966); A. P. Prest, *Public Finance in Theory and Practice* (London: Weidenfeld and Nicholson, 1967). These could be supplemented with Committee for Economic Development, *Budgeting for National Objectives* (New York: C.E.D., 1966); R. Dorfman, ed., *Measuring Benefits of Government Investments* (Washington, D.C.: The Brookings Institution, 1965); S. A. Margolin, *Public Investment Criteria* (Cambridge, Mass.: M.I.T. Press, 1967); I. Sharkansky, *The Politics of Taxing and Spending* (Indianapolis: Bobbs-Merrill, 1969); and C. Wilcox, *Public Policies toward Business* (Homewood, Ill.: Irwin, 1966).

In the United States, there are significant differences in public finance at different levels of government. Useful for an overall understanding is S. B. Chase, ed., *Problems in Public Expenditure Analysis* (Washington, D.C.: The Brookings Institution, 1968). Intergovernmental finances are discussed by the Advisory Committee on Inter-Governmental Relations, *Fiscal Balance in the American Federal System* (Washington, D.C.: U.S. Government Printing Office, 1967); C. T. F. Break, *Intergovernmental Fiscal Relations in the United States* (Washington, D.C.: The Brookings Institution, 1967); and D. S. Wright, *Federal Grants in Aid: Perspectives and Alternatives* (Washington, D.C.: American Enterprise Institute, 1968). Federal finances are the concern of G. Cohn and P. Wagner, *Federal Budget Projections* (Washington, D.C.: The Brookings Institution, 1966); E. S. Flash, *Economic Advice and Presidential Leadership* (New York: Columbia University Press, 1965); R. A. Musgrave, *Essays on Fiscal Federalism* (Washington, D.C.: The Brookings Institution, 1965); D. J. Ott and A. F. Ott, *Federal Budget Policy* (Washington, D.C.: The Brookings Institution, 1969); and A. Wildavsky, *The Politics of the Budgetary Process* (Boston: Little, Brown, 1964). Also at federal level are W. Fellner *et al., Fiscal and Debt Management Policies* (Englewood Cliffs, N.J.: Prentice-Hall, 1963) and C. Green, *Negative Taxes and the Poverty Program* (Washington, D.C.: The Brookings Institution, 1967). Every state has its own financial system, most of which have been written about. Overall views are W. Buckley, *Budgeting by the States* (Chicago: Council of State Governments, 1967) and I. Sharkansky, *Spending in the American States* (Chicago: Rand McNally, 1967). For an intrastate view, compare J. C. Anton, *The Politics of State Expenditure in Illinois* (Urbana, Ill.: University of Illinois Press, 1966) with G. W. Fisher, *Taxes and Politics: A Study of Illinois Public Finance* (Urbana, Ill.: University of Illinois Press, 1969). At metropolitan level, see A. Campbell and S. Sachs, *Metropolitan America: Fiscal Patterns and Government Systems* (New York: Free Press, 1967) and H. S. Perloff and R. P. Nathan, eds., *Revenue Sharing and the City* (Baltimore: Johns Hopkins Press, 1968). For comparative purposes, the basic texts are R. M. Bird and O. Oldman, eds., *Readings on Taxation in Developing Countries* (Baltimore: Johns Hopkins Press, 1967); E. Normanton, *The Accountability and Audit of Governments* (Manchester, England: Manchester University Press, 1960); A. T. Peacock and J. Wiseman, *The Growth of Public Expenditure in the United Kingdom* (London: G. Allen and Unwin, 1967); and A. R. Prest, *Public Finance in Underdeveloped Countries* (New York: Frederick A. Praeger, 1962).

The literature on PPBS grows rapidly. The student has a choice of three readers —J. W. Davis, *Politics, Programs, Budgets* (Englewood Cliffs, N.J.: Prentice-Hall, 1969); H. H. Hinrichs and G. M. Taylor, eds., *Program Budgeting and Benefit-Cost Analysis: Cases, Texts and Readings* (Pacific Palisades, Calif.: Goodyear, 1969); and F. J. Lynton and E. G. Miller, *Planning, Programming, Budgeting* (Chicago: Markham, 1968); and a collection of papers published by the Joint Economic Committee, *The Analysis and Evaluation of Public Expenditures: The P.P.B. System*, 3 vols. (Washington, D.C.: U.S. Government Printing Office, 1969). Two symposia in the *Public Administration Review* in the December 1966 and the March 1969 issues are landmarks, as were F. C. Mosher, *Program Budgeting: Theory and Practice* (Chicago: Public Administration Service, 1954) and A. D. Novick, *Program Budgeting* (Cambridge, Mass.: Harvard University Press, 1965) before them. These could be supplemented by staff papers issued regularly by the Rand Corporation, which fathered PPBS, and specialized texts such as R. L. Chartrand, K. Janda, and M. Hugo, eds., *Information Support, Program Budgeting and the Congress* (New York: Spartan, 1968) and H. H. Hartly, *Educational Planning-Programming-Budgeting: A Systems Approach* (Englewood Cliffs, N.J.: Prentice-Hall, 1968).

Economic planning and budgeting are closely allied in public finance, and both merge into developmental planning. The United Nations has accumulated much descriptive material in its regional workshops, much of which is available from the UN under the classifications TAO and IBRW. The classic work, which contains an extensive bibliography, is A. Waterston, *Development Planning: Lessons of Experience* (Baltimore: Johns Hopkins Press, 1965). The National Planning Series of Syracuse University should be read along with other comparative and general studies, such as J. Hackett and A. M. Hackett, *Economic Planning in France* (Cambridge, Mass.: Harvard University Press, 1963); E. E. Hagen, *Planning Economic Development* (Homewood, Ill.: Irwin, 1963); A. H. Hanson, *The Process of Planning: A Study of India's Five Year Plans 1950–64* (New York: Oxford University Press, 1966); J. E. S. Hayward, *Private Interests and Public Policy: Experience of the French Economic and Social Council* (London: Longmans, 1966); U. K. Hicks, *Development Finance: Planning and Control* (New York: Oxford University Press, 1965); and M. F. Millikan, *National Economic Planning* (New York: Columbia University Press, 1967).

Public Service

As in public finance, the literature on public-personnel administration, including comparative civil services, is extensive, and choice is correspondingly more difficult. For an introduction to research designs in public-personnel administration, the student could consult W. S. Carpenter, *The Unfinished Business of Civil Service Reform* (Princeton: Princeton University Press, 1952); C. E. Goode, *Personnel Research Frontiers* (Chicago: Public Personnel Association, 1958); and W. S. Sayre and F. C. Mosher, *An Agenda for Research in Public Personnel Administration* (Washington: National Planning Association, 1959). Major texts include F. A. Nigro, *Public Personnel Administration* (New York: Holt, Rinehart and Winston, 1959); and N. J. Powell, *Personnel Administration in Government* (Englewood Cliffs, N.J.: Prentice-Hall, 1956), both badly in need of revision, more so than O. G. Stahl, *Public Personnel Administration* (New York: Harper & Row, 1970) and R. T. Golembiewsky and M. Cohen, *People in Public Service: A Reader in Public Personnel Administration* (Itasca, Ill.: F. E. Peacock, 1970). Less revelant, but worth consulting, are P. Pigors *et al.*, eds., *Readings in Personnel Administration* (New York: McGraw-Hill, 1959); G. Strauss and L. Sayles, *Personnel* (Englewood Cliffs, N.J.: Prentice-Hall, 1960); and several introductions on the top executive, public or private, in C. I. Barnard, *The Functions of the Executive* (Cambridge, Mass.: Harvard University Press, 1938); J. D. Glover and R. M. Hower, *The Administrator* (Chicago: Irwin, 1949); D. Marvick, *Career Perspectives in a Bureaucratic Setting* (Ann Arbor, Mich.: The University of Michigan Press, 1954); F. C. Mosher, *Democracy and the Public Service* (New York: Oxford University Press, 1968); R. K. Ready, *The Administrator's Job* (New York: McGraw-Hill, 1967). The professionalization of public service is the special attention of C. L. Gilb, *Hidden Hierarchies* (New York: Harper & Row, 1966) and F. Ridley, ed., *Specialists and Generalists* (London: G. Allen and Unwin, 1969). For an amateur's view, see C. Frankel, *High on Foggy Bottom* (New York: Harper & Row, 1968).

In contrast to normative and formal descriptive approaches, which dominated public-personnel administration before the 1950s, several behavioral studies are available—M. Crozier, *The Bureaucratic Phenomenon* (Chicago: University of Chicago Press, 1964); R. Dubin, ed., *Human Relations in Administration* (Englewood Cliffs, N.J.: Prentice-Hall, 1961); S. W. Gellerman, *The Management of Human Relations* (New York: Holt, Rinehart and Winston, 1966); R. T. Golembiewski, *Organizing Men and Power* (Chicago: Rand McNally, 1967); M. Haire, *Psychology in Movement* (New York: McGraw-Hill, 1956); A. P. Hare *et al.*, eds., *Small Groups* (New York:

Alfred A. Knopf, 1965); J. Pfiffner and M. Fels, *Supervision of Personnel* (Englewood Cliffs, N.J.: Prentice-Hall, 1964). The mechanics of public-personnel administration are dealt with by the many publications of the Public Personnel Association, among which are I. Baruch, *Position-Classification in the Public Service* (1941), K. O. Warner and J. J. Donovan, eds., *Practical Guidelines to Public Pay Administration* (1965), and K. O. Warner, *Collective Bargaining in the Public Service* (1967), plus a new series, entitled Policies and Practices in Public Personnel Administration, which includes J. J. Donovan, ed., *Recruitment and Selection in the Public Service* (1968), F. M. Lopez, *Evaluating Employee Performance* (1968), and F. A. Nigro, *Management-Employee Relations in the Public Service* (1969).

Recently in the United States, there have been several studies of bureaucratic elites, particularly top federal public-service positions, in recognition of growing bureaucratic power and the difficulties of finding both within and without the United States Civil Service qualified persons, following the rejection of a Senior Civil Service in the 1950s (see P. T. David and R. Pollock, *Executives for Government* [Washington, D.C., The Brookings Institution, 1957]). They include J. J. Corson and R. S. Paul, *Men Near the Top* (Baltimore: Johns Hopkins Press, 1966); Committee for Economic Development, *Improving Executive Management in the Federal Government* (New York: C.E.D., 1964); F. P. Kilpatrick *et al., Source Book of a Study of Occupational Values* (Washington, D.C.: The Brookings Institution, 1964); D. T. Stanley, *The Higher Civil Service* (Washington, D.C.: The Brookings Institution, 1964); W. L. Warner *et al., The American Federal Executive* (New Haven: Yale University Press, 1963). Also receiving prominent attention are industrial relations—M. R. Godine, *The Labor Problem in the Public Service* (Cambridge, Mass.: Harvard University Press, 1951); W. Hart, *Collective Bargaining in the Federal Civil Service* (New York: Harper & Row, 1951); W. B. Vosloo, *Collective Bargaining in the United States Federal Civil Service* (Chicago: Public Personnel Association, 1966); K. O. Warner, ed., *Developments in Public Employee Relations* (Chicago: Public Personnel Association, 1965); and K. O. Warner and M. L. Hennessy, *Public Management at the Bargaining Table* (Chicago: Public Personnel Association, 1967). On the issue of political rights, P. S. Ford, *Political Activities and the Public Service* (Berkeley: Institute of Governmental Studies, 1963) and M. Grodzins, *The Loyal and the Disloyal* (Chicago: University of Chicago Press, 1956) should be compared with some questioning of the moral and legal basis of the Hatch Act in the 1969 and 1970 issues of the *Public Administration Review* and *Civil Service Journal* (Washington, D.C., issued by the Civil Service Commission). To round off federal personnel policies, see H. L. Case, *Personnel Policy in a Public Agency: The T.V.A. Experience* (New York: Harper & Row, 1958). No outstanding texts on state personnel practices exist, but at local-government level, see the International City Managers Association, *Municipal Personnel Administration.* (Chicago: I.C.M.A., 1960) and the Municipal Manpower Commission, *Governmental Manpower for Tomorrow's Cities* (New York: McGraw-Hill, 1962).

For comparative analysis of public bureaucracies and the different concepts of public service outside the United States, consult the following.

Great Britain and the British Commonwealth: G. E. Caiden, *The Commonwealth Bureaucracy* (Melbourne, Australia: Melbourne University Press, 1967); F. Dunnill, *The Civil Service: Some Human Aspects* (London: G. Allen and Unwin, 1956); E. N. Gladden, *British Public Service Administration* (London: Staples, 1961); E. N. Gladden, *Civil Services of the United Kingdom 1855–1970* (London: Frank Cass, 1967); J. E. Hodgetts and D. C. Corbett, eds., *Canadian Public Administration* (Toronto: Macmillan, 1960); R. J. Polaschek, *Government Administration in New Zealand* (Wellington: Oxford University Press, 1958); W. A. Robson, ed., *The Civil Service in Britain and France* (London: Hogarth, 1956); R. N. Spann, ed., *Public Administration in Australia* (Sydney: N.S.W. Government Printer, 1971).

Western Europe: B. Chapman, *The Profession of Government* (London: G. Allen and Unwin, 1959); M. Crozier, *The Bureaucratic Phenomenon* (Chicago: University of Chicago Press, 1964); R. Gregoire, *The French Civil Service* (Brussels: I.I.A.S., 1965); H. Jacob, *German Administration Since Bismarck* (New Haven: Yale University Press, 1965); F. Ridley and J. Blondel, *Public Administration in France* (New York: Barnes and Noble, 1964).

Communist bloc: J. A. Armstrong, *The Soviet Bureaucratic Elite* (London: Stevens, 1959): A. Doak-Barnett, *Cadres, Bureaucracy and Political Power in Communist China* (New York: Columbia University Press, 1967); M. Fainsod, *How Russia is Ruled* (Cambridge, Mass.: Harvard University Press, 1964); D. Granick, *The Red Executive* (New York: Macmillan, 1960); H. G. Skilling, *The Governments of Communist East Europe* (New York: Crowell Collier & Macmillan, 1966).

Middle East: M. Berger, *Bureaucracy and Society in Modern Egypt* (Princeton: Princeton University Press, 1957); G. E. Caiden, *Israel's Administrative Culture* (Berkeley: Institute of Governmental Studies, 1970); A. Iskandar, *Bureaucracy in Lebanon* (Beirut: Khayats, 1965).

Former British Colonies: A. L. Adu, *The Civil Service in New African States* (London: G. Allen and Unwin, 1965); M. Ahmad, *The Civil Service in Pakistan* (Karachi: Oxford University Press, 1964); R. Braibanti, ed., *Asian Bureaucratic Systems Emergent from the British Imperial Tradition* (Durham, N.C.: Duke University Press, 1966); A. Chanda, *Indian Administration* (London: G. Allen and Unwin, 1967); H. F. Goodnow, *The Civil Service of Pakistan* (New Haven: Yale University Press, 1964); R. S. Milne, *Government and Politics in Malaysia* (Boston: Houghton Mifflin, 1967).

South Asia: N. Dang, *Vietnam: Politics and Public Administration* (Honolulu: East-West Center Press, 1966); H. B. Lee, *Korea: Time, Change, and Administration* (Honolulu: East-West Center Press, 1967); F. W. Riggs, *Thailand* (Honolulu: East-West Center Press, 1966); W. J. Siffin, *The Thai Bureaucracy* (Honolulu: East-West Center Press, 1966).

Administrative Theory

Possibly the fastest-expanding literature in the social sciences concerns administrative theory. Although only a small proportion involves public administration, the student should be conversant with the major writings in the field. No public-administration student should launch himself on the general literature without first digesting E. S. Redford, *Democracy in the Administrative State* (New York: Oxford University Press, 1969); E. O. Stene, *American Administrative Theory* (Lawrence, Kansas: Citizen's Active Society, 1950); and D. Waldo, *The Administrative State* (New York: Ronald Press, 1948); and also some general texts on theory, analysis, and testing, such as R. Brown, *Explanation in Social Science* (London: Routledge and Kegan Paul, 1963); A. Kaplan, *The Conduct of Inquiry* (San Francisco: Chandler, 1964); F. N. Kerlinger, *Foundations of Behavioral Research* (New York: Holt, Rinehart and Winston, 1964); R. R. Stoll, *Sets, Logic and Axiomatic Theories* (San Francisco: Freeman, 1961); and J. W. Yolton, *Theory of Knowledge* (New York: Crowell Collier & Macmillan, 1965). A good introduction to the field is B. Gross, *The Managing of Organiza-*

tions (New York: Free Press, 1964), supplemented by such readers as A. Etzioni, ed., *Complex Organizations* (New York: Holt, Rinehart and Winston, 1962); J. A. Litterer, ed., *Organizations: Structure and Behavior* (New York:John Wiley & Sons, 1963); S. Mailick and E. H. Van Ness, eds., *Concepts and Issues in Administrative Behavior* (Englewood Cliffs, N.J.: Prentice-Hall, 1962); J. G. March, ed., *Handbook of Organizations* (Chicago: Rand McNally, 1965); R. Presthus, ed., *The Organizational Society* (New York: Knopf, 1962); A. H. Rubenstein and C. J. Haberstroh, eds., *Some Theories of Organizations* (Homewood, Ill.: Irwin, 1966); M. Wadia, ed., *The Nature and Scope of Management* (New York: Scott, Foresman, 1966).

Pre-1945 classics of administrative theory with lasting significance include F. W. Taylor, *Principles of Scientific Management* (New York: Harper & Row, 1911); H. Fayol, *General and Industrial Management* (London: Pitman, 1949); M. P. Follett, *Dynamic Administration* (New York: Harper & Row, 1942); F. J. Roethlisberger and W. J. Dickson, *Management and the Worker* (Cambridge, Mass.: Harvard University Press, 1939); L. Gulick and L. Urwick, eds., *Papers on the Science of Administration* (New York: Institute of Public Administration, 1937); and C. I. Barnard, *The Functions of the Executive* (Cambridge, Mass.: Harvard University Press, 1938). Postwar classics now include H. A. Simon, *Administrative Behavior* (New York: Crowell Collier & Macmillan, 1947); A. Maslow, *Motivation and Personality* (New York: Harper & Row, 1954); J. March and H. A. Simon, *Organizations* (New York: John Wiley & Sons, 1958); R. Likert, *New Patterns of Management* (New York: McGraw-Hill, 1961); C. Argyris, *Integrating the Individual and the Organization* (New York: John Wiley & Sons, 1964); and H. Wilensky, *Organizational Intelligence* (New York: Basic Books, 1967). In addition, the following are in widespread use: D. Cartwright and A. Zander, eds., *Group Dynamics: Research and Theory* (New York: Harper & Row, 1953); E. D. Chapple and L. R. Sayles, *The Measure of Management* (New York: Crowell Collier & Macmillan, 1961); R. Dubin, *The World of Work* (Englewood Cliffs, N.J.: Prentice-Hall, 1958); A. W. Goulder, *Patterns of Industrial Democracy* (New York: Free Press, 1954); G. C. Homans, *The Human Group* (New York: Harcourt, Brace Jovanovich, 1950); H. Koontz and C. O. O'Donnell, *Principles of Management* (New York: Alfred A. Knopf, 1959); R. V. Presthus, *The Organizational Society* (New York: Alfred A. Knopf, 1962); M. Weber, *The Theory of Social and Economic Organization* (New York: Oxford University Press, 1947); and S. S. Wolin, *Politics and Vision* (Boston: Little, Brown, 1960). Most of the seminal works in administrative theory have already been listed in previous sections. To them should be added the following:

Administrative functions: L. R. Bittel, *Management by Exception* (New York: McGraw-Hill, 1964); T. Caplow, *Principles of Organization* (New York: Harcourt, Brace Jovanovich, 1964); G. R. Terry, *Principles of Management* (Homewood, Ill.: Irwin, 1956).

Decision making: M. L. J. Abercombie, *The Anatomy of Judgment* (London: Hutchinson, 1965); K. Deutsch, *Nerves of Government* (New York: Free Press, 1963); P. C. Fishburn, *Decision and Value Theory* (New York: John Wiley & Sons, 1964); M. Komarovsky, ed., *Common Frontiers of the Social Sciences* (New York: Free Press, 1957).

Administrative behavior: R. M. Bellows, *Creative Leadership* (Englewood Cliffs, N.J.: Prentice-Hall, 1959); B. Berelson and G. A. Steiner, *Human Behavior* (New York: Harcourt Brace Jovanovich, 1964); R. T. Golembiewsky, *Behavior and Organization* (Chicago: Rand McNally, 1962); C. E. Redford, *Communications in Management* (Chicago: University of Chicago Press, 1958); L. R. Sayles, *Behavior of Industrial Work Groups* (New York: John Wiley & Sons, 1958); L. R. Sayles, *Managerial Behav-*

ior (New York: McGraw-Hill, 1964); W. G. Scott, *The Management of Conflict* (Homewood, Ill.: Irwin, 1963); G. A. Steiner, *The Creative Organization* (Chicago: University of Chicago Press, 1965); W. H. Whyte, *The Organization Man* (New York: Simon and Schuster, 1956). Of particular interest in public administration are D. Mc-Gregor, *The Human Side of Enterprise* (New York: McGraw-Hill, 1960); and R. Presthus, *Behavioral Approaches to Public Administration* (University, Ala.: University of Alabama Press, 1965).

Administrators: C. Burger, *Executives Under Fire* (New York: Crowell Collier & Macmillan, 1966); E. Dale, *The Great Organizers* (New York, McGraw-Hill, 1960); M. Dalton, *Men Who Manage* (New York: John Wiley & Sons, 1959); R. H. Guest, *Organizational Change* (New York: Dorsey, 1962); D. McGregor, *The Professional Manager* (New York: McGraw-Hill, 1967).

Administrative dynamics: C. Argyis, *Organization and Innovation* (Homewood, Ill.: Irwin, 1965); W. G. Bennis, *Changing Organizations* (New York: McGraw-Hill, 1966); P. M. Blau, *The Dynamics of Bureaucracy* (Chicago: University of Chicago Press, 1963); M. E. Dimock, *Administrative Vitality* (New York: Harper & Row, 1959); D. R. Hampton *et al., Organizational Behavior and the Practice of Management* (Glenview, Ill.: Scott, Foresman, 1968); C. Press and A. Arian, eds., *Empathy and Ideology* (Chicago: Rand McNally, 1966); W. E. Scott, *Human Relations in Management* (Homewood, Ill.: Irwin, 1962).

Organizational Theory: C. I. Barnard, *Organization and Management (Cambridge, Mass.:* Harvard University Press, 1952); W. W. Cooper *et al., New Perspectives in Organization Research* (New York: John Wiley & Sons, 1964); A. Etzioni, *A Comparative Analysis of Complex Organizations* (New York: Free Press, 1961); A. Etzioni, ed., *Readings on Modern Organizations* (Englewood Cliffs, N.J.: Prentice-Hall, 1969); M. Haire, ed., *Modern Organization Theory* (New York: John Wiley & Sons, 1959); H. J. Leavitt, ed., *The Social Science of Organizations* (Englewood Cliffs, N.J.: Prentice-Hall, 1963); N. P. Mouzelis, *Organisation and Bureaucracy* (Chicago: Aldine, 1968); R. L. Peabody, *Organizational Authority* (New York: Atherton, 1964); W. G. Scott, *Organizational Theory* (Homewood, Ill.: Irwin, 1967); J. D. Thompson, *Organizations in Action* (New York: McGraw-Hill, 1967); V. A. Thompson, *Modern Organization* (New York: Alfred A. Knopf, 1961).

Organization as social system: W. G. Bennis and P. E. Slater, *The Temporary Society* (New York: Harper & Row, 1968); B. J. Biddle and E. J. Thomas, eds., *Role Theory: Concepts and Research* (New York: John Wiley & Sons, 1966); R. L. Kahn *et al., Organizational Stress* (New York: John Wiley & Sons, 1964); R. Katz and R. L. Kahn, *The Social Psychology of Organization* (New York: John Wiley & Sons, 1966); R. Likert, *The Human Organization* (New York: McGraw-Hill, 1967).

Organizations as social structure: M. Crozier, *The Bureaucratic Phenomenon* (University of Chicago Press, 1964); A. Downs, *Inside Bureaucracy* (Boston: Little, Brown, 1967); D. Martindale, *Institutions, Organizations and Mass Society* (Boston: Houghton Mifflin, 1966); G. Vickers, *Towards a Sociology of Management* (London: Chapman and Hall, 1967).

Administration and mathematics: A. Battersby, *Mathematics in Management* (Middlesex, England: Penguin, 1968); S. Beer, *Cybernetics and Management* (London: English Universities Press, 1959); S. Beer, *Decision and Control* (New York: John Wiley & Sons, 1966); D. J. Clough, *Concepts in Management Science* (Englewood Cliffs, N.J.: Prentice-Hall, 1963); L. W. Hein, *Quantative Approach to Managerial Decisions* (Englewood Cliffs, N.J.: Prentice-Hall, 1967); T. L. Whisler and S. F. Harper, *Performance Appraisal Research and Practice* (New York: Holt, Rinehart and Winston, 1962); N. Wiener, *The Human Use of Human Beings* (New York: Doubleday, 1954).

Unified theory: H. Koontz, ed., *Toward a Unified Theory of Management* (New York: McGraw-Hill, 1964); M. E. Mundel, *A Conceptual Framework for the Management Sciences* (New York: McGraw-Hill, 1967).

Research methods: R. N. Adams and J. J. Preiss, *Human Organization Research: Field Relations and Techniques* (New York: John Wiley & Sons, 1964); J. D. Barber, *Power in Communities* (Chicago: Rand McNally, 1966); H. Guetzkow, *Simulation in Social Science* (Englewood Cliffs, N.J.: Prentice-Hall, 1962); E. J. Meeham, *The Theory and Method of Political Analysis* (Homewood, Ill.: Dorsey, 1965); H. J. Morgenthau, *Scientific Man Versus Power Politics* (Chicago: University of Chicago Press, l965).

Comparative and Development Administration

Indispensable reading is M. J. Esman and J. D. Montgomery, "Systems Approaches to Technical Cooperation: The Role of Development Administration," *Public Administration Review* XXIX, No. 5. (September-October 1969), pp. 507–539, which traces the history of postwar efforts, suggests a program for the 1970s, and provides an extensive bibliographic note, including a table of bibliographies. A second indispensable source is the monographs and papers issued by the Comparative Administration Group, several of which are being combined into books of readings. The classic volume remains J. LaPalombara, *Bureaucracy and Political Development* (Princeton: Princeton University Press, 1963), whose 1967 paperback edition contains over six hundred references compiled by G. D. Brewer to 1966. The volume is second in a series sponsored by the Committee on Comparative Politics of the Social Science Research Council, entitled Studies in Political Development issued by the Princeton University Press. Other titles include L. Binder *et al., Crises in Political Development* (1966); J. S. Coleman, ed., *Education and Political Development* (1965); J. La-Palombara and M. Weiner, eds., *Political Parties and Political Development* (1966); L. W. Pye, ed., *Communications and Political Development* (1963); L. W. Pye and S. Verba, *Political Culture and Political Development* (1965); R. E. Ward and D. A. Rustow, *Political Modernization in Japan and Turkey* (1964). A new series was begun by the Duke University Press at the end of the 1960s for the Comparative Administration Group. The planned titles include E. Bock and B. Chapman, eds., *Comparative European Bureaucratic Development;* R. Braibanti, ed., *Political and Administrative Development* (1969); J. Heaphey, ed., *Spatial Dimensions of Development Administration;* A. Kornberg and L. D. Musolf, ed., *Legislatures in Developmental Perspective;* M. Landau, ed., *Organization Theory and Comparative Analysis;* F. W. Riggs, ed., *Frontiers of Development Administration;* F. W. Riggs, ed., *Comparative Bureaucracy: An Historical Perspective;* C. Thurber, ed., *Development Administration in Latin America;* D. Waldo, ed., *Temporal Dimensions of Development Administration;* E. W. Weidner, ed., *Development Administration in Asia.* To these should be added two other C.A.G.-sponsored projects, R. T. Daland, ed., *Comparative Urban Research* (Beverly Hills, Calif.: Sage Publications, 1969); and B. M. Gross, ed., *Action Under Planning* (New York: McGraw-Hill, 1967); and a new series sponsored by Rutgers University, entitled Studies in Comparative International Development and issued by Sage Publications in annual volumes. Other notable collections include F. Heady and S. L. Stokes, eds., *Papers in Comparative Public Administra-*

tion (Ann Arbor, Mich.: Institute of Public Administration, The University of Michigan, 1962); J. D. Montgomery and W. J. Siffin, eds., *Approaches to Development: Politics, Administration and Change* (New York: McGraw-Hill, 1966); N. Raphaeli, ed., *Readings in Comparative Public Administration* (Boston: Allyn & Bacon, 1967); W. J. Siffin, ed., *Toward the Comparative Study of Public Administration* (Bloomington, Ind.: Department of Government, Indiana University, 1957); I. Swerdlow, ed., *Development Administration* (Syracuse: Syracuse University Press, 1963).

Methodological problems of comparability are discussed in a short introductory text, F. Heady, *Public Administration: A Comparative Perspective* (Englewood Cliffs, N.J.: Prentice-Hall, 1966); two methodological primers: G. Heckscher, *Study of Comparative Government and Politics* (London: Macmillan, 1958) and R. C. Macridis, *The Study of Comparative Government* (New York: Doubleday, 1955); and two readers: H. Eckstein and D. E. Apter, eds., *Comparative Politics* (New York: Free Press, 1963) and R. C. Macridis and B. E. Brown, eds., *Comparative Politics* (Homewood, Ill.: Dorsey, 1968). Methodological and theoretical contributions are provided in G. Almond and J. S. Coleman, eds., *The Politics of Developing Areas* (Princeton: Princeton University Press, 1960); G. Almond and S. Verba, *The Civic Culture* (Princeton: Princeton University Press, 1963); G. Almond and G. B. Powell, *Comparative Politics* (Boston: Little, Brown, 1966); D. E. Apter, *The Gold Coast in Transition* (Princeton: Princeton University Press, 1955); S. N. Eisenstadt, ed., *Comparative Social Problems* (New York: Free Press, 1964); S. N. Eisenstadt, *Essays on Comparative Institutions* (New York: John Wiley & Sons, 1965); J. L. Finkle and R. W. Gable, eds., *Political Development and Social Change* (New York: John Wiley & Sons, 1971); L. W. Pye, *Aspects of Political Development* (Boston: Little, Brown, 1966); R. E. Wraith and F. Simpkins, *Corruption in Developing Countries* (London: G. Allen and Unwin, 1963). For an application of economic theory to political development, see W. F. Ilchman and N. Uphoff, *The Political Economy of Change* (Berkeley: University of California Press, 1969) and *The Political Economy of Development* (Berkeley: University of California Press, 1971).

International systems are well covered in the literature on international relations, but some studies merit special attention—"Symposium: Towards an International Civil Service," *Public Administration Review,* No. 3 (1970), pp. 206–263; D. S. Cheever and H. F. Haviland, *Organizing for Peace: International Organizations in World Affairs* (Boston: Houghton Mifflin, 1954); E. Luard, *The Evolution of International Organizations* (London: Thames and Hudson, 1966); M. A. Kaplan, *System and Process in International Politics* (New York: John Wiley & Sons, 1957); H. G. Nicholas, *The United Nations as a Political Institution* (New York: Oxford University Press, 1967); S. C. Suffrin, *Technical Assistance: Theory and Guidelines* (Syracuse: Syracuse University Press, 1966); F. Tickner, *Technical Cooperation* (New York: Frederick A. Praeger, 1966). On foreign aid, in particular, see L. D. Black, *The Strategy of Foreign Aid* (Princeton: Van Nostrand, 1968); E. S. Mason, *Foreign Aid and Foreign Policy* (New York: Harper & Row, 1964); and J. D. Montgomery, *The Politics of Foreign Aid* (New York: Frederick A. Praeger, 1962) are recommended, together with the more specialized E. W. Weidner, *Technical Assistance in Public Administration Overseas* (Chicago: Public Administration Service, 1964).

Studies of national systems have been listed under the section on comparative public bureaucracies. The numerous country studies that exist in the literature of comparative politics, government, and administration are omitted, mainly because most are outdated and are not truly comparative or developmental. Among those that are of the most lasting academic significance are A. F. Alderfer, *Local Govern-ment in Developing Countries* (New York: McGraw-Hill, 1964); H. G. Barnett, *An-thropology in Public Administration* (New York: Harper & Row, 1956); M. J. Esman, *The Politics of Development Administration* (Pittsburgh: University of Pittsburgh Press, 1963); J. C. Honey, *Toward Strategies for Public Administration Development in Latin America* (Syracuse: Syracuse University Press, 1968); R. J. May, *Federalism and Fiscal Adjustment* (New York: Cambridge University Press, 1969); F. W. Riggs, *The Ecology of Public Administration* (Bombay: Asia Publishing House, 1961); R. P. Taub, *Bureaucrats Under Stress* (Berkeley: University of California Press, 1969).

The modernization assumption behind development administration is debated in D. E. Apter, *The Politics of Modernization* (Chicago: University of Chicago Press, 1965); C. E. Black, *The Dynamics of Modernization* (New York: Harper & Row, 1966); S. N. Eisenstadt, *Modernization: Protest and Change* (Englewood Cliffs, N.J.: Pren-tice-Hall, 1966); M. J. Levy, *Modernization and the Structure of Societies* (Princeton: Princeton University Press, 1966); M. Weiner, *Modernization: The Dynamics of Growth* (New York: Basic Books, 1966). Development administration is considered by R. E. Asher, ed., *Development of the Emerging Countries* (Washington, D.C.: The Brookings Institution, 1962); M. J. Esman and F. C. Bruhns, *Institutional Build-ing in National Development* (Philadelphia: University of Pennsylvania Press, 1965); F. W. Riggs, *Administration in Developing Countries* (Boston: Houghton Mifflin, 1964); P. E. Sigmund, ed., *The Ideologies of the Developing Nations* (New York: Frederick A. Praeger, 1967); K. Younger, *The Public Service in New States* (New York: Oxford University Press, 1960). Some references to economic development and planning have been listed in the public finance section. To them should be added H. F. Alderfer, *Public Administration in Newer Nations* (New York: Frederick A. Praeger, 1966); A. O. Hirschman, *The Strategy of Economic Development* (New Haven: Yale University Press, 1958); A. O. Hirschman, *Journeys Toward Progress* (New York: Twentieth-Century Fund, 1963); A. O. Hirschman, *Development Pro-jects Observed* (Washington, D.C.: The Brookings Institution, 1967): C. H. Hunt, *Social Aspects of Economic Development* (New York: McGraw-Hill, 1966); M. S. Huq, *Education and Development Strategy in South and Southeast Asia* (Honolulu: East-West Center, 1966); A. M. Scott *et al., Simulation and National Development* (New York: John Wiley & Sons, 1966); J. Tinbergen, *Essays in Regional and World Plan-ning* (New Delhi: National Council of Applied Economic Research, 1966).

For the social indicators of progress, see R. Bauer, *Social Indicators* (Cambridge, Mass.: M.I.T. Press, 1967); B. M. Gross, *The State of the Nation: Social System Accounting* (London: Tavistock, 1966); B. Russett *et al., World Handbook of Polit-ical and Social Indicators* (New Haven: Yale University Press, 1964). The policy implications of social indicators in foreign aid are discussed in L. B. Pearson *et al., Partners in Development* (New York: Frederick A. Praeger, 1969), which is a good review of international efforts to promote development.

Some Useful Addresses

Administrative Staff College, Greenlands, Henley-on-Thames, Oxfordshire, England

American Academy of Political and Social Science, 3937 Chestnut St., Philadelphia, Penn. 19104

American Bar Association, 1155 E. 60 St., Chicago, Ill. 60637

American Civil Liberties Union, 156 Fifth Ave., New York, N.Y. 10010

American Institute of Planners, 917 15 St., N.W., Washington, D.C. 20005

American Political Science Association, 1527 New Hampshire Ave., N.W., Washington, D.C. 20036

American Public Welfare Association, 1313 E. 60 St., Chicago, Ill. 60637

American Society of Planning Officials, 1313 E. 60 St., Chicago, Ill. 60637

American Society for Public Administration, 1225 Connecticut Ave., N.W., Washington, D.C. 20036

Center for Governmental Studies, Suite 906, 1701 K St., N.W. Washington, D.C. 20036

Center for the Study of Democratic Institutions, P.O. Box 4068, Santa Barbara, Calif. 93103

Center for the Study of Public Choice, Virginia Polytechnic Institute, Blacksburg, Va.

Committee for Economic Development, 477 Madison Ave., New York, N.Y. 10022

Comparative Administration Group, Social Science Research Institute, No. 101, 1914 University Ave., Honolulu, Hawaii 96822

Congressional Quarterly Service, 1735 K St., N.W. Washington, D.C. 20006

Council of State Governments, 1735 De Sales St., N.W., Washington, D.C. 20036

Ecole Nationale d'Administration, 56 Rue des Saints-Peres, Paris 7^e, France

Hochschule für Verwalt Ungewissenschaften, Frhr. Van Stein Str. 2, Speyer, Germany

Institute of Juridical Administration, 40 Washington Square S., New York, N.Y. 10012

Institute for Local Self-Government, Claremont Hotel, Berkeley, Calif. 94705

Institute of Public Administration, 55 W. 44 St., New York, N.Y. 10036

Inter-University Case Program, Inc., 131 Stadium Pl., Syracuse, N.Y. 13210

International Association of Assessing Officers, 1313 E. 60 St., Chicago, Ill. 60637

International City Management Association, 1140 Connecticut Ave., N.W., Washington, D.C. 20036

International Institute of Administrative Sciences, 25 Rue de la Charité, Brussels 4, Belgium

International Political Science Abstracts, 27 Rue Saint-Guillaume, 75—Paris 7e, France

Municipal Finance Officers Association, 1313 E. 60 St., Chicago, Ill. 60637

National Academy of Public Administration, 1225 Connecticut Ave., N.W., Washington, D.C. 20036

National Academy of Sciences, 2102 Constitution Ave., N.W., Washington, D.C. 20418

National Association of Housing and Redevelopment Officials, 2600 Virginia Ave., N.W., Washington, D.C. 20037

National Civil Service League, 1028 Connecticut Ave., N.W., Washington, D.C. 20036

National Education Association, 1201 Sixteenth St., N.W., Washington, D.C. 20036

National Industrial Conference Board, 845 Third Ave., New York, N.Y. 10022

National Institute of Public Affairs, Suite 610, 1825 K St., N.W., Washington, D.C. 20006

National League of Cities, 1612 K St., N.W., Washington, D.C. 20006

National Municipal League, 47 E. 68 St., New York, N.Y. 10021

National Planning Association, 1666 Connecticut Ave., N.W., Washington, D.C. 20036

New York City—Rand Institute, 545 Madison Ave., New York, N.Y. 10022

Public Administration Branch BTAO, United Nations, New York, N.Y. 10017

Public Administration Service, 1313 E. 60 St., Chicago, Ill. 60637

Public Personnel Association, 1313 E. 60 St., Chicago, Ill. 60637

Royal Institute of Public Administration, 24 Park Crescent, London, W.1., England

Tax Foundation, Inc., 50 Rockefeller Plaza, New York, N.Y. 10020

The Brookings Institution, 1775 Massachusetts Ave., N.W., Washington, D.C. 20036

The Rand Corporation, 1700 Main St., Santa Monica, Calif. 90406

The Urban Institute, 2100 M St., N.W., Washington, D.C. 20037

Washington Center for Metropolitan Studies, 1717 Massachusetts Ave., Washington, D.C. 20036

Index

Acephaly, 255
Administration, definition of, 99–100, 232
Administrative Behavior, 45, 46, 68, 69, 70, 71, 225, 236–237
Administrative law, 31
Administrative-polities classification, 262–264
Administrative-process school, 232–233
Administrative reform movement, 32–34, 123–127
Administrative Regulation, 41
Administrative roles, 236
The Administrative State, 41, 225
Administrative systems, 244–272
    bases of comparison, 244–245
Administrative theory, 225–243
    administrative-process, 232–233
    behavioralism, 234–235
    bibliography, 329–332
    decision-making, 236–237
    empiricism, 234
    integration of, 238
    mathematics, 237–238
    schools of, 231–240
    social-system, 235–236
Agraria-industria model, 260–261
Almond, G. A., 253–254, 255, 268, 288
Appleby, P. H., 46, 67
Apter, D., 252–253, 255
Assumption theory, 231
Authority, types of, 102

Bailey, S. K., 230–231, 242
Barnard, C., 68, 81, 236
Beard, C. A., 36, 41
Behavioralism, 45, 234–235, 258
Better Government Personnel, 38
Biller, R. P., 19
Bock, E., 45
Brady, J. R., 262
Brownlow, L., 38, 39, 119–122
Budget, national, 188–193
Bureaucracy:
    assumption of neutrality in, 94–102
    depoliticized, history of, 84–89
    theory of, 47, 235, 258–259
Bureaucrat, image of, 200
Bureaucratic arrangements, bibliography, 319–321
Bureaucratic infrastructures, 59–60

Bureaucratic power, 102–105
    bases of, 103–104
Burnham, J., 102

Cameralism, 31
Career service concept, 207–210
    alternatives to, 207
    open and closed career systems, 208–209
Case-study approach, 45
Central personnel agency, 211–212
Cephaly (*see* Polity)
The City Manager, 37, 63
Civil rights, 286–287
Civil Service Abroad, 38
Classification of public employees, 217–218
Cleveland, F. A., 35, 36
Coleman, J. S., 254
Communal authority, 6
Communication, 255
Comparative administration systems, 256–264
Comparative political systems, 249–256
Comparative public administration, bibliography, 332–334
Complete weapon system, 161
Computers, 72
Conflicts of loyalty, 91–92
Conservation of nature, 149–150
Contract system, 163–167
    bibliography, 323–325
    and Department of Defense, 165–167
Contractors, private, 154–163
    characteristics and problems, 159–163
    conflict of interest, 158–159
Controls on public service, 203–206
Cost-benefit analysis, 196
Crecine, J. P., 72
Credit, national, 184–185
Cross cultural approach, 47–48
    See also Comparative public administration
Currency, debasement of, 183–184

Dahl, R. A., 257
Decentralization movement, 125–126
Decision-making, 17–18, 46, 236–237
    applied theory, 74
    factors of, 71

Decision-making (*cont.*):
    models for, 74–75
    and problem-solving, 68–75
Decisions, programmed and nonprogrammed, 71
Defense, national, 134–135
Definitions, 230
de Grazia, A., 238
Democratic Administration, 41
Depoliticization:
    assumptions of, 94–102
    concept of, 89–93
    See also Politicization
Descriptive-explanatory theory, 230
Development, meaning of, 287
Developmental administration, 264–272
    bibliography, 332–334
    major concerns of, 268–272
    meaning of, 267–268
Dewey, J., 37, 76
Dimock, M. E., 64
Dror, Y., 75, 78

Easton, D., 251, 252, 253, 288
Economic planning, 142–143
    development, 143
    macrocollectivist, 142
    post-Keynesian adjustment, 142–143
Economic regulation, 141–142
Eisenstadt, S. N., 47
Elements of Public Administration, 41
Empiricism, 234
    vs. principles approach, 37–38
Employee organization (*see* Unionization)
Employment conditions, 217–221
Environmental control, 146–152
Esman, M. J., 267–268
Etzioni, A., 75
External relations, 133–134

Factual judgments, 69
Fayol, H., 232–233
Foreign aid, 265–266
Foreign relations (*see* External relations)
Friedrich, C. J., 38
The Frontiers of Public Administration, 64
Functional expertise, 131–153
    bibliography, 321–323
    impact of, 152–153
Functionalism, 255
The Functions of the Executive, 68, 236

Galbraith, J. K., 179
Gaus, J. M., 64
Goodnow, F., 33–34, 35, 69
Government:
    machinery of, 107–127
        definition, 116–118
        formal and informal structures, 116–118
    new functional areas of, 287–288
    public expenditures, 179–183
    techniques of meeting costs, 183–188
Government by Merit, 38
Governmental Problem-Solving: A Computer Simulation of Municipal Budgeting, 72
Governmental Reorganizations, 45, 122
Gross, B. M., 238
Gulick, L., 36, 38, 39, 46, 64, 119–122, 233

Handbook of Organizations, 238
Hawthorne experiments, 234
Hayek, F. A., 40
Herring, P., 65–66, 118
Heterocephaly, 256
Heuristic methods, 73–74
Hitch, C. J., 81
Hopkins, H., 38
Human-behavior school, 234–235
    See also Behavioralism
Humanitarianism, 136–137
Hypotheses, 230

Ilchman, W. F., 270–271
Institutionalism, 255–256, 258
Instrumental theory, 231
Integration school, 238
Interest aggregation, 255
Interest articulation, 254–255
International systems, 247–249
Internationalism, 43
    ideology of, 247–249
Introduction to the Study of Public Administration, 37, 63

Jacksonian democracy, 87–88

Kaufman, H., 257
Keynes, M., 142–143
Kissinger, H. A., 81
Klein, B., 74
Koontz, H., 232, 238

Labor movement (*see* Unionization)
Landau, M., 16–17
La Porte, T., 242–243
Lasswell, H. D., 76–77, 288
Law and order, 134
Leiserson, A., 41
Lewis, B. W., 174
Lindblom, C. E., 75
Litchfield, E. H., 238
Living constitution (*see* Government, machinery of)
Logic, 76

Macridis, R., 252, 253
Macroplanning, 271, 295
Management, meaning of, 232
Management science, 72–73
The Managerial Revolution, 102
The Managing of Organizations, 238
March, J. G., 70, 238
Marini, F., 277
Marx, F. M., 41
Mathematics school, 237–238
Mayo, E., 234
Measuring Municipal Activities, 194
Merriam, C. E., 37, 38, 39, 119–122
Metacephaly, 256
Microplanning, 271, 295–296
Military complex, 135, 285–286
    complete weapon system, 161
Models:
    building of, 72–73, 259–264
    decision-making, 74–75
Models of Man, 70
Modernization, 255
Mosher, F. C., 14, 45, 122
Municipal Research, 35

National development, 139–140
National socialization, 139
National symbols, 138
National unity, 138
Nationalism, 137–140
Neutrality (*see* Depoliticization)
The New Deal, 38, 63, 64, 118–122
The New Public Administration, 277
The New Science of Management Decision, 71
Nomothetic approach, 258, 262–264
Nonbureaucratic organizational theory, 236

Nonrational action, 18
Normative theory, 231

Officialdom, nature of, 201–203
Operations research, 196
Organizational society, 226–227
Organizations, 238
Orthocephaly, 256

Papers on the Science of Administration, 36
Parker, R. S., 15
Parson, T., 253, 254
Personal well-being, 151–152
Personnel:
    positive administration of, 210–213
    supervisors, 213
Planning-programming-budgeting systems (PPBS), 193–198
    program demands and budgets, 197–198
    suboptimization, 195–196
Policy analysis, 75–81
Policy and Administration, 46
Policy, and politics, 67
Policy sciences, 75–81
Political control, 113–116
    See also Authority
Political functions, 254
Political institutions, 255–256
Political roles, 253–254
Political science, 249–256
    descriptive vs. comparative, 250–251
    general system theories, 251–253
    political-culture theories, 253–256
    and public administration, 279–280
The Political Systems of Empires, 47
Politicization, 82–106
    measurement of, 105–106
    See also Depoliticization
Politics and Administration, 34
Politics-administration dichotomy, 38–42, 62–64, 99
    bibliography, 317–319
The Politics of the Budgetary Process, 192
Politics:
    definition, 99–100
    and public administration, 38–42
    of reorganization, 118–123
Polity (cephaly):
    tonic characteristics, 256
    types of, 255–256
POSDCORB formula, 46, 233, 237

Postulates, 230
Powell, G. B., 254, 255
Price, D. K., 15-16
Principles approach, 36-38, 40, 232-233
The Principles of Public Administration, 36
Prismatic-sala model, 261-262
Problem-solving, 68-75
Problems of the American Public Service, 38
Procephaly, 255
Professional journals, bibliography, 300-304
Propositions, 230
Public Administration, 45, 288
Public administration:
    as academic discipline, 12-19, 62-63
    autonomy of, 44-45
    coercive power of, 7
    comparative political systems, 249-256
    comparative systems, 256-264
    crisis in confidence, 276-277
    cultural context of, 17-18
    decision-making approach, 17-18
    developmental systems, 264-272
    ecological approach (*see* Prismatic-sala
        model)
    economic-management functions,
        140-143
    environmental-control functions,
        146-152
    evolving concepts of, 282-289
    expansion of, 23-26, 43-44
    expectations of, 9
    in ferment, 278-282
    general theory of, 283-284
    history of, 30-42
    international systems, 247-249
    internationalism, 43-44
    judgment of performance of, 8-9
    meaning of, 3-22, 226
    nation-building functions, 137-140
    new academies for, 292-294
    new approaches to, 288-289
    new patterns in, 275-297
    new realism, 45-46
    peculiarities of, 6-9
    and politics, 8, 38-42
    practice vs. academic study, 279
    prejudice against, 4-6
    priority of activities, 7
    problems of theory, 228-229, 240-243
    and public-policy making, 61-68
    restructuring of, 280-282
    roles of, 25-26
    shifts in emphasis, 19-22

Public administration (*cont.*):
    size and multiplicity of, 7-8
    social-welfare functions, 144-146
    study of, 23-49
        in America, 32-42
        American vs. British approaches, 32
        basic approaches, 27-28
        bibliography, 311-314
        goals of, 28-30
        history of, 245-246
        philosophical bases, 41-42
        reasons for, 26-30
        since 1940s, 42-49
    subject matter of, 9-12
    systems, classification of, 246-247
    traditional functions, 133-137
    unavoidability of, 6-7
*Public Administration and Policy Develop-
    ment: A Case Book,* 45, 77
*Public Administration and the Public
    Interest,* 118
Public administrator, new image for, 289-291
Public bureaucracy, 60-61
Public entrepreneurs, 167-175
    bibliography, 323-325
    extent and form of, 169-170
    operational considerations, 170-174
    reasons for, 168-169
Public finance, 176-198
    bibliography, 325-327
Public interest, concept of, 169-175
Publicness, 18-19
    definition, 283
Public-personnel administration, 210-213
    bibliography, 327-329
    and unionization, 214-216
Public Policy and General Welfare, 41
Public-policy making, 53-81
    arena of, 55-61
    bibliography, 314-317
    estates in, 15-16
    problems of, 57
    and public administration, 61-68
Public Policy Making Reexamined, 78
Public-policy problems, 285-287
Public propriety, 101
Public servants:
    international, 248
    self-controls, 205-206
Public service, 199-221
    academic studies of, 200
    bibliography, 327-329
    career service concept, 207-210

Public service (*cont.*):
  controls on, 203–206
  employment conditions, 217–221
  promotion in, 218–219
  recruitment, 218
  rewards of, 219–221
  work atmosphere, 220
Public-service ideology, 19th century Europe, 85
Public services, decision to contract, 155–159
Public works, 135–136

Quade, E. S., 196

Rationality, 111–112
  movement toward, 109–111
  and post-rationality, 112–113
  and pre-rationality, 109
Rationalization, process of, 108–113
Recruitment of public employees, 218
Reorganization, politics of, 118–123
Research and development, 148–149
Research movement, United States, 34–38
Ridley, C. E., 194
Riggs, F. W., 44, 48, 255–256, 257, 260, 261–264, 288
The Road to Serfdom, 40
Roosevelt, F. D., 38, 39, 118–122
Rule adjudication, 255
Rule making, 255

Sayre, W. S., 36–37, 257
Schelling, T. C., 73
Scientific analysis, 34–38
  vs. politics, 39
Self controls on public servants, 205–206
Sharkansky, I., 288
Sharp, W., 257
Shils, E., 255
Siffin, W. J., 282
Simon, H. A., 17, 40, 45, 46, 47, 68–72, 74, 75–76, 194, 225, 233, 236–237, 238, 279, 288
Smithburg, D. W., 45, 70, 288
Snyder, R. C., 252, 253
Social-system school, 235–236
Social welfare, 144–146
Societal redundancy, 295

Spoils system, 87–88
Staff relations, 213–217
Stein, H., 14, 45
The Strategy of Conflict, 73
Supracephaly, 256
Surpluses in public enterprises, 187–188
Sutton, F. X., 260
Systems analysis, 73
  in PPBS, 195–196
  theory of, 236

Taxation, 136, 185–187
  direct and indirect, 187
Taylor, F. W., 35, 232
Teaching materials, 36
Tead, O., 41
Technology, 286
Textbooks, bibliography of, 304–334
Theory:
  categories of, 230–231
  constituents of, 230
  need for, 229–231
  of public administration, 47
Third World (*see* Developmental systems)
Thompson, V. A., 45, 70, 288
Tonic polities, 256, 262
Truman, D. B., 15
Turbulence, environmental, 285
  coping with, 294–297

Unionization, 214–216
Urban design, 150
Urbanism, 286
Urwick, L., 36

Value judgments, 69
Vickers, G., 81
Von Mises, L., 40

Waldo, D., 17–18, 41, 47, 225, 238, 241
Weber, M., 47, 102, 235, 254, 260
White, L. D., 37, 38, 63, 64
White, O., 289
Wildavsky, A., 192
Willoughby, W. F., 35, 36
Wilmerding, L., 38
Wilson, W., 33, 34